Television's *Outlander*

ALSO BY MARY ELLEN SNODGRASS
AND FROM McFARLAND

Rachel Carson: A Literary Companion (2021)

Edwidge Danticat: A Companion to the Young Adult Literature (2021)

Marion Zimmer Bradley: A Companion to the Young Adult Literature (2020)

Lee Smith: A Literary Companion (2019)

Coins and Currency: An Historical Encyclopedia, 2d ed. (2019)

Gary Paulsen: A Companion to the Young Adult Literature (2018)

World Epidemics: A Cultural Chronology
of Disease from Prehistory to the Era of Zika, 2d ed. (2017)

Brian Friel: A Literary Companion (2017)

Settlers of the American West: The Lives of 231 Notable Pioneers (2015)

Isabel Allende: A Literary Companion (2013)

Leslie Marmon Silko: A Literary Companion (2011)

Peter Carey: A Literary Companion (2010)

Jamaica Kincaid: A Literary Companion (2008)

Kaye Gibbons: A Literary Companion (2007)

Walter Dean Myers: A Literary Companion (2006)

World Shores and Beaches: A Descriptive and Historical
Guide to 50 Coastal Treasures (2005)

Barbara Kingsolver: A Literary Companion (2004)

August Wilson: A Literary Companion (2004)

Amy Tan: A Literary Companion (2004)

World Epidemics: A Cultural Chronology of Disease
from Prehistoryto the Era of SARS (2003; paperback 2011)

Who's Who in the Middle Ages (2001; paperback 2013)

Encyclopedia of World Scriptures (2001; paperback 2011)

Television's *Outlander*

A Companion, Seasons 1–5

MARY ELLEN SNODGRASS

McFarland & Company, Inc., Publishers

Jefferson, North Carolina

LIBRARY OF CONGRESS CATALOGUING-IN-PUBLICATION DATA

Names: Snodgrass, Mary Ellen, author.
Title: Television's Outlander : a companion, seasons 1-5 / Mary Ellen Snodgrass.
Description: Jefferson, North Carolina : McFarland & Company, Inc.,
Publishers, 2021 | Includes bibliographical references and index.
Identifiers: LCCN 2021014563 | ISBN 9781476682990 (paperback : acid free paper) ∞
ISBN 9781476642697 (ebook)
Subjects: LCSH: Outlander (Television program) | BISAC: PERFORMING
ARTS / Television / Genres / Science Fiction, Fantasy & Horror |
LITERARY CRITICISM / Science Fiction & Fantasy
Classification: LCC PN1992.77.O985 S66 2021 | DDC 791.45/72—dc23
LC record available at https://lccn.loc.gov/2021014563

BRITISH LIBRARY CATALOGUING DATA ARE AVAILABLE

ISBN (print) 978-1-4766-8299-0
ISBN (ebook) 978-1-4766-4269-7

Front cover image: Caitriona Balfe and Sam Heughan
in *Outlander*, Season 2, 2016 (Starz/Photofest)

Printed in the United States of America

*McFarland & Company, Inc., Publishers
Box 611, Jefferson, North Carolina 28640
www.mcfarlandpub.com*

For those buried at Culloden,
God rest ye well.

Acknowledgments

Gabrielle Geiger, French teacher, Stuttgart, Germany
Joseph Parks Hester, philosopher, Claremont, North Carolina
Sharyn Hughes, language consultant, Queensland, Australia
Ewart Oakeshott, antiquarian, Ely, England
Àdhamh Ó Broin, Gaelic tutor, Cowal, Scotland
Lotsee Patterson, archivist, Apache, Oklahoma
Mark Schumacher, reference librarian, UNC–Greensboro, North Carolina

Special thanks go to reference librarians Martin Otts and Beth Bradshaw of the Patrick Beaver Library in Hickory, North Carolina, and to my publicist and consultant Joan Lail.

Table of Contents

Set me as a seal upon thine heart, as a seal upon thine arm: for love is strong as death.

—Song of Solomon 8:6

Preface

The present work guides the viewer, media and culture specialist, and researcher of gender studies, literature, and military history through five years of quality historical fiction found in the first five seasons of the *Outlander* television series. The 125 topics illuminate broad subjects—deception, crime, law, circles, fire and heat, couples, anachronisms—as well as the particulars of the Fraser story. Dominant themes, especially rape, prisons, and violent death, account for much of the screen action and a preponderance of positive and negative criticism. Overviews of specifics—music, dance, food, the British Army, the American Revolution—incorporate detailed scenes and their nuances. Genealogies explicate the family quirks of the Bourbons, Stuarts, and Hanoverians along with the fictional backgrounds of the Dunsanys, Browns, MacKenzies, and Frasers. The implications of Maroons, piracy, slavery, indenturing, and Native American history characterize the involvement of fictional families in greater social and racial movements as they developed in Haiti and Jamaica, along the Cape Fear River, and into the North Carolina frontier.

Integral to the protagonists' success as proto–Americans, entries on clans, colonialism, homosexuality, witchcraft, Christianity, clergy, taxation, and altruism reveal causes of conflict at the personal, state, and universal levels. Literary discussion of allegory, storytelling, details, coincidence, Gothicism, and foreshadowing illustrate methods of scripting that enhance a long-running series. The mesmerizing appeal of *Outlander* draws on unique elements of the grotesque, heirlooms, dueling, makeup and costuming, healing, and weapons as well as individual events as ominous as the battles of Prestonpans, Culloden, and Alamance Creek and unforeseen time travel through Craigh na Dun.

A glossary enlarges on 300 terms as specific and essential as Gaelic slang and Cherokee names. The words and phrases define usage in identified episodes, as with these models:

> **costume**—fichu, stock, wellies, sporran, breeks, robe rouge, tatterdemalion
> **culture**—dall, whist, Hogmany, cribbage, bawbee, gill, A&P, Samhain, turner
> **food**—Pavlova, oolong, grog, K-rations, vinho de porto, bannock, black pudding
> **foreign language**—smout, frau, braw, danke, da locum, soiree, eau de femme
> **government**—Francis Stephen, dry county, affidavit, Gaberlunzie tokens, tanist
> **healing**—la grippe, morbid sore throat, zam gau, necrosis, anisomelia, in flux
> **inventions**—astrolabe, composing stick, cutthroat razor, tolbooth prison
> **literature**—Procrustes, Brahan seer, danu, gang thegither, deo gratias, Jonah
> **music**—schlaf Kindlein, lilt, ceilidh, eisd ris, multure, waulking wool

sex—wee man, nether mouth, radge, soixante-neuf, swive, cockstand, rake
superstition—tannasg, selkie, fenghuang, old nick, La Dame Blanche, conjure
warfare—sgian dubh, stand down, thousand-yard stare, tulach ard, quick-march

The guide to place names combines the fictional—Fort William, River Run, Ardsmuir Prison, Lallybroch, Castle Leoch, Fraser's Ridge—with essential locales in the narrative, e.g., Jamaica, Corrieyairack, Carfax Close, Wilmington, Gold Coast, Versailles, Ocracoke, and Rose Hall.

A compendium of herbalism lists patients with healers, 54 medicinal plants, and their use in treating chronic cough, measles, aching amputation, and scurvy. A collection of 32 wise sayings includes speakers and episodes. An historical chronology lists events beginning with the founding of Harvard College in 1636 and the outlawing of witchcraft in England in 1653 and ending with the U.S. moon landing in 1969. A separate listing of primary and secondary sources, both print and electronic, precedes the index, which presents major entries in boldface, including fostering, whisky, prophecy, and Paris. Additional terms itemize characters—Uncle Lambert, Faith Fraser, Elias Pound, Lizzy Wemyss—alongside historical figures—Herman Husband, Steve Bonnet, Monsieur Foret, Hector Cameron, Governor William Tryon—and actors, notably Lotte Verbeek, Duncan McTavish, Tom Jackson, Colin McFarlane, Thapelo J. Sebogodi, Tobias Menzies, and stars Caitriona Balfe and Sam Heughan. The companion assists the viewers in separating fact from fiction and incorporating aftereffects of the 1746 Jacobite Uprising with the formation of the United States.

Introduction

A classic historical fiction for television, *Outlander* weaves love and war into an enduring narrative. The series continues to outrank competition with engrossing scripting, casting, quality costuming and makeup, and cinematography, all based on meticulous research. The near magic relationship between stars Sam Heughan and Caitriona Balfe as the Frasers, Claire and Jamie, draws fans to a solid marital relationship forged during intrigues and conflict on sea and land. Surviving a two-decade separation and an attempted assassination by Laoghaire, a calculating rival, the union builds strength from stalwart family and service to a frontier North Carolina community through Claire's medical care and Jamie's protection and loyalty.

In 2014, I came upon the first episodes of *Outlander* on Netflix with no knowledge of Diana Gabaldon's fictional octad by the same name. To connect my North Carolina family with the Frasers, I researched John, Charles, and William Robinson's background as members of the Regulators and continued with my birth in Wilmington during World War II and my 76-year residency in the southern end of fictional Fraser's Ridge. Currently, I live five miles northeast of Isaiah Morton and Alicia Brown, the Brownsville lovers and prospective parents whom Jamie aids in escaping a virulent father. To further my work on a viewing companion, I avoided reading Gabaldon's novels and concentrated on the five-season screen version. My months of repeat viewings began with closed captioning and included scripts in English and French for full effect. Unfortunately, transfer of seasons four and five from quality presentation on Netflix to Starz subjected fans to an awkward, amateurish network that tends to interrupt episodes with advertisements for grade B series. Another obstacle, the absence of translated episodes limits full immersion in dialogue.

From the beginning, *Outlander* builds on romance. A controlling triad enters the debut with characters drawn together on Samhain eve, a threshold between the living and spirits in the world beyond. During a thunderstorm and electrical blackout on Wednesday night, October 31, 1945, Claire Beauchamp Randall, a veteran military nurse for Allied forces, unknowingly appears at a second floor window in the gaze of two pedestrians: Frank, her husband, sees a lone Highlander in kilt and tam staring at Claire outlined in candlelight. Intervening in the fixed observation, Frank addresses the Highlander, who vanishes. Frank pursues the watcher's identity by questioning Claire about her relationship with Scots casualties during World War II. The implication reveals a disparity between two husbands: Frank's suspicion of adultery and the Highlander's pure, unwavering adoration. To the consternation of viewers, nothing identifies the Scot as Jamie Fraser, Claire's second husband, but the trio forecasts the off-kilter love triangle to come.

Dramatic energy, the primary determiner of *Outlander* success, propels the intricate storyline through multiple cliffhangers and resolutions as dire as threats of burning at the stake for sorcery, jailing in the Bastille, a whirling Atlantic vortex, and abduction and gang rape by depraved outlaws. To prevent extreme action from taking over, scripting humanizes characters with idiosyncrasies—Claire's need to tend the sick, Roger's misgivings about militarism, Jocasta's silent grief for daughter Morna, Murtagh's compassion for the frontier underdog, and Jamie's ferocity at threats to his household. Individual tells—the giveaways that poker players catalog on each other—reveal Stephen Bonnet's self-pity, Laird Colum MacKenzie's disappointment in his brother Dougal's poor judgment, Geillis Duncan Abernethy's mania for Scots independence, and Marsali Fraser's acceptance of Claire as her anatomy teacher and ma. Viewer responses attest to their involvement in primary and secondary character lives and concern for their welfare.

Within the sweeping chronicle, weaknesses emerge in casting, setting, and plotting, especially the stagy homosexuality of the Duke of Sandringham, Sophie Skelton's impersonal performance of Brianna, and Mary Hawkins's whimpers and dependence on rescue. The commanding view from Fraser's Ridge glows fake, like a Thomas Kinkade scenario that fails by a long shot to resemble the stately Blue Ridge Mountains of North Carolina. There's the leaves-with-car-keys-after-an-argument before a driving accident, a guilt-pointing ploy common to early television soaps and 1950s film. One of the most disappointing episodes in season three rounds up too many loose ends with Caribbean reunions and concludes with a poorly filmed resolution set in a rinky-dink cave with pool water undulating in crayola hues. Geillis Duncan's beheading produces a floppy corpse looking more like Raggedy Ann than the original.

A serious flaw in "Famous Last Words," repetitions of the gimcrackery of sepia film, clacking projector, hands clutching a noose, and eyes peering through a burlap bag impede narration, violating the vested interests of long-term fans. Such fascination with gee whiz screen experiments, similar in lapse to the make-believe media interviews in the *M*A*S*H* series and *The West Wing,* suggest that producers get bored with their own success and dream up alternatives to stretch their imagination. For a five-season all-star TV epic, the variations fracture continuity and cohesion. Fortunately for fans and media history, the Frasers move on.

In contrast to gimmicks, ideas stand firm as the *Outlander* backbone. A sturdy thematic development builds on second-wave feminism, the refusal of women to accept scorn, menace or exploitation. Claire and her sisterhood are equal to deriders as arrogant as Dr. Thorne, Dr. Simms, and Professor Jackson; the taint of violators like Phillip Wylie, Lionel Brown, Arvin Hodgepile, and Stephen Bonnet; or threats by Dougal MacKenzie, Buck MacKenzie, Captain Black Jack Randall, or even husband Jamie Fraser. Coercion as a lifestyle distresses secondary characters, leaving Jenny Fraser Murray husbandless with a farm to manage, Ulysses to defend his mistress from a killer, Rose Brown with a broken wrist, and Fanny Beardsley with a fatherless infant to rear. The unanswerable questions of African slavery, indentured servitude, and the uprooting of First Peoples receive scant coverage primarily because fundamental American sins defy solving on the fly. The Frasers do what most citizens did in the American past—treated people of color with respect, comforted the abused on a one-to-one basis, and left society's wrongs to institutional and political correction.

Essential to visual appeal, the architecture of medieval Scots castles and forts and the grandeur of Versailles, Belmont, Helwater, and Tryon's Palace receive less screen time than simpler chapels, farmsteads, and the clinic and feeding station at l'Hôpital des

Anges. The spartan respite at Father Anselm's abbey offers the Frasers a haven to mend their spiritual hurt much as the wilderness cabin enfolds Brianna and Roger MacKenzie, eventually becoming a respite from vile memories and a place to safeguard their son Jemmy. A move to the big house on Fraser's Ridge turns the dwelling into a community center and surgery for healing Josiah and Keziah and for dispensing advice on conception, nutrition, and the antisepsis that cures Jamie's infected snakebite. In *Outlander's* unpredictable style, Claire's professional work space also provides Marsali with a setting for exterminating Lionel Brown, the monster who ravages the Fraser family.

The electronic pulse following each episode attests to viewer plunge into the fictional *Outlander* microcosm. Amid a deluge of fan comments and musings, questions on social media and at book clubs focus on favorite characters:

- Does Briana learn she had a sister named Faith?
- Is Jenny aware of Ian's decision to become a Mohawk?
- Why doesn't Phaedra attend her mistress before the wedding?
- Do Letitia and Mrs. Fitz survive the Clearances?
- How can Claire enjoy impromptu coitus without foreplay?
- Does Jocasta know that Ulysses loves her?
- Does Fiona continue her grandmother's part in dancing with the Druids?

The predominance of female character conflicts attests to earnest concern over women's fate.

For fans seeking more of the chronicle, season six may answer the questions that crop up on online *Outlander* sites:

- Did Castle Leoch survive British ruin?
- Will Young Ian see his wife again?
- What happens to Wee Bonnie? Phaedra? Johiehon's baby?
- Does Jocasta give money to the family members on her list?
- Will Claire revisit Joe Abernethy in Boston?
- Do the Beardsley twins thrive as members of the militia?
- Will Roger and Brianna establish a school on Fraser's Ridge?
- Does John Quincy Myers continue to live rough in the wild?
- Will Brianna meet her brother, the ninth Earl of Ellesmere?
- How does Ulysses survive in England?
- Does Young Ian send frontier news to the Murrays?

Hovering in the distance, the smeared newspaper obituary predicting death to the Frasers in a house fire leaves to the future a troubling prospect.

Essential to scholars studying *Outlander,* the themes of marriage, feminism, war, pioneering, and democracy offer myriad choices for discussion and debate. Researchers around the world—Berlin, Queensland, El Paso and Austin, Puerto Rico, Dublin, Utrecht, Ontario, Warwick, Pretoria, London, Glasgow, Tübingen, Rome, British Columbia, Sweden, Barcelona, Williamsburg, and Fayetteville, North Carolina—peruse the television adaptation of Gabaldon's novels from the perspectives of literature, media, linguistics, medicine, psychology, archeology, and military history. Quality online analyses from Genevieve Valentine of the *New York Times,* Amy Wilkinson for *Entertainment Weekly,* Yvonne Villarreal for the *Los Angeles Times*, Carolina Hallemann at *Town & Country,* Meredith Carey for *Conde Nast Traveler,* Erika Mailman on staff at the *Washington Post,*

Alexandra Macon for *Vogue,* Jennifer Vineyard at *Elle,* and Laura Prudom, Andrea Rei-her, and Diane Gordon at *Variety* offer valuable insight into the development of major subjects, particularly homosexuality and male rape. Additional commentary from *Hollywood Reporter,* the *Guardian, Glamour, Express, Philadelphia Inquirer, Oprah Magazine, Radio Times, New York Post, Vanity Fair,* and especially Kayla Kumari Upadhyaya for *AVClub* and Amber Dowling at *IndieWire* broadens the researcher's point of view, encompassing the fields of women's studies and cultural history.

The Companion

Acupuncture/Acupressure

The medical focus in the *Outlander* TV chronicle incorporates ancient, medieval, and Renaissance practices and the enthusiasm of American doctors in the 1960s for alternative medicine. In the episode "The Doldrums," immigrant Yi Tien Cho (played by Gary Young) applies expertise in Chinese healing to spare Jamie from crippling bouts of seasickness while he serves as supercargo on the French brig *Artemis.* The acupuncturist authenticates his remedy by describing its value against nonstop vomiting and twisting of the testicles, which must be removed. The secret treatments attempt to save Claire's professional pride, an extension of the remorse on Jamie's face with her first view of prosthetic needles bristling from his face. His stealth indicates willingness to suffer in silence rather than risk losing Claire again.

A more successful regimen than Claire's ginger tea to alleviate nausea, the insertion of steel needles demonstrates ancient alternative medicine from China dating to 100 BCE and from Korea and Japan around 500 CE. A traditional Asian therapy, it appeared first around 2600 BCE in a compilation, *The Yellow Emperor's Classic of Internal Medicine.* The fundamental Taoist text on wellness and treatments of illness supplanted shamanism with recommendations of balanced *chi* (energy) as the watchword of health. One journalist, television critic Genevieve Valentine of the *New York Times,* complained that "the vaguely-Asian flute music that accompanies his scenes (a rare misstep from composer Bear McCreary), his water calligraphy, the acupuncture" bogged down the characterization of Yi Tien Cho with obvious stereotypes about mystic Chinese beliefs (Valentine, 2017).

In season four, set in the North Carolina outback, Claire ventures from herbalism to acupressure, a self-healing therapy based in the interconnection of human tissue. Her skilled compression of John Grey's orbital sockets relieves fever and headache, symptoms of measles that he contracted at Cross Creek (Fayetteville), North Carolina. Like acupuncture, the alternative cure opens body meridians to a flow of healing energy. Holding fingers firmly to pressure points in John's eye cavities, she relieves his suffering by promoting blood circulation. The method, derived from Indian massage, also applies to nausea and vomiting from motion sickness and early pregnancy, both of which afflict the Frasers. As though forcing a homosexual obsession from John's mind, simultaneous with his relief comes a deluge of confused feelings about his bisexuality and jealousy of Jamie's contentment with Claire.

See also Epidemics; Healing.

Source

Coleman, Tyrese. "How Outlander Has Avoided the Stereotypes of Its Source Material," *BuzzFeed News* (22 October 2017).
Kosin, Julie. "*Outlander* Season 3 Episode 9: Jamie & Claire Are Separated Again," *Bazaar* (12 November 2017).
Valentine, Genevieve. "'Outlander' Season 3, Episode 9: Sailing Takes Them Away," *New York Times* (12 November 2017).

Allegory

Touches of allegory mark the *Outlander* TV saga with abstract analogies to epic and political movements. Examples epitomize the age of British imperialism—the fall of James III with the decline of European monarchy and the expansion of colonialism in the New World by uprooting first people from ancestral lands and installing indenturing and African slave labor as the basis of Britain's agricultural wealth. On a more complex level, the building of Tryon's Palace in New Bern on North Carolina tax levies compares with the boy kidnappings by Geillis Duncan's Portuguese sex bondsmen on the Portuguese ship *Bruja* and the smuggling and sale of a white woman by Stephen Bonnet to Captain Howard, a paradox yielding surprising insight into issues of sordid crime, greed, and corruption.

Character names, like the cast of John Bunyan's classic allegory *Pilgrim's Progress,* affirm personal traits. The *Outlander* script populates its cast with Dr. Thorne, the prickly obstetrician; Ronald MacNab, an abuser of son Rabbie; Sandy Travers, the intended bride of Frank Randall, who helps him "cross over" from his first marriage; and Father Fogden, the ditzy lapsed priest who takes advice from a coconut. By basing narration on moral principles, the allegorist elevates theme and motif above character and action. The result is a multidimensional work with the resonance of the films *Mulan, The Wizard of Oz, The Little Mermaid, Pocahontas,* and *Beauty and the Beast,* pivotal studies of gender traditions.

Episode six of season five reaches a height of symbolism with a late-in-life courtship and marriage. Jocasta Cameron selects Duncan Innes as her fourth husband because of his lack of Jacobite fervor and his opposition to risky alliances. By wedding a calmer, more homebound man, she ends a fevered affair with Murtagh FitzGibbons Fraser, the epitome of the idealistic man of principle and action. On withdrawal from her den, Murtagh leaves behind a family crest for a wedding gift, a medieval symbol of clan φιλία (*philía*), a form of brotherly love based on lineage and community. Jocasta's regret that third husband Hector Cameron accidentally shot and killed her last child Morna grieves her mind. She blames the transportation of Louis XV's gold out of the country for robbing her of three daughters and eyesight, a handicap that conceals from her conscious mind the investment in slaves to work River Run. In a pensive moment of regret, Jocasta fondles Morna's hair ribbon, a frail tie to the Scots past.

In a parallel to Jocasta's regretful wedding, Claire and Jamie clash over the value of vengeance to family and personal pride. Because he finds Claire fighting off the groping of rake Phillip Wylie in Jocasta's stable, Jamie threatens to kill the fop with a dirk. To save the nuptial reception from violence, he chooses instead to defeat Wylie at a game of whist, a symbolic battleground like games of chess with Joseph Duverney and John Grey, and pledges for ante Claire's silver and gold wedding rings. When he returns the jewelry, Claire wallops him on the jaw for risking her prized wedding tokens to redeem his manhood from shame and defeat. Their equanimity revitalized, they make passionate love as a ritual offering to their marital vows.

The explosion of tensions from a heated coupling in a horse stall yields a romantic effulgence that restores the couple's serenity. The script builds hidden significance from the name of the pedigreed Arabian Lucas, who bears a blood tie to undefeated British thoroughbred Eclipse and a literary connection with St. Luke, author of the beloved gospel story in Luke 2:1–20 of Baby Jesus and his birth in straw. Contrasting Wylie's vanity, the concluding scenario represents a loving husband and wife who value affection and humility over a show of style and prominence. A lesser nuance connects Claire with St. Luke, a middle eastern physician, because of her selfless medical career.

See also Names.

Source

Apperley, Tom. "Counterfactual Communities: Strategy Games, Paratexts and the Player's Experience of History," *Open Library of Humanities* 4 (2018): 1–22.

Brigley Thompson, Zoë. "From Safe Spaces to Precarious Moments: Teaching Sexuality and Violence in the American Higher Education Classroom," *Gender and Education* 32:3 (2018): 1–17.

Obey, Erica. "Tall, Dark, and a Long Time Dead: Epistemology, Time Travel, and the Bodice-Ripper," *Worlds Enough and Time: Explorations of Time in Science Fiction and Fantasy.* Westport, CT: Greenwood, 2002.

Pollard, Tony. "Shooting Arrows," *Writing Battles: New Perspectives on Warfare and Memory in Medieval Europe.* New York: Bloomsbury, 2020: 177.

Altruism

The place of humanitarianism in the televised *Outlander* saga reveals a magnanimous side of the eighteenth-century Highlander's ethos. Aspects of kindness take numerous forms:

affection—Roger's purchase of a charm bracelet for Brianna

alms—Dougal's gift of a bag of grain to a starving member of the MacKenzie clan

amiability—Ian Murray's welcome of an English sister-in-law to Lallybroch

benevolence—Hamilton Knox's toss of coins to the poor

clemency—Jamie's freeing of Hercules from Abandawe

comfort—Claire's assistance to Maisri and Rose Brown, both victims of male abuse

concern—Claire's tonsillectomies to rid the Beardsley twins of sore throats

consideration—Adawehi's sharing of herbal remedies with Claire

cordiality—John Quincy Myers's welcome to Jamie with a gift of jerky

decency—Jenny's prayers for the dead members of the Watch

devotion—Ulysses's rescue of Jocasta from Gerald Forbes

forgiveness—Father Anselm's pardon of Claire's sins

generosity—Murtagh's wedding gift to Jocasta

gentleness—Louise de Rohan's cradling of Claire's dead baby

good will—the Frasers' invitation to their Cherokee neighbors

grace—Claire's kiss on Hugh Munro's cheek

heart—Mother Hildegarde's gentle explanation of Faith's death

honesty—Young Ian's apology for insulting Uncle Jamie

hope—Claire's supply of a love potion to Laoghaire

hospitality—Jocasta's welcome of niece Brianna to River Run

humanity—Brianna's compliments to Phaedra

leniency—Jamie's decision to spare Captain Jack Randall for kidnapping Claire

mercy—Jamie's release of Novelli from the pillory

pardon—Governor Tryon's forgiveness of Jamie's insolence

    patience—Frank's willingness to begin marriage again with Claire
    philanthropy—Jamie's payment of cash to Lesley for traveling with the family
    pity—Claire's search for a wet nurse to feed Wee Bonnie
    rescue—Jamie's saving of Willoughby from starvation and the purchase of
       Temeraire from slavery
    solicitude—Kezzie's abandonment of his pants to the kittens' bed
    succor—Willie's offer to rescue Jamie from Wentworth Prison
    sympathy—Mrs. Fitz's assurance to Claire that Jamie will return
    tact—John Grey's identifying Brianna as his fiancée
    tenderness—Jamie's rescue of Adso from starvation
    thoughtfulness—Jamie's sharing of rum with two condemned prisoners
    tolerance—Brianna's visit to Stephen Bonnet's jail cell
    understanding—Hal Melton's decision to send Jamie home to Lallybroch
    welcome—Jamie's acceptance of Lizzy into the Fraser family

The variety of kindnesses illustrates aspects of the Greek concept of ἀγάπη (*agapē*), any form of charity that expects nothing in return.

    The season one nuptial opens with Ned's purchase of a wedding dress, the blacksmith's shaping of a ring from a door key, and Dougal MacKenzie's bribing of a Catholic priest, all of which speed the Frasers down the aisle. A day after the wedding, the couple welcomes Hugh Munro, a beggar formerly tortured and muted by Algerian Muslim proselyters, who sliced out his tongue. Claire kisses Hugh on the cheek in thanks for a wedding gift—a dragonfly in amber—and in pity for his suffering. After acknowledging Claire's disclosure of time travel, Jamie demonstrates a more personal humanity by accepting without complaint the limitations of a crippled Highlander and pregnant Englishwoman. Even though he is apolitical, based on Claire's warnings of disaster, he concocts a clever method of derailing the bonnie prince's ambition to muster a Jacobite army to prevent disaster in northern Scotland.

Body and Soul

    With less sympathy for women's needs in 1744, Jamie still has much to learn about equality in marriage. Pettishly, he misinterprets Claire's professional philanthropy as domestic desertion. Because of her belief in the Hippocratic Oath as it is administered to Harvard Medical School graduates, she avoids frivolous Frenchwomen's activities at tea, cards, and gossip and anticipates the carnage of the 1789 French Revolution. Already heavy with pregnancy, she elects to spend long hours nursing poor patients at l'Hôpital des Anges, a fictional Paris charity near Notre Dame Cathedral. Her skill at urinoscopy, preparation of the dead for burial, surgical removal of a splinter, and treatment of scrofula, burns, broken bones, and diabetes earns the regard of Mother Hildegarde, admirably played by Frances de la Tour, an approval that Claire requires to feel essential and integral to healing and self-worth.

    Problematic therapies enable Claire's rescue of Jamie from starvation and potential suicide. In the "Wentworth Prison" episode in 1744, he undergoes what gender critic Emma Nagouse of the University of Sheffield terms "a psychological, emotional, and spiritual self … splintered in the aftermath of his assault," a demonstration of Captain Black Jack Randall's bravado in disempowering a chained prisoner (Nagouse, 2017). Claire's husband languishes from post-traumatic shock and humiliation at his loss of masculinity, which the Old Testament author Jeremiah expressed after 586 BCE in Lamentations 3:14–15 (KJV). The unnamed biblical victim broods, "I was a derision to all my people; and their song all the day. He hath filled me with bitterness," a description of Jamie's mental state.

To relieve her patient's dolor, Claire attempts a visceral catharsis to counteract what Nagouse calls "the rape myths that sustain the silence surrounding this crime" (Nagouse, 2018, 143). After securing Jamie's sanity through role-play of rapist and victim, lavender oil fragrance, and counseling, in Paris, Claire continues to treat his nightmares with *Humulus lupulus* (hops) and *Valeriana officinalis* (valerian), traditional aromatics and soporifics from Master Raymond's pharmacy. She soothes her mate with news of her unexpected pregnancy, a timely gift to the couple to salvage their romance and hope for the future. The couple remain intimate, even though Claire's oversized abdomen appears awkward in bed.

Sparing and Saving Lives

Out of pity for congenital impairment, before the Battle of Culloden on April 16, 1746, Claire arranges euthanasia by yellow jasmine liquid for Jamie's crippled uncle Colum MacKenzie, laird of Castle Leoch. A victim of terminal wry limbs akin to Toulouse-Lautrec syndrome, a disease causing brittle bones, he labors to walk even small distances. After Claire treats his pain with sacral massage, at the end of his tolerance, she offers assisted suicide in the form of deep sleep induced by drinking the vial of poisonous *Gelsemium sempervirens*. Her instructions leave to Colum time and place of his death and make no judgment on his choices.

With less candor, Claire repeats the dosage for Rufus, a seriously wounded slave at River Run who faces a barbarous lynching sanctioned by Southern law. At the end of the boy's life, Jamie prays for his soul and asks God's forgiveness for himself and Claire, both of whom venerate Catholic dictates forbidding suicide and murder. A more personal dilemma, Brianna Randall's pregnancy, causes Claire to abandon twentieth-century laws criminalizing abortion and to suggest expulsion of the fetus in the early stages of development. Her dispassionate instructions indicate the ability to dissociate herself from the role of Christian mother and future grandmother.

Medical risks follow Claire from Boston to Edinburgh and across the Atlantic to the West Indies. A day after Claire's arrival at Jamie's Edinburgh shop in 1766, her selflessness recurs in surgical relief of a brain bleed in the sneak thief John Barton, a potential rapist. He dies after trepanning, an easing of cranial pressure with a drill. At sea, against Jamie's admonition, Claire opts to treat three hundred survivors of a shipboard epidemic of typhoid fever, which had no antidote in the mid–1700s. Out of love for fourteen-year-old aide Elias Pound, she blames herself for his death from the contagion and volunteers to stitch his corpse into a canvas shroud for burial at sea. In Elias's final delirium, she poses as his birth mother and calls him home, a euphemism for joining his deceased mama in heaven. The brief farewell dramatizes Claire's inborn mothering urges.

Parenting and Forgiving

Youths like Rufus and Elias bring out the best in the Frasers. Jamie confesses his fault in the hemorrhage that kills Geneva Dunsany, whom he impregnates impersonally on her command. At Brownsville, North Carolina, Claire chides Alicia Brown for attempting to shoot herself to end her longing for Isaiah Morton and kill their unborn child. Claire joins Jamie in rescuing Rabbie MacNab from abuse and in parenting the motherless Fergus,

Young Ian Murray, and Fanny Beardsley's biracial infant and the grandmothering of Germain, Joan, and Felicité Fraser and Jeremiah "Jemmy" MacKenzie. The Big House on Fraser's Ridge offers the Frasers a chance at rearing Wee Bonnie Beardsley, an Afro-American newborn, but Claire, out of pity for Lucinda Brown, chooses to surrender the little girl to the wetnurse who still mourns the death of her premature infant. The decision authenticates Claire's deep commitment to surgical ethics and to compassion for the defenseless.

Throughout the saga, Jamie's greatheartedness involves him in danger and in grace, which he confers on his former girlfriend Annalise de Marillac, the widow of a rival dueler who dies of smallpox. From a soldier's perspective in a murky barn at Corrieyairack, Jamie justifies release of sixteen-year-old William John Grey from an attempted assassination with a knife to Jamie's throat. The act of mercy defines much of ensuing action, securing a lifelong friendship with the stepfather/uncle/widower who rears Jamie's motherless son William "Willie" Ransom and shields Brianna from an arranged marriage at River Run with attorney Gerald Forbes. On the way west from Wilmington, North Carolina, an unwise rescue of felon Stephen Bonnet confutes Jamie's benevolence. By offering Bonnet transportation, Jamie unleashes a murderer and smuggler, thief of Claire's wedding ring, brutalizer of Brianna, and stalker of Jemmy, whom Stephen believes to be his son.

Jamie's humanity forgives the poor from spitting at the militia and releases married seducer Isaiah Morton from the custody of Lionel Brown, an outraged father in Brownsville. Jamie sets Isaiah on the way to an adulterous relationship with Alicia Brown, who bears his child. Perhaps Jamie sees in Isaiah his own ill-planned marriage to Laoghaire MacKenzie MacKimmie, an abused and twice-widowed mother rearing fatherless daughters Joanie and Marsali. After arranging with attorney Ned Gowan for alimony and sparing Laoghaire imprisonment for firing a pistol into Jamie's left shoulder, Jamie chooses to flee the area with Claire, his rightful spouse. In North Carolina, he can continue to support a faux second family without having to quarrel with the indomitable Laoghaire. Their permanent separation also enables him to enjoy stepfatherhood of Marsali Fraser, Fergus's wife. At the wedding in Haiti, Father Fogden blesses Claire and Jamie, ostensibly for their union and good will to the newlyweds.

See also Healing; Parenting.

Source

Del Mar Rubio-Hernández, María, and Irene Raya Bravo. "The Erotization of the Male Body in Television Fiction: *Outlander* as a Case Study," *Oceánide* 10 (2018): 1–9.

Doran, Sarah. "How Outlander Fans Helped Diana Gabaldon Change the TV Portrayal of Jamie Fraser's Assault," *Radio Times* (1 June 2017).

Javaid, Aliraza. "Feminism, Masculinity and Male Rape: Bringing Male Rape 'Out of the Closet,'" *Journal of Gender Studies* 25:3 (2016): 283–293.

Nagouse, Emma. "The Lamentation of Jamie Fraser: *Outlander*, Male Rape and an Intertextual Reading of Lamentations 3," *The Shiloh Project* (11 September 2017).

_____. "To Ransom a Man's Soul': Male Rape and Gender Identity in *Outlander* and 'The Suffering Man' of Lamentations 3," *Rape Culture, Gender Violence, and Religion*. London: Palgrave Macmillan, 2018, 143–158.

American Revolution

An historical crucible uniting Highlander recovery from the Battle of Culloden on April 16, 1746, with the ousting of English imperialists from North America, seasons four and five of the *Outlander* TV epic format shifting fictional loyalties. At the end of episode one, Maureen Lee Lenker, a TV critic for *Entertainment,* identifies North Carolina violence as "the early rumblings of what we know will build to the American Revolution" (*ibid.*). At the core of conflict, Scots-Americans reject the English demand that the New World requite the debts of the old. The focus of their ill will, Tryon's Palace at New Bern, North Carolina, revives Highlander hatred of greed and preying on peasants via high taxes and duties collected by unscrupulous agents and sheriffs.

Producer Matthew B. Roberts stated of the worst of the war for independence from 1775 to 1783: "Being at the center of the birth of America is often a bloody and violent and heartbreaking matter" (Vincenty, 2020). Claire, a time traveler well acquainted with facts from the eighteenth century, warns Jamie that fighting in Governor William Tryon's Rowan County Militia places him on the losing side. Of the contretemps, actor Sam Heughan confided, "I think they obviously know from history what's coming," but Jamie views his involvement as a means of assuring his daughter a free country (*ibid.*). Brianna's gallop to the militia encampment at Alamance Creeks warns Jamie that the Regulator loss of combat on May 16, 1771, against the Redcoats sparks a national upheaval.

A fictional citizen effort, in fall 1772, the Committee of Safety that vigilante Richard Brown forms consists of an *ad hoc* militia and source of communication. Television reviewer Amanda-Rae Prescott commented, "These groups, which were initially formed to stop criminal activity in rural areas, also became the new outlet for the defeated Regulators' anti-government agitation" (Prescott, 2020). The fifth state to organize a provincial response to revolutionary crisis, North Carolina followed Georgia, Maryland, Delaware, and Massachusetts and preceded formation of patriot committees in New York and New Jersey.

In 1882, John Dalton Whitford, a columnist for the *New Berne Weekly Journal,* expounded on Tryon's vanity and dismissal of settler unrest as the causes of war: "He did not know the period was so close at hand for this country to boldly assert its independence and to have sufficient strength to maintain it … and to aid in establishing the great American Republic" (Whitford, 1882). As actions worsened against slavery, importing European goods, and violating provincial regulations, subsequent North Carolina Governor Josiah Martin of Dublin, Ireland, fled New Bern in June 1775. After nearly four years in office, he migrated from the Cape Fear River to the British war sloop *Cruizer* in July and continued his administration offshore. Patriots burned his refuge at Fort Johnston, the beginning of North Carolina's open revolt.

See also Militia; Regulators; Tryon's Palace; Weapons.

Source

Lenker, Maureen Lee. "*Outlander* Recap: Is It the American Dream or Nightmare?" *Entertainment* (4 November 2018).
Prescott, Amanda-Rae. "*Outlander* Season 5 Episode 11 Review: Journeycake," *Den of Geek* (3 May 2020).
Vincenty, Samantha. "Everything We Know about Outlander Season 5," *Oprah Magazine* (7 February 2020).
Whitford, James Dalton. "Rambles about Town: Tryon's Palace," *New Berne Weekly Journal* (3 December 1882).

Anachronism

The *Outlander* TV chronicle splices futurist details with period culture and social expectations, an auditory jolt of jazz sax at Castle Leoch (1:3), Claire's hangover and delight in Bob Hope (1:7), Brianna's requests for Eggo Toaster Waffles (3:2), and, in season five, sepia film clips (5:8), Jamie's first microscopic view of sperm (5:8), and PB&J sandwiches (5:11). The emersion of time traveler Claire Randall in eighteenth-century Scotland and North America requires constant monitoring of conversation and behavior to avoid confusing people with language and feminist concepts from the previous two centuries. Because of her training in Allied combat nursing, she follows World War II protocols that demand antisepsis against infection (1:1) with iodine (1:1), merthiolate (1:1), cautery (5:5), and penicillin (3:8, 3:11, 5:2). In frustration, she swears, "Jesus H. Roosevelt Christ," an allusion to the role of American president Franklin Delano Roosevelt in rescuing England from German bombardment (1:1).

In season three, Claire's wise introduction of penicillin injections with a hypodermic syringe (3:8) reduces Jamie's fever from a gunshot wound to his left shoulder. On reuniting with Brianna in season four, mother and daughter recall past treats—hamburgers with all the trimmings (4:10) and peanut butter and jelly sandwiches (4:10). In the performance of Claire's medical role, she misses aspirin (4:10) and toilets that flush (4:10). At her clinic at the big house, she grows bread mold for extraction of penicillium, an antibiotic fungus (5:2), and conceals an autopsy (5:2) to determine Leith Farrish's cause of death. While diagnosing Aaron Beardsley's illness, she identifies apoplexy by the modern term, "stroke" (5:3). During Jemmy's cold, Brianna and Roger wish for baby aspirin and boxes of tissues (5:6). Claire's recognition of a fellow time traveler results from Wendigo Donner's mention of Beatles drummer Ringo Starr (5:12).

BITS OF CULTURE

Jamie Fraser recognizes the time warp that summons terms unfamiliar to his era—Christmas stockings (1:8), commando raids (2:9), bicycle (3:6), camera (3:6), fizzle (3:9), Jell-O (3:6), and photograph (3:6). He admires the workings of a zipper (3:6, 3:11), which befuddles Mamacita in Hispaniola. At the Wilmington playhouse, Claire accidentally refers to chopping down cherry trees (4:8), part of lore from George Washington's boyhood. At Fraser's Ridge, Brianna mentions Appalachian frontiersman Daniel Boone (4:9), who was alive but not a legend in 1770. Claire, Roger, and Brianna keep to themselves references to the Easter rabbit (1:5), jazz records (4:10), Led Zeppelin (4:10), L-O-V-E (5:1), the Mashed Potato and Twist (5:1), cut a rug (5:1), Elvis (5:1), Nancy Drew (5:2), Scarlett O'Hara (5:3), antivenin (5:9), and Never My Love (5:12).

Vernacular mention of entertainment and literature recalls the tippler's toast Geronimo (1:5) to wool waulkers. From the 1939 movie *The Wizard of Oz*, Claire rewords "There's no place like [home]" (1:4) and recites "I'm going to miss you most of all" (2:7). The episode "Not in Scotland Anymore" (2:2) rephrases Dorothy's assurance to Toto that they aren't in Kansas. While playing chase with children at Castle Leoch, Claire thinks about bread crumbs (2:11) from "Hansel and Gretel," a nineteenth-century fairy tale by the Grimm brothers. Geillis Duncan Abernethy retrieves the Strange Case of Benjamin Button (3:12) and, from the 1942 film *Casablanca*, recites "of all the gin joints in all the towns in all the world" (3:12), a sarcasm directed at meeting Claire at Rose Hall, Jamaica. Varied situations involving Brianna and Roger MacKenzie summon "Are You Going to San Francisco" (4:7), Lewis Carroll's "Down the Rabbit Hole" (4:7), pull out of a hat (4:11), Jeremiah was a bullfrog (5:2), and Smokey the Bear (5:2). Roger's ineptitude with a rifle calls to mind the Tufty Fluffytail Club (5:2), a British animal monitor created in 1953 by the Royal Society for the Prevention of Accidents to Children.

TROUBLED TIME LAPSES

Anachronisms pop out of Claire's mouth without warning. At the Black Kirk, she miscues Jamie with Germany (1:3), which she quickly replaces with the historically correct "Prussia." Other out-of-time terms prove crucial to the action, especially sadistic (1:16) and sadist (2:9), psychological terms for spousal abuse that came into use in the 1890s, and *crème de menthe* (3:7), an after-dinner digestive formulated in France in the 1880s. Claire's reliance on a pocket mirror (3:11, 5:3) employs silvered glass, first manufactured in the 1830s. The scene of her beach rescue on Hispaniola reprises a handy use of reflected light in a TV episode of *Dr. Quinn, Medicine Woman.*

Additional oops in the scripts incorporate "Comin Thru the Rye" (3:6), a Robert Burns poem from 1782, the Scots hymn "Abide with Me" (5:2) from 1847 at Leith Farrish's burial, and the Victorian wedding custom of something old, something new, something borrowed, something blue, and a sixpence in the shoe (5:1), which Jamie cites to his daughter. A contrast in expectations on Jamie's fiftieth birthday on May 16, 1771, allies Claire's "Happy Birthday to You" (5:7), composed in 1893, with "Clementine" from the late nineteenth century (5:7), a mournful frontier ballad that Roger sings to Jemmy. A wisp of gallows humor from Brianna before the Battle of Alamance Creek declares her competent to sing "Clementine" if something happens to Roger (5:8).

On a North Carolina beach, Claire and Brianna's day at the shore reminds them of a less polluted world and a time before whaling reduced the sea's whale population (5:10). Brianna recalls how much she admires novelist Herman Melville's sea classic *Moby-Dick* (5:10), which she pretends to read aloud to Stephen Bonnet from a book on animal husbandry. After revealing time travel to Young Ian, in fall 1772, Claire recognizes script that Otter Tooth wrote in ballpoint pen (5:11) and introduces her entire family to peanut butter and jelly sandwiches, which Jamie eats with fork and knife (5:11).

See also Costume; Music; World War II.

Source

Herrera, Hannah. "Shifting Spaces and Constant Patriarchy: The Characterizations of Offred and Claire in *The Handmaid's Tale* and *Outlander*," *Zeitschrift für Anglistik und Amerikanistik* 67:2 (2019): 181–196.
Murillo, Stella. "Half-Ghosts and Their Legacy for Claire, Jamie and Roger," *Adoring Outlander: Essays on Fandom, Genre and the Female Audience.* Jefferson, NC: McFarland, 2016, 144–161.

Animals

In a departure from human behaviors and instincts, according to Caroline Hallemann, a journalist for *Town and Country*, the *Outlander* TV saga "is no stranger to animals," from maggots on the bite of a pit viper, Colum's caged pets, and whales leaping along the North Carolina shore to Willie's pony Rosy and a buffalo charging Brianna MacKenzie in the Fraser backyard (Hallemann, 2019). Episodes incorporate animal transportation, appraisal, harvesting, and care, from Jamie's tumble from a horse in the dark to Brianna's dog Smokey in the photo at Abandawe, Ulysses's honking mule Clarence, Father Fogden's goats and chickens, Claire's gray cat Adso, and Yi Tien Cho's claim on Manzetti's hawksbill for turtle soup and his apology for killing Arabella the goat. At Castle Leoch, Claire receives a wardrobe from Mrs. Fitzgibbons that includes fur-trimmed winter riding cloaks, neck pieces, and hoods that rival the furs of Letitia MacKenzie. The dungeon lab contains pharmacopeia left by Davie Beaton, a deceased apothecary, leech, charmer, or medic in the medieval Celtic tradition. Critic Sarah Stegall describes his collection as "rather revolting remedies … horse dung, sheep's testicles, worms," nature-based curatives that contrast Claire's reliance on wild flora (Stegall, 2016, 100).

For Jamie, early life on a farm introduces him to the care of horses, which he trains, curries, breeds, and diagnoses for splints, swayback, and hoof abscess. He describes a winter of free-roaming rustling when he subsists on grass in the absence of food, a reduction of human diet in pursuit of herding wealth. The scripts impose an implausible naiveté on a 22-year-old adult, a seasoned mercenary for four years. Inconceivably, he confuses equine mating front to back with coupling with his human bride, who directs him to the missionary position. On a post-wedding ride with War Chief Dougal MacKenzie's band, Rupert recites the tale of the waterhorse, a mystic kelpie that Claire mentions to frighten the mulatto Tebbe. The story alludes to the warmth of the Fraser marriage and foretells Scotland's touristy Loch Ness monster lore.

Human Conflicts

Complications in the action retrieve human-animal relations at key moments. After battling Lord Simon Lovat over the Jacobite cause in season two, episode eight, Jamie retreats to the stable and admits to envying beasts their carefree existence, a suggestion of the Jungian concept of the unconscious mind and subhuman instinct. In France, he serves as a purchasing agent assessing stance, age, and promise in thoroughbred steeds. At the English estate of Helwater, grooming and saddling horses indirectly results in Jamie's siring of son William "Willie" Ransom by Geneva Dunsany, a skilled equestrienne who demands his bedroom skills to end her virginity. The alliance of Jamie with animal breeding enhances his symbolic value as a sex object and husband.

The incarceration of Claire and Geillis Duncan in Thieves Hole, a subterranean cell at Cranesmuir in 1743, affirms period accommodations for suspected criminals and sorcerers, whom wardens treat with inhumanity and disrespect. At a break in the witch trial, Claire admires a murmuration of starlings, one of a series of bird images that suggest the Celtic reverence for flight and freedom, from heron to American eagle to the songbirds on her window in Boston. The introduction to the seventh episode, season two, inexplicably pictures a heron that delights young Bree. A segue to Claire's birthing of Faith fails to legitimize the episode's opening scene, which connects improbably to visions of blue wings, a representation of healing. The wings take on lamentable meanings in Mother Hildegarde's revelation that Claire's stillborn infant has joined the angels. The wing metaphor returns in season three, episode thirteen when Claire approaches death amid the sunken white sails of the French brig *Artemis*.

Horse and Dog

In a saga dependent on horseback riding, mounts epitomize the character of Jamie, Claire, and Dougal. During the long lope from Lallybroch to Beaufort Castle in season two, episode eight, Claire's fancy-footed white horse diverts in style and color from Jamie's more dashing black steed. Later glimpses of the white horse's prissy footwork suggest that the horse suits the elite or a lady of Claire's stature and breeding. By seating Dougal on a white gelding mottled with gray spots, the coloring implies the splotched nature of the MacKenzie war chief, who dies ignobly under Jamie's dirk after threatening to kill his nephew. (Inexplicably, the distinctive mounts follow the Frasers to North America and enjoy more screen time, particularly Finley, the victim of a *tskili yona*'s claws.)

At Lallybroch, two dogs, Lucas and Bran, guard the premises. The latter bears the name of a Welsh mythic hero and king of Britain. Another vital mammal, Bouton, the infection sniffer at l'Hôpital des Anges, lends a precious touch to nursing the desperately

infected among the Paris poor. The small, scruffy terrier snaps to work at Mother Hildegarde's command to "allez" and locates an abscess in a man's broken leg (2:7). By endearing the dog to viewers, the series prefigures Bouton's devotion to guarding Claire during
her lethal experience with puerperal fever and anticipates second daughter Brianna's first
word, dog (3:6). The insertion of small animals into the second season advances from
the conscientious Bouton to the vicious Colette, Louise's monkey, which bites the bonnie
prince's hand, and the plasticky caged snake in the Star Chamber, a borrowing from the
more realistic *I, Claudius* TV series.

Mild and Wild

The action turns rabbits into a multi-use symbol as harbingers of survival for Jamie
and as food for post-war inmates at Ardsmuir Prison who snare them on the heath. In
the wild, Jamie handily skins his catch for dinner. During a flash forward to the Randall home in Boston, Claire amuses Brianna with a stuffed bunny in her playpen. On the
Culloden battleground in 1746, a rabbit looks toward Jamie, suggesting a flicker of frisk-
iness in a battered body. Outside Rose Hill, Jamaica, fortuneteller Margaret Campbell
divines the battlefield rabbit's significance to Jamie and addresses the Frasers in their
daughter's voice. At streamside with Adawehi, Claire and her fellow healer exchange
Cherokee and English words for the animal—*tsistu*/rabbit. The prompt causes Adawehi
to intuit Brianna's landing in eighteenth-century North Carolina. The rabbit returns in
two forms to the season five finale, again as a symbol of endurance.

Unlike the peaceable rabbit, the Gothic touch of wolves baying at Claire outside
Wentworth Prison suggest abandoning Jamie as sacrificial lamb after Captain Black Jack
Randall tosses Claire to the bone pile. A cattle stampede—a staple of American cowboy
film—unleashes on Jack and his soldiers a bestial chaos that threatens his survival. Witty
in its show of bravura and brute strength in a stone lockup, the event returns at Versailles
in mention of the jailbreak during an informal audience with Louis XV. Playacting sympathy for Jack's physical complaints, Jamie pretends to remember the animal explosion as
sheep rather than cattle, a smirking demotion of Jack's heroic wounding.

While rehabilitating in a cave near Lallybroch, Jamie survives on fish and rabbit
and aids the fatherless Murray family by aiming his arrow at an antlered stag, a reminder
that the renegade retains the laird's masculine influence and agency. In Jenny's kitchen,
his hacks with a cleaver signify the unremitting terrorism of Redcoat insurgency and the
outlawing of weapons and dissolution of clan homesites during the 1746 post–Culloden
Clearance. To his shame, Jamie views Corporal MacGregor lopping Fergus's left hand
with a saber and rushes to save the boy from bleeding from the stump. The lingering
camera pan on a dismembered hand furnishes gratuitous Gothicism at the expense of
decorum.

New World Fauna

The West Indies and Carolinas introduce domesticated and feral beasts, including
goats, the expensive Arabian stallion named Lucas, squirrels, an eagle, a mass of birds
marking the Beardsley trading post with ill omens, smokepots aimed at an invasion of
locusts, a mountain lion's cry and call of a mourning dove, and a huge Haitian snake
crawling over Claire's middle, which foretokens Geillis Duncan Abernethy's slither over
Young Ian. An easy target for Brianna's rifle, wild turkeys supply frontier families with

an edible bird that joined New Spain's chocolate and Andean potatoes in the Columbian exchange of American foodstuffs to sixteenth-century Europe. Young Ian's half-wolf, half-dog Rollo, won from a sailors' dice game, augurs a dicey future for the Frasers, who must learn by experience how to avoid crime and violence in the wilderness after Stephen Bonnet's river pirate raid. At Fraser's Ridge, Claire works up a dinner of trout to replace the meat bag stolen by the *tskili yona* (evil bear), an insane man's crazed attempt at shape-shifting. Significantly, the Cherokee rechristen Jamie with a feral name—*yona dihi* (Bear Killer), the result of struggle between a human stalker and animal spirit.

The promise of a smokehouse on the Fraser property foretells an easier time, when Jamie and Young Ian's tracking and fishing will supply them with fresh meat and jerky, a favorite snack that Claire ate in Boston. The hunting trek with William "Willie" Ransom over Fraser's Ridge verifies Jamie's New World skills at tracking and skinning a stag for the table as well as cooking venison liver for supper, a hunter's reward for his son. On the flash forward to Roger and Brianna's drive in North Carolina toward the gathering of the clans at Grandfather Mountain, they cover roads built on the trails left by animal tracks through the forest.

Animals continue to impact families with danger and adequate food harvested close to home. Marsali Fraser exhibits strength and knowledge in removing the liver from a slaughtered goat and in disjointing a pig, a training session she applies to Geordie's dislocated shoulder. On the recruitment of militia, Jamie and Claire encounter a macabre situation at the trading post of Aaron and Fanny Beardsley, who pen a billy and nanny goats indoors to keep them warm. The protection proves insightful. After Fanny gives birth and abandons her biracial daughter, Claire relies on goat milk to feed the baby. The short-term change of nutrition keeps the child content until the Rowan County Militia reaches Brownsville, home of Lucinda Brown, a willing wetnurse.

At an evocative moment in season five, episode eight, the Fraser grandparents are teaching Jemmy MacKenzie his numbers during a game of hide-and-seek when a boar charges from the brush. Young Ian's quick shot of an arrow into its neck kills the wild pig and supplies pork for a family dinner. More meals from the wild in episode nine treat Jamie with roasted bites of pit viper and feed the neighborhood a hearty dinner after Claire shoots a raging bison. On the coast in "Mercy Shall Follow Me," she collects sponges for the clinic and a conch shell to grind into calcium for patients. At pirate Stephen Bonnet's Ocracoke residence, a large fish entree connects him with marine life and his sale of Brianna to Captain Howard.

See also Storytelling.

Source

Hallemann, Caroline. "See the First Photo of Sam Heughan Introducing Outlander's Newest Furry Cast Member, ADSO," *Town & Country* (24 May 2019).

Stegall, Sarah. "The Beaton: Healing as Empowerment for Claire Beauchamp," *Outlander's Sassenachs: Essays on Gender, Race, Orientation and the Other in the Novels and Television Series*. Jefferson, NC: McFarland, 2016, 97–104.

Architecture

To survey social levels, the *Outlander* TV series emphasizes the stone, thatch, and whitewashed buildings of eighteenth-century Scotland from Edinburgh to the Highlands. The hideout where Claire Randall first encounters War Chief Dougal MacKenzie's Jacobite band illustrates the bare-bones stone cottage with thatched roof, a spare shelter common to the poor since feudal construction in the 1100s. Without adequate indoor light, she examines a dislocated shoulder under meager fireplace illumination. In witnessing an eviction of Scots cottagers by the Watch, she questions why attackers fire the flammable covering. The same impermanent style of construction marks the barn, animal enclosures, and craft space for women waulking wool, an icon of period fiber work complete with its own space and work song.

In a tourist view of fictional Castle Leoch on the Firth of Forth in late October 1945, Frank Randall's flashlight flits over neglected walls and thick wood doors belonging to the historic Doune Castle, Perthshire. Trailing vines and spider webs indicate centuries of neglect and abandonment. On arrival to Leoch 202 years in the past, Claire views the thatched sheds and outbuildings of a four-story stone mansion. Roman arches frame the doorways; stone sills line the latticed windows overlooking a courtyard busy with domestic chores conducted on muddy ground. Crenellations and lookout towers enable MacKenzie garrisons to prevent attackers from approaching. Thrust into Davy Beaton's surgery, Claire discovers an in-house prison below the main floor level outfitted with shelving and work tables for concocting remedies and treating patients.

THE FRASER ESTATE

The homes of Dougal and Jamie juxtapose less wealth than Laird Colum MacKenzie's estate. Jamie's home, Lallybroch, offers a fictional version of Medop (Midhope) Castle at Hopetoun Estate near Linlithgow. Period design depicts a mid-level eighteenth-century mansion of unassuming proportions. Begun in 1458 by Laird John Martyne, the floor plan features a four-story stone tower with garret on the west wall. Three corner bartizans or turrets supported by corbels in late medieval style offered the additional protection of arrow slits. Vantage points enabled security forces to halt undermining of the walls and the displacement of earthworks to cause battlements to collapse.

At Martyne's death, on April 4, 1478, Henry Levingstone, moderator of the Presbyterian synod, acquired the baronial Midhope mansion. It passed in 1582 to a knight, Alexander Drummond of Carnock, Lord Midhope, and his wife, Marjory Bruce, who remodeled the tower in 1587. Under entailment, at the death of their eldest son, Judge Alexander Drummond of Midhope, on July 15, 1619, Robert of Fife, the Drummonds' next son, became laird. When Midhope passed from Robert and wife Marjory Elphinstone Drummond to George, 4th Earl of Linlithgow, and wife Henrietta Sutherland Livingstone and on to John and Margaret Hamilton Hope in 1678, a few architectural treasures upgraded the Hopetoun mansion. Additions included the entrance arch beneath a three-step wall and family crest, Renaissance front door capital, oak stair, painted and gilded ceiling beams, paneling, plastered cornices, walled garden, and underkitchen.

Opposite the Firth of Forth, Midhope grew into a castle in 1710 under the control of antiquary, geographer, and physician Robert Sibbald, wife Anna Orrock, and daughters Eupham, Katherine, and Elizabeth. With the addition of a three-story house on the east wing, the manse acquired a crested coat of arms and two-room dovecote housing 2,000 doves, a table delicacy and focal bird for *Outlander* action. A steep gabled roof coordinated slate with turrets. Into the mid–1800s, the structure housed grooms and carters, gardeners, joiners, gamekeepers, foresters, and Hopetoun Estate workers before the dereliction of the empty château in the early twentieth century.

SCENES OF STRIFE

At another screen setting east of the Firth of Clyde in Ayrshire, the Lord Simon Lovat's fictional compound at Beaufort Castle ironically derived from men loyal to Robert I the Bruce at the Battle of Bannockburn on June 23, 1314, where Scots defeated England's Edward II. As a reward, Robert Boyd and wife Joanna Montgomerie accepted the 200-acre parcel and Kilmarnock Castle, later known as Dean Castle. Their war-like son Thomas Boyd fortified the estate in 1350 with a four-story keep and three-story archers' tower. An imposing crenellated structure with walls nine feet thick, in 1467, the edifice featured a great hall, gatehouse, corbeled gables, battlements, gun-loops, terraced gardens, and orchard. After the Battle of Culloden on April 16, 1746, the British decapitated William Boyd, the security guard for the bonnie prince, at Tower Hill, London. His ghostly head appeared to roll across the floor in a specter predicted by the fictional seer Maisri and Claire Fraser.

Overlooking the south coast of the Firth of Forth on the port of Linlithgow, the curtain wall of Fort William provides fictional grounding for Jamie's scourging and Captain Black Jack Randall's interrogation of Claire Randall. An historic courtyard castle known as Blackness, the four-story crenellated stronghold was the plan of George Crichton, sheriff of Stirling, who built a free-standing five-floor tower at center in 1449. James II annexed the property in 1453. Thickened and reinforced in 1537 by architect James Hamilton of Finnart with a covered caponier (dry moat) and gunports for small cannon fire, it served as an armory. The North Tower incarcerated Catholic plotter Cardinal David Beaton and Earl Archibald Douglas, a traitor to James V. Stout fortification in 1553 braced the walls to withstand artillery.

After the military defortified gates and dungeons in 1580, the Livingstones acquired Blackness Castle from the Stewarts in 1600. Under assault by English statesman Oliver Cromwell's siege batteries, the structure wavered. The chapel collapsed in June 1650 and yielded to the English. Charles II restored the prison in 1660; after the Act of Union, the British Army garrisoned Blackness in 1707. The South Tower became a main residence and the walled keep a munitions dump. Blackness Castle served as a prison for captives of the Napoleonic wars and as a cinematic setting for the Mel Gibson *Hamlet* and for the films *Ivanhoe, Outlaw King, The Bruce,* and *Mary Queen of Scots.*

PLACE OF HEALING

Just as torture alters the fictional hero's life, Father Anselm's medieval stone abbey resets architectural expectations from military to Benedictine, a brotherhood devoted to hospitality. Decor marked by white-washed walls, groined ceilings, crucifixes, and candles projects a monastic piety suited to treating the sick, both physically and spiritually. Filmed at Aberdour Castle, which Alan and Countess Anicea de Mortimer erected at Fife in 1126, the trapezoidal tower house castle with arrow slits, timbered ceilings, and carved monograms—EWM and CAM—for Earl William Morton and Countess Anne Morton adapted to demands of a half millennium. In the spirit of the episode "To Ransom a Man's Soul," St. Fillan's Church took shape in 1140 to honor an eighth-century monk who treated the mentally ill.

In the hands of William Douglas of Liddesdale, James Douglas of Dalkeith, and Joan Stewart, the deaf mute daughter of James I, in the early 1300s to mid–1400s, Aberdour Castle acquired a massive beehive dovecote, source of epicurean meals. In 1635, designers molded mantelpieces, painted Renaissance ceilings with foliage and fruit in tempera, and hung tapestries featuring heraldic devices. Chronicles record domestic details—a brewery, apple orchard, and corner sundial. In 1740, planners terraced gardens along a steep grade, source of horse chestnuts, mulberry trees, water lilies, and lavender for the fictional Jamie's healing, a specialty of Benedictine monks like Father Anselm and Brother Paul.

Religious Retreats

Simple venues create charm and atmosphere for *Outlander* as well as authentic Scots history. For the Frasers' wedding, Glencorse (or Glencross) Old Kirk, at Penicuick in Midlothian seven miles south of Edinburgh provided a Gothic stone edifice with post and lintel entrance and tiled roof. Lighted by candelabra and lancet windows, the one-room sanctuary and its three descending stone stairs encompassed the unyielding attitude of church fathers concerning custom and Catholic dogma. In 1370, John de Bothwell received from King David a land grant that passed to Richard de Bothwell and his heir Francis Bothwell, an attorney, and grandson Adam Bothwell, bishop of Orkney and husband of Margaret Murray. Begun in 1616 under a great-grandson, Judge John Bothwell of Alhammer, the original parish church burned during possession by his widow, Maria Carmichael. A decade before the christening of their son William Bothwell, Alexander Bothwell and Jonet Trotter Bothwell of Glencorse House rebuilt the edifice in 1665 with new nave, heraldic paneling, and front stairs to two lofts. By 1699, the floor plan expanded to a cruciform chancel with a round window and timbered spire. Until its abandonment in 1885, the setting accommodated worship and churchyard burials.

At a turn in Jacobite fate, Jamie and his followers withdraw to Tullibardine Chapel of St. Salvator north of Gleneagles, Perthshire, to tend Rupert MacKenzie, who requires surgery to remove a musket ball from his right eye. Built around 1446 near Tullibardine Castle, the structure occupies land acquired in 1284 by William de Moravia (Murray). Featuring timbered collar-beam roof, romanesque windows, aumbries, statuary niches, and walled cemetery, it was the private worship place of David and Margaret Colquhoun Murray of Dumbarton. When the stone chapel passed to their grandson Andrew and Margaret Barclay Murray in 1500, he enlarged the rectangular plan with arched transepts and a bell tower. The edifice and its Murray and Stewart coat of arms, burial vault, piscina basin, holy water stoup, and lancet and rose windows suffered damage by the British in retaliation against George Murray's leadership of the Jacobites at the Battle of Prestonpans on September 21, 1745. Because he fled to Holland and his brother William Murray died in the Tower of London in July 1746, the Drummond family took control of the property.

See also Castle Leoch; Craigh na Dun; Forts and Prisons; Fraser's Ridge; Lallybroch; l'Hôpital des Anges; River Run; Versailles.

Source

Colvin, Howard. *Architecture and the After-life.* New Haven: Yale University Press, 1991.

Gavin, Anne. "Outlandish Locations: A Look at Midhope Castle—Outlander's Lallybroch," *Outlander Cast* (17 April 2019).

MacGibbon, David, and Thomas Ross. *The Ecclesiastical Architecture of Scotland.* Edinburgh: D. Douglas, 1897, 330–337.

Mitchell, Hilary. "14 Scottish Places All 'Outlander' Fans Must Visit," *BuzzFeed* (21 May 2015).

Tabraham, C.J. *Scotland's Castles.* London: B.T. Batsford, 1997.

Birthing

Childbirth, which fictional con man Archibald Campbell identifies as "woman's curse," recurs as a secondary theme in the TV epic *Outlander* (3:12). When Jenny Murray's fetus appears to be breech, time traveler Claire readies herself to bring a "footling" (2:13). Curiosity about Jenny's pregnancy implies Claire's desire to have children, even though she fears she's barren after failed attempts to conceive a twentieth-century baby with husband Frank Randall. She appears adequate to superintend Jenny's heavy contractions, groans, and swollen fingers, but struggles to turn baby Margaret Ellen "Maggie" Murray during the birth. In the thirteenth episode, Jenny describes deep coital penetration as a man's desire to return to the womb, a non sequitur that the script fails to establish. On the gallop to find Jamie, she empties breast milk to ease the pain of engorgement, a discomfort she characterizes as one of the inconveniences of bearing and feeding infants.

The superb rendering of Claire's fictional 1744 labor and delivery in season two, episode seven reveals actor Caitriona Balfe in a range of emotions—joy at motherhood, disbelief that her daughter was born dead. The rising panic gives way to hysteria and a lengthy period of delirium and shivering from puerperal fever, which plunges Claire near death. The mystic appearance of Master Raymond extends the two healers' friendship. Rescued from the infectious afterbirth, Claire appears restored. The lapse into extreme anger transposes the grieving mother into the betrayed wife. A reunion with Jamie precedes one of the most heartrending scenes in the TV series, ending in clasped hands over a tiny headstone. On Claire's reunion with Jamie after two decades' absence, he recalls his first child and her red hair, a unifying element in the family that solidifies the love of a father for two daughters.

Sisters in Birth

Season three, episode one epitomizes Claire's waddling walk and domestic chores in her final weeks of a second pregnancy in November 1968. Filming segues to April 16, 1746, and scenes of Jamie's agony from a saber slash to the left thigh after defeat at the Battle of Culloden. A normal cycle of symptoms—waters breaking, contractions, dilation—follows Claire to a Boston hospital, where Dr. Thorne offers imperious and unnecessary advice on avoiding panic. As the birthing reaches conclusion, forcible anesthesia overrules the mother's wishes, a frequent complaint of second wave feminists who weary of supercilious obstetricians dominating medical choices. Claire retrieves control of motherhood in delight at Brianna's first breastfeeding, a Madonna-and-child pose revisited at Lallybroch after Jenny Murray produces Young Ian and in North Carolina at the bonding of Petronella Mueller with baby Clara.

Extending the arrival of progeny in episode two, the series turns Jenny's next lying-in to a vehicle for the black arts. In 1752, Fergus's shooting a crow to avoid harm to the child retrieves from William Shakespeare's tragedy *Macbeth* the warning that "the raven himself is hoarse/That croaks the fatal entrance of Duncan/Under my battlements" (I, v, 3). Just as Shakespeare chose the black bird as a harbinger of King Duncan's assassination, Fergus fears that a raven on the gate at Lallybroch bodes ill for Young Ian, newly born. While Jamie conceals the babe, Jenny's lie to the Redcoats imparts a falsified sorrow for a stillborn child, an echo of Jamie's grief at the birth and death of Faith Fraser in 1744.

Mothers in Duress

At Rose Hall, Jamaica, Geillis Duncan Abernethy fills in the story of her delivery of a son at the Duncan home in Cranesmuir and of rescue by War Chief Dougal MacKenzie, who substitutes Granny Joan MacClellan's remains at the witch pyre. The episode models how an unwanted babe delights William John and Sarah MacKenzie, a barren couple, while serving the evil ends of a self-absorbed pair of lovers. The series revives the importance of Dougal and Geillis's offspring to Roger MacKenzie, the baby boy's twentieth-century descendant. At the birthing of Roger and Brianna's boy Jeremiah, Brianna trusts Phaedra, the domestic slave at River Run, to follow the progress of pregnancy and delivery.

Season five elides the birth of Fergus and Marsali Fraser's daughter Joan, moving on to Claire's assistance to Fanny Beardsley, the fifth wife of Aaron Beardsley, who holds her in bondage by beatings until she conceives a child. At the baby's arrival in episode three, Jamie recognizes negroid features and skin tone of the laborer who sired her. When Fanny disappears overnight, Claire feeds "Wee Bonnie" goat milk until the couple can locate a nursing mother in Brownsville (5:3). Lucinda Brown's gratitude at having an infant to feed—whatever the race—illustrates the suffering of mothers whose children die at birth, a loss she shares with Ellen and Claire Fraser. Juxtaposed to fearful, tragic parturition, Felicité Fraser's arrival in the woods dramatizes a loving union and a husband willing to serve as midwife.

Source

DuPlessis, Nicole M. "Men, Women and Birth Control in the Early *Outlander* Books," *Outlander's Sassenachs: Essays on Gender, Race, Orientation and the Other in the Novels and Television Series.* Jefferson, NC: McFarland, 2016, 82–96.

Gregor, Walter. *Notes on the Folk-Lore of the North-East of Scotland.* Sydney, Wales: Wentworth, 2019.

Sinn, Shannon. "The Raven and Crow of the Celts," *Living Library* (23 March 2018).

Bonnet, Stephen

Fierce, narcissistic smuggler and brigand Stephen Bonnet fills in the gap in series villainy. His demise occurs after the death of Captain Black Jack Randall, who succumbs to Jamie's dirk at the Battle of Culloden, Scotland, on April 16, 1746, and, in season three, the beheading of Geillis Duncan Abernethy in 1766 at Abandawe, a cave under a stone circle in Jamaica. Equally savage, but less sexually perverse, the fictional psychopath/pirate/murderer tosses the passenger Marion and her child into the sea to ward off a smallpox epidemic aboard his ship, the *Gloriana*. To preserve his crew, he apprehends another mother and sickly child, Morag and Jeremiah MacKenzie, whom sailor Roger Wakefield conceals in the hold. Little caring whether the pair lives or dies, Stephen tosses a coin to decide their fate, a glimpse of specie that becomes an ongoing icon of his melodramatic pursuit of Jemmy MacKenzie.

A career in banditry, human trafficking, and smuggling precedes Bonnet's capture and death sentence, the standard destiny of buccaneers during the Golden Age of Piracy. Essential to the script, his charismatic personality and gift for duplicity win Jamie's friendship and a sip of rum from his flask in the Wilmington jail. After eluding hanging on the gibbet, Stephen slips onto the Frasers' wagon and shares space alongside a haunch of venison and Gavin Hayes's shrouded remains. The sudden rise of the canvas over the corpse terrifies Lesley that a ghost follows them to Gavin's burial. Again, the pirate disarms the Frasers with bonhomie.

A Dual Personality

In later episodes, the charming Irish felon compounds his crimes with river rapacity, murder, and sex crimes. The TV series depicts luck and guile that free Stephen from the noose during an uproar in the crowd. To convince Jamie Fraser to trust him, the smuggler poses as a friend of Gavin Hayes and talks his way into free wagon transport away from road patrols by assisting at the wayside burial of Gavin's corpse. On his parting from the couple, his insincerity takes the form of a warning of thieves in the forest. His depravity continues along the Cape Fear River northwest of Wilmington, North Carolina, where he overtakes a barge and seizes Claire Fraser's wedding ring, an iron round that satisfies his fascination with circlets, an icon the series relates to the noose.

Reviewers EllenandJim [*sic*] characterize Stephen's return to the Cape Fear region as "a pantomime of violence and grief distanced from us by stylization in the acting [picturing] an ungrateful ruthless but debonair Mr. Bonnet" (EllenandJim, 2019). The *Outlander* TV narrative imposes on Jamie sincere regret for being hoodwinked and outmanned by the winsome freebooter, especially after learning that his and Claire's 20-year-old daughter Brianna suffered sexual assault and possible impregnation by Stephen. The jailhouse confrontation between the mother-to-be and her assailant discloses a tinge of humanity in Stephen, who furnishes her a red gemstone to help support the unborn child she says is his. The camera's lingering shot on a ring of jail keys poses a cliffhanger by suggesting that Stephen may escape an explosion by which the Regulators demolish the Wilmington stockade.

Pursuit to the End

Suspense until season five conceals Bonnet's survival. Reappearance in elegant garb revives his evil gambling over a bitch fight, blinding a victim with a knife, and pursuing Brianna and her son Jeremiah. John Grey's revelation that Stephen survived destroys wedding day elation for Brianna, who conceals that she knows he is alive. Secret knowledge invades marital intimacy, destroying the mood and forcing the bride to hide her worries. Her relationship with the rapist bedevils her marriage, causing Roger to question her motives for visiting Stephen's jail cell, lying about Jeremiah's paternity, and forgiving Bonnet's crimes.

A second blow to wedlock causes a rift in the Frasers. Jamie's gambling with Phillip Wylie using Claire's rings as ante results in a future smuggling deal with Stephen, but outrages her for risking another loss of her jewelry. As Jamie lies feverish from snakebite, he passes on a duty to kill Stephen to Roger. The narrative creates multiple ironies in the pirate's recompense—capture and trial leading to a death sentence by drowning, the demise he foresees in nightmares. Brianna's rifle bullet to his head creates a paradox—does she murder him out of pity or vengeance?

Historical Model

The name Stephen Bonnet suggests an historical basis in the exploits of Barbadian pirate and murderer Major Stede Bonnet (July 29, 1688–December 10, 1718), a career that one reviewer terms "violence as a way of life" (EllenandJim, 2019). A West Indian aristocrat born in Bridgetown, Barbados, to comfortable English sugar planters Sarah Whetstone and Edward Bonnet, he was the grandson of Thomas Bonnet, a pioneer New World investor. At age six following his father's death, Stede came into his inheritance of a cane mill, two windmills, and 520 cleared acres farmed by 94 slaves southeast of Bridgetown. After wedding Mary Allamby on November 21, 1709, he appears to have served the King's Guards as a major based on his property and the acreage from Mary's dowry rather than military expertise.

After the loss of Allamby Bonnet, the first of Mary and Stede's four children, in 1715, Stede chafed at island life. In spring 1717 at age 29, he pretended to join a party of Jacobite privateers to hunt down Spanish sea rogues at St. Thomas. Under the alias Captain Edwards, he initiated a sea dog's career in August 1717, decades before the TV series felon's appearance. With a hired crew, Stede contracted the building of the 60-ton Bermuda sloop *Revenge,* a name replete with the disgruntlement evident in *Outlander*'s anti–British Jacobites. After abandoning three- and four-year-old sons Stede, Jr., and Edward and baby daughter Mary, he embarked from Carlisle Bay south of Bridgetown with six cannon.

A maritime dictator impeccably dressed in fashionable suit, silk cravat, and powdered periwig, much like the fictional Stephen's foppery, Stede and seventy to eighty crewmen burned the Barbadian galley *Turbet* to quell rumors of piracy. On the South Carolina coast off Charleston, he seized and rifled Boston merchant Thomas Porter's brig *Elizabeth* and, on August 26, 1717, Barbadian captain Joseph Palmer's sloop *Industry*. Instead of sharing the loot from the *Anne, Endeavour,* and *Young,* Stede allotted his men wages, a peculiarity depicted in the *Outlander* series with the payment of Roger Wakefield at his request in small gemstones rather than coins or paper bills. After departure from eastern Long Island, New York, Stede sought the shallow-draft Pamlico Sound within the North Carolina Outer Banks, a hideout during hurricane season.

A CLUMSY PIRATE

Throughout much of his oceanic career, Stede lounged in his cabin and read volumes about navigation, weaponry, and seamanship, leaving command to the quartermaster Robert Tucker. Crew avoided Stede's surly, unpredictable moods, an idiosyncrasy he shared with the fictional Stephen Bonnet, who dominates his peers, terrorizes underlings, and philanders freely in Wilmington at Madame Sylvie's brothel. On the way to the Bahamas to trade indigo, tobacco, flour, sugar, molasses, rum, Madeira wine, slaves, cotton, tar, pistols, and personal items with merchant smugglers, Stede suffered shrapnel wounds and lost up to forty crewmen during pursuit by a Spanish man-o'-war in the Florida straits. At the pirate stronghold at Nassau, New Providence, he recuperated and refurbished the ten-cannon *Revenge* with two more guns.

In September 1717, Edward "Blackbeard" Teach and some 400 men took control of the *Revenge* and its two tenders. A month later, partners Blackbeard and Stede ransacked eleven ships between the Bahamas and the Virginia coast. At Delaware Bay off Philadelphia, Stede had two crewmen flogged, a serious punishment like the fictional Black Jack Randall's double lashing of Jamie Fraser in October 1739, which stirs observers to anger at British occupation forces. On November 28, 1717, off St. Vincent, Blackbeard captured his famed 200-ton flagship, the frigate *Queen Anne's Revenge,* and armed her with 31 cannon. In a general revolt against authority, he may have chosen the ship name as a salute to the last Stuart monarch, the bonnie prince's aunt, and in support of the Jacobite cause.

From April 5 until the end of the piracy season in December 1717, Blackbeard looted

28 merchant ships along Honduras in the Gulf of Mexico. At Belize, he resumed collaboration with Stede on March 28, 1718, following Stede's defeat by the 400-ton merchantman *Protestant Caesar* at Roatán Island in the Bay of Honduras. The Barbadian's ineptitude as a seaman and criminal caused his 300-man crew to desert and sail with Blackbeard. While Blackbeard held Stede under guard, Stede threatened noncompliant men with marooning on an island and made his victims walk the plank, an execution that the *Outlander* TV series resets as Captain Stephen Bonnet tossing sick passengers out the window of his quarters. The freebooting entourage sailed back to the South Carolina coast in mid–May 1718 and, for two weeks, blockaded Charleston by looting ten vessels for valuable medicines and holding prisoners for ransom.

SEEKING CLEMENCY

On June 10, 1718, the *Queen Anne's Revenge* ran aground at Topsail Inlet (Beaufort) east of Morehead City, North Carolina. At Bath, North Carolina's first colonial capital, in early summer 1718, Stede wangled amnesty from Governor Charles Eden, an anti-piracy politician who reputedly accepted bribes from Blackbeard. Eden assigned Stede a privateer's license to patrol Spanish sea traffic in the Virgin Islands on behalf of England and France. The chance to rob Spanish treasure fleets proved irresistible.

On return to captaincy in July 1718, Stede found himself cheated and robbed by his partner, who fled from Ocracoke, the island where the fictional Bonnet owns a residence. Stede renamed his sloop the *Royal James,* a salute to the dethroned James III, and hired Blackbeard's 25 rejects. Under the alias Captain Thomas, Stede built a criminal career from theft, kidnap, and murder. Flying a black flag showing a skull, single bone, heart, and dagger, he sailed a three-sloop flotilla from Delaware Bay to Wilmington. He moored his leaky flagship for repairs in August, the beginning of hurricane season on the mid–Atlantic coast and the most dangerous for balky treasure ships loaded with Spanish doubloons.

To end the constant preying on transatlantic shipping, on September 28, 1718, a merchant and militia officer, Colonel William Rhett, fought Stede at the five-hour Battle of Cape Fear River, a musket vs. cannon combat. The stalemate ended with surrender of the *Royal James,* announced by a knot tied in its flag. Before Stede could blow up the powder magazine, Rhett's 130-man navy seized the sloop. The militia nabbed 29 survivors of Stede's 46-man crew, a larger company than the band of the *Gloriana* pictured in *Outlander.*

TRIAL AND HANGING

On October 3, 1718, in Charleston, South Carolina, a favorite coastal target of Blackbeard, Stede entered arrest on Tradd Street at the house of night watchman and provincial councilman Nathaniel Partridge. Three weeks later, Stede escaped with his sailing master David Herriot and sought provisions in the swamps. The governor offered £700 (currently worth $168,932.47) for Stede's apprehension at a time the amount equaled seventy times the average income of £10 per annum. Upon the shooting death of Herriott by musket ball and the wounding of two slaves among the wetland Maroons on Sullivan's Island four miles south of Charleston, Rhett's posse recaptured Stede.

In November, boatswain Ignatius Pell testified that Stede took no role in the crew's piracy. To Judge Nicholas Trott, the popular folk hero stated that piracy was "contrary to my Inclination" and that he had slept during the boarding of the stolen sloop *Fortune* and the offloading of swag (*Tryals,* 1719, 39). In private, some colonial opinion exonerated Stede as a liberally educated "Gentleman, a Man of Honour, a Man of Fortune," but Attorney-General Richard Allein dubbed him "a common Robber" and "*Archipirata*" (*ibid.,* 9). On the damaging affidavit of Herriott before his death, a 23-man jury returned to the admiralty court a guilty vote against Stede on November 10 for looting the sloops *Fortune* and *Francis* and 18 murders.

The next day, Stede altered his plea to guilty of raiding thirteen ships and wrote Governor Johnson offering to amputate his own four limbs in exchange for a pardon. The visual image of multiple limb loss recurs in *Outlander* during Stephen's threats to maim Roger Wakefield if he refuses to sail to Philadelphia on the *Gloriana.* The judge postponed Stede's execution seven times because of pressure from citizens pitying the felon's mental instability. At age thirty on December 10, 1718, he died on the Charleston gallows at White Point (the Battery) and, alongside his crew's remains, went to a watery grave in the swamp, which the TV series alters to the bizarre death by drowning in a rising tide.

See also Fraser, Brianna; Crime; Jacobites; Maroons; Piracy; Rape.

Source

Butler, Lindley S. "Stede Bonnet," *South Carolina Encyclopedia.* Charleston: University of South Carolina, 2016.
Crawford, Amy. "The Gentleman Pirate," *Smithsonian* (31 July 2007).
EllenandJim. "Outlander, Season 4, from *Drums of Autumn*: The Colonialist American Past, a Book of Fathers & Ghosts," *EllenandJim* (10 February 2019).
Johnson, Charles. *A General History of the Pyrates.* London: Thomas Warner, 1724.
Lenker, Maureen Lee. "*Outlander* Recap: Is it the American Dream or Nightmare?," *Entertainment Weekly* (4 November 2018).
The Tryals of Major Stede Bonnet and Other Pirates. London: Benjamin Cowse, 1719.
Woodard, Colin. *The Republic of Pirates.* Orlando, FL: Houghton Mifflin, 2007.

Bonnie Prince Charlie

The sobriquet of the historic exile Charles Edward Stuart (September 31, 1720–January 31, 1788), the bonnie prince attempted to reframe Britain's monarchy from Anglican Hanoverian to Catholic Stuart. His prime fault, in the estimation of Celtic expert Christy Jackson Nicholas, allowed greed to thwart ambition and the reclamation of the Scottish crown. His fictional persona on the *Outlander* TV series depicts his plotting as devoid of rationale, justified by a preposterous sense of merit, and incaution with other people's money and lives.

The prince was born on December 31, 1720, at Rome to estranged parents, members of the doomed Jacobite succession. The elder son of James Edward Stuart and Maria Clementina Sobieska, a Silesian princess of Polish ethnicity, the prince came of age in Rome at the Palazzo Muti east of the Tiber River and resided part-time at the family's summer estate. He absorbed the disillusion of Jacobites who had expected Lord Mar to defeat the Hanoverian Duke of Argyll and to seize Edinburgh Castle in October 1715, five years before the prince's birth. The dismal strife brought down a Scots Hero, Rob Roy MacGregor, admirably played on screen in 1995 in the film *Rob Roy* by actor Liam Neeson.

A Depressing Coming of Age

Disunion between the Stuart parents inflicted an impression of rejection and melancholy on the bonnie prince and caused him to over-value loyalty, a trait that dominates his fictional maneuvering with Jamie Fraser at Maison Elise in Paris and with the Jacobites in the field. In 1744, the prince crusaded for the divine right of kings and led the 1745 Jacobite rising, a doomed effort to dethrone the Hanoverian George II, whom parliament selected to rule Great Britain. Launched on August 19, 1745, the last pro–Stuart rebellion elicited from the king a reward of £30,000 for the prince, an amount worth $65,189,700 today. The conflict ended in the Scottish highlands at Culloden Moor on April 16, 1746, with some two thousand Scots dead and others burned to death or bayonetted, an execution vivified in the *Outlander* TV episode "The Battle Joined."

Legend and folksay attended the bonnie prince throughout a glamorous life, leaving historians to muddle over his true nature. A prince regent at age 23, he used ample charisma to build a French coalition, the subject of fictional sessions with Jamie Fraser, Murtagh Fitzgibbons Fraser, and Joseph Duverney, finance minister of Louis XV from 1736 to 1758. The negotiations picture the demeaned young pretender conducting confabs at a Paris night spot and groveling for funds from Louis XV, Le Comte St. Germain, the Duke of Sandringham, and private English and French backers.

Jamie easily manipulates the prince's idealistic plans for a Stuart restoration by posing as a candid Scots informer and monitoring stolen mail. After a fictional encounter with tacksman Duncan Kerr, a demented Highlander dying of age and fever, Jamie avers to Lord John Grey that the transfer of funds from the French crown never happened. The hidden treasure remains a pipe dream conjured by Charles Stuart until Jocasta reveals Hector Cameron's role in whisking French gold out of Scotland after the Culloden debacle of 1746.

THE 1745 UPRISING

The bonnie prince's arrival via the warship *Elisabeth* on the isle of Eriskay on July 23, 1745, mobilized Jacobite forces composed of clan loyalists from the Camerons and MacDonalds, most of them Catholic. The British navy turned back the prince's troop ship, which bore cash, weapons, and seven hundred recruits. By August, when the British raised the reward for the capture of the Bourbon prince, Charles posted an equal amount for the capture of George II. After taking Edinburgh on September 17 and receiving homage at Holyrood Palace, before the Battle of Prestonpans six days later, the fictional prince voices a divisive opinion—his pity for British wounded, whom he identifies as brothers to the Scots. The statement appalls Jamie, who advises against giving preferential treatment to Redcoats.

On September 21, 1745, at Prestonpans on Scotland's southeastern shore, the prince and lightning fast Jacobites overwhelmed the English. The TV series depicts Jamie as the heroic leader of 6,000 clan warriors, who confound Redcoats still sleeping in tents and rout them in ten minutes. A lively folk song, "Johnnie Cope," mocked British General John Cope for the humiliating defeat by a Highlander whom the fictional British remember as "Red Jamie," the embodiment of Satan (3:1). In the aftermath on the way to Nairn in the dark, the prince gets lost, a fitting description of his clueless leadership of Jacobite forces.

Clad in highland tartan at the head of 4,500 men, the historical bonnie prince enjoyed a brief series of victories at Carlisle in November and Derby on December 4, 1745, a period that Scots dubbed "Charlie's year" (Duffy, 2007). On the approach to London, the fictional Jacobite high command rejects the prince's demand to press on and capture the capital. On December 26, he regroups to the far west at Glasgow. By January 17, 1746, the impassioned Jacobite cause rallied some twelve thousand men—a mix of Gaels, lowlanders, Irish, French, Welsh, and English, who defeated the British troops at Falkirk.

On fallback to Inverness, a stronghold of Stuart support on the Moray Firth, the fictional juggernaut abandons a night attack on April 15, 1746, during a birthday party for the Duke of Cumberland and wilts from poor leadership, exhaustion, and hunger. Against the advice of his generals, the prince exerts leadership and urges his staff to take London. In a risky setting, he faces the Duke's army at Culloden on April 16, a pivotal victory for British imperialism. Despite humanitarian intentions, the fictional Jamie and Claire's attempt to assassinate the mad prince by poisoning his tea with yellow jasmine fails to intervene in history. While cannon and artillery pound the Jacobites, the prince takes Jamie's horse and slips away, a humorous departing comment on Charlie's narcissism.

A Failed Life

On Claire's return to Jamie in 1766, she fills in details of the historical bonnie prince disguised in women's garb fleeing to the Isle of Skye on June 28, 1746, under the name Betty Burke. Scots émigrés carried to the American colonies the myths of Culloden and the scuttled prince as well as the bravery of Flora McDonald, who served a sentence in the Tower of London for aiding and abetting treason. Poet Robert Louis Stevenson recounted the national loss in his "Skye Boat Song" (1892). After the bonnie prince's five months as a fugitive, with the help of his younger brother Henry, Charlie escaped to France by the war frigate *L'Heureux* (Happy) on September 18, 1746. London media began stoking a long-lived tradition of heroism in the face of certain execution on the block or gibbet or before a military firing squad.

The historic prince's quixotic dream of a Stuart restoration crumbled from his heavy drinking, womanizing, and debauchery, tendencies that the fictional prince displays in the TV series with his frolics at Maison Elise. Just as the fictional prince withdrew from his pregnant mistress, the historical Louise de la Tour d'Auvergne, the real prince abandoned his cousin Marie Louise, whom he impregnated with son Charles, and, in 1748, left France under official orders. He disapproved of his illegitimate daughter Charlotte Stuart, child of Clementina Walkinshaw, his Scots mistress. Withdrawal of papal support from Clement XIII ended the Stuart succession and buoyed George III to rule on October 25, 1760.

The television series depicts the fictional bonnie prince as an hysterical, self-pitying religious fanatic and schemer incapable of accepting reality or prudent advice. Oddly, he achieves the respect of Louis XV, his father's cousin, but of few close observers. Jamie declares him a loon; Sandringham calls him an ass; General Murray rates him an imbecile. Murtagh Fitzgibbons Fraser, Jamie's guardian, opts to slit the royal throat. The prince's grand projection of victory for the exiled King James III lacks pragmatic details to convince Joseph Duverney, the historical French finance minister, to draw Louis XV into an ephemeral victory plan. The impromptu drop into the Fraser house at night further satirizes a romantic fool who suffers a monkey bite on the hand from Colette while he lurks in the home of Jules de Rohan, the cuckolded husband.

In a change of strategy, the real Charles Edward Stuart converted to Anglicanism.

Wedlock at age 51 with twenty-year-old Belgian princess Louise of Stolberg-Gedern on March 28, 1772, failed to produce harmony or children. Under the alias the Count of Albany, the bonnie prince retired and lapsed into spousal abuse and alcoholism. Before his demise from a stroke at age 67 at his birthplace in Rome, he depended on daughter Charlotte for nurse care. He left unacknowledged a three-year-old grandson and namesake, Charles Edward Stuart.

See also Culloden; Hanoverian Dynasty; Stuart Dynasty.

Source

Duffy, Christopher. *The '45: Bonnie Prince Charlie and the Untold Story of the Jacobite Rising.* Columbus, OH: Phoenix, 2007.

Nicholas, Christy Jackson. *Stunning, Strange and Secret: A Guide to Hidden Scotland.* Meath, Ireland: Tirgearr, 2014.

Oates, Jonathan. *Battles of the Jacobite Rebellions: Killiecrankie to Culloden.* Havertown, PA: Pen and Sword Military, 2019.

Royle, Trevor. *Culloden.* New York: Pegasus, 2017.

Bourbon Dynasty

Season two of the fictional TV saga *Outlander* contrasts the heavy-handedness of the British Hanoverian dynasty under George II with the *Ancien Régime,* the overly fastidious reign of Bourbon king Louis XV. Louis adopted the absolutism of his great-grandfather, the Sun King Louis XIV, who had ruled 72 years, the longest reign in Europe's history. Among the elder king's accomplishments, the Château Versailles set an example of Bourbon extravagance that followed the dynasty to the patriot revolt at the Bastille on July 14, 1789.

Known as *le bien-aimé* (the Well-Beloved), Louis XV was born at Versailles. He came to the Bourbon throne at age five and remained in power for 58 years. In creative mode, he augmented his great-grandfather's palace with private apartments for the royal family. A highlight of the refurbishments, the *Bassin de Neptune* situated a massive fountain and pool in the gardens adorned with sculptures of the mythic sea god, water nymphs, a tusked narwhal, and small sea creatures. The water feature became a focal point of grand entertainments highlighted by fireworks like those that delight the fictional Clarence Marylebone, Duke of Sandringham, in 1744.

A sybarite who dresses fashionably in the TV series *Outlander*, the fictional Louis XV proudly serves New World chocolate a decade after French engineer Dubuisson constructed a steam table grinder to end the hand milling of cacao beans. The screen king also expresses pleasure in a 1,000-tree orangerie, a highlight of Versailles planted in cubical *cache-pots* in 1686 under Louis XIV. In the episode "La Dame Blanche," he demands control of the trial in the Star Chamber of Le Comte St. Germain and Master Raymond, whom he charges with practicing the black arts. To balance majesty with humanity, the fictional Louis XV labors publicly at a delayed bowel movement, a token of his leanings toward a sedentary life and rich food rather than the beneficial roughage of cereal grains, which he disdains as peasant food. To entertain his entourage, he makes light humor at the expense of Captain Black Jack Randall, an ongoing French badinage of the English army.

During Europe's second-longest reign, historical absolutism set the tone of obdurate monarchy until the storming of the Bastille, the start of the French Revolution on July 14, 1789. Louis XV defended the divine right of kings, a philosophy of unconditional rule

Louis XIV=Maria Theresa of Spain=Françoise d'Aubigné, Countess of Maintenon

September 5, 1643-September 1715 |

|

Louis, Grand Dauphin=Maria Anna Victoria of Bavaria

|

Louis, Duke of Burgundy=Marie Adelaide of Savoy

|

great grandson

Louis XV, the Well-Beloved=Marie Leszczynska

January 15,1710-May 10, 1774 |

|

Louis XVI=Marie Antoinette

born at Versailles, August 23, 1754

guillotined at Place de la Concorde, Paris,

January 21, 1793

that dominates the *Outlander* dialogue of fictional Stuart pretender Bonnie Prince Charlie. With her knowledge of the future, in 1744, Claire Fraser anticipates bloody streets and more scenes like the corpses of a poor woman and child left in a Paris roadway. The female klatch dramatizes the classism that preceded unrest leading to mass murder and the guillotine, the site of royal executions in 1793 of Louis XVI and Marie Antoinette.

As represented by baby-faced actor Lionel Lingelser in the TV series, the fictional king at age 33 retains a remarkably youthful appearance and vigor at his *lever*, an early morning reception by the court, attendants, and guests. His historical appeal to female subjects extended to a series of official mistresses, including Marie de Mailly in 1742 and, in 1745, the wily, forceful Jeanne, Madame de Pompadour. Louis's neglected consort, the Catholic princess Marie Leszczynska, bore eight girls and two boys, the producers of three French kings, Louis XVI, Louis XVIII, and Charles X.

Like Claire Fraser and Mother Hildegarde, the fictional goddaughter of Louis XIV, the real Polish queen sponsored Catholic benevolence at hospices and clinics and a convent school at Versailles for poor girls. Ethnic resentment against Poles emerges in Bonnie Prince Charlie's outburst about having to retreat to "god-forsaken Poland" (2:6). Countering the demeaning of Charles Stuart, editors at the *Scotsman* argued, "There is no way that such a man could have mobilised the support he did, or completed the gruelling odyssey from the Highlands to Derby and back" ("Outlander," 2019).

See also Bonnie Prince Charlie; Star Chamber.

Source

Bell, Carrie. "'Outlander' Postmortem: All Hail King Louis XV!" *Yahoo Entertainment* (14 May 2016).
Bernier, Olivier. *Louis XV.* Tokyo: New Word City, 2018.
"*Outlander*'s Depiction of Bonnie Prince Charlie 'a Travesty,'" *Scotsman* (13 February 2019).

British Army

In movie style, the *Outlander* TV series depicts a fictional military arm of the United Kingdom that manages imperial missions around the globe. The high command chafes to put down Highlanders after three unsuccessful uprisings in 1689, 1715, and 1719. The army's aim is to halt the 1745 revolt and to extend colonialism to profitable sites in the Western Hemisphere. Online analyst Katharine Trendacosta, a reviewer for the Electronic Frontier Foundation, envisions cocky army officers as "dandies at best and sociopathic at worst" (Trendacosta, 2014).

A prancing patrol of occupation forces at the Lallybroch mill demeans all Scots for their rural milieu. A surveillance squad ridicules local folkways banning crows as emblematic of death. At Ardsmuir Prison, Major John Grey impresses Jamie Fraser as a too-young warden strutting and posturing about. After Jamie and company retrieve Gavin Hayes's body from the gallows, Redcoats at a highway stop insist on stabbing the corpse to ensure that it's dead. The Frasers consider such defilement a sacrilege, a typical show of English inhumanity.

Critic Courtney A. Hoffman, on staff at the Georgia Institute of Technology, distills the saga conflicts into "tension between clan patriarchies and English occupation" as viewed by fictional nurse Claire Randall Fraser, the well educated twentieth-century time traveler (Hoffman, 2017, 8). To the dismay of some United Kingdom residents, the former Allied nurse sympathizes with War Chief Dougal MacKenzie and his Jacobite band and with the Highlands regiment led in 1745–1746 by husband Jamie Fraser. To questions about cast loyalties in current times, three actors—Sam Heughan (Jamie), Graham McTavish (Dougal), and Grant O'Rourke (Rupert)—concur with the Yes vote for Scottish independence.

CORRUPTER OF MEN

Screen torment visualizes the all-male military as an outlet for homoeroticism and the rapacity of Captain Jonathan Wolverton "Black Jack" Randall, a relentless sociopath. A muting of colors in a flashback to Jack's abuse of Jamie and Jenny Fraser emphasizes the red of British uniforms, the color that inflames Scots anger at insurgent troops known for brutality and suppression of human rights. Jenny empowers herself by cleverly mocking Jack, a torturer and potential rapist unable to achieve an erection. The laughter shields her from sexual assault, but not from a clout to the head.

In a gender swap, Jack abandons his assault on Jenny and transfers his depravity to her well-muscled brother Jamie. The shift in retribution discloses Jack's sociopathology and the acting out of carnal possession through one hundred lashes. To Randall's dismay, a British soldier embarrasses him by fainting. The collapse of 49-year-old Brian Fraser beside the Fort William pillory dramatizes Scots helplessness under military persecution. The sudden death from apoplexy gnaws at Jamie, causing his loathing of Redcoats.

Episodes accord limited expertise to the British military. Ironically, according to Swedish scholar Moa Hågbäck of Linnaeus University, Lord Thomas and the British high command that Claire meets at Brockton Inn taunt Scots for their dress and speech and present themselves "as the cultivated superior in pursuit of cultural salvation for their inferior" (Hågbäck, 2019, 49). Multiple scenes picture Jamie's ease at overpowering guards outside the Duke of Sandringham's Belmont manse, sentries in the British camp paying no attention to commando raiders, and a uniformed messenger easily overtaken by two Lallybroch women, who steal and read an official sealed communication. Jamie's fierce attack on Prestonpans earned him the nickname "Red Jamie" and identification as "the devil himself" (3:2).

In contrast to arrogant British soldiers, Jeremy Foster, an exemplary army officer, provides what aid he can to Claire, even when outnumbered by Highlanders. The brief mention of the historical Archibald Campbell, the third Duke of Argyll and colonel over an infantry regiment, suggests the power of a noble title, which can determine Jamie's release from a second flogging. The series recycles the name for the brother of Margaret Campbell, a terrorized victim of his cruel beatings.

STANDOUT VICTIMIZERS

Season three, episode two demonizes the fictional Corporal MacGregor, a member of the ninth-century clan that produced Jacobite Rob Roy MacGregor. The self-important Scots corporal fights on the Redcoat side and abets harassers of residents at Lallybroch in 1752 after the alleged stillbirth of Jenny's son Ian. As proof that all Highlanders do not think alike, he browbeats the Murray family, belittles Ian for depending on a wooden leg, demands the family produce Red Jamie and the Dunbonnet, and tracks Fergus into the woods.

A penchant for anti–Gallic sentiments turns MacGregor against Fergus, a young French boy whom he belittles as a frog eater, a predominant slur against people who eat frog legs. The corporal cripples Fergus by shearing off his left hand with a saber. The hand lies palm up, as though beseeching rescue from a soulless warrior. Rather than aid the child, MacGregor directs his underlings away, leaving Fergus to bleed to death. The attack on the vulnerable correlates the corporal with Beatrix Potter's villainous Farmer MacGregor, nemesis of Peter Rabbit.

COLONIAL REDCOATS

Season five at Fraser's Ridge, North Carolina, highlights the historical primacy of Governor William Tryon, the proverbial fly in the buttermilk. In full redcoat dress, in 1770, he flaunts his authority at a frontier wedding. Deliberately seated on the aisle, he stands out from humbler guests with the insouciance of an aristocrat. Actor Tim Downie characterizes his part as Tryon as "the figurehead of the machine. He's part of the world's greatest army to the world's greatest empire," an achievement of influence and power that negates his humanity (Vincenty, 2020).

Posturing suits Tryon, who epitomizes British self-assurance. Wading into the after-ceremony crush, he targets Colonel Jamie Fraser with unsubtle arrogance and demands that back country militiamen track and kill Murtagh FitzGibbons Fraser, leader of the Regulators. With similar chutzpah, he rides off from the festivities amid a squad of soldiers, leaving Jamie to ponder the possibility of a British repossession of Fraser's Ridge. Lieutenant Hamilton Knox remains behind with a squad to spy on Jamie to ensure his obedience. His discovery of Jamie's loyalty to godfather Murtagh Fitzgibbons Fraser forces Jamie to asphyxiate Knox and conceal the murder as suffocation from vapors from a faulty flue.

The arcing of *Outlander* toward the American Revolution discloses murderous British attitudes toward New World settlers. At the Battle of Alamance Creek on April 16, 1771, artillery officers gleefully prepare cannon and swivel guns for use against poorly armed peasant rabble. With ill-concealed pleasure, Tryon obligates Jamie to dress like a Redcoat officer. The merciless felling of Regulators and an offhand command to hang three captives illustrates Tryon's intent to parlay his army victory into success as governor of North Carolina and New York.

See also Militias; Regulators; William Tryon; Tryon's Palace.

Source

Danilova, Nataliya, and Kandida Purnell, "The 'Museumification' of the Scottish Soldier and the Meaning-making of Britain's Wars," *Critical Military Studies* (2019): 1–19.

Hågbäck, Moa. "[..] If Only You Behaved Like the Loyal British Subjects You're Supposed to Be: National Identities and the Function of the Past in Starz's *Outlander*," master's thesis, Linnaeus University, 2019.

Hoffman, Courtney A. "How to Be a Woman in the Highlands: A Feminist Portrayal of Scotland in *Outlander*," *The Cinematic Eighteenth Century*. New York: Routledge, 2017, 103–117.

Trendacosta, Katharine. "Is the UK Missing Out on *Outlander* Because of the Scottish Referendum?," *Gizmodo* (18 September 2014).

Vincenty, Samantha. "The True Story Behind *Outlander*'s Villainous Governor Tryon," *Oprah Magazine* (17 February 2020).

Swaminathan, Srividhya, and Steven W. Thomas. *The Cinematic Eighteenth Century*. New York: Routledge, 2017.

Brown Genealogy

The bartering spirit of the Brownsville Browns and their grudges and zeal for a fight contrast an act of altruism toward a mixed-race infant. When Jamie and Claire Fraser arrive at the trading center in north central North Carolina, they find surly brothers Lionel and Richard Brown still spoiling to punish Alicia Brown for taking a married lover, Isaiah Morton of Granite Falls.

Alicia's adultery ruins Lionel's business deal with her suitor, trader Elijah Ford, who offers ten acres and tobacco for her hand in marriage. Lionel's abuse of second wife Rose results in a broken wrist and animus toward Claire for publishing birth control information in the newspaper. Allied with marauder Arvin Hodgepile and his band, Lionel meets his end in the Fraser's Ridge surgery after Marsali Fraser poisons him with an injection of water hemlock, a quick death for Claire's rapist.

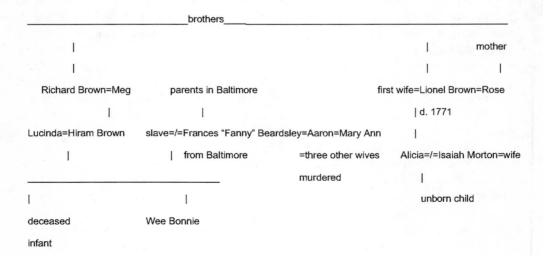

Source

Burt, Kayti. "*Outlander* Season 5 Ending Explained," *Den of Geek* (10 May 2020).
Ingham, Alexandria. "*Outlander* Season 5: Who Is Lionel Brown in The Fiery Cross?," *Claire&Jamie* (December 2019).

Burial at Sea

To dramatize the dilemma of infected sailors in season three, episode ten, the *Outlander* TV historical fiction depicts British naval traditions regarding multiple shipboard deaths and consigning corpses to the deep. At the height of a fictional typhoid fever epidemic fever on the man-o'-war *Porpoise,* Acting Captain Thomas Leonard despairs at a loss of eighty sailors coded DD—"discharged dead"—from an original crew of four hundred (3:10). After Claire Fraser transfers from the French brig *Artemis* to the naval vessel, she warns Leonard that more men will die from septic conditions before the outbreak ends. She observes the "stitch to wake the dead," a last gesture to Jim Quigley's corpse, and stands at attention to honor the deceased being jettisoned in sailcloth shrouds into the Atlantic (Parker, 2017).

A leveling device, the crew's emotion at the funeral for twelve sailors unites survivors in a crusade to save others, whatever their rank. Leonard's homily from the Book of Common Prayer and the Lord's Prayer incorporates Christian belief in the certainty of demise and immortality. As contagion lessens, one death grieves Claire more than the others. Critic Amber Dowling, a reviewer for *Indiewire,* describes the friendship of fourteen-year-old Elias Pound with the ship's doctor as a "pseudo mother-son relationship" (Dowling, 2017). His unexpected death personalizes for her the loss of a friend. In his last moments, she play-acts the summons of a mother to "come home," a merciful leave-taking (3:10).

Compartmentalization enables Claire to justify dissociation as a necessary mindset for a doctor battling an epidemic. She follows a shipboard regimen by stitching through Elias's nose into the canvas shroud as a precaution against burying a living person, a common motif in Gothic fiction. By returning his lucky rabbit's foot, she honors a gift from his deceased mother and pays genuine respect for a veteran of seven years at sea. With the removal of hats, she and the crew honor the flag-draped remains as they slide overboard into the sea.

Ocean committal dates to the beginning of marine travel and transport in Egypt, Greece, and Rome. The dignified marine ritual includes among the famous British Pacific Ocean burials Sir Francis Drake, Elizabethan England's privateer and victim of dysentery. He entered the deep in his armor and in a lead coffin off Portobelo Bay, Panama, on January 28, 1596. Against Muslim, Hindu, Jewish, and Catholic preference for land interment, from the 1700s, Anglican dogma approved a watery burial for British colonials. A second historic seaman, Captain James Cook, the explorer murdered by islanders in Hawaii on February 14, 1779, received the traditional naval burial off Kealakekua Bay.

Typically, the crew's sail maker sews shrouds that engulf the body in uniform. The ritual begins with the halting of the ship and the dropping of the hammock- or canvas-wrapped remains overboard. Inclusion of cannon balls ensures that the corpse reaches the sea bottom. Viewers refer to the deep-ocean burial as "sleeping with the fishes," a metaphor dating to Homer's *Iliad* and repeated by novelist Herman Melville in *Moby-Dick* and in the film *The Godfather.* If the deceased is unrecoverable, in lieu of a burial, sailors scatter flowers and wreaths while the vessel circles the site.

Source

Bell, Bethan. "Burial at Sea," *BBC News* (19 December 2016).

Dowling, Amber. "'Outlander' Review: Tumultuous Waters Rip Claire and Jamie Apart," *IndieWire* (19 November 2017).

Parker, Emily. "*Outlander*, Season 3, Episode 10—'Heaven and Earth,'" *Sweatpants & Coffee* (21 November 2017).

"Sir Francis Drake's Body 'Close to Being Found off Panama,'" *BBC News* (25 October 2011).

Castle Leoch

A Gothic given, the setting of the televised *Outlander* chronicle places Claire Beauchamp Randall, the damsel in distress, within stereotyped androcentric confines staffed by women domestics. Suited to clan militancy, female residents at Castle Leoch restrain their opinions and respect males, especially "himself," the semi-official title of Laird Colum Ban Campbell MacKenzie (1:1). The fictional Castle Leoch supplants Eilean Donan Castle, the historical MacKenzie stronghold that Robert Stewart built at Ross on River Teith northwest of Edinburgh near Stirling, Scotland. From 800 to 1266 CE, its regiment shielded residents from Viking raids and the Norwegians who colonized the Hebrides and northern mainlands. To stem Jacobite uprisings, the British razed the original castle on May 10, 1719, with an offshore bombardment and undermined walls by exploding twenty-seven barrels of gunpowder.

Arrival at the estate's central courtyard in early November 1743 leaves Claire feeling trapped in stone battlements by a 100-foot gate tower and kitchen that she had visited with husband Frank Randall before Samhain 1945. Amy Wilkinson, a reviewer for *Entertainment Weekly,* explains cinematic techniques—a "flashback to Claire walking the same path with Frank—a nice narrative device used throughout the episode to keep Frank at the fore, just as he must be in Claire's mind" (Wilkinson, 2014). Her residence requires a bath and makeover by housekeeper Glenna "Mrs. Fitz" Fitzgibbons in period dress and attendance at an evening meal for a polite interrogation in the Great Hall at the laird's table.

PAIRED OUTSIDERS

Claire is not the castle's sole outlander. For the fictional Jamie Fraser, Colum and Letitia's homestead offers a refuge from the British occupation regiments, which pursue Jamie on a false charge of murder. Like Claire, he conceals his true identity and reason for living his uncle's castle, where he first visited in 1737. Safe in the corral training colts for Auld Alec, he lives in the stables under the alias Mr. MacTavish. He survives on Colum's largesse until he can return home to Lallybroch. The outsider's identity shared with Claire establishes reasons for their friendship and eventual marriage.

Claire's iffy relationship with the laird results in promotion to castle healer after the death of herbalist Davie Beaton, a post she equates with house arrest because of Colum's suspicion that she spies for the British. Although empowered as a medical wizard, she shudders at her stone cell and at War Chief Dougal MacKenzie and other lustful men who lurk in its shadowy passages. Nonetheless, the dank chamber allows her intimate medical examinations of the bullet wound in Jamie's right shoulder. Salvation of Tammas Baxter from poisonous lily of the valley berries with a dose of belladonna raises her reputation as a miracle worker. Still, she longs to escape and return to husband Frank in the twentieth century.

The Way Out

Before the MacKenzies' gathering for a boar hunt and cyclical tribute to the laird, Claire studies the architecture, internal intrigue, and layout of the grounds, stable, lookout towers, and herb beds. The fourth episode depicts her scrutiny of castle security, which consists of beacons and armed sentries at guard posts. She counts the number of steps to safe spots out of view of watchers. In secret, she gathers apples and other foodstuffs, which the kitchen staff leaves unguarded. By gauging the degree of drunkenness at the MacKenzie clan gathering, she aims to flee castle environs. In preparation for flight, Claire marks the grounds with a ribbon and fichu (scarf) during games with Hamish and other children, trail leavings that she compares to the breadcrumbs in the Grimm Brothers' witch tale "Hansel and Gretel."

Castle Leoch epitomizes the layer of male protection that eighteenth-century women depend on. After a first quarrel with husband Jamie, Claire retreats to their quarters to plot response to a husbandly whipping for disobedience. Significantly, within her bedroom domain, she negotiates freedom from patriarchy and a future of affection and sexual satisfaction based on equality rather than feudal debasement of women as possessions and carnal playthings. After a witchcraft trial at Cranesmuir threatens Claire with burning at the stake, the Frasers flee and never return to Castle Leoch.

See also Architecture.

Source

Osborne, Kristin O'Neill. "This Noble Ruin: Doune Castle's Relationship to Popular Culture and Heritage," Dissertation, Ohio University, 2018.
Webb, Claire. "Discover the Real Castle Leoch and Outlander's Stunning Scottish Locations," *Radio Times* (29 June 2017).
Wilkinson, Amy. "Outlander Recap: Castle Leoch," *Entertainment Weekly* (17 August 2014).

Celtic Beliefs

On October 31, 1945, in the *Outlander* TV chronicle, the reclamation of timeless divinity at Inverness restores resilience and majesty to the "old ones," who anchored a communal faith imbued with liturgy and prophecy (2:8). Analyst and essayist for the *University Times* Victoria Sharpe, on staff at the University of Guelph in Ontario, praised archeological probes corroborating the female divine: "Notions of a great goddess and earth mother were actually appropriate concepts for the earliest objects of worship in past societies," which preceded the concept of standing armies (Sharpe, 1998, 36). In the rigidly androcentric clans of eighteenth-century Scotland, devout female Druidism redeemed the Great Mother, a Paleolithic nature goddess. Into the Bronze Age, aboriginal Celts revered her at monumental stone shrines like Craigh na Dun and through mystic divination, vernacular verse, chant, quest tales, and balladry like the bardic narratives that the fictional Welsh harper Gwyllyn sings at Castle Leoch.

According to Marija Gimbutas, anthropologist and author of *The Language of the Goddess*, adoration of a peace-loving agrarian matriarchy evolved into spiritual and planetary reverence. The divine matriarchy affirmed life and the benefits of nature through ceremonies as old as ring dance at the fictional Craigh na Dun, a stone shrine open to the sky and effulgent with concentrated womanly powers at the annual Samhain observance. The concept flourished around 7000 BCE in Moldova, Ukraine, and Romania from the Black Sea to the Danube River. Beliefs remained viable in the arts through sculpted fetishes of fleshy womanly bodies, knitting and fiber weaving, and customary circle dance, the foundation of the *hora,* a Balkan folk ritual at weddings and celebrations.

Across Gallia and Iberia from 2500 BCE, Anatolic, Balkan, and Slavic migrants forced the primal faith to yield to a belligerent sky or sun god, the source of Egyptian, Norse, and Greek pantheons of the lusty male deities Osiris, Odin, and Zeus. Translator and essayist Don Riggs called suppression of the earth mother an undermining of female divinity to the level of fairy, a demotion to a magical sprite known as wee folk. The *Outlander* supernatural incorporates other versions in *ban druidhs* (witches), changelings, and selkies (3:3). Prophecy in northwestern Europe and Britannia in 600 BCE derived from Celtic Druids who meditated on ancient wisdom and lore, the source of visions in Maisri, Margaret Campbell, Mrs. Graham, Duncan Kerr, and Master Raymond. Sisterhoods focused academic research on the power of monoliths like Craigh na Dun and on curative herbs, the origin of mortal strengths that Claire shares with herbalists Geillis Duncan Abernethy and Master Raymond and clairvoyant Cherokee Adawehi.

REVERING THE OLD ONES

Celtic matriarchy remained dynamic for 650 years, until General Aulus Plautius led 20,000 Roman legionaries to Kent, England, in May 43 CE. Proclaiming the Christian faith, the Romans bruited the androcentrism of a warlike civilization through violent hagiography, e.g., the X-shaped crucifixion of St. Andrew and chivalric lore of St. George and St. Michael, both of whom Jamie Fraser reveres. In 431, the Ecumenical Council of Ephesus legitimized a theological basis for elevating the Virgin Mary to an anti-patriarchal demigoddess. As *Theotokos* (God bearer), she evolved into Queen of Heaven, the universal comforter, and the source of mariology and female regeneration in sci-fi maven Marion Zimmer Bradley's Arthurian novel *The Mists of Avalon.*

Through time travel, *Outlander*'s main healers and nature consultants—Claire and Geillis—freshen and enliven rituals and herbal therapy extolling the maternal mediator. In the fictional observance of Samhain on October 31, 1945, Mrs. Graham and her sisterhood of midnight votaries embody fertility and reproduction, elements that bond womanhood with midwifery and all living things. To encompass nature, participants spread their arms wide to air and sky. As icons of the earth mother, emblems reflect exaltation of the virginal huntress Artemis/Diana, goddess of the moon, and expand with Christian mariolatry and Wicca, models of endurance and female bounty into the current age.

FICTIONAL DRUIDIC BELIEFS

In secret, Scots mystic, otherworldly practices flourish into modern times among women's sodalities. The primal deity occupies an intimate interiority with female devotees and practitioners of palm reading, sky reading, and tea leaf analysis. The TV saga elucidates female intuition in Claire and Jamie. In her first moments in eighteenth-century Scotland on November 1, 1945, she orders a band of unknown Scotsmen to stand back while she realigns a dislocated shoulder with arm bones, an allegorical repositioning of male thinking about gender and power. On the two-day ride toward Castle Leoch, she halts to treat Jamie a second time to stop bleeding from a bullet wound that allows an outflow of sacred ichor to deplete his strength. He expresses true gratitude for female knowledge of anatomical harmony and wellness.

The streaming of ἀγάπη (agapē or divine love for humankind) takes metaphorical form in the sacred fount at St. Ninian's Spring, a fluid image commemorating an eighth-century missionary to the lowland Picts at Galloway in southwestern Scotland. A refreshing drink from a covert Druid meeting site frees Claire Randall of War Chief Dougal MacKenzie's suspicions of sassenach espionage(1:6). For Geillis Duncan's near-naked revel by the full moon, chanting and gestures toward a campfire and her pregnant belly epitomize a revival of faith. Ironically, Faith is the name that Mother Superior Hildegarde bestows on Claire's daughter by illicit baptism, a secret violation of Catholic dogma at a time when pregnant women might incur one to four stillbirths each in a lifetime. Evidence of bigotry arises in misogyny and public accusations of enchantment, the experience of Claire and Geillis in 1743 at a Cranesmuir court and its all-male panel, who secure the alleged enchanters in a rocky pit that dehumanizes female suspects.

Return to Nature

For Jamie, failure of the mercenary mode of life sends him to stream-side to skip stones and review his options. The appearance of Laoghaire, a false sprite, elicits his loyalty to Claire, the true female psyche. At the transformation of his destiny through earthly affliction, he spends six years in a cave, welcomed by Mother Earth. Before Mary MacNab consoles him with mutually satisfying lovemaking, he witnesses a form of human sacrifice in the cropping of Fergus's left hand by Corporal MacGregor, a British version of the standard Roman stage role of *miles gloriosus* (egotistical soldier). The trial by ordeal worsens with Jamie's volunteering for another prison sentence at Ardsmuir, which he shares with fellow traitors to the Crown.

After the Frasers' quest across the Atlantic Ocean, their peaceful hermitage at Fraser's Ridge introduces them to folk society with the Cherokee, who live pagan style—in accord with ancient animistic beliefs about the outdoors. A cabin residence replaces a brush shelter, gradually directing the Fraser household toward a bigger, more inclusive home at the big house for their growing family. Once more, the rise of willful manhood in the Rowan Count Militia and British Army muzzles the divine female, leaving Marsali, Lizzy, Mrs. Bug, and Brianna at home with the children while the men foresee conflict, represented by their burning Celtic cross. Womanly agency rounds out the finale with Marsali in command of a syringe of poison, which kills marauder Lionel Brown.

See also Craigh na Dun; Dance; Superstition; Witchcraft.

Source

Crosby, Janice C. *Cauldron of Changes: Feminist Spirituality in Fantastic Fiction.* Jefferson, NC: McFarland, 2000.

Evans, Richard, ed. *Prophets and Profits: Ancient Divination and Its Reception.* New York: Routledge, 2017.

Garfinkle, Robert A. "The Moon in Mankind's History and Lore," *Luna Cognita.* New York: Springer, 2020, 1–50.

Sharpe, Victoria. "The Goddess Restored," *Journal of the Fantastic in the Arts* 9:1 (1998): 36–45.

Christianity

In a violent, unpredictable era, Christian values permeate the *Outlander* television epic with a god-fearing humanity, personalized by Jamie's hearth blessing and his intoning St. Patrick's prayer for the dying in fall 1772 to a Dutch girl burned in a cabin fire. After seeing his son's back wounded by one hundred strokes of the cat-o'-nine-tails in 1739, Brian Fraser urges Jamie to pray for strength before the second flogging at Fort

William. In private, Jamie prays for the lost, including his friend Taran MacQuarrie, who dangles long at the end of a noose before expiring, and insists on burying fellow ex-con Gavin Hayes in hallowed ground. In fealty to the family's Catholicism, Jamie is scrupulous about blessing the souls of two Scots crucified on X-shaped crosses in a mockery of the death of St. Andrew, the national patron. The rent collectors' discovery of the two Highlanders left to rot and the nail in Jamie's hand at Wentworth Prison emulate the sufferings of Christ. The white × covering the Jacobite flag brandishes the Greek letter chi, an abbreviation for *Christos,* the Greek honorific for "anointed one."

Scots Highlanders give voice and gesture to their Christianity with cruciform signs, oaths, recitations of scripture, sculpture, and veneration of the Virgin Mary, saints, the eucharist, and shrines. A partly obscured speech features Father Bain banishing Satan with a version of the standard rubric: *Dominus Jesus Christus. Da locum. Recite, Libera nos, domine deus* (Lord Jesus Christ. Give place. Repeat, Free us, Lord God). By challenging Father Bain's authority during exorcism of lily of the valley poisoning from Tammas Baxter, Claire raises her repute as a healer. Her boldness incites controversy in 1743 that reemerges at the Cranesmuir witch trial under the scurrilous charges of prejudiced witnesses.

Righting Sins

Although Claire professes a "nominal" Catholicism, an earnest conference with Captain Black Jack Randall at Brockton Inn reveals her belief in atonement and redemption, even for a vicious sociopath (1:1). Later, she upends overt piety by fooling Fletcher Gordon, a showy Christian governor of Wentworth Prison who leaves his office to eat dinner and read his bible. Claire's phony performance as a dutiful Christian convinces Sir Fletcher that Jamie deserves to reconcile with his family. At a low in Claire's faith, genuine spiritual need surfaces during her harborage at Father Anselm's abbey confessional. TV analyst Laura Byrne-Cristiano lauded his accessibility: he's "pretty much what you would want in a priest" (Byrne-Cristiano, 2015). Claire unloads guilt for causing anguish to both her husbands. Candid about time travel, attempted rape, and bigamy, she convinces her confessor of sincere repentance. Author Diana Gabaldon declared the scene beneficial: "Claire really needed that extra spiritual boost to give the walk into the darkness more power" (Bell, 2015).

Father Anselm, a gracious confessor, surprises Claire by proclaiming the events in her two marriages marvels and miracles (1:16). He ends with the standard *Te absolvo* (I forgive you) in the name of the trinity. Claire's revival of forgiveness after a first major argument with Jamie readies her for combatting her husband's prison torture and rape and exonerating him for sodomy by a monster. Departure from Scotland at the end of season one carries two implied blessings on the couple—embarking for France on the two-masted *Cristabel* (beautiful Christian) and celebrating a first pregnancy, nature's blessing on the Frasers.

Childhood Training

More devout than his wife, Jamie displays a Catholicism derived from conventional Christian upbringing that compels him to thank Christ after he reunites with Claire on a Haitian beach and rescues her from drowning off Les Perles, Georgia. In the frigid waters of the Lallybroch millpond, he calls on St. Michael, defender of Christians in impossible situations. Before the bonnie prince in la Maison Elise, Jamie grooms royalty for duping by pretending to acknowledge the divine right of kings, the Stuart philosophy of absolutism. The prince expresses his loyalty to the Vatican by offering verbal rebuke to the Duke of Sandringham for ridiculing the work of Pope Benedict XIII. Historically, when the bonnie prince began claiming victories for his Jacobite army, in summer 1745, the British revived anti–Catholic laws by banning Highlander ownership of horses and weapons and by prohibiting assembly for worship or political discussion.

At the grave of Faith Fraser in 1744, Jamie lays an iconic apostle spoon of St. Andrew on the headstone. Andrew, patron of Scotland, embodied Scots Christianity, a spirituality recognized in the joining of the parents' hands. Before leaving son William "Willie" Ransom at Helwater, England, Jamie lights a candle venerating St. Anthony, the patron of the lost, and commemorates his siblings, parents, and godfather. Evidence of deep reliance on the almighty recurs in season four, where Jamie prays for the soul of Rufus, the poisoned slave, and begs God's forgiveness and patience with the plantation South. On the retreat of the Jacobites from London to Inverness in February 1746, Jamie's quiet moment in the army camp reveals his foreknowledge of Claire's second pregnancy by praying for her and asking succor for her womb and safety from harm. At his daughter's wedding at Fraser's Ridge in 1770, he grouses that the priest spoke no Latin. In a better humor on return of the Rowan County Militia, Jamie prays *deo gratias* (thanks to God) for Claire while she sleeps (5:3).

At Helwater, the baptismal scene in season three, episode four consecrates William "Willie" Ransom to his birth father. At a home altar lit by a candle, Jamie sanctifies the boy's anecdotal conversion from Anglicanism to a "stinking papist" with water and the cross sign (3:4). The ritual concludes with a new name—William James—and the gift of a carved snake, a symbol of regeneration and a reminder of the death of Jamie's elder brother Willie in 1726. Describing his son to Claire, Jamie reveals a depth of conscience by blaming himself for the death of Geneva Dunsany, whom he did not love.

Jenny Murray, another Fraser reared in the pious Lallybroch household, chooses for her wedding St. Martin's Day or Martinmas (November 11), the feast day of St. Martin of Tours, a Roman monk and patron of children and beggars. While searching for Jamie, she supplicates for the souls of two unburied members of the Watch killed in an ambush. On Jamie's departure to the Jacobite army, she offers him a good luck rosary that once brought him home from war in France. When Claire returns in 1766, Jenny scolds her brother for having two wives, a serious sin against the sacrament of marriage.

Faith and Choices

For Roger, a Presbyterian, Father Alexandre Ferigault's dedication to Catholic dogma places him in unnecessary jeopardy from pagan Indians. During treatment for fever, Ferigault fell in love with Johiehon, the Mohawk mother of their biracial baby. He considers his sin a lapse from grace that prevents him from baptizing their daughter. Roger restates the sin as normal human need. To his attempts to keep the priest from submitting to torture, Ferigault refuses any philosophy but strict church doctrine, which results in lopping his left ear, a symbolic refusal to listen to reason. By tossing a keg of gunpowder, Roger intervenes and produces a conflagration that quickly burns Ferigault and Johiehon alive, a merciful end to a ghastly slow roasting.

Season five develops Jamie's Christian beliefs by enacting the mercy killing of Aaron

Beardley, a wicked tormentor of five wives and two indentured servants, Josiah and Keziah Beardsley. After viewing Kezzie's ear damage and Fanny's terror of Aaron, Jamie commiserates with the fifth wife and servants for living with a physical and spiritual crippler. Before the Frasers leave the Beardsley property, Jamie replaces a fallen crucifix on the mantle and asks permission from Aaron to end his pain. The dramatic taking of life inspires Jamie to plan his own euthanasia if he should lie helpless from stroke.

Episode five depicts Claire in a quandary over time's web. In place of Graham Menzies, a pre-surgical patient who succumbs to anaphylaxis from allergy to penicillin, she attends the perpetual adoration, an uninterrupted liturgical ritual where Catholics venerate the sanctified host. The concept derived from fourth century CE comfort to the sick and dying. Claire undergoes an apotheosis—realization that her twentieth-century experience with Graham caused her to travel to Scotland, meet Roger, and reconnect with Jamie, an overturn of perpetual adoration to ongoing love for her husband.

An overarching theme declares unpredictable past and future, especially the MacKenzie family's intent to return toddler Jemmy to a safer twentieth-century milieu. Episode seven plunges the Regulators and Redcoats into combat on May 16, 1771, after the Reverend Caldwell delivers a truce proposal, but fails to halt the Battle of Alamance Creek. Still suffering an overwhelming grief at losing his godfather, Jamie's request for last rites indicate Christian faith as he faces death from an infected snakebite. Roger can suggest only a prayer for the sick in English because he knows no liturgy in Latin, which the church abandoned under Pope John XXIII in 1967.

See also Literature.

Source

Bell, Carrie. "*Outlander* Author Diana Gabaldon on the Season-One Finale, and What Changes to the Book Were Hard to Swallow," *Vulture* (1 June 2015).

Byrne-Cristiano, Laura. "'Outlander' Season 1, Part 2: Superfans Talk Must Haves," *Hypable* (31 March 2015).

Reiher, Andrea. "'Outlander' Recap: 'Perpetual Adoration' Slows Season 5 Action Down," *Variety* (15 March 2020).

Royle, Trevor. *Culloden*. New York: Pegasus, 2017.

Circles

The recurrence of circles in the *Outlander* TV series creates venerable spaces with wedding rings, ritual, dance drama, and rescue. The circle illustrates a primeval pattern dating to caveman, based in part on the shape of the sun and moon and adopted by Native Americans as an emblem of continuity. According to expert Christy Jackson Nicholas, at one time, "Stone circles and chambered cairns dominated the land" and mirrored a culture that respected animism, the presence of god in nature (Nicholas, 2014, 3). At fictional Craigh na Dun, circle dance compounds the spiritual power of individuals honoring the Samhain harvest and the authority of the old ones, a common name for Druids. The round predicts a major narrative conflict between Claire's marriages to two husbands, both symbolized by wedding rings. As prophecy, the circlet also prefigures Claire's elevation to Lady Broch Tuarach, a title linking her to Lallybroch's round tower and the Fraser family.

In the episode "America the Beautiful," set in the New World, the brief view of aborigines piling stones and celebrating the power of the eternal round in 2000 BCE lacks dignity. The TV version of prehistory cheats first peoples of intelligence and ingenuity by picturing ragged dress, unfocused eyes, and the jerky movements of savages. A more believable ring dance resurfaces outside Rose Hall, Jamaica, where Maroons perform voodoo rites in West African style with animal costumes, chant, gesture, frenetic steps, and a rooster sacrifice. Subsequent presentation of circles tends toward focused drama, for example, the Cherokee bear dance, led by healer Adawehi. A mix of verisimilitude and prophecy, group animation imitates the shapeshifter's ursine movements and mimics attacks with bear claws, a real threat to the tribe and their neighbors.

FRASER MEMORIALS

The burning of the Celtic sun cross visualizes the syncretism of Druidism with Christianity as a halo or aura, a saintly glow sometimes accorded to St. Columba, St. Declan, or St. Patrick, Christianizer of Ireland. On a pragmatic note, the four stone arms encircled with a nimbus strengthens the sculpture against the elements. At Jamie's call for volunteers at Fraser's Ridge, immigrants surround him at the fiery cross to pledge allegiance to the Rowan County Militia and its colonel. Circles like the one Murtagh Fitzgibbons Fraser makes from stones in the first episode of season five and the fireside enclosure that Regulators form around him before the Battle of Alamance Creek on May 16, 1771, continue to strengthen and unify Scots-Americans far from their Celtic upbringing.

Additional rings suggest the easing of Claire's concerns. In season five, episode five, as a volunteer at the perpetual adoration of the communion wafer, she replaces deceased patient Graham Menzies, a victim of anaphylactic shock from penicillin allergy. The church altar displays the Eucharistic host as a disc in a sunburst, which recalls Claire's summation of ancient circle lore as universal in nature. The next episode presents in a new light her wedding rings—one silver, one gold. They represent Jamie's willingness to risk her treasures in a gamble on whist against Phillip Wylie, a fop and womanizer. After the Frasers kiss and make up, the heirlooms become unifiers. Jamie admits to too much pride and makes a ritual overture to Claire by replacing the bands on her fingers with a promise to leave them there, a miniature altar vow on a par with their marriage.

THE HEALING ROUND

Such cracks in the Fraser family circle yield a paradox—fractures of unity that restore the need to come together. Because Roger dangles from a noose, Jamie retrieves him in time for Claire to perform a tracheotomy, a small hole in the airway that revives his breathing. Beyond her help after the Battle of Alamance Creek, in episode seven, Jamie crouches alone at a fire surround to mourn godfather Murtagh, who arrives dead at the field hospital from a single bullet hole. Jamie honors his beloved surrogate parent with a cairn, a prehistoric pillar composed of stones that mourners add one by one to yield a conical folk obelisk. Because the prehistoric mound illustrates permanence, the grave marker implies an unending commemoration and a landmark guiding a wanderer home.

In the aftermath of loss and serious illness, Jamie and son-in-law Roger Mac vow to pursue vengeance against pirate Stephen Bonnet, a tontine guaranteeing death for a psychopath. With the aid of Young Ian Murray, the men form a threesome, but the stalker outwits them. His ultimate capture and court judgment places him at a stake in rising tidewater. Brianna surprises her husband by shooting Stephen in the head. The neat hole in his skull removes from the Fraser household a *bête noir,* placing a female sharpshooter in the coterie of male riflemen.

See also Stephen Bonnet; Craigh na Dun; Dance.

Source

"Cairns of Scotland," www.scotland.com/blog/cairns-of-scotland.
Devine, Thomas M. "La nation écossaise s'est construite dans la lutte contre l'angleterre," *L'Histoire* 2:468 (2020): 13–23.
Halleman, Caroline. "*Outlander* Author Diana Gabaldon Sees Claire's New Ring as the Show's Way of 'Apologizing,' to Readers," *Town & Country* (10 December 2018).
Nicholas, Christy Jackson. *Stunning, Strange and Secret: A Guide to Hidden Scotland.* Meath, Ireland: Tirgearr, 2014.

Clans

The *Outlander* TV series attains stature for investigating the survivalism of marginalized peoples as colorful and interrelated as Scotland's clans. The social concept developed from Celtic tribalism and feudalism. The word itself derives from archaic *cland*, Gaelic for "descendants," who recognize arbitrary male authority and clan jurisdiction of a chief over an extended family. Critic Srividhya Swaminathan, an English professor at the University of Texas at Austin, salutes the television production for satisfying "interest not only in the cinematic spectacle of the eighteenth century but also in the complex ways that issues of race, ethnicity, gender, sexuality, class, and nation might be represented on the screen" (Swaminathan, 2017, 1).

Unified by the lineage of a common male ancestor, scions treasure songs, folk narratives, genealogy, banners and heraldic lore. Under an escutcheon or coat of arms, defenders issue a motto or battle cry emblematic of pride and accomplishment, such as the Fraser adage "Je suis prest" (I am ready) and the MacKenzie "Luceo non uro" (I shine not burn) and the slogan *tulach ard* (the high hill) (1:3, 1:1). The MacKenzie clan, a twelfth-century lineage, built Eilean Donan Castle in 1297 as a stronghold of the far western highlands. All members in good faith lived on common acreage superintended by a tacksman or lease manager such as Rupert MacKenzie and Duncan Kerr. Out of fealty, members pledged loyalty to Colum Ban Campbell MacKenzie, the autocratic laird.

The fictional gathering in the fourth episode, season one, involves the Castle Leoch staff and kin in field hockey, a wild boar hunt, feasting, bagpipe music and dance, plaids and crest badges, and a ritual of oaths. Kin drink from a loving cup to demonstrate constancy to their leader and judge. The power of clan law enables his brother, War Chief Dougal MacKenzie, to thwart Redcoat Captain Black Jack Randall by transforming Claire Beauchamp into a Scots citizen: she joins the Fraser clan in late fall 1743 by wedding James Alexander Malcolm MacKenzie Fraser. Still an outsider, she accommodates manners, dress, and speech to clan demands and makes friends with housekeeper Glenna "Mrs. Fitz" Fitzgibbons, Hamish MacKenzie, and Tammas Baxter and other patients.

Property, for example Beaufort Castle in Aberdeenshire, epitomizes the longevity of clans. To Jamie, Horrocks's attempt at blackmail gains no promise to sell Fraser land, which has been in family ownership since the 1100s. Political manipulation of small clans concerns Jamie in season two, episode eight. He fears that MacKenzie neutrality will influence the choices of lesser groups to avoid a fourth Jacobite uprising. Before the disastrous Battle of Culloden on April 16, 1746, the British mustered some fifty Highland military companies such as the Black Watch and the Gordons as local police forces. The Cameron Highlanders, led by Laird Donald Cameron, became the last division to wear the kilt. The despised treachery of some Scots against the clans draws opprobrium to fictional Corporal MacGregor, the turncoat Highlander who harries Ian Murray, amputates Fergus's left hand, and leaves the boy in the woods to bleed to death.

Tribal outlines take shape once more at Fraser's Ridge in the opening of season five. To flesh out the Rowan County Militia, Jamie dresses in kilt, brooch, dirk, and sword to light a Celtic cross. With a brief speech, he musters the faithful, interdependent immigrant frontiersmen whose prosperity in the diaspora depends on unity. To restore peace in the North Carolina piedmont, he must ally with Governor William Tryon's suppression of the Regulators, Scots-Americans and others who conspire against dishonest sheriffs and tax collectors. At the death of Regulator leader Murtagh Fitzgibbons Fraser at the Battle of Alamance Creek on May 16, 1771, Claire removes the tartan scrap and crest from his body and saves it as an honorarium to a faithful Highlander. Jamie cements his alliance with settlers by lighting the cross once more and donning the kilt for the roundup of Lionel Brown's gang.

See also Heirlooms; Kilts; MacKenzie Genealogy.

Source

Cornelius, Jim. "The Doom of the Clans," *Frontier Partisans* (16 April 2016).

Hix, Lisa. "True Kilts: Debunking the Myths about Highlanders and Clan Tartans," *Collectors Weekly* (15 November 2017).

Stewart, Malcolm. "The Decline of Scottish Clans," *The Corvette* 3:2 (2016): 7–22.

Swaminathan, Srividhya, and Steven W. Thomas. *The Cinematic Eighteenth Century*. New York: Routledge, 2017.

Clergy

For a largely secular narrative, the *Outlander* TV series requires the services of numerous fictional clergy, each individualizing understanding and performance of ritual, notably, anti-woman judges at the Cranesmuir witch trial and nuns who volunteer at a Paris hospice. TV critic A.J. Delgado stated that Scots clergy "were largely responsible for keeping the peace, law, education, charity for the poor and weak, civil rights, and morality" (Delgado, 2014). At first, Father Bain, the Cranesmuir catechizer and disciplinarian, hovers on the villain list for ordering the amputation of tanner's boy Novelli's hand for stealing bannocks. At the witchcraft hearing, the priest confesses vanity and hubris and reveals that he accepts human frailties. As God's servant, he exonerates Claire for saving Tammas Baxter by countering lily-of-the-valley poison with a dose of belladonna. Amid fractious witch-burners, Bain appears contrite and willing to accept Claire's medical miracle as divinely inspired.

Season one introduces a chapel priest sickened by conducting services in an unheated stone chapel, a fictional setting at Glencorse (or Glencross) Old Kirk, at Penicuick in Midlothian seven miles south of Edinburgh. Sour and surly, the priest bandies scripture with Willie on setting marriage banns. A folk tradition from 1215, the public announcement required three weeks notice, reputedly to prevent spur-of-the-moment or forced marriages. The priest brandishes a ridiculously small knife and angers Dougal, the MacKenzie war chief, at interruption of wedding plans for Claire to Jamie, a ruse that changes her from Englishwoman to a Scot. A rapid shift in atmosphere and purpose sets the priest at the altar, where he conducts the wedding in ecclesiastical Latin after learning that Dougal plans to reward him with casement windows for the chapel. From the altar setting amid candelabra and sonorous Latin, the paltry architecture takes on a romantic glow.

The Ministry in Action

Clergy joins patient care at l'Hôpital des Anges in Paris in 1744. At the request of supervisor Mother Hildegarde, Father Laurentin anoints Claire's forehead to absolve her from sin before she dies of puerperal fever. Against the policies of the Catholic hierarchy, Hildegarde increases the air of mercy by baptizing and naming Claire's stillborn child. A second absolution at Father Anselm's Benedictine abbey occurs by accident after he finds Claire spiritually slogging through her faults and fears of losing Jamie to suicide. Limited reproduction of the confession ends with Anselm's kind acceptance of her tangled lives two centuries apart. Unlike Bain, who looks for reasons to allot maximum penalties, Anselm expresses awe at Claire's adventures and forgives her with Christly clemency.

Additional clergy present alternate views on protocol. In Haiti, Father Fogden, once a missionary to Cuba, contends with minutia at the union of Marsali and Fergus. In an unfunny dialogue, the priest declares it necessary that the groom have a penis as well as a surname. Jamie ends the predicament by declaring his foster son "Fergus Claudel Fraser," an identity welcoming both husband and wife to the extended Fraser family. Jamie reaffirms his foster son in the opening segment of season five. After Gavin Hayes's hanging in Wilmington in the opening of season four, Fergus negotiates with a local minister for burial rights. The clergyman's demand for "recompense" to redeem Hayes's sins convinces Jamie that the ministry remains corrupted by greed and bribery (4:1).

GODLINESS VS. PRAGMATISM

On Fraser's Ridge, superstition takes a ghastly form after Petronella and baby Clara's death from measles unhinges settler Gerhard Mueller. A German minister, Pastor Gottfried (derived from the German for "God's peace"), warns Claire of insanity at the Mueller residence. Despite good intent, he cannot halt Mueller from murdering and scalping Adawehi, the Cherokee healer, whom Gerhard calls a sorcerer. The episode lapses into Indian revenge, flaming arrows, and destruction of the Mueller cabin, a Hollywood stereotype of Native American retribution. The Muellers totter into the yard and die from arrow wounds that Gottfried cannot have prevented with his limited influence on the ruthless, superstitious Gerhard.

At Shadow Lake, New York, Father Alexandre Ferigault risks his survival over a point of Catholic doctrine. Fallen from grace because he broke vows of celibacy with Johiehon and fathered a biracial child, he refuses to baptize their French-Mohawk baby and accepts execution by slow roasting over fire. Roger MacKenzie, his own life agitated by the rejection of a marriage proposal to Brianna and by her father's misidentification of the man who raped her, careens toward an ultra-selfish stance of serving his own needs first. Compelled to action, he hurries Ferigault's slow death by tossing on a cask of gunpowder. To Roger's amazement, Johiehon leaps onto the pyre with her lover, a testimonial to love and sacrifice beyond merciless Catholic strictures.

PROTESTANTS AND CATHOLICS

As a humorous jab at Jamie's cradle Catholicism, in 1770, the fifth season offsets his rigorous home training with a Presbyterian son-in-law. The Rev. David Caldwell, the historical pastor who weds Brianna Randall to Roger MacKenzie at Fraser's Ridge, follows the standard liturgy. To Claire, Jamie complains that vows in English defeat his intent for a proper Latin ritual. The Frasers look more favorably on Caldwell an hour before the Battle of Alamance on May 16, 1771, when he attempts to negotiate a truce with Governor William Tryon.

The dig at Jamie's staunch Catholicism recurs in the wild after he lies ill from snake-bite. Roger can offer no last rites in Latin, but can utter a prayer for the sick—the *de profundis* taken from Psalm 130. The eloquent words, like those that Claire utters when she reclaims her husband's soul at Father Anselm's abbey and that Jamie intones at his baptism of Willie Ransom, attest to the power of the layman as a substitute for clergy. The narrative contrasts the unnamed priest who consoles Claire at the perpetual adoration of the host in Boston by clarifying the meaning of loss, a turning point in her reclamation of faith.

See also Christianity; Literature.

Source

Delgado, A.J. "*Outlander* Slams Christianity," *National Review* (8 September 2014).
Donelan, Carol. "'Sing Me a Song of a Lass That Is Gone': Myth and Meaning in the Starz Original Series Outlander," *Quarterly Review of Film and Video* 35:1 (2018): 31–53.

Coincidence

The *Outlander* TV epic relies heavily on the Dickensian ploy of coincidence. People and objects make impromptu appearances, reverting Geillis Duncan's skeletal remains to Claire and Joe Abernethy's examination, placing Jamie at Murtagh Fitzgibbons Fraser's Woollam's Creek forge after years of separation on two continents, Lionel Brown's crushing the hypodermic syringe during treatment of Isaiah Morton at the Battle of Alamance Creek, and, during a game of chess, a message divulging to Lieutenant Hamilton Knox the colonel's former incarceration with his godfather at Ardsmuir Prison. In the view of critic Kayla Kumari Upadhyaya, unexpected simultaneity and discoveries ground the narrative, particularly the typhoid fever epidemic that draws Claire away from the brig *Artemis* to the naval man-o'-war *Porpoise*. The analyst characterizes "an underlying message that an invisible thread forms between us and the people we touch—whether in good or bad ways—and remains through time" (Upadhyaya, 2018).

Objects take on special meaning, especially Jamie's prosthetic glove on the day of his duel with Jack Randall and Claire's quiet matins in the Benedictine abbey chapel at the canonical house. The pre-dawn prayer at 2:00 A.M. anticipates her release from mental suffering and self-blame by a confession to Father Anselm. Simultaneous with Claire's need of a rescuer for Jamie from Wentworth Prison comes Marcus MacRannach, who recognizes her heirloom Scots pearls, the bride's wedding gift from a guest. Marcus, like Murtagh, treasures memories of Ellen MacKenzie, to whom he gave the pearls when she married Brian Fraser. Along with Claire's receipt of Ellen's boar tusk bracelets from Jenny, the heirlooms serve as key connections to character values in the previous generation.

Birth and Death

The intense discussion of stepfatherhood in the first episode of season two develops into a suave sermonette. To Frank Randall's outrage in 1968 at Claire's pregnancy by another man, the Rev. Reginald Wakefield poses the New Testament model of Joseph's parenting of the Virgin Mary's child, conceived by the Holy Spirit. An interruption by six-year-old Roger MacKenzie in the adult conversation places a visible model of step-parenting, this one an orphan who loses parents Marjorie and Jerry MacKenzie in World War II. The child's ability to accept a surrogate father appears to help Frank think of Claire and Jamie's child as a secondhand nuclear family, ironically, growing into Brianna Randall, the woman whom Roger marries.

An audacious example of synchroneity, Jamie's moments in a noose at Wentworth Prison end dramatically with the sound of Captain Jack Randall's clattering hooves and postponement of the execution. A slick cliffhanger, the intrusion plays on viewer sympathy for the hero and fear for his demise in a degrading mass hanging that has already taken outlaw Taran MacQuarrie. The last minute of Jamie's reprieve changes nothing for the next victim in line: colonial savagery continues to expunge more Scots rebels and criminals. Contributing to concurrence, the villain's tossing of Claire out a prison trapdoor reunites her with Taran's remains.

FATEFUL MEETINGS

Compressed action recurs in season three, episode eight with Young Ian's swim to Selkie Island. On his discovery of the MacKenzie treasure box, the Portuguese crew of the *Bruja* arrives by sea to retrieve sapphires for Geillis Duncan Abernethy's use in restoring the Stuart monarchy. At her Jamaican residence, Rose Hall, in episode thirteen, she refuses to accept as accidental a meeting with Claire in Kingston's governor's palace, where the Frasers also encounter Archibald and Margaret Campbell and John Grey. From false logic, Geillis accuses Claire of following her to the West Indies. TV critic Kayla Kumari Upadhyaya characterizes the episode "The Bakra" as misguided and muddled with character reunions and antipathies: "This dramatic crossing of paths at the party should be thrilling, but it mostly just feels tedious, and it never eclipses the episode's glaring problems" (Upadhyaya, 2017). The coincidence sets in motion the Caribbean phase of Ian's deliverance and the Frasers' unplanned arrival on the shores of Les Perles, Georgia.

Concurrence affects the falling action of season five. Roger's near-tragic reunion with Morag MacKenzie, the mother of Jeremiah whom Roger rescued from Stephen Bonnet aboard the *Gloriana,* results in an uneven fight with her surly husband, William "Buck" MacKenzie. Nearly lost in the post-combat savagery of the Battle of Alamance Creek on May 16, 1771, Roger survives lynching by Claire's on-the-spot tracheotomy. In a later episode, Young Ian's surprise introduction during a game of hide and seek occurs too neatly, stopping a wild boar from attacking the Frasers and grandson Jemmy. Into August, trauma haunts Roger until he shares with Young Ian Murray their mutual sufferings and suicidal urges. Season five, episode eight ends with the two men aiding each other in finding the way back to normality.

See also Dueling.

Source

Upadhyaya, Kayla Kumari. "*Outlander* Bungles the Conflict in 'Savages,'" *AVClub* (2 December 2018).
_____. "*Outlander* Peddles a White Savior Narrative in Jamaica," *AVClub* (3 December 2017).
Valentine, Genevieve. "'Outlander' Season 3, Episode 11: The Most Unlikely Places," *New York Times* (26 November 2017).

Colonialism

The *Outlander* TV episodes incorporate colonial themes and motifs that influence and impact each other, forcing viewers to rethink the paradoxes of two contrasting eras separated by two centuries. According to analyst Srividhya Swaminathan, the sequence is "an assemblage of criss-crossing narratives of piracy, slavery, and sexual taboos, as well as royal families, colonial encounters, and revolutionary movements" epitomized by the Jacobites, North Carolina Regulators' anti-tax revolt, and anticipation of the French Revolution and American Revolutionary War (Swaminathan, 2017, 4). Historic encounters introduce fictional characters to George II and III, Louis XV, the bonnie prince, radical Quaker Herman Husband, North Carolina governor William Tryon, Court Judge Richard Henderson and hatchet man Edmund Fanning, and Cherokee and Mohawk chiefs.

The series opening episodes in November 1743 depict Jamie as a handsome, physically active, and heroic mercenary during Continental wars in his teens. On a rent collection tour with his uncle, War Chief Dougal MacKenzie, displays of Jamie's scarred back demean him and threaten his hyper-masculinity. To further the Jacobite cause of returning a Stuart to the throne, Dougal turns his nephew into a spectacle of British savagery. An object of pity and outrage, the network of scourge marks from October 1739 permanently establishes Jamie's colonized body as Redcoat loot. Described by film experts Gemma Goodman and Rachel Moseley, both on staff at the University of Warwick, the dehumanized torso "resembles a relief map of a territory, with ridges, rivers and trails etched upon it—… a landscape" (Goodman and Moseley, 2018, 67). The diagram prefigures the Frasers' flight from pirates and kidnappers to Caribbean plantations that enrich British owners and Governor John Grey through the labor of black Africans.

EUROPEAN GREED

The English rapacity for New World land and resources permeates seasons two through four, beginning with Father Fogden's description of the bungled English invasion of Santiago, Cuba, in August 4–5, 1741. TV reviewer Kayti Burt summarizes imperialism as "the powerful elite controlling, killing, and using the vulnerable masses to sustain and grow their own power and wealth" (Burt, 2018). Part of the Columbian exchange delights Louis XV, who, in 1744, enjoys sipping chocolate from cacao grown in Central America. In contrast to his trivial joys, at the Frasers' Jamaican landfall, they see firsthand the humiliation of slave branding and marketing in Kingston and the vivid West African spirit of Maroons, whose secret rituals energize their company through indigenous dance, masking, prophecy, and prayer.

Season four introduces a real regional map of North Carolina, replete with the high country, roads, and waterways that entice immigrants. Governor William Tryon's land grant of 10,000 acres on the Appalachian frontier offers Jamie a beginning for his household. An introduction to New World settlement informs Jamie about human bondage, Regulators, and Tryon's Palace, the derisively named governor's residence at New Bern. Its elegance and cost arouse a virulent revolt among Scots-American smallholders, whom corrupt tax agents and sheriffs fleece of their money and possessions. Similar in outcome to post–Culloden land divestments in the Highlands, American class warfare again places Scots on the losing side after Jamie's Rowan County Militia battles the tax protesters.

THE IMMIGRANT'S PERSPECTIVE

Into season five, Jamie and fellow Scots-Americans epitomize the hunger of deracinated Highlanders for land and autonomy from Tryon, a clever manipulator of settlers. Reviewer Genevieve Valentine, a critic for the *New York Times,* remarked on opposing aspects of imperialism—"everyday violence … generally loaded ground for storytelling" such as the *Outlander* series and folk songs about military recruitment (Valentine, 2017). At Aunt Jocasta's nuptials at River Run in 1771, Tryon divulges that he plans to move north to become governor of New York. But first, he must end dissension in North Carolina with an anti-peasant war fought with cannon and artillery.

The colonial battle between anti-tax Regulators and the Redcoats on April 16, 1771, places in jeopardy the least prepared colonizers. Because of the near strangulation of Captain Roger MacKenzie, Tryon allots him 5,000 acres in the backcountry as compensation. Only Jamie, Claire, Brianna, and Roger know that the future holds a major revolution that wrests the American colonies from George III and bureaucrats like Tryon. At an aha moment in Roger's mulling over his career as an Oxford history professor, he realizes that reading about the colonial past and living it places him at the scene of life-changing struggles for independence from England.

See also Jamaica; Land Grants; Maroons; Piracy; Regulators; Slavery; Tryon's Palace.

Source

Burt, Kayti. "*Outlander* Season 4 Episode 1 Review: America the Beautiful," *Den of Geek* (5 November 2018).

Goodman, Gemma, and Rachel Moseley. "*Outlander*: Body as Contested Territory," *Conflicting Masculinities: Men in Television Period Drama*. New York: Bloomsbury, 2018.

Swaminathan, Srividhya, and Steven W. Thomas. *The Cinematic Eighteenth Century*. New York: Routledge, 2017.

Valentine, Genevieve. "'Outlander' Season 3, Episode 11: The Most Unlikely Places," *New York Times* (26 November 2017).

Combat Nursing

Few critiques of the televised *Outlander* series identify it as an anti-war saga. The symptoms of Post-Traumatic Stress Disorder in Claire Randall reveal a psyche that broods over flashbacks to six years of field tourniquets and amputations. At Inverness on October 28, 1945, she recognizes a swath of black on lintels as cockerel blood, which honors St. Odhran's feast. Intercutting of Claire's service to the British army during World War II pictures her clamping a femoral artery before drinking champagne straight from the bottle on May 8, 1945, during the commotion of VE Day. Subsequent time travel ends her post-war second honeymoon with husband Frank and thrusts her into November 1743, a savage era of clan violence and sedition against the English King George II, a strife fraught with more amputations, tourniquets, and bleeding.

In reference to the fictional nurse's resetting 202 years into the past, novelist Diana Gabaldon applauded Claire's field training. The author noted how Allied nursing equips Claire for the past with "three basic pillars that modern medicine rests on, and that's antisepsis—which is germ theory—antibiotics and anesthesia [which] came into common use in the general population during World War II, because of their use in the battlefield" (West, 2014).

When her first eighteenth-century combat approaches at Prestonpans on September 21, 1745, Claire relives chatting with American veterans of D-Day, June 6, 1944. With the voice of experience, she rakes Angus Mohr, a Scots infantryman, for neglecting his feet, which can become gangrenous from marching. She re-envisions a stark existential episode in a jeep that leaves her alone in the dark amid German artillery fire. Within earshot, a wounded soldier calls for his mama, a maternal motif that accompanies Claire's treatment of injured and exhausted men, including Jamie, Ross, Kincaid, Angus, Rupert, British casualties, and the child soldier Fergus.

Prestonpans

In whatever century they occur, readiness defines nursing duties. While awaiting farm boy Richard Anderson to lead the Jacobites over a bog to Prestonpans at Tranent, Claire and her fellow nurses—Alice McMurdo, Allina Clerk, and Molly Cockburn—stock before-combat supplies. Reminiscent of the TV series *Mercy Street, The Crimson Field, China Beach,* and *ANZAC Girls,* Scots volunteers organize and sterilize clamps and scalpels, tear and roll bandages, stoke fires, stir honey into water to stabilize blood pressure and rehydrate, and prepare bedding for casualties. Fergus recognizes the gender divide between soldiery and field stations and balks at supplying hearths to heat water, a task he demeans as woman's work. The tense wait depicts the noncombatant role of females and children as nerve-wracking.

The arrival of wounded friends and some Redcoats tests Claire's steely advice to accept the part of healers and perform what treatment they can. In the background, Alice McMurdo prays the first two verses of Psalm 91 from the King James translation:

> He that dwelleth in the secret place of the most High
>   shall abide under the shadow of the Almighty.
> I will say of the Lord, He is my refuge and my fortress:
>   my God; in Him will I trust.

Alice places her faith in God, a convention of war literature that reminds people of their shortcomings in the face of suffering and mortality. The motif returns in season five, when Claire rages at the loss of twentieth-century patient Graham Menzies from anaphylaxis brought on by an allergy to penicillin.

Patient Needs

Post-Prestonpans on the gallop to Inverness, Claire continues to treat the wounded ambushed by Redcoats. In a dark chapel set at the historic Glencorse (or Glencross) Old Kirk, at Penicuik in Midlothian seven miles south of Edinburgh, she plucks a musket ball from Rupert MacKenzie's right eye and bandages his forehead with a patch. On-the-spot surgery saves the Highlander's life and affords him material for jokes about winking at Claire. The worsening saga transforms her into a metaphysical angel at Culloden, where Jamie lies among the few moribund men who survive the slaughter of April 16, 1746. Two decades later, she travels with the Rowan County Militia and intervenes before Alicia Brown can kill herself and her unborn child. Claire's experiments with bread mold produce penicillium for he Beardsley twins' tonsillectomies.

The demand for nursing in the *Outlander* narrative seems unending. The website "Lord, Ladies, and Lore" comments that Claire "finds herself caring for the injured and ill in Britain during the 1940s, in Scotland during the 1700s, and finally in America as the country is involved in the Vietnam War" (Quick, 2018). Preparation of the medical tent at Alamance Creek on May 16, 1771, readies her once more for post-combat casualty treatment, this time with Brianna's help. Integral to Claire's box of herbs she values laudanum, juniper, belladonna, and pennyroyal for fighting infection and controlling pain.

Familiar faces deepen Claire's sorrow at the outcome of war. This time she knows by name militiaman Isaiah Morton, pierced through the right lung, and Regulator leader Murtagh Fitzgibbons Fraser, who arrives at the tent already inert from Hugh Findlay's rifle shot to the chest. To prevent therapy for Isaiah, Lionel Brown spitefully crushes a glass and metal hypodermic syringe. In the aftermath of a one-sided suppression of the Regulators, Claire redesigns the syringe for local artisans to manufacture before the onset of the American Revolution. The season finale turns the new syringe into the appropriate device for Marsali's execution of a monster.

See also Healing.

Source

"Claire Fraser Becomes a Doctor: Medical Education and Developments from 18th Century Scotland to 20th Century America," *LordsLadiesandLore* (2018).

Lagerwey, Jorie. "The Feminist *Game of Thrones*: *Outlander* and Gendered Discourses of TV Genre," *Women Do Genre in Film and Television*. London: Routledge, 2017, 198–212.

Larson, Mary. "A Brief History of Nursing and Diana's Impressive Choices for Claire," *Outlander Cast* (1 September 2015).

McAllister, Margaret, and Donna Lee Brien. *Paradoxes in Nurses' Identity, Culture and Image: The Shadow Side of Nursing.* Abingdon, UK: Routledge, 2020.

West, Kelly. "*Outlander*'s Diana Gabaldon on Setting World War II as Claire's Backstory," *Cinemablend* (29 July 2014).

Conception

The full panorama of male-female relations forces the *Outlander* TV narrative to investigate human conception and the growth of families, such as Aaron Beardsley's murder of fourth wife Mary Ann because she gave him no child and Rose Brown's refusal to copulate with her violent husband Lionel to avoid impregnation. Claire's failure to conceive in her marriage to Frank Randall casts doubt that she can produce babies with second husband Jamie Fraser. He accepts her warning that they may be barren, a blow to his dynastic plans. He gracefully digests the news with a comment on the dangers of parturition, the cause of his mother Ellen's death in 1730. By coincidence, the news of Claire's conception reaches him as he recovers from the despair of rape trauma and affirms his manhood.

Analyst Nicole M. DuPlessis, a literature expert on staff at Texas A&M University, explains that "by discussing and depicting the ravages of reproduction in the eighteenth century, *Outlander* establishes—and history verifies—that some have the motivation to limit conception," a strategy corroborated by Master Raymond's prescription of contraception for Claire's maid Suzette (DuPlessis, 2016, 86). Before the voyage to Le Havre, France, the onset of Claire's pregnancy symptoms—vomiting at the entrance to Wentworth Prison and the Benedictine abbey and collapsing in Murtagh's grasp—foretells the announcement of good news. The possibility of a child boosts Jamie through a difficult post-traumatic breakdown. Both Frasers caress Claire's rounded belly and anticipate a propitious birth, a nuclear family pose preceding heartbreak.

During the months of waiting, Claire counsels Louise de Rohan on aborting the fetus sired by the bonnie prince by taking a risky barberry and hellebore concoction. Claire advises on creating a loving home for the child, despite illicit paternity, a foreshadowing of her own situation on return to the twentieth century from the Battle of Culloden on April 16, 1746. Jules de Rohan's response at the Fraser dinner indicates that Louise has duped her husband into accepting the unborn fetus as his. The motif of child rescue continues with Jamie's retrieval of Willie from Lord Ellesmere's knife because he refuses to believe that Geneva was a virgin bride. More questionable conceptions affect the womanhood and choices of Mary Hawkins, lover of Alex Randall; Alicia Brown, Isaiah Morton's amour; and Brianna Randall, handfasted wife of Roger Mackenzie and rape victim of Stephen Bonnet.

An Inexact Science

Because of the loss of infant Faith Fraser in 1744 to stillbirth, Claire seems less eager to try again. At her bedside on the march, Jamie prays for his wife and the future of their family, a fond speech delivered in Gaelic. On the frantic early morning gallop away from the British attack on the Jacobites at Culloden, he reveals his calculation of Claire's lunar cycle and his assurance that a second fetus has formed in her womb. A poignant announcement on the day that he prepares to die, the second pregnancy forces a twenty-year separation and Claire's rearing of Brianna with Frank Randall in the twentieth century. When Claire awakens from anesthesia in a Boston hospital, she fears that her second baby has died, a qualm shared by other women who have lost infants at birth.

The series makes humorous reference to the Friedman or rabbit test, a 1931 development in conception testing to prove the implantation of a fertilized ovum in the uterus. A whimsical salute to the frisky life of a second daughter crops up with the appearance of a rabbit among heaps of Jacobite corpses at Culloden. In babyhood, Brianna treasures a stuffed rabbit as her favorite toy. As though conceived a second time, her voyage to the past to join her parents coincides with a subsequent rabbit sighting by midwife Adawehi, a clairvoyant who knows that the grown daughter will reunite with her mother and Jamie. The trope recurs in the season five finale with the rabbits that Claire sees while awaiting rescue from gang rape. At home once more, she receives dual hugs from Brianna and Marsali, who has adopted Claire as her "ma" (5:12).

Later impregnation focuses on a contrasting couple, beginning at Helwater, England. To ease Geneva Dunsany's fear of losing her virginity to grandfatherly husband Lord Ellesmere, she blackmails Jamie into deflowering her. The felonious maneuver bodes ill for the mother-to-be. In critic Du Plessis's evaluation, the plot "punishes her for her risk; Geneva dies in childbirth" (*ibid.,* 88). In informing Claire of the coercive arrangement, Jamie claims guilt for siring a bastard son who killed the mother, a woman he did not love. The loss violates his sense of honor, a fact he conceals from Brianna when he tells her of her brother, William Ransom, the 9th Earl of Ellesmere.

A New Generation

A promising mating in Haiti rewards the Frasers with grandparenthood. Before Marsali MacKemmie's wedding to Fergus, her concerns about coitus and conception draw her closer to Claire, a wisewoman who can supply birth control information and connubial experience. The announcement of an addition to the family delights the Frasers, who consider the baby their first grandchild despite the fact that neither Marsali nor Fergus share their blood. On learning about Brianna's pregnancy, Claire at first asks about availability of contraceptives and Roger MacKenzie's attempt at *coitus interruptus* before learning about Brianna's rape by Stephen Bonnet. In private conversation with Lord John Grey about his foster son William, Brianna declares her intent to keep her infant and love it. John asks permission to touch her abdomen and smiles at the fetal movement, a fascination that he shares with Jamie before the birth of Faith in Paris.

In seasons four and five, two more conceptions for Fergus and Marsali MacKenzie bring joy simultaneous with Aunt Jocasta's machinations to supply niece Brianna with a respectable husband to extend the MacKenzie legacy. Masking an unmarried state with a bogus engagement to John Grey, the action depicts Grey gallantly squiring Brianna to the Wilmington jail and his pretense of engagement to rescue her reputation. During the last stage of pregnancy, Brianna piques prisoner Stephen Bonnet's interest in the fetus, which she identifies as his. DuPlessis comments that "Brianna and Roger struggle with intimacy in a new marriage shared with an infant of uncertain parentage," a predicament that recurs in season five, episode five (*ibid.*, 95). More troubled conceptions relieve Aaron Beardsley's longing for a child after his wife Fanny couples with a slave and begets a biracial daughter, whom Jamie names Wee Bonnie. In a narrative balance, Marsali anticipates the birth of a fourth child conceived at the prompting of husband Fergus Fraser, a proponent of family life in a man who grew up motherless in the bawdy atmosphere of Madame Elise's brothel.

Source

DuPlessis, Nicole M. "Men, Women and Birth Control in the Early *Outlander* Books," *Outlander's Sassenachs: Essays on Gender, Race, Orientation and the Other in the Novels and Television Series*. Jefferson, NC: McFarland, 2016, 82–96.
de Waard, Jolien. "Adapting Claire's Feminist Beliefs and Female Agency: A Comparison Between the First *Outlander* Novel and Its Television Adaptation," bachelor's thesis, Utrecht University, 2018.

Costumes

Costumes in the *Outlander* TV historical fiction combine with spot-on casting to create vivid characters in period dress, including the outfitting of Duncan Kerr in rags, John Grey's sapphire fob, Ned Gowan in the Cranesmuir court with a Battenberg lace tie, Claire shaded by a respectable umbrella in Kingston, and Colonel Fraser in tailored frock coat with leather collar and lapels. Ensembles infuse authentic details as elegant as Isobel Dunsany's afternoon mourning dress and John Grey's signet ring, as illustrative as Hugh Munro's Gaberlunzie tokens and Brianna's hippie prairie skirt and boots, as symbolic as Claire's necklace shaped like dogwood, the North Carolina state flower, and as suggestive as Redcoat officers' gorgets reclaimed by Cherokee interpreter Raven of Keowee and Kaheroton, a Mohawk brave. After actor Sam Heughan proposed wire rims for Jamie, he explained the character's need: "It's a weakness of Jamie's. He doesn't have many" (Hellemann, 2020).

Women typically exhibit gendered markings. In 1743, outfits provide time traveler Claire Randall with a clue to her milieu on the outskirts of eighteenth-century Inverness. Star Caitriona Balfe connected female attire with women's status: "Once you're sucked into these corsets, you realize just how repressed women were. Your ability to emote, vocalize and be physical is so restricted, purely because of the clothes" (Fretts, 2015, 18). Brianna MacKenzie learns a similar lesson during her abduction by Stephen Bonnet, who supplies her with a fussy, but elegant polonaise, a chic cutaway gown, stomacher, and draped overskirt. The gold-toned costume sets up the female as property, an objectified chattel intended to be admired for the sake of male esteem.

Womanly Status

Dialogue points up the madonna/whore dichotomy of period women, who choose fichus, bum roles, stomachers, and shifts appropriate to their status and reputation. Upon Claire's abrupt arrival among War Chief Dougal MacKenzie's band of outriders, the men assume that her knee-length white dress without corset is a standard shift or underdress, a possible indication of a prostitute at work. Because Jamie's wounded shoulder demands dressing, she tears strips from her hem for bandaging and sling. After defending herself against defaming, season one builds subtle humor from the purchase of her wedding dress at a brothel.

Like a visual tutorial, Mrs. Glenna Fitzgibbons's garbing of Claire in standard Scots dress replaces the French brassiere and tap pants of the mid–1940s with shapeless shift, corset, bum roll and panniered skirt to broaden the hips, and suede lace-up shoes. The modular nature of her outfit involves knit wrist warmers, a fichu at the neckline above the triangular torso shaper or stomacher, and sleeves tied on to the shoulders. The scriptwriter of *Outlander* makes no mention of Claire's clothing sources, which seem high in quality for outfitting an unexpected guest of Castle Leoch. A noteworthy outfit, the fur-edged cloak she snuggles in during the rent collection prefigures Brianna's hooded coat. Claire's favorite knitted shoulder wrap, which follows her to North Carolina, serves as a V-shaped frame for creamy complexion and sable curls and an on-the-spot sling to nestle Wee Bonnie. The addition of a rabbit fur vest stresses the abundance of the wilderness and the value of wild animal hides and furs to settlers.

Men's Outfits

Whatever the setting and vigor of action, Jamie manages to look neatly tailored in his wardrobe. His early outfitting favors a loose, unattractive shirt with a stock tie at the neck that usually appears grimy and ungainly. The everyday garment evidences the barbarism of flogging, which stains a blackish red across the back, an anticipation of his cave attire at Lallybroch and his rags at Ardsmuir Prison in 1752. In the final segments of season one, tattered pants and bare feet mark the victims who precede Jamie to the gibbet, heightening viewer expectations of a grisly death for Taran MacQuarrie and his compatriot, both grimly made up with filth, beards, and sweat. The camera views Jamie's haggard, ill-shaven visage through Taran's jerking limbs and validates the final struggle of Scots victims against spiffily dressed Redcoats, who seem unperturbed by executions.

To exhibit his dependence on Highlanders, the historical Prince Charles Edward Stuart wore a white silk vest embroidered with scrolls over bias-cut tartan trews (leggings), which covered him from high waist to the soles of his feet. His clan costume incorporated the traditional kilt, an outfit duplicated onscreen for the fictional bonnie prince. Upon his introduction in season two, second episode, the *Outlander* version of Prince Charles decks himself in crimson satin and white lace shirt, a departure from Jamie's true-blue jacket and simple white shirt and stock tie. At Versailles, Jamie favors a tan coat finely figured with tan-on-tan embroidery, a contrast to the prince's exhibitionist finery.

Military uniforms dominate much of the male wardrobe. Close-ups of Captain Black Jack Randall's soldiers marching toward Lallybroch detail boots, puttees, and the familiar gold-trimmed red coats and tricorn hats, a dominant mark of colonial repression and the arrogance that precedes his groping of Jenny Fraser. Prominent red coats with gold epaulets maintain an imperial presence on the English man-o'-war *Porpoise* and among regiments in Jamaica and North Carolina. Hats take on symbolic meaning when the crew removes them to honor the dead.

Dramatic Changes

Season two makes a rapid swap of costumes, with Frank burning the Scots corset and dress that Claire wore on restoration through the stones on April 16, 1746, and her reappearance in 1940s suit and pullover sweater. With a leap backward to 1744 and the France of Louis XV, the second episode outfits her in lavish baroque costumes suitable to Versailles, notably, her *robe rouge,* a sweeping ball gown constructed from fifteen yards of red fabric (2:2). To accommodate a fashionable milieu while diverting the Jacobite plot, Jamie wears clean shirts and a wardrobe of embroidered vests and shiny cavalry footwear less droopy than the mercenary's boots with wide collars. His tasteful outfits offset the overdone suits and lacy cuffs of Monsieur Duverney, Le Comte St. Germain, and Louis XV, a clichéd male peacockery that Marsali later calls "dandy" (3:13).

Tight jackets and wide peplums obscure Claire's pregnancy; gloves and Dior platter hats proclaim her sense of style. *New York Times* TV critic Jennifer Vineyard admired "basket panniers and pads underneath the silk skirt to give her that eighteenth-century look" (Vineyard, 2018). Her choice of color blocking in lustrous silk or taffeta juxtaposes restrained taste alongside the garish modes of dress and aristocratic accessories of Annalise de Mauriac and Louise de la Tour, Marquise de Rohan. Similarly, the demimonde, the courtesans working for Madame Elise, adorn their shapes in furbelows, ruffles, and florid fabric in imitation of their betters.

Outlander's TV hairdos, jewelry, and wardrobes parallel the seriousness of court politics. At the Star Chamber hearing, Claire's sedate blue-green gown with impeccably fitted neckline and waist presents her with calm demeanor to face down an unrelenting enemy. A long sable curl at the right shoulder draws attention to the loadstone, which turns black at the pivotal moment of death by poisoning. The long back drape establishes her matronly command of an eerie situation—a private trial of St. Germain in the French royal palace that Claire and Master Raymond settle with poison. The sophisticated look acknowledges her self-control.

The third season epitomizes the fancy fare of guests at the governor's mansion in Kingston, Jamaica, as opposed to Claire's homely twentieth-century maternity wear for daily and dress-up occasions. The obligatory floppy tie at the collar contributes a stereotype of demure mother-to-be laced up tight for obedient domesticity. Claire's outfitting follows with a model's coat over white slip featuring appliquéd rose, a sweetie-pie decoration that disappeared along with slips within two more decades. Claire's unappealing wardrobe sets Geneva Dunsany apart for her over-ruffled peignoir, made from a chaste white fabric and lace, the markings of a virginal aristocrat.

North American Tastes

Introduction of Southern plantation era finery puts Jocasta Cameron in luscious at-home and entertainment outfits, some topped with lacy fluff common to modest elderly women. Phaedra's skill with stitchery suggests that she frequently modifies outfits for "Miss Jo." The arrival of Roger and Bree to Scotland points up teen tastes from the late 1960s, especially her tan corduroy Mao cap. In Boston, Claire's ingenuity with a Singer sewing machine results in her batsuit—a fitting travel costume stitched from waterproof raincoat material and furnished with pockets to secure coins and medical necessities. The arm slits on her cloak give her a vulnerable look for the final steps to Jamie's print-shop and a reunion after two decades apart. The scene, repeated in episode six, transfers concern for Claire to Jamie's surprising collapse, a fainting motif usually relegated to the female protagonist.

A visual delight, the opening episode of season five at Fraser's Ridge places costume above other elements of drama, especially Jamie's fatherly suit for giving the bride away and the unpacking of his kilt, dirk, and plaid to answer Tryon's call to arms. At the center of her wedding, the bride stands out in demure ecru embroidered with forget-me-nots and finished with a modest pleated bustle. Unfortunately for star Caitriona Balfe, the camera cheats her of a full-length portrait. More stunning than Jocasta in a lace-topped great aunt's dress, Claire glows in a quietly majestic mother-of-the-bride gown in another blue color block style. The rich brocade prepares for Jamie's stylistic transformation into "a Scot" in warrior's uniform, brooch, and sporran (5:1).

Clothes for the Times

The connection between Claire and blue, introduced in the episode "Faith," establishes the heroine's motherly charm and her link to healing, a conjunction that Master Raymond introduces at l'Hôpital des Anges when he saves her from puerperal fever. In addition to allying Claire with artists' views of the Virgin Mary, the color symbolism communicates an affinity for nurse care, which Claire learned during six years at the Allied front during World War II. Claire's subdued outfit at Jocasta's nuptial celebration asserts a quiet grandeur suitable to a frontierswoman and highlights her strongest qualities, self-reliance and modesty. The effect deviates from the powdery makeup and foppery of Phillip Wylie, a lecher who attempts to molest Claire in the barn. Her aggressive shove that sends him backwards into horse manure awards him a deserved comeuppance. As a badge of victory, Jamie jerks away the patched mole that Wylie left on her neck.

The fifth season tends to stress mechanical sewing not yet available. Camera close-ups reveal machine stitchery, the most glaring on Jamie's brown leather coat with close gathers on the shoulders. The blunder carries little weight to the meaning of episode seven, in which Tryon forces on Colonel Fraser a British army uniform. The wordless promotion of a militia colonel to a British officer dismays Jamie's wife and men. With a determined gesture, in anger at the battle that kills his godfather, Jamie removes the coat then thrusts it at Tryon's feet, a public rejection of imperialist morals and aspirations. Star Sam Heughan characterized the psychological impact of the coat as an enemy—"the occupation of Scotland, the suppression of his culture, Black Jack Randall, Wentworth Prison" (Kosin, 2020).

See also Kilt; Native Americans.

Source

Fremont, Maggie. "*Outlander* Season Premier Recap: Take a Vow," *Vulture* (14 February 2020).
Fretts, Bruce. "Behind 'Outlander,' on Starz, True Hearts in the Highlands," *New York Times* (16 April 2015): 18.
Hallemann, Caroline. "*Outlander*'s Caitriona Balfe Shares a Rare Behind-the-Scenes Video of Sam Heughan," *Town & Country* (23 April 2020).
Kosin, Julie. "Sam Heughan on *Outlander*'s Devastating Double Loss," *Elle* (30 March 2020).
Vineyard, Jennifer. "'Outlander' Takes Manhattan," *New York Times* (2 November 2018).

Couples

The smash success of Claire and Jamie's passion for each other in the *Outlander* TV saga gains diversity by modeling pairs who founder or deviate from social standards, especially the high-toned public behavior of Governor William Tryon with "Her

Excellency" Margaret Tryon and the breath of melancholy when Ulysses mentions his mistress, Jocasta Cameron Innes (5:6). In Boston, Jerry and Millie Nelson represent the 1960s cutesiness common to early TV sitcoms the ilk of Lucy and Desi Arnaz and Ozzie and Harriet. In juxtaposition, the arranged affairs of the eighteenth century that join Geneva Dunsany and Lord Ellesmere base relationships on courtesy, family name, and financial arrangements. In the style of an Old World patriarch, Ellesmere thinks of Geneva as "mine," a pronoun echoing the rapacity of the duke in Robert Browning's "My Last Duchess" (3:4). Other couples accentuate the individuality of relationships:

couple	*relationship*	*offspring*
Aaron/Fanny Beardsley	abusive marriage	none
Aaron/Mary Ann Beardsley	coercion and murder	none
Abernethy/Geillis Duncan	marriage for money	none
Alardyce/John Grey	gay pair	none
Alexandre Ferigault/Johiehon	doomed by canon law	infant daughter
Alex Randall/Mary Hawkins	lovers	son
Alicia Brown/Isaiah Morton	passionate romance	pregnancy
Annekje Johansen/husband	shipboard couple	none
Arthur/Geillis Duncan	marriage of convenience	none
Brian/Ellen Fraser	loving alliance	Willie, Jenny, Jamie, one stillbirth
Brianna/Roger MacKenzie	troubled early marriage	Jemmy
Charles Edward Stuart/Louise de Rohan	passionate affair	pregnancy
Claire Beauchamp/Frank Randall	strained open marriage	none
Claire Beauchamp/Jamie Fraser	arranged union that develops equality	Faith, Brianna
Colum/Letitia MacKenzie	stately platonic wedlock	none
Dougal MacKenzie/Geillis Duncan	lovers	son
Dougal/Letitia MacKenzie	dynastic arrangement	Hamish
Dougal/Maura MacKenzie	neglected marriage	four daughters
Duncan Innes/Jocasta Cameron	companionable union	none
Ermenegilda/Father Fogden	illicit affair with a married woman	none
Fanny Beardsley/slave	secret romance	"Wee Bonnie"
Fergus/Marsali Fraser	devoted union	Germain, Joan, Felicité, a fourth pregnancy
Frank Randall/Sandy Travers	open affair	none
Geneva Dunsany/Jamie Fraser	one-night affair	William "Willie" Ransom
Gerhard/Rosewitha Mueller	close frontier couple	two sons
Gillian/Greg Edgars	separation ending in murder	none
Hector/Jocasta Cameron	amicable business partners	Morna, Seanag, Clementina

couple	relationship	offspring
Hiram/Lucinda Brown	loving couple	deceased daughter, "Wee Bonnie"
Ian/Jenny Fraser Murray	established farm family	Jamie, Maggie, Ian, Janet, Matthew
Isobel Dunsany/John Grey	platonic marriage	none
Jerry/Millie Nelson	typical 1960s marriage	children
Jonathan/Mary Randall	match of financial convenience	none
Jerry/Marjorie MacKenzie	wartime marriage	Roger
Jocasta Cameron Innes/Ulysses	one-sided adoration	none
Jocasta Cameron/Murtagh Fitzgibbons Fraser	infrequent liaisons	none
Jules/Louise de Rohan	lapsed couple reunited by pregnancy	none
Laoghaire/Simon MacKimmie	hurtful relationship	Joan, Marsali
Lionel/Rose Brown	abusive husband	none
Louisa/William Dunsany	formal model of a couple	Geneva, Isobel
Margaret Campbell/Yi Tien Cho	newly formed tie	none
Margaret/William Tryon	public models of probity and manners	one
Mary/Ronald MacNab	union troubled by domestic violence	Rabbie
Murtagh Fitzgibbons Fraser/Suzette	brief fling	none
Simon Lovat/kitchen maid	womanizer and his conquest	Brian Fraser
Young Ian Murray/Mohawk wife	failed arrangement	Unknown

COMPLEX DUOS

Table conversation on Haiti informs Claire of the brief passion of Father Fogden, a missionary to Cuba, who violates his priestly vow of celibacy. On August 4, 1741, the day the English invaded the island at Santiago, he eloped with Ermenegilda, a married woman. The affair produced no children. Ermenegilda's death burdens Fogden with sad memories and a hostile mother-in-law, Mamacita. Claire turns her overnight stay with Fogden into the source of a priest and altar for Marsali MacKimmie's marriage to Fergus. At the nuptials, Jamie claims Fergus as son Fergus Claudel Fraser, a waif whom the Frasers fostered in Paris. At the amicable ceremony, Father Fogden blesses both couples and sanctions their devotion.

In antithesis to her nephew Jamie's belief in love, Aunt Jocasta Cameron manipulates couples to avert scandal and produce socially acceptable mates. At River Run, she attempts to foist her pregnant niece Brianna onto a reputable suitor—the wimpy attorney Gerald Forbes, egotistical Lieutenant Wolff, or the closeted gays Judge Alardyce and Lord John Grey. The list equates with Forbes's box of unset jewels—sapphire, emerald, topaz, and diamond—four sparkling possibilities to enhance Jocasta's social standing in the Cape Fear community. To Brianna's insistence on a love match, Jocasta voices a pragmatic demand for a husband before the birth and poses as a model her older sister Ellen MacKenzie, who conceived a child before wedding Brian Fraser. Jocasta's dismissal of romance prefigures her final marriage to Duncan Innes, a suitor she barely tolerates.

LOVE TRIUMPHS

Much anxiety dissipates in season five with the reunion of the Frasers—Claire, Jamie, and their twentieth-century daughter Brianna, who meets her birth father for the first time in Wilmington in 1770. He takes part in a Victorian custom—something old, something new, something borrowed, something blue, and a sixpence for her shoe, apparently a pre-wedding ritual passed on by Claire. In an interview with *Vogue* journalist Alexandra Macon, star Caitriona Balfe praised the frontier wedding scene because it alleviates Claire's doubt that she will see her daughter marry. After reuniting with her Highlander husband, "She felt like she had sacrificed all of these moments to spend her time with Jamie" (Macon, 2020).

Season five satisfies narrative romance with a grand celebration of love—the Frasers, Murtagh and Jocasta, Fergus and Marsali, and the Roger MacKenzies, who seem the least enthralled with the end of their special day. A subsequent nuptial day justifies Jocasta's rejection of Murtagh's suit in favor of Duncan Innes, a peaceable man who will relieve his bride from tumultuous memories of wedlock to Hector Cameron. At Murtagh's cairn, Jocasta sings "The Flowers of the Forrest," a farewell ballad honoring the precious man she might have wed. TV critic Andrea Reiher, a writer for *Variety,* explained, "She lost everything because of her late husband Hector's Jacobite obsession, and she won't go through that again" (Reiher, 2020). The bitter scene dramatizes a mature choice based on peace rather than passion.

The triumph of love in episode nine opposes the misogynistic ostracism of Eve as the seducer and betrayer who costs Adam an easy life in the Garden of Eden. The *Outlander* version pictures husband and wife apart, with Jamie waylaid by a pit viper in the wilderness. Meanwhile, Claire dyes clothing with indigo, the color of healing. Struggling to reunite with her, Jamie wants to spend his final moments in her care and in their bed, the site of mutual passion. When he sinks toward a passageway to the afterlife, he has a choice—die or return to his wife. Claire perceives his need and stimulates him sexually, reviving the bliss of their union. Jolted back toward life, he chooses to remain on earth with Claire, not out of ardor, but because she needs him. His revitalized body assures him a chance to keep her safe during the coming war. Thus, they become each other's deliverance.

See also Marriage; Matrilineage.

Source

Macon, Alexandra. "An Exclusive First Look at Brianna and Roger's Huge *Outlander* Wedding," *Vogue* (7 February 2020).
Reiher, Andrea. "'Outlander' Recap: Why Jocasta Feels It Is 'Better to Marry Than Burn,'" *Variety* (22 March 2020).

Craigh na Dun

A suitable locale for magic in a subdued fantasy, Craigh na Dun is a monument to female questing that addresses real issues in women's lives, especially the consequences of combat. Because of its centrality to the *Outlander* TV series, the stone round recurs in introductions to each fictional episode. On October 31, 1945, in the aftermath of World War II, the apostles of the Celtic shrine draw army veterans Claire and Frank Randall into a mythic, other-worldly milieu. Within the monoliths, women garbed like eighteenth-century Druids have their own battlefields to mourn, a ubiquitous affliction among female mortals. The dynamics coincide with spirits walking on earth at Samhain and nature energized with potency and fecundity. The dancers whirl like dervishes seeking communion with lost souls.

Craigh na Dun contributes to a sense of universality, a generic need for enclosed space to house liturgy and religious communion. In a scene parallel to the fictional Scots landmark, the open-air motif portrays the sanctuary of an aboriginal New World race. In occluded surroundings in 2000 BCE, communicants join in stacking stone pillars and performing a ring dance, perhaps to some celestial phenomenon or nature cycle. Filmed in an ambiguous state of awe, the repeated pagan motif lures the crudely clad adults into tentative celebration. Their ceremony reflects a circular perspective on history in which conflict and sorrow chain all humankind into a repeated state of regret and anticipation.

AFTER SAMHAIN NIGHT

As a foreshadowing, the main scenario pictures Claire Randall examining forget-me-nots, a simple blue wildflower with a fortuitous name suggesting the grief of two husbands who can't let her go. On Samhain, the observation of a fluid ritual lighted by bud-shaped lanterns draws her into the private world of Scots Druidesses. Epitomized and directed by fortune-telling housekeeper Mrs. Graham, Fiona's grandmother, caller of the dance, participants flutter gauzy, neutral-colored robes topped with modest loose drapes that reveal necks and shoulders. Amid an irregular sequence of Neolithic dolmens or menhirs, the women intone an eerie chant that sets the pace for an annular course, the original sacrament of humankind begun around 4000 BCE. Like the future that awaits Claire, the figures swirl, indistinct, yet trancelike, a testimonial to the ten women who commit themselves to their own path.

Claire's tumble back two centuries reminds her of a car wreck in the dark and her sense of disequilibrium, which wrests her from a familiar place in history. After learning of her origins in "The Devil's Mark," Jamie generously offers to escort her back to the mystic site. Arrival at the stones forces a decision—new love over old. On departure from the Battle of Culloden on April 16, 1746, the crucial choice of leaving Jamie in a combat zone to spare harm to their unborn child sets Claire again in the granite enclosure, an inexorable time divider. Fittingly, the Frasers repeat wedding vows before the central pillar, a pagan foreshadowing of the Christian altar. The pillared landmark epitomizes the round smallpox inoculation that frees her and Geillis Duncan from lethal illness and mirrors the iconic iron wedding band that Claire never removes.

A CIRCLE OF PEACE

Whisked from Craigh na Dun within earshot of British cannon roar to 1948, Claire can only scream her sorrow and crouch on the roadway, babbling about the outcome of an eighteenth-century battle that continues to agonize Scots. Her arrival at Jamie's printshop in Edinburgh in 1766 begins the second stave of a consuming romance, a cycle of passion that introduces two more metaphysical time-altering passages: the imitation of the dolmen ring above a liquid portal at Abandawe near Rose Hall, Jamaica, and on the

Mohawk trail outside Shadow Lake, New York. A dissimilarity, the separate arrivals of Brianna Randall and Roger MacKenzie through the Scots circle contribute to the image of enduring wedlock and female choice and of unavoidable bloodshed in whatever era they reside.

At Fraser's Ridge in season five, the idea of a timeslip influences Roger, who plots to remove danger by spiriting wife Brianna and son Jemmy to the twentieth century. In the final moments of Murtagh FitzGibbons Fraser's discussion with Jamie of a clash with the British army, the elder godfather bends to the ground to arrange stones in a miniature Craigh na Dun. The revival of the thematic round proposes an escape for the influential Regulator, whom Governor William Tryon wants to hang as an example to colonial tax protesters. Without much chance of success, Murtagh poses the stones as a means of returning to the distant future to offset warfare.

See also Celtic Beliefs; Circles; Dance; Matrilineage.

Source

Avina, Alyssa. "*Outlander*: 10 Things That Are Historically Accurate (And 10 Things That Aren't)," *Screenrant* (24 April 2019).

Crouch, David. "Places around Us: Embodied Lay Geographies in Leisure and Tourism," *Leisure Studies* 19:2 (2002): 63–76.

Potter, Mary-Anne. "'Everything and Nothing': Liminality in Diana Gabaldon's *Outlander*," *Interdisciplinary Literary Studies* 21:3 (2019): 282–296.

Crime

The merger of rebellion and everyday felony steeps the opening season of the televised *Outlander* historical drama. By categorizing Scots as "superstitious barbarians," fictional British occupation forces exonerate what scholar Moa Hågbäck of Linnaeus University termed the victimizing of the "underdeveloped, uncivilised savage," a rationalization of a global land grab in Scotland, the West Indies, and North America (Hågbäck, 2019, 49). In the first episodes, War Chief Dougal MacKenzie's outrider band gleefully engages in a skirmish with Redcoats at Cocknammon Rock, revealing the arrogant intent of English insurgents on November 1, 1743. At the corral of Auld Alec, Jamie confesses to rustling and jailbreak, both of which summon English garrisons. Because he considers occupation troops Scotland's enemy, he clouds questions of criminality with a gleeful patriotism.

Felonies bring Dougal and Geillis Duncan together, encouraging her to divert £1,000 from Arthur Duncan's private receipts for use by the Jacobites. Her slick theft, worth $239,664.87 in current value, contrasts the misdemeanor of the tanner's boy Novelli, who risks losing a hand for stealing bannocks. Jamie's intervention enables the boy to flee nailing to the Cranesmuir pillory, a sentence that bloodies his left ear. Claire's outrage at child abuse for a minor theft places twentieth-century jurisprudence above the casual sentencing by Arthur Duncan, the town procurator fiscal, and Father Bain, the Catholic confessor and disciplinarian. Neither the representative of law or religion exhibits compassion for a boy's mischief or pity for his suffering and terror.

A resetting of action in France in season two examines the *Ancien Regime* and its corruption 46 years preceding the French Revolution. Juxtaposing the splendor of Versailles against the squalor of l'Hôpital des Anges, the social milieu appears to accommodate multiple forms of lawlessness, from beggary, street gangs, rape, adultery, mail theft, and highway robbery to bribing a harbormaster to conceal two deaths from smallpox.

The Frasers embroil themselves in malfeasance and justify crimes to attain a greater good: impeding an epidemic and halting a fourth Jacobite rebellion. Even Mother Hildegarde, the hospital supervisor, excuses her misconduct of baptizing and naming Faith, a stillborn child, to allow burial in consecrated ground.

Anti-British Crime

In the third season in 1766, Claire teases out of Jamie his continued involvement in sedition and illicit business, which involves immigrant Yi Tien Cho and Young Ian Murray in avoiding the British duty on alcohol. Confession of smuggling whisky, cognac, brandy, rum, and French wine extends complicity in avoiding English taxes. Episode seven creates dramatic irony out of excise agent John Barton, who dies from a tussle with Claire and lies ripening in a barrel of crème de menthe, the color of envy and financial thievery. The fiasco results from Sir Percival Turner's extortion and Barton's breaking and entering at Madame Jeanne's brothel to obtain Jamie's ledgers. In an androcentric society, however, Claire risks arrest for killing a man not her husband. Such women incur suspicion based on gender rather than evidence.

A broader view of crime continues into fictional and historic events in the New World, where Jamie Fraser applauds the American theft of the anthem "God Save Great George Our King." Capital punishment opens the fourth season with ex-con Gavin Hayes's hanging for killing a cuckolded husband. Simultaneously, the flight of pirate and smuggler Stephen Bonnet from the gibbet prefigures a series of wrongdoings targeting the Frasers and their company on the way up the Cape Fear to River Run. The introduction of plantation law outlines multiple levels of criminality: the slave Rufus's crime of striking a white person, Overseer Byrne's crime of hooking Rufus in the torso and suspending him from a tree, and Jocasta Cameron's crime of letting the slave live. In a furor, neighbors thronging on the front lawn break windows and threaten arson. To rescue Rufus from lynching, Claire violates the Hippocratic Oath, which dictates "Do no harm" (4:2). The difficult decision illustrates choices that still cluster around capital punishment, mob rule, and assisted suicide.

Colonial Crimes

A mix of criminalities involves John Grey in sodomy with Judge Alerdyce, a serious infraction that Brianna Randall uses to blackmail Grey into marrying her. Cultural historian and journalist Rictor Norton summarized the popular recoil from homosexuality:

> Sodomy was a crime set apart, wholly different in nature from all other crimes, a crime committed by a different race from mere mortals, a crime which merited a severer form of punishment than even the most violent murder or rape [Norton, 2009].

Simultaneously, Governor William Tryon charges Murtagh Fitzgibbons Fraser for forming Scots-American landowners into the Regulators, a vigilante group that wars against corrupt North Carolina sheriffs and tax agents. The muddle of individual self-defense and civil rights forecasts the American Revolution and a complete overturn of colonial lawlessness by the U.S. Constitution. Significantly, the issues of slavery and sexual privacy remain unsettled until the nineteenth through twenty-first centuries.

At an unexpected occurrence in season five, the series inserts Lieutenant Hamilton Knox's anger at Ethan MacKinnon, a Regulator incarcerated in Hillsborough, whom the Redcoat officer stabs in the gut with a saber. Jamie accuses Knox of executing an unarmed prisoner without a trial. The on-the-spot asphyxiation of Knox and concealment of the murder muddles the view of Jamie as heroic villain against English colonialism. Further discussion of crimes against persons heightens Jamie's concern for Josiah Beardsley, a branded thief who could fall prey to thief takers. In a worsening of malefaction, Bonnet broadens his felonies to include rigged gambling and human trafficking, which he conducts with Captain Howard at the rate of £6 ($1,074.32) for the sale of Brianna Mackenzie. Jamie reaches a heroic height by chasing Lionel Brown's gang for abducting, beating, and gang-raping Claire. With no remorse, he orders, "Kill them all" (5:12).

See also British Army; Clergy; Democracy; Jacobites; Piracy; Jack Randall; Regulators; Smuggling; Violent Death.

Source

Hågbäck, Moa. "[..] If Only You Behaved Like the Loyal British Subjects You're Supposed to Be: National Identities and the Function of the Past in Starz's *Outlander*," master's thesis, Linnaeus University, 2019.

Norton, Rictor. "Popular Rage (Homophobia): The Gay Subculture in Georgian England" (16 August 2009), http://rictornorton.co.uk/eighteen/homophob.htm.

Culloden

The *Outlander* TV production, a popularized fiction on a par with Michael Shaara's war novel *The Killer Angels,* reprises the Battle of Culloden and its invalidation of Scots rights to property and full citizenship. Initiated by Bonnie Prince Charlie in 1744, the fourth and final Jacobite rebellion and last battle fought in Great Britain sought the downthrow of George II, an anti–Catholic Hanoverian. To enthrone King James III, a Catholic Stuart exile in Rome, Italy, the prince began securing funds, volunteers, and armaments for the pro–Stuart rising. On his first view of Scotland, he arrived at the isle of Eriskay on July 23, 1745, and, with the backing of clans Cameron and MacDonald, he launched an eight-month offensive. His staff mobilized a Jacobite army on August 19, 1745. The fighting force consisted of lowland Scots, Gaels, and French in service to the French military along with six hundred Royal Scots under John Drummond, an Irish brigade of five regiments and cavalry, and Welsh and English recruits, including deserters from the British army.

To the epicenter of violence, generals George Murray and Niall Drummond led the first ranks in clan order: Athol men, Camerons, and two lines of Stewarts followed by Frasers, McIntoshes, Faquharsons, McLeans, McLeods, Chisholms, Clanronald, Keppoch, Glen Garry, and the Duke of Perth's troops. The second line consisted of the Highland Horse, Benerman, Glenbucket, French Scots, Kilmarnock, Irish piquets (advance men), and Lewis Gordon's regiment. All preceded Prince Charles leading the reserve. The fifteen battalions totaled 6,411 against a British force of 8,000 marching from Aberdeen plus 2,000 Hessian mercenaries as loyalist backup.

While the Redcoats received supplies from the Royal Navy, prospects for a Jacobite victory dimmed from a dearth of horses, oatmeal, and provisions. On April 16, 1746, in the tragic trouncing of Highland forces at Culloden Moor east of Inverness, ten Redcoat cannon and six mortars of the Royal Artillery commanded by William Augustus, the Duke of Cumberland, the youngest son of George II, slew 2,000 Scots, 80 percent of whom fought without swords. On a flat, boggy battlefield, the 7,600 surviving Redcoats seized 154 Jacobites and 222 French allies. French painter David Morier captured the one-sided confrontation in "An Incident in the Rebellion of 1745."

In the aftermath, Cumberland's vengeance took the form of rigorous Disarming Acts that stripped Scots of dirks and claymores, Gaelic language, bagpipe music, plaids, and clan authority, membership, and property. After execution of rebel leaders and the incineration of survivors in barns, some 936 survivors left for the British colonies under the Traitors Transported Act of 1746. The recruiting of reprieved Jacobites such as the fictional Jamie Fraser to the British military of North America produced one of the ironies of colonial history.

The Film Version

With a limited number of actors, the TV depiction of Culloden depends upon spirited high command debate of a night raid at Nairn and remorse at the slim chance that an amateur military can free Scotland from England's draconian rule. As described by *Variety* critic Laura Prudom, "The inevitability of it is barreling down on them, it feels like a pressure cooker—no matter what they do, no matter what they try, fate is stronger than their will" (Prudom, 2016). Self-defense by sword, pistol, and French and Spanish firelocks (muskets) with ball shot, grape shot, and state-of-the-art bayonets requires last-minute drilling. At Kingussie, Jamie demands strict order; Murtagh Fitzgibbons Fraser teaches march commands and shows Fergus how to load and fire a pistol.

In conflict with the fictional Jacobite leadership, War Chief Dougal MacKenzie disputes European methods in favor of the savage Highland raid. By clever filming in clouds of smoke, the actors recreate the exhilaration of victory at Prestonpans, top level conferences at Culloden House, and the dreaded debacle at Culloden. In drifting snowflakes, shielded by fumes from artillery and volleys of musket fire, Scots warriors move close to the enemy's bayonets and sabers for deadly hand-to-hand bouts with dirk and sword.

Close-ups shrink the one-hour confrontation and reduce the combatant-strewn field to Jamie's monomaniac charge on a Redcoat with a fistful of turf, a symbolic taste of Scots soil to choke the aggressor. In a private duel, "Red Jamie" battles Captain Black Jack Randall, who delivers an arcing wound to Jamie's left thigh. Jamie's killing blow to Jack strikes his left torso. Both men totter toward exhaustion. Post-battle camera pans of a plain of corpses heighten the mechanical stockpiling of Jacobite weapons, emptying of sporrans, and brief dispatching of survivors with saber and bayonet and by burning alive.

Ironically shielded by Jack's body from freezing weather, Jamie survives the long day. A bobble of the Adam's apple reveals him alive, his perception distorted by the approach of a rabbit, a token glimmer of life and his unborn daughter Brianna's love of bunnies. In an existential state between life and death, he experiences an illusion—Claire, a metaphysical angel in white, a shimmering echo of the elf Arwen, played by Liv Tyler in *The Lord of the Rings*. Some joshing with Rupert MacKenzie muffles rifle shots that dispatch Scots traitors one by one. Among ragged, demoralized Jacobites, Jamie's last-minute statement of his full name draws Hal Melton's attention. In one of the epic's memorable cliffhangers, Hal saves the infamous "Red Jamie" from the firing squad.

Culloden in Memory

After 57 years of rebellion form 1689 to 1746, the repercussions of an iconic defeat dishearten Highlanders, causing Fergus to brand his foster father a coward. In the genocidal backlash by "Butcher Cumberland," Scots endure interrogation, unforeseen arrests, and property searches for dirks, muskets, claymores, targes, and pistols, one discharged by Fergus at an ill-omened raven. Jamie, his left thigh seriously slashed, abandons hope for his homeland. Pursuit reduces him to a troglodyte for six years under the aliases "Red Jamie" and "the Dunbonnet," a sartorial attempt to conceal his red hair. To excoriate Jacobite traitors, Corporal MacGregor plagues the Murray family and waylays Fergus, severing his left hand with a saber and leaving him to die of hemorrhage. The series inserts the turncoat Scot to illustrate choices Highlanders made to ally with the winning side.

Culloden's post-war miseries—known as the Highland Clearances—force Jamie to reassess his life. The lopping of Fergus's hand so distresses his foster father that Jamie sinks to his knees in regret that he can't insulate the household from SS-style persecution. In the twentieth century, Claire makes a pilgrimage to burial sites and talks to Jamie's spirit at the Fraser headstone, which lies alongside markers for MacKintosh, MacGillivray, MacLean, MacLaghlan, Atholl Highlanders, Stewarts of Appin, Campbell, Cameron, Donald, and mixed clans. To Jenny's questions in the third season, Jamie conceals the conception and birth of daughter Brianna, while he tries to explain why Claire left before the battle.

The follow-up to defeat protested the 1707 Act of Union that consolidated the United Kingdom. The loss broke Jacobite and Highlander spirits and initiated a period when rents rose and Scots struggled with debt. According to expert Christy Jackson Nicholas, the Crown troops freely raped, burned crofts, slaughtered, salted farmland, imprisoned, "stole from, killed, arrested, and transported thousands" as indentured servants in North America, the fate of the fictional Gavin Hayes, Lesley, and Murtagh Fitzgibbons Fraser (Nicholas, 2014). On approach to River Run, Aunt Jocasta Cameron's home on North Carolina's Cape Fear River, Jamie explains to Claire that his uncle Hector Cameron, an historic survivor of the Battle of Culloden and a relative of the fervid Jacobite Donald Cameron of Lochiel, joined Jocasta in the Scottish diaspora to begin again in the New World by planting tobacco and indigo. The effort to build a frontier home heartens the Frasers to do likewise, but causes Jamie to compare the British hounding of Highlanders to the displacement and genocide of first peoples in the Americas.

In caustic recollection in season five, Jocasta Cameron relives her family's flight from northern Scotland to the coast, where Hector Cameron accidentally shoots daughter Morna. Although the couple manages to export French gold sent by Louis XV, the bars arrive too late to spare Highlanders a catastrophe and the Camerons the burning deaths of Seonag and Clementina and their children. The money funds River Run, a grand mansion in Bladen County on the Cape Fear River that enriches the family through slave-operated agriculture. In tortured recall of leaving Morna's corpse in the mud beside dead Redcoats, Jocasta accepts her blindness as a punishment and grips a blue hair ribbon, a relic of her daughters' lives after Culloden. Her wretchedness corroborates tacksman Duncan Kerr's claim that the gold is cursed.

See also Bonnie Prince Charlie; British Army; Disarming Acts; Jacobites; Weaponry.

Source

Nicholas, Christy Jackson. *Stunning, Strange and Secret: A Guide to Hidden Scotland*. Meath, Ireland: Tirgearr, 2014.

Oates, Jonathan. *Battles of the Jacobite Rebellions: Killiecrankie to Culloden*. Havertown, PA: Pen and Sword Military, 2019.

Prudom, Laura. "'Outlander' Stars Break Down the Desperate Deals of 'The Hail Mary,'" *Variety* (25 June 2016).

Royle, Trevor. *Culloden*. New York: Pegasus, 2017.

Dance

The *Outlander* TV series incorporates dance to vivify traditions of Scots and other cultures, as with a circle ritual among North American aborigines in 2000 BCE, Murtagh Fitzgibbons Fraser's Scots sword dance, Brianna's introduction to ceilidh dancing at Grandfather Mountain, Jamie's slow dance with Claire in her dreamscape, and Otter Tooth's painting himself for a war dance to influence the Mohawk. Central to the ethnic overview, Mrs. Graham leads a troupe of ten Druidesses in chanting to the heavens, spreading arms wide, and processing around Craigh na Dun until sunrise on Samhain eve 1945, a magical time for summoning the Earth Mother. More balletic celebrations follow the sacred opening of each episode. At Castle Leoch, reels to bagpipe skirls end a tense positioning of Jamie as Laird Colum MacKenzie's ally, but not a rival to Colum's brother, War Chief Dougal MacKenzie, for clan control. The rapid turns of partners release stress and renew delight in the clan gathering, which recurs in Roger MacKenzie and Brianna Randall's visit to North Carolina's Grandfather Mountain calling of the clans.

A private sacrament in season one, episode ten pinpoints evil in Celtic dance. At the forest ritual Geillis Duncan enacts to the earth deity, she dances alone and in private among three fires for the purpose of manipulating enemies. During a fruitful time in her womanhood, she raises a firebrand to honor nature, the female body, and the source of her fertility, which she dedicates to the Jacobite cause. She identifies the purpose as freedom from marriage to Arthur Duncan and furtherance of an affair with Dougal. As a result of Geillis's summoning the great Celtic mother, Dougal's wife Maura dies of fever. In view of banqueters at the castle Leoch great hall, Geillis poisons Arthur with cyanide. The double deed presents the religious and civil sides of Geillis's evil—sorcerer and murderer.

In the third season, Jamie stresses the centrality of jigs and reels to his first Hogmanay after release from indenture to the Dunsanys at Helwater, England. Cinematography draws food, decorations, fiddlers, candlelight, and fellowship into the celebration of the New Year, a homey scene similar in importance to the December 31 party at the Red House in the film version of George Eliot's *Silas Marner*. Like Silas, Jamie uses the holiday spirit as reason for risking greater involvement in normality. His rejuvenation begins with marriage to Laoghaire MacKimmie and stepfatherhood to her daughters, Joan and Marsali, but the short-lived wedlock with a sexually frigid woman sends him to Edinburgh to initiate a lone bachelorhood in a brothel. At his reunion with Claire and flight to Jamaica, the couple encounter a voodoo blood ritual, a vibrating whirligig of Maroons outside Rose Hall. The spiritual communing with divinity ironically overthrows Geillis Duncan Abernethy before she can kill the Frasers' daughter Brianna as a sacrifice to the Stuart dynasty.

Dance in season five spreads family joy. A wedding celebration at the big house for Brianna and Roger MacKenzie revives community spirit with reels on the lawn. The figures represent the roots of American square dance, especially the "Virginia Reel." Solo dance presents Jamie in a new light at Brownsville, where he performs a highland fling to entertain the Rowan County Militia. Actor Sam Heughan explained to *Collider* the androcentric battle preparation filled with symbols: "The shaking of the leg would show the shaking off of the shackles of the British, and the hands above the head were the stag's horns. It's a very patriotic dance, so it felt like the right dance to do" (Radish, 2020).

In contrast to spirited reels and solo jigs, polite minuets and sarabandes before Duncan Innes's marriage to thrice-widowed Jocasta Cameron dramatize the dominance of European arts among elite colonists. The occasion brings guests to an outdoor flower-decked pavilion to display fashionable dress and shoes and fussy choreography. In view of River Run, the sedate performance of tightly figured social protocols displays the courtly etiquette gendered by male bowing to female curtseys. The emphasis on convention and decorum forces John Grey to satisfy single women who flirt with an unmarried man without recognizing the politesse of a closeted homosexual.

See also Circle; Craigh na Dun.

Sources

Radish, Christina. "Sam Heughan Talks 'Outlander' Season 5, What's Next for the Frasers, and His 'Bloodshot' Role," *Collider* (16 February 2020).
Salto, Cattia. "*Outlander*: Dance of the Druids," *Terre Celtiche* (1 April 2018).

Deception

Lies and deceit become a way of life in the *Outlander* TV narrative for characters who weather perilous wars and intrigues. Trickery flourishes as twisted as Claire's bigamous marriage, as calculated as Jamie's stampeding Lionel Brown's horses from Brownsville, as manipulative as Jenny's lies about a stillborn child, and as endearing as Claire's pose as the mother of Elias Pound during his delirium with typhoid fever. At Cranesmuir, Claire's melodramatic collapse enables Jamie to rescue the tanner's boy Novelli from pillory impalement by his left ear. Claire improves on the subterfuge by pretending to faint from the sight of blood while Jamie removes the nail and sets the boy free. By way of explanation, Jamie identifies Claire's weakness at bloody scenes, a sight gag belied by the opening scenes of her stopping a hemorrhage from a femoral artery at an Allied combat aid station during World War II. The girlish collapse anticipates Jamie's actual faint in season three, episode six, a conversion of a feminine stereotype of delicate sensibilities.

The rapid shift of identities during time travel dazzles Claire, who passes from Randall to Beauchamp to sassenach to Fraser to Malcolm and back again. Briefly, by extension, she compounds Jamie's alias at Lallybroch by becoming Mistress MacTavish. At a second meeting with Clarence Marylebone, the Duke of Sandringham, at Castle Leoch, she pretends that she has never met the duke, her husband's proposed rescuer. The ruse works a second time at her introduction to the duke at Belmont. In an *Outlander* recap, producer Ron Moore exonerates Claire by lambasting Sandringham as "this guy who keeps everybody dancing, where you never can tell which way he's going to go" (Bucksbaum, 2016). The comment reasons that life among liars and deceivers requires adversaries to adopt similar hoaxes.

VARIED PLOYS

Claire's foil, herbalist Geillis Duncan is both temptress and trickster. She exults in the malleability of husband Arthur Duncan, the town fiscal (treasurer), whom she cons into lowering the penalty on the tanner's son Novelli from amputated hand to one ear nailed at the Cranesmuir pillory for an hour. She worsens her scheme by laughing at male naiveté. Deception imperils Claire and Geillis from Laoghaire MacKenzie's prank letter sending Claire on an emergency mission to the Duncan house. Under arrest for witch-craft by steely wardens, the women await trial in the open air thieves' hole. Geillis admits lethal trickery of Arthur Duncan by slowly killing him with white arsenic and cyanide, the twisting of herbal lore for the sake of regaining her freedom.

The TV epic seethes with cunning. Jamie, upon receipt of a forged letter from the bonnie prince, blurts *a mhealltair mhallaichte* (cursed deceiver, 2:8). Betrayal threat-ens the Watch, Lallybroch's protection squad that follows Horrocks's directions into a certain-death trap to earn the grifter his exoneration for deserting the British army. To free Jamie from Wentworth Prison, Claire performs a *tour de force* charade of "Chris-tian duty" and proper English breeding, a convincing appeal to the governor, Sir Fletcher Gordon (1:15). By pretending to pity a condemned prisoner from a good family, she wins Gordon's grudging sympathies. The chicanery results in receipt of Jamie's belongings and collapse at the exit, a testimonial to the cost of playacting compassion for a family friend. The finale, achieved by stampeding nineteen shaggy cattle through the prison's back entrance, enables Murtagh FitzGibbons Fraser and Rupert MacKenzie to liberate Jamie without deceit—straightforward muscle and retreat by wagon to Father Anselm's Bene-dictine abbey.

Season two resets plot and characters in the Boston home of a tragically misaligned couple. By opening on Frank Randall's confrontation with his wife in 1948 at the fireside of the Rev. Reginald Wakefield's guest room, the sorrowing husband expresses confusion and grief before flickering light, a suggestion of modifications of truth and simmering emotion. The revelation of Claire's pregnancy further skewers Frank, sending him into a frenzy of destruction and rage in the minister's storage shed. His anger spent on a stash of rubbish, he stands at the parsonage hearth to discuss a pragmatic solution to a sterile man rearing Jamie's child. The sham proves untenable: his Harvard associates doubt the Ozzie and Harriet marriage after Sandy Travers offers a better life as his mistress.

Marital Complicity

By entitling the third episode of season two "Useful Occupations and Deceptions," the *Outlander* TV script advances Jamie and Claire's dissuading the bonnie prince from dethroning the Hanoverian George II, an anti–Catholic Anglican. From purloining the prince's correspondence and deciphering coded letters, one in musical staffs, the High-lander intervention inches along. Jamie's clever decoding precedes a more sinister strata-gem in the fourth episode, "La Dame Blanche," which portrays tampering with the cotter pin in the Frasers' carriage wheel. Unaware of her mythic reputation as a white witch, Claire scares off a street gang by revealing her light complexion, a pose she later scorns until it becomes more useful to her rescue in the finale of season five.

In contrast to Claire's reputed enchantments, her skill at herbalism provides a sci-entific duplicity. To prevent Le Comte St. Germain from investing in the Jacobite cabal, she mimics smallpox in his warehouse workers by sending Fergus to spike their wine with rosemary, rose madder, and bitter cascara followed by brushing mashed nettles on their clothes to raise a rash. The flimflam integrates gut pain, vomiting, inflammation, and contact dermatitis, a confusing trio of symptoms suggesting lethal contagion. Fer-gus's part in infecting the winery workers incriminates the Fraser's foster son, a pick-pocket who is already well versed in criminality. On the way to the warehouse, Fergus rides Jamie's black horse, a hint at the real deceiver.

Of the alteration in Jamie Fraser from honest wine merchant to double-dealer, actor Sam Heughan remarked on "discovering a side of the character I didn't know was there. He's playing someone else—he's learning to be quite deceptive, and he does it very well" (Prudom, 2016). The lead-up to the Battle of Culloden on April 16, 1746, forces characters into extremes of lying and antipathy. In a grim fraternal word battle, War Chief Dougal MacKenzie, the eternal narcissist, accuses his dying older brother Colum of betrayal by falling from a horse and destroying Dougal's hero worship. The silence that follows Colum's demise forces out a mix of selfishness and regret in Dougal. Unable to disburden himself of unfinished family business, Dougal grips his brother's hand and weeps, discovering too late Colum's suicide.

Greater Stakes

Blatant perfidy in season three threatens Jamie's household and the peace of Lallybroch. From 1746 to 1752, Jenny, Ian, and the Murray children deny their connection with Red Jamie, their ill-famed relative. His capture by Redcoats at the Lallybroch gate requires playacting by brother and sister when Jenny Murray pretends to betray "the Dunbonnet" in exchange for English blood money. A parallel of Judas's receipt of thirty pieces of silver from the Roman hierarchy, the scenario poses another comparison of Jamie to the forsaken Christ. The camera focuses on Jamie's brown tam, a protection that falls unheeded in the road.

At a new life in Edinburgh, Jamie professes candor, but initiates marital fraud by concealing from Claire his remarriage. At his smuggling operation, he hides from brother-in-law Ian the presence of runaway Young Ian at the printshop. Claire questions the overt misinformation, a lead-in to the "kebbie-lebbie" in episode eight (3:8). Judging the lie from a mother's perspective, she scolds Jamie for worrying the Murrays about their son's welfare. The time traveler's sudden meeting with Laoghaire and daughters Joanie and Marsali MacKimmie inflates charges of prevarication too flagrant to excuse. The evasion threatens to end the Fraser reunion. Only a bullet wound and emergency surgery redirect Claire to the Hippocratic Oath and a vow to minister to the injured, an honorable act the antithesis of Jamie's sham.

Colonial Risks

Season five heightens the cost of deception to murder and ruination. After Lieutenant Hamilton Knox realizes that Jamie shared Murtagh's prison cell at Ardsmuir, the revelation motivates Jamie's brutal asphyxiation of an admirable career soldier. Jamie's aplomb concludes with pocketing a homeless kitten and strolling past Knox's corpse in the street. In episode six, Jamie requites an insult to Claire by threatening Phillip Wylie with a knife. The man-to-man vendetta ends with a triumph at whist and Jamie's claim on Lucas, the Arabian stallion. Using the horse as collateral, Jamie retreats under his old alias "Alexander Malcolm" and plots a business deal with pirate Stephen Bonnet, a villain too underhanded to fall for ordinary guile.

The trickery that ends Bonnet's crimes begins with his kidnapping Brianna and assaulting Claire. During Brianna's captivity at the pirate's Ocracoke residence, she uses his ignorance as a ploy to teach him about vengeance. By pretending to read the story of Captain Ahab and his pursuit of the white whale in Herman Melville's *Moby-Dick,* she discloses Bonnet's need for payback against members of society who have belittled him.

To save son Jemmy from Bonnet, she involves Eppie, a prostitute at Sylvie's brothel, in an escape plot. The scenario concludes with a conundrum—Brianna shoots Bonnet before he drowns in a rising tide. Roger questions her motive—mercy or revenge.

The final deception, Lionel Brown's abduction of Claire, shields heinous battery and gang rape. By exploding Jamie's still and luring the Fraser men away from home, Lionel quickly overwhelms Claire and rides away with his gang. On the way to Brownsville, he ignores rumors of her metaphysical powers and laughs in anticipation of debauching the woman who introduced his wife Rose to birth control. Too late to spare Claire a grievous assault, Jamie leads his militia into the felons' camp and orders execution for all. Because Lionel survives for questioning, Marsali uses her opportunity to exterminate a sneaky cut-throat, an overturn in his rough-handed dodge that leaves him vulnerable to a pregnant woman.

See also Fire and Heat; Rescue.

Sources

Bucksbaum, Sydney. "'Outlander' Team Breaks Down That Violent Act of Revenge and 'Powerful' Scene Viewers Didn't See," *Hollywood Reporter* (18 June 2016).

Hesse, David. *Warrior Dreams: Playing Scotsmen in Mainland Europe.* Manchester, UK: Manchester University Press, 2014.

Prudom, Laura. "'Outlander' Stars on 'Surprising' Season 2 Twists, Parisian Politics and Changing History," *Variety* (8 January 2016).

Democracy

The development of the democratic ideal in the fictional *Outlander* TV series follows the Highlander metamorphosis—from diaspora fleeing English oppression to the formation of a Scots-American citizenry in piedmont North Carolina. Season three progresses from the Frasers' failed stratagem in France––to subvert rebellion against the Redcoats and prevent cultural collapse in Scotland––to a pilgrimage across the Atlantic toward an emerging republic. A lengthy, obstacle-fraught adventure moves higgledy-piggledy from a microcosm of shipboard plague to an island respite on Haiti with Father Fogden and Mamacita, a deranged priest and his waspish mother-in-law. After the Frasers reunite for the final leg to Jamaica, framed as the rescue of Young Ian from kidnappers, they encounter the Kingston slave market. Claire and Jamie demonstrate twentieth-century ethics by setting free one African, Temeraire, the beginning of their disavowal of period bondage and flesh markets.

A false murder charge against Jamie at Kingston presses the couple into a frantic race compounded of outsized Gothic events. From house arrest at Rose Hall, Claire hurries him to the voodoo gathering that joins West African religion to Margaret Campbell's predictions of slave emancipation. Maroon celebrants epitomize revolt by dismembering Archibald Campbell, Margaret's tormentor, and seizing his periwig, a minor pun on the name "Archibald." Narrative pacing thrusts the Frasers into a subterranean portal for Claire's defeat of European divine right of kings with a single slice through the neck of Geillis Duncan Abernethy, the deluded champion of Stuart restoration. The beheading lops off centuries of noblesse oblige and leads the Frasers to unique contributions to the American experiment in democracy.

A heart-pounding swirl whisks the couple into near drowning within the "eye of the storm," a metaphor for Old World struggles against monarchy and intrigue (3:13). Safe at last on the shores of Les Perles, Georgia, the survivors begin an allegorical pilgrimage by advancing northwest toward a wilderness rich with resources and possibilities. At first, they pass through the evils of pirate attack, Governor Tryon's taxation to fund an elegant mansion, and Aunt Jocasta Cameron's token escape from Scotland to the plantation South. The Frasers' values, still in the formative stage, press them west to the Appalachias, an Edenic getaway from the turmoil yet to come from the Regulator Movement, frontier criminals, and the American Revolution.

Andrea Reiher, a TV critic for *Variety*, isolated Jamie's noble aim: "As a modern cover of 'America the Beautiful' played ironically over the montage…. He liked the idea of playing a small part in helping [Brianna's] future country throw off the ruling fist of England" (Reiher, 2018). On the way west, Claire introduces Jamie to fundamentals of democracy in Katharine Lee Bates's lyrics to "America" and the constitutional ideal of "pursuit of happiness" (4:1). By season five, a fallback on family and community gives the couple a rest before Jamie must don his kilt, light the fiery cross, and take up his motherland's battles against Redcoat imperialism.

Season five enacts a painful truth about American democracy: it demands a high price from citizens, both fictional and historical. The struggles of the Rowan County Militia to recruit volunteers precede losses on both sides during the Battle of Alamance Creek on May 16, 1771. Differences in idealism cost the Scots-American community the lives of Bryan Cranna and Murtagh Fitzgibbons Fraser and the back-shooting of Isaiah Morton. The Roger MacKenzie's near hanging reduces a loving husband into a traumatized mute. The script illustrates how Jamie, Roger, and Young Ian adopt vigilantism to halt smuggler Stephen Bonnet from seizing Roger and Brianna's son Jemmy and from selling Brianna in a human trafficking deal. The *ad hoc* formation of a Committee of Safety introduces an interim problem for patriots: how to stop criminals from widespread felonies in the name of independent policing. In lieu of police, Jamie resorts to a frontier mainstay—vigilantism and the extermination of thugs.

See also American Revolution; Maroons.

Source

Nurczynski, Melissa Anne. "Fortune Favors the Brave," master's thesis, University of Texas at El Paso, 2019.

Reiher, Andrea. "'Outlander' Season 4 Premiere Recap: Jamie and Claire Meet 'America the Beautiful,'" *Variety* (4 November 2018).

Details

Numerous items in the *Outlander* TV narrative indicate meticulous research, especially of period details, such as a wagon load of pitchforks and hay reapers transported to a Jacobite war zone, the knuckles-to-forehead salute on the British man-o'-war *Porpoise*, a macramé backdrop for a frontier wedding at the big house, the popularity of Chad and Chip as boys' names in Boston, and the T branded on Josiah Beardsley's right hand as punishment for stealing cheese. On the Frasers' wedding night, Jamie admires the tones of Claire's brown hair, a foretokening of her many charms during their long marriage. At the MacKenzie gathering at Castle Leoch, Geordie bleeds to death in the shade of a forked tree, a representation of the departure from life to the beyond and a parallel of the tree that marks the boundary of Fraser's Ridge. For the MacKenzies, a failed attempt at time travel returns them to family along a "road less traveled" (5:11). While the Randalls discuss seeing one of two movies—*The Searchers* and *Carousel*—the downhill dialogue raises the subject of a merry-go-round marriage and their search for an end to misery, perhaps in divorce.

In the second season, episode seven, Louis XV, like his great grandfather before him, makes a show of wealth and power that extends to sexual privileges among his citizens. To Claire, a petitioner, he displays pride in his 1,000-tree orangerie and in the hot chocolate he acquires from New Spain. On her way out of the French royal palace after judging the king's inquiry into sorcery, she remembers to claim her gift orange, which recurs in her dissociative state in the season five finale. At the tiny headstone for Faith Fraser in the convent garden, the inscribed year 1744 summarizes a stunted life. Placement of the apostle spoon of St. Andrew lessens Jamie's grief at leaving their stillborn infant in French soil.

New World Rewards

Season four investigates the methods of obtaining and staking a land grant. For 10,000 acres of western North Carolina, Jamie must sign a deed, swear a loyalty oath, and place sharpened stakes along the perimeter, the boundaries that delineate European from native Cherokee holdings. His carving of F.R. on peripheral trees establishes the divide between Fraser's Ridge and the property of indigenous tribes. John Quincy Myers, a knowledgeable mountain man, explains the land pride of a people who ousted the Tuscarora in 1713. Because of heavy blood spillage and enslavement of 950 Indians as a result of the Tuscarora War (1711–1715), the former residents abandoned the Carolinas and migrated to New York, leaving the Cherokee to new insurgencies by the English and European immigrants.

The focus of the first episode of season five on a family wedding introduces a host of details that demonstrate prosperity in Rowan County, North Carolina. The bride's buttermilk-hued prairie dress, topped with Ellen MacKenzie Fraser's pearls, acknowledges the Scots family and their heirlooms as input to North American culture. The big house, replete with fretwork and molding and the beginnings of a roofed front porch, welcomes all comers to the festivities. In the yard, a low fire bakes new bricks. Across the lawn, a Scots reel prefigures American square dance as couples form and reform circles and lines. One curious anomaly, Spanish moss (*Tillandsia usneoides*), a tropical and subtropical draping in the trees, has either been imported from the Carolina swamps for the occasion or inadvertently relocated to the Piedmont. In episode eleven, the familiar melancholy call of the mourning dove (*Zenaida macroura*) laments the separation of Brianna and Roger Mackenzie from their home in North Carolina and their return to Boston.

Killing with Kindness

A sober component of episode three introduces Christ in the Beardsley family. At Fanny's stumble when her water breaks, a crucifix falls from the trader's walls. After Claire and Jamie tend a newborn and treat Aaron for gangrene and torture, Jamie replaces the crucifix above the hearth. To Aaron's refusal to repent of his evildoing against five wives and two indentured servants, Jamie chooses to end his suffering with the sign of the cross and a bullet to the head. The mercy killing holds special meaning for Jamie, who fears that he, like his father Brian, may die of apoplexy and lie helpless. The scene reminds both Frasers of the heavy burden of mortality and foreshadows a major loss of Murtagh Fitzgibbons Fraser on May 16, 1771, at the Battle of Alamance Creek. Inexorably, heavy grief assaults Jamie on his fiftieth birthday, when he takes stock of his losses.

A cautionary tale, season five, episode ten concludes the extended Fraser family's longing for reprisal. In extensive views of the psychopathic Stephen Bonnet, the narrative unfolds his self-pity for being orphaned and his craving for fine manners. By kidnapping Brianna and forcing her to teach him etiquette, he begins refining social behavior by removing his elbows from the table. Sudden mood swings shift him from charming host and audience for a version of Herman Melville's novel *Moby-Dick* to fornicator and trafficker in dissolute women. By ending the tale with his near drowning off the coast of Wilmington and Brianna's choice to shoot him in the head, the episode leaves uninterpreted details of his madness and the recompense for his crimes.

See also Makeup.

Source

Bianchi, Diana, and Adele D'Arcangelo. "Translating History or Romance? Historical Romantic Fiction and Its Translation in a Globalised Market," *Linguistics and Literature Studies* 3:5 (2015): 248–253.

Karda, Ni, and Made Fany Renjana. "The Exposures of Scottish Culture in Diana Gabaldon's *Outlander*," *Jurnal Ilmiah Mahasiswa FIB* 1:4 (2015).

Potter, Mary-Anne. "'Everything and Nothing': Liminality in Diana Gabaldon's *Outlander*," *Interdisciplinary Literary Studies* 21:3 (2019): 282–296.

Disarming Acts

After five centuries of Scots struggle to attain independence, in 1716, 1725, and 1746, a series of British disarming legislations targeted Jacobites and ended hope of a Stuart monarch. The British parliament outlawed possession and use of swords, knives, daggers, and firearms. The second act bolstered peacekeeping through confiscation of weaponry by Redcoat garrisons at Inverness and fictional Fort William. After a significant triumph at Prestonpans on September 21, 1745, Jacobites rearmed with flintlock muskets and bayonets seized from the routed British army. The decisive Scots defeat at Culloden Moor on April 16, 1746, curtailed Jacobitism with the stalking and slaughtering of escaped Highlanders and execution of Lord Simon Lovat of Beaufort, the fictional Jamie's grandfather.

Further disarming by the Act of Proscription of August 1, 1746, enforced by the victorious Duke of Cumberland, youngest son of George II, demolished the feudal clan system such as that willed to the fictional Hamish MacKenzie and prevented Highlanders from rearming. Punishments ranged from jailing to indenturing in the British colonies for seven years for clansmen owing court fines. For wearing the highland kilt and tartan, speaking or teaching Gaelic, or playing bagpipes anywhere in Scotland, the Dress Act of 1746 threatened six months imprisonment and servitude in the colonies. Cumberland also set fire to Linlithgow Palace, the twelfth-century setting for the fictional Wentworth Prison, where Claire and Murtagh Fitzgibbons Fraser engineer Jamie's rescue from Captain Black Jack Randall with a cattle stampede, an emblematic overthrow of British military tactics with a Highlander strategy from the Scots wild.

Deracinated Highlanders

For some 75 years, the clearances of land produced evictions, unemployment of tacksmen, elevated rents, and arson to cottages. Of the homes and furnishings, Doune Castle near Stirling—the fictional Laird Colum MacKenzie's Castle Leoch—fell to ruin as did Midhope, the location of the Frasers's Lallybroch. Only the Duke of Argyll saved his district. Rural transformation and cultural collapse fueled a Scots diaspora that depopulated the highlands as far south as Arran and north into the Hebrides. In the estimation of tourism specialist LuAnn McCracken Fletcher, an English professor at Cedar Crest

College in Allentown, Pennsylvania, the suppression of picturesque and historical elements exoticized the "distinctive Highland and Gaelic culture" for romantic recreations in fiction, art, tourism, film, and television (Fletcher, 2019, 192).

The *Outlander* TV series visualizes the result of anti–Highlander legislation and the emigration of families like the fictional Frasers. Under the Heritable Jurisdictions Act of 1746, Jamie and other lairds and titled nobles lost judicial rights to Crown officials, sheriffs, and investors. Following the assisted suicide of Laird Colum MacKenzie and his brother Dougal's murder the morning before the Battle of Culloden, Jamie's fostering powers over Hamish MacKenzie and the leaderless clan go unclaimed. The authority gap remained unhealed until the legend of Jacobite Rob Roy MacGregor and the writings of Sir Walter Scott in the 1810s and 1820s revived national pride.

A COLLAPSING CULTURE

The third season features Lallybroch's residents left defenseless after the seizure of arms and eviction of Gaels and their herds from communal fields. Antiques expert Lisa Hix summarized debilitation caused by the Dress Act of 1746, which forbade male Scots from wearing "the manly garb of [their] forefathers":

> Clothes commonly called Highland Clothes [that is to say] the Plaid, Philabeg, or little Kilt, Trowse, Shoulder Belts, or any part whatsoever of what peculiarly belongs to the Highland Garb; and that no Tartan, or party-coloured Plaid or Stuff shall be used for Great Coats, or for Upper Coats [Hix, 2017].

The ban remained in effect for 35 years. While the film hero Jamie disguises himself as the Dunbonnet and hides in a cave from 1746 to 1752, he feeds his family on game he snares or kills with bow and arrow rather than musket. He regrets the uprooting of fellow Scots and the arbitrary arrests of the elder Ian Murray, whose absences for questioning leave the household to women, servants, and children. Dialogue depicts the crude Redcoat mockery of Ian's leg amputation, a representation of Highlands crippling.

Post-Culloden genocide precedes cruel acts, including the killing of Highlanders that Claire mentions in season three, episode thirteen. A meticulous Redcoat search for an illegal pistol at Lallybroch in episode two puts at risk the newborn Ian, whom Fergus protects from a folk curse by shooting an ominous raven. Claire's return to Jamie after twenty years apart elicits his regret at the loss of dirk and sword and hope in the printing press, a newfound weapon. By issuing seditious leaflets and circulating them among papists, he maintains and energizes an underground coterie of Jacobites and Catholics until fire destroys his printshop. Ned Gowan restates the criminality of weapons possession in season three, episode eight after Laoghaire shoots Jamie with a pistol. After emigration to North Carolina, Jamie finds disgruntled Highlanders like Brian Cranna, Ethan MacKinon, Lee Withers, and Murtagh Fitzgibbons Fraser retaining their belligerence toward the British and forming the Regulators, a New World revision of Jacobite defiance of British taxation.

See also Culloden; Regulators; Scots Culture.

Source

Fletcher, LuAnn McCracken, ed. *Literary Tourism and the British Isles: History, Imagination, and the Politics of Place.* Lanham, MD: Lexington Books, 2019.

Hix, Lisa. "True Kilts: Debunking the Myths about Highlanders and Clan Tartans," *Collectors Weekly* (15 November 2017).

Mackenzie, Alexander. *The History of the Highland Clearances.* Edinburgh: Mercat Press Books, 1883.

Dueling

A civil settlement of male quarrels, vendettas, lies and affronts to personal and family honor, dueling typically involved gentlemen from military backgrounds. George K. Zhukov, author of *Post-Napoleonic Warfare & Small Arms,* justified the mechanics of dueling: "The censure of society—and possible *social* death—was feared over the possibility of actual death," a likelihood that causes the fictional Duke of Sandringham to hire Jamie as backup in settling a debt to the MacDonalds (Zhukov, 2018). From the late Middle Ages, an arranged trial by combat of challengers and their seconds began with selection of a site twenty paces wide and a choice of pistols, slender rapiers, or swords. Duelers could halt the face-off after drawing first blood, after felling the opposition, or at death, the end of Henry de Bohun's duel with Robert the Bruce, who killed his opponent at Bannockburn with a battleaxe.

Renaissance philosophy yielded erudite discussions of two-man combat. In 1409, the Italian monograph "Fior di Battaglia" (Flower of Battle) established rules that remained the *code duello* for more than two centuries, when survivors flaunted manly scars. From the mid–1600s to the mid- to late 1900s, church and civil laws in the Holy Roman Empire prohibited settling disgrace, aspersions, and disputes by arms backed by chain mail and armor. In 1777, the Irish *code duello* replaced blades with firearms; in 1865, fist fighting under the Marquess of Queensberry rules supplanted weapons.

The romantic nature of man-to-man combat suited filmmakers of *Barry Lyndon, Highlander, Rob Roy, Three Musketeers, Eugene Onegin, Poldark,* and *Roots.* In fictional Jamie Fraser's *Outlander* code of honor, dueling evidences manhood and expertise with weapons. Annalise de Marillac remembers him in his youth as a man of the blade and challenger of her previous husband. In 1744, Jamie's nagging hatred of Captain Black Jack Randall pushes him toward a match-up in the Bois de Boulogne, a forested section free of policing west of the Paris gendarmerie. The issue of Frank Randall's ancestry renews Jamie's animosity toward Claire, who fears that Jack's death will erase Frank from history. The eruption of Jamie's macho payback forces him to negotiate a year's grace with his wife, a dialogue that ends with the vicious command "Do not touch me" (2:5).

In one of the *Outlander* TV series' numerous coincidences, about the time that Claire goes into labor, Jamie violates his promise to her, this time to punish Jack for sodomizing Fergus. TV critic Sydney Bucksbaum, a journalist for the *Hollywood Reporter,* explains, "They've sold a piece of their souls for each other. It's something they can weather together" (Bucksbaum, 2017). A hard-fought struggle worsened by Jack's taunting, the clash pictures expertise on both sides, a means of elevating epic implications. Jamie's plunge of the sword into Jack's crotch recalls Claire's fear that descendent Frank Randall may never be born. Reviewer Sarene Leeds, a writer for *MarketWatch,* remarked on the erotic nature of the contest, which continues at Culloden: "Even when Jack delivers a crippling blade wound to Jamie's thigh, and the Highlander eventually lands the fatal stab to his adversary's chest, you still feel their carnal history with every physical blow" (Leeds, 2017).

Source

Bucksbaum, Sydney. "'Outlander' Producer Defends Graphic Rape Scene: 'We Wanted to Do It Justice,'" *Hollywood Reporter* (21 May 2016).

Leeds, Sarene. "'Outlander' Season 3 Premiere: One Relationship Ends in a Sexually Charged Duel," *MarketWatch* (10 September 2017).

Zhukov, Georgy K. "In *Outlander* Season 1, the Duke of Sandringham Has a Duel in Which They Appear to Fire Blanks at Each Other," *Reddit* (2018).

Dunsany Genealogy

The initial appearance of Helwater mansion and its stuffy, pretentious family in the *Outlander* TV chronicle suggests the kind of employment Jamie Fraser will encounter as stable groom and Scots "other." The historical setting, Gosford House, a real three-story estate begun after 1790 east of Edinburgh in East Lothian, Scotland, presents a grimly aristocratic exterior accessed by a double rank of steps leading to a portico above four columns. The addition of molded architraves over windows and neoclassic adornments at corners suggests a family who depend on incidentals to justify their belonging among the Lake District elite. Geneva and her son Willie demand obedience from underlings, ironically including Willie's father Jamie.

The side note of colonnades connecting to pavilions compounds the grandeur of a double inner stairway, marble hall, Palladian windows, baroque fireplace, and art gallery, essentials featured in the films *Downton Abbey, The Buccaneers,* and *House of Mirth.*

See also Helwater.

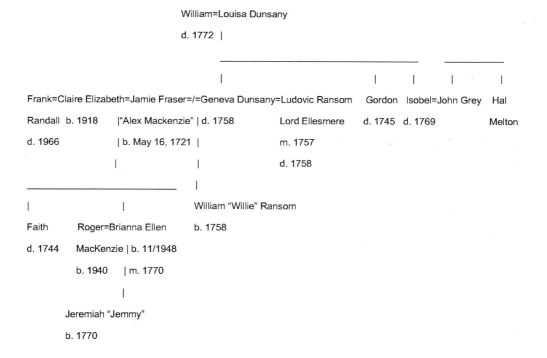

Source

Carey, Meredith. "*Outlander* Filming Locations around the World," *Conde Nast Traveler* (27 January 2019).
Raterink, Eline. "The '*Outlander*-effect' on Social Media: Screen Tourists' Perceptions of Scottish Cultural Heritage Sites," master's thesis, Radbaud University, 2019.

Epidemics

The effects of contagion in Europe, the West Indies, and colonial North America stagger fictional characters in the *Outlander* TV chronicle, killing Geillis Duncan Abernethy's English husband and Jocasta Cameron's first husband John from flux (dysentery or gastroenteritis), a disease first described by the Greek doctor Hippocrates in the fifth century BCE. Fear of an epidemic at sea on the pirate ship *Gloriana* causes Stephen Bonnet to toss overboard passengers who appear ill with smallpox, a contagion that struck India in 1500 BCE. The deaths of two sailors from the merchantman *Patagonia* threaten crew members and onlookers at Le Havre, France, with *le petit variole* (smallpox). Claire's quick assessment of the infection in two corpses prevents a civic disaster, but requires the burning of the ship and its cargo. Owner Le Comte St. Germain accuses her of deliberate destruction of his wine business and launches a secret vendetta. After threatening her and her unborn child with poisoned wine, he dies by a similar means in the Star Chamber of Louis XV. Jamie later credits Claire with applying twentieth-century training to stem an eighteenth-century pestilence, proof that time travelers can alter history.

Before reaching the West Indies, Claire transfers from the French brig *Artemis* to the English man-o'-war *Porpoise* to treat sailors infected with typhoid fever, a virulent form of salmonella that felled Egyptians as early as 4533 BCE. Without modern medicines, she relies on quarantine and sanitation with grog and alcohol, clean decks, fresh air, and alimentation with cereal or ship's biscuit thinned with goat's milk. The demanding hands-on treatment saves some crewmen, but not those already diseased. Burial at sea rids the decks of corpses. The loss of fourteen-year-old Elias Pound, the naval aide, saddens her for an infection she diagnosed as exhaustion.

The New World suffers a range of epidemics, many of which decimate native tribes and newcomers like Virginia settler Isobel Dunsany Grey. At River Run in North Carolina, Jocasta's second husband, Hector Cameron, dies from a putrid sore throat, a common term for diphtheria, caused by the *Corynebacterium diphtheriae* bacterium, which swept Iberia in the early seventeenth century. He and other diphtheria patients expire of pneumonia or asphyxiation after a false membrane forms over the airways.

Plasmodium infection at Fraser's Ridge begins with Lizzy Wemyss, who arrives in the port of Wilmington ill with malaria, a common disease of slaves imported to the plantation South from West Africa. Intermittent fever borne by the female *Anopheles* mosquito weakens her with fatigue, a symptom that can accompany headache, chills, nausea, and muscle aches. For a likely cure, Claire selects Jesuit bark (*Cinchona*) from her stock of dried herbs. The treatment derived from the Quechua Indians in Lima, Peru, in the 1600s.

The spread of the measles virus (*Morbillivirus Paramyxoviridae*) in Cross Creek (Fayetteville), North Carolina, kills patients from pneumonia, the source of the rapid demise of Petronella Mueller and her newborn daughter Clara. Gerhard Mueller's misguided vengeance against the Cherokee results in his murder alongside wife Rosewitha, whom fiery arrows kill. The arrival of John Grey through a measles outbreak threatens his survival with fever and head pain. Claire treats fever and inflammation with rest and willow bark tea (*Salix alba*), a natural cure that dates to ancient Sumer (Iraq) in 3500 BCE. She soothes headache with acupressure to the ocular lobes. Quarantine spares his son William from infection.

See also Acupuncture/Acupressure.

Source

Greenberg, Stephen J. "Claire Fraser, RN, MD, OMG: History of Medicine in the *Outlander* Novels and Series," *Journal of the Medical Library Association* 108:2 (April 2020): 310–313.

Walbert, David. "Disease and Catastrophe," *Anchor,* https://www.ncpedia.org/anchor/disease-and-catastrophe.

Euthanasia

The theme of medical ethics impacts Claire's surgical career, which takes shape in 1955 to be practiced in the eighteenth century. To spare patient suffering, she is not disinclined to abort Brianna's fetus nor to assist in suicide, the method by which Jamie dispatches Aaron Beardsley from paralytic stroke, sparing him surgery on a gangrenous foot. With the Battle of Culloden looming on April 16, 1746, she accepts a plea from Laird Colum Mackenzie to end his extreme pain from genetically misshapen limbs known as Toulouse-Lautrec syndrome. At Culloden House, the choice of liquid yellow jasmine (*Gelsemium sempervirens*) allows Colum to select his own time to swallow an oily alkaloid neurotoxin that suppresses respiration and muscle action and results in cardiac arrest. Belying Claire's description of a gentle soporific, the final stage causes tremor and extreme convulsions.

At the last effort before the battle between Redcoats and Jacobites, Claire proposes using yellow jasmine to kill Prince Charles Edward Stuart. By pretending to incorporate the poison in his treatment for scurvy, she introduces guile not in keeping with her professional standards. The suggestion bears out War Chief Dougal MacKenzie's statement in season two that poison is a better weapon for women than a dagger, but it is difficult to introduce in combat. His exploding temper forcing Jamie into hand-to-hand combat involves Claire in the struggle. Because Jamie slices his hands by gripping Dougal's dirk blade, Claire completes the final plunge to the gut that kills Dougal, thus mooting the question of poisoning the prince to stop the rebellion.

Claire's third venture into euthanasia follows one of the ghastlier scenes of torture in the *Outlander* TV series. Rufus, a young slave at River Run, writhes suspended on a huge meat hook to the midriff in punishment for lopping the left ear off Overseer Byrnes. According to the *Code Noir,* decreed by Louis XIV in 1685, a slave striking a master earned execution for a crime against a white. She bases trauma treatment on the medical response protocols of ancient Egypt, a Theban concept formulated by Imhotep, Pharaoh Djoser's physician, from around 2635–2600 BCE. Claire applies triage, offering urgent intervention to Rufus rather than to the vengeful overseer. The deft surgery seems successful, but Rufus faces immediate dismemberment by a mob. For heightened melodrama, the episode pictures the end of the grace period at the stroke of midnight.

The hesitant administration of yellow jasmine as a sedative tea and euthanasia for Rufus reveals Claire's fealty to the Hippocratic Oath, a vow attributed to the fifth century BCE compendium *Epidemics* (1:11) written by Hippocrates, an Asclepiad physician from Cos, an island off southwestern Turkey. Adherents swearing to the binding text promised, "ἐπὶ δηλήσει δὲ καὶ ἀδικίῃ εἴρξειν (I will do no harm or injustice)," which Galen later rendered in Latin as "Primum non nocere (First don't harm)" (Cavanaugh, 2017). The oath to Apollo, Asclepius, Hygieia, and Panacea specifically outlawed assisted suicide and abortion by lethal drugs. At the slave's peaceful demise, Jamie's prayer voices Christian forgiveness and clemency and bolsters Claire from guilt and regret. A similar situation in season five, episode eleven requires Roger MacKenzie to end the suffering of a Dutch girl burned in a cabin fire. At the scene, Jamie recites a poignant Gaelic dirge, "Thou goest home."

Source

Cavanaugh, Thomas Anthony. *Hippocrates' Oath and Asclepius' Snake: The Birth of the Medical Profession.* Oxford, UK: Oxford University Press, 2017.

"Greek Medicine," https://www.nlm.nih.gov/hmd/greek/greek_oath.html.
Hurry, Jamieson B. *Imhotep: The Egyptian Father of Medicine*. Clifton, NJ: African Tree Press, 2012.

Execution

Threats of execution by hanging, beheading, toxins, drowning, and firing squad extend violence from combat to civilian life, a persistent threat to residents of Lallybroch after the Battle of Culloden on April 16, 1746, and to fictional smugglers and North Carolina tax protesters. The execution of the condemned highwaymen from the Watch in the fifteenth episode of season one actuates references to dangling from a rope and ending a criminal career in ignominy. In his final minutes, outlaw chief Taran Mac-Quarrie spouts gibbet-side philosophy about the penis of the condemned and St. Peter, a humorous play on words based on the televised *Outlander's* ongoing genital imagery. For Jamie, a potential death by broken neck leaves him open to Claire's disapproval, a witty understatement that replaces his true sorrow in leaving her. After his temporary release, a sobering glimpse of stigma pictures Taran's remains piled in the Wentworth Prison boneyard among moldering corpses and skeletons, the refuse of English imperialism.

Life in Paris in 1744 presents a time traveler's conundrum—the sufferings of the condemned in the forty-six years preceding the 1789 French Revolution. During Claire's volunteer nursing at l'Hôpital des Anges, she forms a professional companionship with Monsieur Foret, an historical royal executioner, who views criminal demise scientifically. Over a corpse, the two discuss hanging versus drawing and quartering, a more complicated royal retribution. The latter, a grotesque violation of the mortal form, involves bringing the victim to the edge of asphyxiation, then chopping out the beating heart for the entertainment of voyeurs. From the remains, Foret recycles hangman's grease, a salve ironically applied to burned skin.

VICTIMS OF CULLODEN

Historically, the Duke of Cumberland decreed no quarter for Scots involved in the 1745 rising, which killed 76 Redcoats and 2,000 Jacobites on the Culloden Moor battlefield on April 16, 1746. In addition to five months of arson, confiscations, and slaughter miles from the battleground, the cost to Scots traitors entailed 120 executions, 1,100 transportations to the West Indies, 1,150 exiles, and 1,200 shot, clubbed, and bayonetted. The fictional boy soldiers Frederick MacBean and Giles MacMartin quail at a British firing squad, which also takes Gordon Killick and Rupert Mackenzie. For the sake of impact, the camera pictures a single rabbit hopping innocently amid piles of dead and dying, an icon of vulnerability during the unmerciful butchery of Highlanders that reappears in the season five finale to reassure Claire of survival. Those soldiers who lie on pallets face their end propped up for a military death. Out the door, the camera lingers on a field of red poppies, a symbol of Allied sacrifice after World War I. Against the bursts of rifle fire in the background, the flowers bloom like blood spurts.

Historically, emphasis on child soldiery reveals a period detail that increases the pathos of two thousand Scots dead in one short battle. So many awaited trials that, on July 23, 1746, George II established a lottery granting a trial to only one-fifth of the prisoners. Captives as young as three paid the price of rebellion for service during the Jacobite campaign. Of the twenty-eight female sewers, spinners, and knitters destined from Liverpool for Antigua in late October 1747, deportees, including children as young as twelve, gained an unexpected release after French privateers seized the transport cruiser *Veteran*. The French delivered 150 Jacobite rebels to Martinique, the reprieve of the fictional Yi Tien Cho and Margaret Campbell.

POST-WAR VENGEANCE

Highlanders faced arrest for toasting the health of Prince Charlie and for wearing the white cockade, the Jacobite color that Claire identifies in her vision of Lord Simon Lovat's beheading before a spread of white roses. William Cosby, a weaver's seven-year-old, entered Carlisle Prison in November 1745. Three teenagers, fifteen-year-old James Gordon and sixteen-year-old George Barclay and John Bennagh, escaped death penalties. Gordon left prison at age seventeen for indenturing in Jamaica. Denied fuel and utensils, Bennagh starved in prison before he could be transported. Barclay changed sides to fight for the Redcoats. The bewildered hid in barns and caves, much like the fictional Jamie outside Lallybroch. He compares the six years of concealment as the Dunbonnet to just another prison.

On approach to the plantation South, the main characters witness the fictional hanging of Gavin Hayes, an adulterer and murderer. A Wilmington minister refuses to bury him in sacred ground without cash compensation. In the presence of what *Variety* reviewer Andrea Reiher terms "ugliness at every turn," Jamie aids smuggler Stephen Bonnet, an escapee of the gibbet who dogs the family into the future until his sentencing to drown at the stake (Reiher, 2018). Jamie's faulty decisions attest to his inexperience with New World crime and punishment and the salvation of a dangerous man whom his daughter dispatches with a single rifle shot.

Involvement in the Regulator Movement introduces Jamie, a colonel in the Rowan County Militia, to the historical Governor William Tryon. Enraged by the tax rebellion fomented in the piedmont counties, Tryon dispatched General Hugh Waddell to stop the Regulators at Alamance Creek south of Burlington, North Carolina. A quick victory on May 16, 1771, preceded a trial and sentencing of Captain Benjamin Merrill "to be hanged by the neck, that you be cut down while yet alive, that your bowels be taken out and burnt before your face, that your head be cut off, your body divided into four quarters, and this to be at his Majesty's disposal" (Ervin, 1917, 39).

The TV epic inserts more executions, both legal and impromptu. Tryon okays the hanging of "Roger Mac" MacKenzie, a militia messenger whom the Redcoats wrongly identify as a Regulator. The failed execution invades his consciousness, leaving him mute and haunted. After Lionel Brown and his criminal outriders seize and gang-rape Claire, Jamie rushes to her aid. Too late to circumvent a monstrous payback for her published article on birth control, he authorizes executions for all. At her surgery, where Lionel awaits questioning, Marsali Fraser appoints herself his executioner for perverse crimes against women.

See also Rescue; Governor Tryon.

Source

Ervin, Samuel James, Jr. *A Colonial History of Rowan County, North Carolina*. Chapel Hill: University of North Carolina, 1917.

Reiher, Andrea. "'Outlander' Season 4 Premiere Recap: Jamie and Claire Meet 'America the Beautiful,'" *Variety* (4 November 2018).

Feminism

The launching of the *Outlander* TV narrative reprised the second-wave women's movement and sexual revolution that followed the 1960s. Media expert Helen Wheatley, on staff at the University of Warwick, noted the series' focus on female self-determination and control of their own bodies and wealth. For its "textual invitation to a heterosexual, female gaze," the five-season narrative gained an audience of 3.7 million viewers, 59 percent of them women (Moseley, 2017, 225). In 2016, Richard Lawson, a reviewer for *Vanity Fair,* attempted to define the mixed genre: "It's a gentle political thriller, a mournful time-traveling drama, a melodramatic and yet still nuanced romance, a feminist tract, an ode to the ways of old," his take on the forcing of eighteenth-century women into the "madonna or whore" dichotomy (Lawson, 2016). The mix of centuries follows women's issues in the late 1960s by dramatizing supercilious college professors and obstetricians, adultery, divorce, and court placement of children in a mother's care, the judgment that strips Jerry Nelson of his family.

Cinema expert Carol Donelan at Carleton College described *Outlander* programming as "compensation for the marginalization of female characters and viewers in premium cable" (Donelon, 2018, 310). She accounted for the theme song as reference to "the inexplicable 'disappearance' of women—their names, subjectivities, desire—from culture and patrilineal genealogies," the fate of War Chief Dougal MacKenzie's invisible wife Maura, a stereotypical "madwoman in the attic"; of Eppie and other sex workers sequestered in brothels; and of Aaron Beardsley's wives, four of whom he murders (*ibid.*). After maturing, married women lose identity and rights as they pass from their father to their husbands, a motif that Scots rebel Ellen MacKenzie Fraser rejects. Similarly, following Allied service during World War II, gutsy, daring women like British army nurse Claire Randall find society still desultory toward a veteran who survived catastrophic events. In perilous times, she trusts women friends as understanding as Mrs. Fitz, Mother Hildegarde, Louise de Rohan, and clinic aide Marsali Fraser. In broken English, Annekje Johansen, herder on the naval man-o'-war *Porpoise,* outlines an escape plan to foil the Redcoats from using Claire as bait to capture Jamie.

WOMEN'S LIBERATION

Over female lifetimes, under English common law and Christian dogma, men retained women as chattel. The plot makes witty juxtaposition with agrarianism at Laird Colum MacKenzie's court, where he judges three cases involving control of a cow, farmland, and Laoghaire, a wayward thirteen-year-old who has violated the paternal ideal by acknowledging her sexuality. The motif of trading women to wealthy husbands marks the lives of Mary Hawkins, Lizzy Wemyss, and the Browns of Brownsville, who lose a chance to wed Alicia Brown to Elijah Ford, a prosperous tobacco trader and owner of ten acres. Alicia's pregnancy by Isaiah Morton, a married militiaman from Granite Falls, dishonors her family and devalues her on the marriage market in an era that blamed females for their passion and desires much the same way as Mary Hawkins receives family censure and Lord Ellesmere defames his dead wife, Geneva Dunsany.

The fictional men of eighteenth-century Scotland speak openly of cocks, bollocks, cunny/cunt, breasts, shagging, fornication, and Jamie's euphemistic "honeypot," but they contest candor, carnal jokes, and swearing from females with isolated scriptural citations from St. Paul. Claire's aggressive comments to patients and attendants alarm and annoy patriarchal males, who prefer decorum, smiles, or silence from women. During a quiet talk with Geillis Duncan, Claire receives a different view of period females: by marrying fiscal Arthur Duncan, an elderly, sickly, but well-off husband, Geillis finds herself free to do as she wishes. Claire follows her example in 1968 at an Edinburgh pub, where she and Brianna sit at the bar with men to claim female rights.

Various scenarios reveal pro-woman license in period satire, for example, Brighid's tutorial to Young Ian in woman-on-top coitus and Marsali Fraser's complaint about too many pregnancies. At La Maison de Madame Elise, a makeup artist paints a female form in reverse, with breasts on the shoulder blades and false face on the back of the head. The turnabout mocks the fantasies of men who loll in whorehouses to satisfy perverted notions of womankind. The foolish waste of money on gaudy, simpering courtesans advances to Elise's sale of dildos in multiple colors to entertain wives whose husbands seek satisfaction in a make believe milieu. More straightforward brothels distinguish the Highlands, Edinburgh, and Wilmington for investing in plain sex for cash, a less fanciful indulgence that relieves the male urge to copulate.

Female Progress

Claire's emergence from a post–Culloden funk impels her to seek true American-ness through U.S. citizenship and fulfillment by earning a surgical degree from Harvard University. Puerto Rican researcher Ivette López-Cordero explained her interest in "the role of women in the making of history" (López-Cordero, 2019,1). With female doctors still a novelty, Claire forms a friendship with Joe Abernethy, a black pariah among the white elite entering the same profession. The series overplays the smugness of woman-haters like Dr. Simms, Professor Jackson, and Dr. Thorne, all dismissive of female abilities and intelligence. Simms demeans Claire's six-year service to the British military as a combat nurse. Less savory, the eighteenth-century bitch fight at a North Carolina gambling den satisfies male demand for female blood, a disgusting show that Isabel Allende added to her novel *Portrait in Sepia*.

A mother-daughter connection complements soldierly comradery with a female version of amity. After the death of Mrs. Graham, the Rev. Reginald Wakefield's house-keeper, granddaughter Fiona internalizes the lore and Druidic tradition based on the divine earth mother. Respecting Claire's relationship with Mrs. Graham, Fiona passes on the Fraser pearls, a matrilineal heirloom better suited to Claire and her daughter. In a complex family dilemma, after husband Frank's death in a car accident in 1968, Claire, caught in a family restructuring, assuages Brianna's grief over the man who coddled her. Roger encourages Claire to reveal Brianna's siring in Scotland in 1746 and to prepare her for a reunion of their nuclear family in the eighteenth century. The pearls gain worth for the next generation at Brianna's wedding, where the necklace complements a dress home-made by Claire.

An unforeseen clash, Jamie's marriage to Laoghaire pairs Claire with her step-daughter Marsali MacKimmie, who abandons animosity to become Claire's surgical assistant. The settlement of dissension establishes a feminist truism—that women can manage their own problems. Because of Claire's experience with females in disparate centuries, she acquires what Victoria Kennedy, a scholar at Laurier University in Waterloo, Ontario, terms "feminist gains when they imagine the past, but also express longing for aspects of traditional femininity" (Kennedy, 2017). The statement elevates Fiona and

Brianna to a younger generation of activists who treasure women's history as the basis for progress.

See also Matrilineage; Witchcraft.

Source

Bénédic-Meyer, Diane. "La construction d'un tissage émotionnel au féminin dans la série *Outlander*," *TV/Series* 15 (2019).

Donelan, Carol. "'Sing Me a Song of a Lass That Is Gone': Myth and Meaning in the Starz Original Series *Outlander*," *Quarterly Review of Film and Video* 35:1 (2018): 31–53.

Gilje, Paul A. *To Swear Like a Sailor: Maritime Culture in America, 1750–1850.* Cambridge, UK: Cambridge University Press, 2016.

Kennedy, Victoria. "Narrative Pleasures and Feminist Politics: Popular Women's Historical Fiction, 1990–2015," Ph.D. dissertation, Laurier University, 2017.

Lawson, Richard. "*Outlander* Is as Odd and Enveloping as Ever in Season 2," *Vanity Fair* (8 April 2016).

López-Cordero, Ivette M. "A Walk through the Standing Stones: The Historical Novel, Gender and the Supernatural in Diana Gabaldon's *Outlander*," master's thesis, University of Puerto Rico at Mayaguez, 2019.

Moseley, Rachel, Helen Wheatley, and Helen Wood. *Television for Women: New Directions.* London: Routledge, 2017.

Prudom, Laura. "Starz's 'Outlander' Woos Women with Strong Female Protagonist," *Variety* (7 August 2014).

Fire and Heat

Flame and heat zigzag through the *Outlander* TV epic illuminating character traits, as with Claire's ability to strike fire from flint and stone in Haiti, Jamie's relighting of the fiery cross to summon the militia, and Roger's creation of smudge pots to overwhelm locusts with smoke. Flame adds menace to combat episodes, including the Cherokees' fiery arrows that burn Gerhard Mueller's cabin and the Browns' explosion of the Fraser still in season five. By setting the pilot episode at Inverness on Samhain eve, October 31, 1945, the series dramatizes a lightning storm during a power outage. Cinematography introduces dominant light-dark motifs in the Randalls' rented room, which the series reprises in season two, episode one at the Wakefield guest quarters. The overcast night and moonrise increase a mystic glimmer of the Druidesses' lanterns, a ritual ring dance that dates to Celtic prehistory, and anticipates the burning of the stag at the Scots gathering on Grandfather Mountain, North Carolina, an androcentric version of the pre-dawn female ceremony.

On Claire Randall's introduction to Highlanders, limited illumination in a Scots cottage marks her first glimpse of War Chief Dougal Mackenzie's band and her reprise of field nursing protocols to set Jamie Fraser's dislocated shoulder. With a gentlemanly gesture, he offers a fold of his plaid to keep her warm on a gallop into the rainy night, a hint at the rise in desire for his future wife that he repeats on rescuing her from gang rape. By hearthlight at Castle Leoch, she disinfects his bullet wound with a boiled herbal compress to prevent fever and inflammation, a second symbolic strand of the passions that elevate him to Scots warrior, lover, and bicontinental hero.

Before the revelation of twin heat from politics and colonialism, Claire's imprisonment in a damp, cheerless dungeon at Castle Leoch increases her isolation and despair during the first days of MacKenzie hospitality. By venturing out with Dougal's rent collectors, she views socioeconomic conditions in daylight, discovers the fervor of Jacobite fund raising, and witnesses the Watch burning a thatched cottage to punish Redcoat collaborators. The tragedy precedes her obligatory wedding, lit in a crumbling chapel by candelabra. The flickering atmosphere in Glencorse (or Glencross) Old Kirk, at Penicuik in Midlothian seven miles south of Edinburgh resembles the arrival of the ambivalent

Guinevere to King Arthur's bridal reception in the film *Camelot*. As desire and sexual satisfaction arouse love in the newlywed Frasers, the plot outlines the first major marital blowup over female obedience to patriarchal males and Claire's ousting of Jamie into the cold. At their reunion, passion rekindles in a dark bedchamber before a steady hearth flame, a symbol of shared values and a pledge to live in harmony without macho mastery or spousal abuse.

WITCHERY AND FIRE

A third fiery strand infuses *Outlander* with danger from Highlanders enraptured by the supernatural. Friendship with time traveler Geillis Duncan introduces Claire to Wiccan beliefs involving the summoning of the Earth Mother by Geillis's near-naked solo dance before three fires. The ritual celebrates the herbalist's pregnant belly and her lust for Dougal. Claire's discovery of a dead newborn abandoned in a nearby tree prefigures a dual display of fire and heat after Geillis engineers the one-day fever that kills Maura MacKenzie and the cyanide dose that poisons Arthur Duncan. In the wake of three deaths, the constable arrests Geillis and Claire and incarcerates them in a chill underground cell, an iconic reduction of their potential.

Execution by fire thrives in the late eighteenth century *Outlander* epic during an historic period known as the female holocaust, a Christian reign of terror from 1484 to 1782 featured in the documentary *The Burning Times*. The manic woman-hate of James I, author of anti-necromancy propaganda in *Newes from Scotland Declaring the Damnable Life and Death of Dr. Fian, a Notable Sorcerer* in 1591 and the monograph *Daemonologie*, issued in 1597, sparked an era of female duress and grisly deaths. William Shakespeare contributed his own creativity with the Scots tragedy *Macbeth* (1606), in which three weird sisters intone "Double, double, toil and trouble;/Fire burn, and cauldron bubble," an introduction to a stage tragedy filled with mystic evil (IV, i, 10–11).

At the Cranesmuir witchcraft trial in 1744, Claire and Geillis face burning at the stake, which villagers gleefully surround with brush and kindling. Before sentencing, Jamie's arrival at the courtroom separates Claire from Geillis, who admits to judges her fornication with Satan, conception of a demonic child, and Arthur's murder. The women's parting leaves Claire with only a partial understanding of Geillis's fervor for time travel on behalf of the Jacobite cause. The television narrative reduces to storytelling Dougal's replacement of Geillis with the corpse of Granny Joan MacClellan and Geillis's delight at viewing her immolation.

FLIGHT TO FRANCE

The fire and heat motif continues at a northern Scots abbey, a Benedictine retreat from Redcoat pursuit. With prompt care by Father Anselm's monk-nurse Brother Paul, Claire tends the pierced palm and crushed fingers that stifle Jamie's will to live. To revive his spirit, she first bathes him in cold creek water, then forces him to confess his deep humiliation by rapist and torturer Captain Black Jack Randall, who heats a seal red hot to further torture his victim. By revealing the initials JR that Jamie impressed on his left side, he begins healing his wounded dignity. Murtagh excises the circle from his godson's flank and tosses it into the fireplace, thus obliterating the signet, evidence of fiendish sexual torment. In private, Jack still reigns over Jamie's dreams, inhibiting the intimacy with Claire.

In France, the couple make new lives marked by royal glitter and the gauzy idylls of the bonnie prince, who uses Madam Elise's brothel as an office. The diagnosis of two smallpox victims from the crew of the merchantman *Patagonia* forces the burning of a ship and its cargo, the beginning of Le Comte St. Germain's unrelenting hatred of the Frasers. At Jamie's jailing for dueling, Claire reaches a serious low—bedfast for weeks from a stillbirth and puerperal fever, which requires extreme unction and absolution from Father Laurentin. In a mystic parallel, Master Raymond applies hands-on treatment of infection caused by a festering afterbirth. Removal of septic tissue from her uterus reclaims Claire from a high temperature. Therapy restores her blue aura, an icon of healing and balance foreshadowed by the forget-me-nots blooming on Craigh na Dun and the heron she sees in a picture book.

The 1745 Rising

Once more in Scotland, the heat of Jacobite zeal splits clans and arouses vicious altercations among Jamie, his uncle Colum MacKenzie, and grandfather Simon Lovat, the notorious rake of Castle Beaufort. To Simon's threat of sexual violence against Claire, Jamie claims her supernatural power as La Dame Blanche, the white witch, and hurls a bottle into Simon's fireplace. The roaring flame, fed on alcohol, impresses the superstitious old womanizer. To circumvent transfer of Fraser clan property to his grandsire, Claire interrupts a men-only discussion by enacting a vision of Simon. The apparition stands at his hearth awaiting execution by a Jacobite headsman, an historical fact that occurred on April 9, 1747, when Simon was eighty.

To shield Claire and his unborn child from the Battle of Culloden, on April 16, 1746, Jamie forces her back to the twentieth century. He vows to find her, even if he must suffer two centuries in purgatory, a fiery cleansing of the sinful dramatized in Dante's allegory *Inferno* (1472). Before her departure from Inverness in 1948, Frank's incineration of her historic costume reintroduces her to a new/old life. In twentieth-century Boston, symbols of heat and light dog Claire's daily attempts to ignite a gas range, a representation of irrecoverable ardor for Frank, and Frank's battle with a boiler pilot light, an equalizer of the Randalls' misalliance. Frustration inspires her hearth cookery over a living room grate, a recall of eighteenth-century camp cookery with Jamie and training by archeologist Uncle Lambert. At an impasse in the Randalls' discussions, she hurls an ashtray that misses and smashes on the floor, a final expulsion of passion like a crushed cigarette.

Family Heat

The adulthood of Claire and Jamie's daughter introduces a new source of wrath. Claire's vehement arguments with Brianna in 1968 reached a dramatic peak—confession of a marriage in eighteenth-century Scotland and Brianna's conception in 1746 by birth father Jamie Fraser. The mother-daughter set-to continues during a visit to Inverness. At Craigh na Dun, Brianna witnesses the blazing corpse of Greg Edgars, Geillis's husband, whom she sacrifices in a pagan rite to ease her way through the stones. Scholar Marlène Charlier, a researcher at Université de Franche-Comté in Besançon, explained the background: "The Druids burnt sacrificial victims in wicker cages shaped like men, but individuals where killed by strangling, and the throat slit to drain the body of blood" (Charlier, 2019, 17). Abandoning the smoldering corpse, Geillis plunges back through time, proving to Brianna the truth of her mother's fever for Jamie and the conception of their only surviving child.

In the third season, heat and flame vivify the Frasers' reunion in an Edinburgh print-shop after a two-decade separation. By candle- and firelight, passionate bedding reignites libidos and ensures that erotic combustion still anchors their lives. Within a day, however, a fire that consumes the business on Carfax Close compels Jamie to rescue two treasures—the portrait of illegitimate son William "Willie" Ransom and the living form of Young Ian, a pseudo-foster son who witnesses the arson by Harry Tompkins, a corrupt tax collector. With the property razed, Jamie retreats from his Edinburgh identity by snuffing out the existence of Alexander "Alex" Malcolm.

On a reunion at Lallybroch, the *Outlander* TV narrative quickens secondary family rancor. Icy relations with Jenny Murray freeze Claire out of the Fraser household and summon a real witch, Jamie's malicious second wife. Laoghaire's discharge of birdshot into Jamie's left shoulder undermines his health from emergency surgery. To remove five pellets and lower his temperature, Claire treats him with scalpel and penicillin purloined from a Boston hospital. Her mood smolders through several scenes, flickering with anger and disillusion at resuming her past marriage. Troubling to Claire and viewers, the reason for Jamie's marriage to a conniving rival remains unsettled by his vague excuses of a hearty celebration of Hogmanay with Laoghaire's daughters, Marsali and Joanie.

Heat and Light

Ecstatic affairs continue to embroil the Frasers in controversy, thwarting Jamie's attempt to ensure Claire's commitment. Departure to the West Indies on the French brig *Artemis* embroils the couple in Marsali and Fergus's passion for each other. Because Jamie assigns each paramour to a separate cabin, Claire must sleep apart from her husband at a prickly point in their revival of marital ardor. In a wayward moment, she leads him to an airless sail locker. Sharing the stuffy atmosphere, they make heated love and nestle in the afterglow. Once more restored by coitus, Claire enjoys a brief wifely interlude by moonlight and describes for Jamie the cold lunar surface visited by U.S. spacemen on December 21, 1968.

A raging plague at sea pits Claire's Hippocratic Oath against her wedding vows to Jamie. Acting Captain Thomas Leonard of the English man-o'-war *Porpoise* commandeers her to fight an outbreak of typhoid fever that has already claimed eighty out of four hundred crewmen. Amid febrile, dying sailors, she saves some, but loses others to advanced infection. Simultaneously, Jamie's fury at separation from Claire requires his jailing in an airless cell in the *Artemis*. His ferocity attests once more to an abiding passion for Claire, the prime mover of the *Outlander* narrative.

The series depicts Jamie roaring at Captain Raines and Fergus because of Claire's impromptu departure to treat the remaining three hundred English sailors. Jamie's intense bitterness grows while Claire aids in stitching cold corpses into canvas sacks for marine burial. To reunite with Jamie, her leap overboard off Grand Turk places her in a jungly Haitian setting where a thorn pierces her upper right arm. On relocating her fervent mate on the beach, she retreats to his quarters. Hawksbill turtle soup, an established aphrodisiac and erotic stimulus, rebuilds her strength. In a silly state of drunkenness and fever, the couple inject her thigh with penicillin before clasping each other in fervid embrace.

Carolina Home

The New World introduces flame and heat from unexpected sources. In an interlude in Jamaica, the Frasers witness a ring dance lit by firebrands, a cultural remnant of West African voodoo. They rescue Young Ian from Geillis, who soaks him in flammable fluid at the Abandawe cave preparatory to burning him alive. From the Georgia sea islands inland to River Run on the Cape Fear River, Claire and Jamie experience a welcoming warmth. Unfortunately for the times, amid lighted torches raised in threat to Aunt Jocasta Cameron and her plantation, Claire euthanizes the slave Rufus, whose cooling corpse Jamie delivers at midnight to angry planters vowing to dismember the boy. Not willing to make a career based on human torture, the Frasers once more set out to the unknown.

A flash forward to 1968 revisits Brianna's appeal to historian Roger MacKenzie. Her introduction to the Scots Gathering of the Clans in the Blue Ridge Mountains invites a marriage proposal from an old-fashioned beau who demands a virgin bride. A mix of past with present, the tryst of Brianna with Roger discloses his dedication to Highland tradition, which he represents at a night assembly. Clan representatives toss lighted flares into a stag formed of dried branches. The bonfire epitomizes Scots zeal and the flicker of independence that guided Highlanders from the Battle of Culloden to the Scots diaspora.

Flame and heat accompany the Frasers and Young Ian into the North Carolina piedmont to Fraser's Ridge, an idealized pioneer homeplace. Before acclimating to their land grant, Claire encounters a Gothic fireburst—a lightning strike that ignites a pine tree. The theatrical atmosphere introduces her to a fellow time traveler, Otter Tooth, who survives in spirit a savage blow to the cranium and scalping by the Cherokee. Arson recurs during Jamie's absence, when Gerhard Mueller presents to Claire the scalp of Adawehi, a fellow healer he charges with witchery. Claire reverently cremates the remains in her fireplace. The series pictures Mueller's recompense in the attack on his cabin by Cherokee raiders, who impale him and wife Rosewitha with flaming arrows that burn their cabin.

The blaze motif flourishes at Fraser's Ridge, where residents search by lighted brands for a marauding bear. Brianna's mission of mercy to save Claire and Jamie from incineration in their mountain cabin unleashes her anger at Jamie for selling Roger into slavery. Brianna's heated attack concludes a slap to her father's forehead and wishing Jamie in hell, an extreme torment for the damned. On a 700-mile gallop toward Shadow Lake, New York, to rescue Roger from bondage to the Mohawk, the Frasers find him imprisoned for ending the torture of Alexandre Ferigault, a priest defrocked for violating celibacy. At Roger's explosion of a fire with gunpowder, Johiehon throws herself into the conflagration, a representation of passion violated by religious and tribal intolerance.

Source

Borman, Tracy. *Witches: James I and the English Witch Hunts.* New York: Vintage, 2014.

Charlier, Marlène. "La représentation des mythes et légendes dans la série *Outlander*," master's thesis, Université de Franche-Comté, 2019.

Hurley, Laura. "Is *Outlander* Finally Going to Burn Fraser's Ridge in Season 5 Finale?," *CinemaBlend* (3 May 2020).

Food

The least detailed aspect of the *Outlander* TV epic, food and table settings receive scant close-ups or commentary beyond an American Christmas with lobster rolls and

Boston cream pies, a pan of camp gruel for Kezzie Beardsley in season five, Brianna's request for Eggo Toaster Waffles, Stephen Bonnet's fish entree with greens, and K-rations for D-Day survivors. The Lallybroch doocot houses a hidden pistol as well as doves, a table delicacy never served during the series. At Ardsmuir Prison, Jamie recites for prisoners a full menu with pheasant in Burgundy wine sauce, herbs, carrots, turnips, and buttered rolls served to prison warden John Grey. Unlike the thorough grounding in frontier table lore in Laura Esquivel's Gothic novel *Like Water for Chocolate,* the brief views of spit-roasted meat, cheese and bread, figs, and cups of ale, wine, and beer give some indication of hand-held meals.

The televised diet suits the caste at each table. Among British officers at Brockton Inn, slices of venison, cheese, and claret again attest only to meat and drink, not to a full menu. At the Castle Leoch market, baskets of pears, leeks, and beets offer clues to common produce and a source of stuffed cabbage. Jamie's skinning a rabbit precedes dinner over a campfire and anticipates the appetite of the Watch for Jenny's rabbit stew. On the gallop to find Jamie in the fourteenth chapter of season one, Murtagh turns up with a dead duck, which appeals to neither Jenny nor Claire. Jenny demonstrates the pressure of breast milk and explains how a natural flow satisfies an infant, a joy that Claire learns in 1948 from Brianna's first breastfeeding.

Drama on the Menu

In proof of the rift between Frank and Claire Randall in Boston, scenarios of 1968 focus on breakfast and her battles with the gas stove, a symbol of extinguished love. Worsening the scenario, she finds sour milk in the refrigerator and listens to Frank's complaints about American tea bags. He delights in the aroma of bacon and eggs that he missed during wartime rationing, which began in 1939 with standard breakfast items. To wean Brianna from American junk food, he proposes a full English breakfast, which includes black pudding, a sausage made from pig fat, blood, and oats or barley. For an evening with Jerry and Millie Nelson, Claire fails at a Pavlova, a meringue topped with whipped cream and fruit. Frank called her failure "Eton mess," a pun on the term for a dining hall meal (3:2).

A disappointing display of baroque table service, Claire and Jamie's formal banquet in Paris in 1744 again obscures a sizable outlay, revealing baskets of produce beforehand and plates of fruit, a crown roast, and soup alongside wine glasses. At Versailles, grapes share space with pyramids of sweetmeats. At lunch in Paris, cinematography deliberately obscures servings to Jamie and Fergus. Similarly, a quick camera shot of Jamie's post-hangover breakfast delineates little beyond a lumpy bannock. At Beaufort Castle, Laoghaire collects mushrooms for the kitchen, but filming ignores their use. The second season extends the reunion of Claire and Jamie in 1766 at Madame Jeanne's brothel, Jamie's Edinburgh retreat for privacy and hot meals. Pauline's delivery of an evening repast specifies little beyond red wine and a plate of grapes. In an early morning coupling, Jamie rejects food in favor of cunnilingus.

Edible Drama

In the face-off with the Duke of Sandringham at his Belmont estate, action stresses forking delicacies and late-night knoshing on a cherry tart. Meat carving offers Claire a weapon, but few specifics on what the plates contain. At table, she enjoys wine with a dish that, by candlelight, appears to be cake, a reminder of Marie Antoinette's historic gibe "Let them eat cake." Appropriately, the finale for the duke and his lackey Danton happens in the kitchen with Murtagh Fitzgibbons Fraser's gory double ax chop to Sandringham's neck. Of Danton's fall to his victim's butcher knife, star Caitriona Balfe chortled, "I loved how Mary got her justice, finally. And it was by her own hand. That was a wonderful part of that scene" (Bucksbaum, 2016).

Seasons three and four enlighten the brief disclosure of food and drink, as with Claire sipping dew from Haitian plant leaves, her discovery of rotten coconut shells, and Fergus and Marsali's snack on pineapple in the Kingston marketplace. A close-up studies fried plantain with manioc and red beans, Mamacita's Haitian specialty, and Yi Tien Cho's turtle soup, made fresh from a hawksbill. Another close-up of Geillis Duncan Abernethy's guest tray with its tarts, petits fours, and plum pudding visualizes how she drugs Young Ian and extracts information about Dougal's treasure box with sugared truth tea made by a witch doctor.

ACTION MENUS

At Fraser's Ridge, cabin foods tend toward the fresh meat menu—jerky, trout, venison, and a pen-raised pig for Christmas pork chops. The sixth and seventh episodes of season four introduce pantry staples at a time when an eighteenth-century pub breakfast cost six pence and dinner one shilling (12½ pence, currently $21.32). A plate of baked apples in the Frasers' cabin precedes Brianna's Boston farewell to the twentieth century—a thoroughly American peanut butter and jelly sandwich in plastic wrap for her journey to Scotland. Again, visual shortchanging of Brianna's dinner on a tray cheats the viewer of Laoghaire's stew. A flashback of Frank Randall's hangover graces him with Brianna's love in the form of a cream tea with scones, a British tradition that demonstrates efforts to relieve her father's marital funk.

The celebratory season five opening demands food and drink to honor Brianna's 1770 wedding to Roger MacKenzie. Other than a chocolate wedding cake and a pig roasted on a spit, guests seem oblivious to dishes. In Scots tradition, all appear consumed by drink, the source of a round of tongue twisters that ridicules tipsiness. In 1771, at the nuptials of Jocasta Cameron to Duncan Innes, an extravagant fruit display tops out with fragrant, golden yellow pineapples, the colonial symbol of hospitality that appeared on woven brocades, hotel signs, centerpieces, and the finials of fountains, gates, door knockers, bedposts, and balustrades. The confiscation of goats from the Beardsley's trading post provides Wee Bonnie with milk until Claire can locate a lactating mother. Meanwhile, a threat to winter grain requires a smoky battle against a locust influx, proof that Roger MacKenzie has earned the title of captain of the Rowan County Militia by setting up smudgepots in wheat- and cornfields.

At a cheery family gathering, Ian's arrow shot into a wild boar saves the Frasers from harm and provides a feast that he insists on butchering. Lizzy welcomes him home with almond hog's pudding, a spicy English sausage similar to black pudding made from bread or oatmeal, suet, almonds, eggs, and cream for stuffing into pig intestines and boiling. After Jamie's snakebite, he roasts the remains and has a bite. In his backyard, three women collaborate on danger from a bison: Lizzy raises the alarm; Brianna lures it away from Jemmy; Claire fells it with one rifle shot, a three-part testimonial to female agency.

In the aftermath, community members cheerfully butcher buffalo meat. After Young

Ian learns about the time travelers, Claire serves the family a novelty—peanut butter and jelly sandwiches, for which she shells and crushes nuts into paste. On the mustering at the fiery cross, Lizzy packs the Rowan County Militia some salted meat, a hand-held refresher they can devour on the gallop. In a reflection of Claire's involvement in cookery, Jamie sniffs her right arms and locates aromas of cinnamon, clove, onion, garlic, and the dill and vinegar she uses to pickle cucumbers, a condiment that Christopher Columbus introduced to the Western Hemisphere.

See also Whisky.

Source

Bucksbaum, Sydney. "'Outlander' Team Breaks Down That Violent Act of Revenge and 'Powerful' Scene Viewers Didn't See," *Hollywood Reporter* (18 June 2016).

Ervin, Samuel James, Jr. *A Colonial History of Rowan County, North Carolina.* Chapel Hill: University of North Carolina, 1917.

Hallemann, Caroline. "Is *Outlander*'s Fraser's Ridge a Real Place?," *Town & Country* (11 February 2010).

York, Patricia S. "Why the Pineapple Became the Symbol of Hospitality," *Southern Living* (3 March 2017).

Foreshadowing

As a cinema technique anticipating physical and emotional harm to characters, bits and pieces of dialogue and camerawork betoken major themes and events yet to appear in the *Outlander* TV production. Coming attractions emerge from a rotting Highlander slain by Redcoats in the Scots woods, Richard Brown's alliance with thief Arvin Hodgepile and the Committee of Safety, Lionel Brown's discovering the nameplate on Claire's medical equipment, and Jacobite soldiers making their wills on September 21, 1745, before the Battle of Prestonpans. The opening episode depicts Frank Randall's interest in his wife's palm, which Mrs. Graham, the Rev. Reginald Wakefield's housekeeper, examines for predictions of her married life, the narrative's mainstay.

At Castle Leoch in November 1743, Claire's first view of Laird Colum MacKenzie through a semi-open latticed window hints at the finite future of the clan system. An able, reasonable administrator, he must depend on his younger brother Dougal, an irrational master at arms, for the physical operation of an extended household, but he retains a sharp distrust for the aberrant clan war chief. Both men shelter their nephew Jamie, who conceals from Auld Alec, the stable master, scars of two hundred lashes to his back, evidence of the colonial savagery that destroys the Highlands in 1746. Thirty years later, English imperialism harries the Americas into a revolutionary war.

The framework of Jamie's part in salvaging Gaelic culture depends on an arranged matrimony, an echo of the Act of Union in 1707 that joins England and Scotland. In the corral of MacKenzie land, Claire's disruption of Jamie's filly training in the second episode causes a skittish bolt. His remark that the colt is a spirited girl presages marriage to a twentieth-century female given to thinking for herself and refusing to be harnessed. Evidence of independence precedes her reprisal for Jamie whipping her with a belt for disobedience. She states her demands by holding him at knife point, a standoff prefiguring an equitable marriage based on mutual trust, the series' core value.

A PROGRESSION OF VICTIMS

The abrupt emergence of beggar Hugh Munro introduces the controlling motif of torture and human depravity. His legs scarred from hot oil poured by Algerian Islamic extremists and his speech muted by tongue extraction anticipate combat memories of the elder Ian Murray, who returns from France minus his right lower leg, and Jenny's self-silencing of memories of sexual abuse by Captain Jack Randall in her own bedroom. The sufferings prepare for Corporal MacGregor's chopping Fergus's left hand at the wrist with a saber and the boy's accommodation of permanent handicap. All four examples of victimization precede the barbarity that the Randall perpetrates on Claire's body and Jamie's left palm, right flank, genitals, and dignity, a violation that Libby Hill, a reviewer for the *New York Times,* called "uncompromising, pushing well past the audience's point of comfort" (Hill, 2015).

After Claire undergoes threat of Randall's knife at her left nipple in Wentworth Prison, she gamely faces a complex rehabilitation project. She begins with realigning hand bones and retrieving Jamie from self-loathing by removing a brand marking him with the initials JR. In Hill's review, she summarizes Jamie's sufferings compared to Ian's diminution to a pegleg: "[Jamie's] been made less of a man, less of a human being, and more than that, he's unconvinced that it's possible to be made whole again" (*ibid.*). After the combat traumas Claire tackled in the opening scenes, maimed bodies center her in physical repair and emotional restoration. The shift in character focus implies that strong males like Jamie require more therapy than females—Jenny, Mary Hawkins, Brianna, Marsali, and Claire—after gendered violence.

In the intro to season two, episode eleven, colonial overreaching moves beyond Scotland and France to the West Indies and the plantation South. The puffs of hairpiece powder on a peruke conclude with the wig stand's tumble and the lurch of male finery to the floor. The overly theatrical scene augurs the decapitation of Clarence Marylebone, the shifty Duke of Sandringham, for various deceits, including dispatching Danton to rape Mary Hawkins in a Paris alley. The concept of dehumanizing treatment broadens during the voyage to the New World, where the Frasers witness the auction and genital humiliation of Temeraire, an enslaved African, and the kidnap, rape, and murder of young boys, a double challenge ended by a *deus ex machina,* a storm that floats the couple along Les Perles, Georgia. A new locale places the Frasers again amid slaves and introduces them to a New World concern, deracinated first peoples. The extent of anti-human topics almost topples the TV series.

FORESEEING THE FUTURE

On the way to Fraser's Ridge, overriding devotion to family once more stabilizes episodes with the foretelling of shapes and shadows in Jocasta Cameron's limited vision. In season five, occluded vision reveals unbearable memories of Morna's post–Culloden death in 1746 and the sorrow that causes the plantation mistress to reject Murtagh Fitzgibbons Fraser as a fourth husband. Her sobbing farewell foretells grief at his cairn after his shooting at the Battle of Alamance Creek on May 16, 1746. Preceding the reunion of the Frasers with their daughter in North Carolina, Jamie's dream of a diamond-shaped birthmark on Brianna's neck pairs with Claire's discussion of motherhood with Cherokee healer Adawehi and a glimpse of a rabbit, Brianna's favorite toy. To account for future challenges, producer Ronald Moore asserted the value of feeling character discomfort vicariously, a description of Brianna's revelation of rape in a Wilmington inn and Jocasta's disclosure of her three daughters' deaths in Scotland.

Foreshadowing of war against the British again strains the boundaries of one man's agency. The disparity between joys and portents introduces Jamie's attempt to retaliate against Brianna's rapist, serve the Rowan County Militia, and appease Governor William

Tryon, the bestower of 10,000 acres of land. Jamie's son-in-law Roger MacKenzie's singing the mournful "O My Darlin' Clementine" before he sets off to war hints at the near loss of Jamie's captain to the Redcoats. The obvious rise of revolt and Richard Brown's invitation to join the Committee of Safety anticipates Jamie's inability to avoid the American rebellion.

See also Animals; Conception; Forts and Prisons; Prophecy.

Source

Brinson, Susan L. "TV Rape: Television's Communication of Cultural Attitudes toward Rape," *Women's Studies in Communication* 12:2 (1992): 23–36.
Faircloth, Kelly. "*Outlander*: Damn This Show Took a Dark Turn," *The Muse* (18 May 2015).
Hill, Libby. "'Outlander' Season 1 Finale Recap: Jamie Is Broken," *New York Times* (30 May 2015).

Forts and Prisons

A social disparity between the 1700s and 1900s emerges in attitudes toward jailing, prison, and mercy. Claire Fraser and Geillis Duncan's incarceration in the fictional Cranesmuir Thieves' Hole by wardens at the end of the tenth episode introduces anti-witch prejudice with an iron-barred underground cell held shut with a bulky padlock. Under the open sky, cold and rats threaten the women, who have no blankets or food and no hope of escape. The prospect of such inhumane imprisonment so outrages Taran MacQuarrie, leader of the Watch, that he prefers shooting people than betraying them to the British.

The military stance of Redcoats at fictional Brockton Inn and Fort William introduces the *Outlander* TV saga's critique of the British army. Separated by rank, the higher echelon enjoys a private dining room and servings of venison, cheese, and claret. After Captain Black Jack Randall takes custody of prisoner Jamie Fraser, the Fort William courtyard provides a stony backdrop for the second scourging, which brings on Brian Fraser's apoplexy. Brianna's touristy visit in 1968 with historian Roger Mackenzie as guide casts a chill over the walk-through, which reviews brutal excess preceding her introduction to her ex-con birth father.

Gothic Settings

Fortification architecture continues to dominate season one as Claire ponders the impossible task of breaking Jamie out of Wentworth Prison, filmed at Linlithgow Palace northeast of Glasgow. Cinematography exaggerates a Gothic horror replete with dank underground levels, torchlight, rats, and a dump spot for gibbeted corpses. Amid the cadavers and debris of the boneyard, the action reveals Taran MacQuarrie's remains, recently hanged on the prison gallows. The camera introduces the quadrilateral outlines and central tower, arrow slits, and lookout posts, which face Linlithgow Loch. Claire's insistence on scouting the dungeon alone identifies extremes of courage in an androcentric milieu built on British might over the vulnerable. The stone walls, iron grating, uneven steps, and flambeaux envelop her in Gothic ambience menaced by lewd calls from male prisoners, a lurid companionship among the doomed.

Season two refers frequently to the Bastille Saint-Antoine, a moated, eight-towered fort more strategic in design than Wentworth. Begun by Charles V on April 22, 1370, under the name "St. Anthony's Bastion," the original security gate of the city walls developed into the royal state prison and munitions store. When threats from the English increased during the Renaissance, the French heightened security and staffed a police interrogation and detention center. After the fictional Murtagh Fitzgibbons Fraser and Jamie enter the Bastille under arrest for brawling at a formal dinner party, they find the dire structure in service to the *ancien régime* as a state penitentiary holding 1,194 people. Much despised by libertarian citizens and former prisoners and dealers in anti-monarchy publications and pornography, the Bastille became a rallying point for oppressed classes. By July 14, 1789, the storming of the infamous lockup ignited the French Revolution, the outcome of a republican movement to bring down the despotic Bourbon dynasty.

Outlines of Torment

Season three investigates eighteenth-century punishment in detail. At Craigmiller Castle, setting of fictional Ardsmuir Prison in 1752, Jamie and his godfather and other traitors to the British crown begin bondage in grubby surroundings worsened by hunger, cold, filth, and vermin. Close-ups of wrist and ankle chains, ragged and patched garments, and huddled postures of defeated Jacobites marched to new locations in the colonies in 1756 impress on viewers the pre-nineteenth-century movement to humanize court judgments and punishments, a pervasive theme in the works of Charles Dickens, a court reporter and social novelist of *A Tale of Two Cities*. A revealing shift to Helwater estate in England and Jamie's aprons and groom's uniforms stress a vast change in amenities for an indentured servant serving the wealthy.

New World lockups particularize colonial jailing. At Wilmington, pirate Stephen Bonnet, rebel Murtagh, and others languish in a city jail more open to light and air than the penitentiaries in Scotland. Rescue by the Regulators implies that the confines collapse easily when surrounded by exploding gunpowder. In season five, Jamie's release of Bryan Cranna and other captives of the British in Hillsborough requires little more than prying loose a single lock. For the jailing of Isaiah Morton at Brownsville, rope alone secures his hands until Jamie sets him free.

See also Gothic.

Source

Donelan, Carol. "'Sing Me a Song of a Lass That Is Gone': Myth and Meaning in the Starz Original Series *Outlander*," *Quarterly Review of Film and Video* 35:1 (2018): 31–53.

Leach, Yvonne D. "*Outlander* from Book to Screen: Power in Gender," *Outlander's Sassenachs: Essays on Gender, Race, Orientation and the Other in the Novels and Television Series*. Jefferson, NC: McFarland, 2016, 130–152.

Ormond, Melissa. "Gender, Fantasy, and Empowerment in Diana Gabaldon's *Outlander*," master's thesis, DePaul University, 2009.

Fostering

The issue of bloodlines in the *Outlander* series reveals a number of alliances between orphans and their foster parents, particularly Jamie's harborage with the MacKenzies at Castle Leoch, his proposed guardianship of heir Hamish for the sake of Laird Colum and the clan, the rearing of Wee Bonnie by Lucinda and Hiram Brown, Claire's mothering of Elias Pound, and the adoption of Geillis Duncan and Dougal MacKenzie's son by William John and Sarah, a childless MacKenzie couple. Just as support of two uncles bridged the gap between Jamie's outlawry and respectability, his housing and rearing of Claudel, a Paris brothel factotum, precedes a strong father-son relationship. During the siphoning of information from the bonnie prince, Jamie implicates the lone pickpocket and mail thief. Jamie renames him Fergus, the identity of the vigorous medieval king who defeated King Cole in the fifth century CE.

Over a lengthy Paris residence with Jamie, Claire, and Murtagh Fitzgibbons Fraser, the fictional Fergus becomes a son and comforter following the death of Faith in child-birth. After two weeks recuperation, he requests that Claire come home from l'Hôpital des Anges to reinstate her parental role. He awards her a bouquet of blue cineraria, an extension of the blue forget-me-nots that lure her to the stones and of the cerulean aura that promises healing of afterbirth infection. Their closeness uplifts her during Jamie's incarceration in the Bastille and enables Fergus to discuss Jamie's broken promise to avoid dueling—child rape by Captain Black Jack Randall. The boy's emotional needs sal-vage Claire from self-pity, rage at Jamie, and mourning for Faith and illustrate the recip-rocal rewards of fostering.

COMING-OF-AGE

On departure from Lallybroch to join the Jacobite army at Kingussie, Fergus perches on the rim of manhood. He insists on becoming a soldier and riding out with the Fra-sers on a small mule. While volunteers prepare for heavy-duty combat nursing, his wise-mouth rejection of women's work in the Prestonpans field clinic injects a humorous atmosphere. Armed with a knife on September 21, 1745, he terrifies Claire with his secret departure to combat. The plot reveals much about the stress of warfare on grown men in the boy's exhaustion after a fifteen-minute knife battle that kills a Redcoat. Claire's moth-ering calls for scolding, a hug, and promise of food and rest, but the scene indicates that a violent coming-to-maturity will never rid Fergus of the specter of his first kill.

Before the Battle of Culloden on April 16, 1746, Fergus rejects a mission to take the deed of sasine away from the action to safety at Lallybroch. Jamie completes a folk adop-tion by calling the boy *mon fils* (my son) and by giving him a surname, "Fraser," at Fer-gus's marriage to Marsali MacKimmie in Haiti. In the aftermath of defeat by Redcoats, Fergus's feisty defense of his Scots father costs him amputation of his left hand, a savage saber attack by Corporal MacGregor, a turncoat Scot, that brings Jamie to his knees. At the boy's bedside, affection leads to Jamie's vow of lifelong parenting and support for Fer-gus, who grows even more attached to his Scots family. By wooing and wedding Marsali in the West Indies, he forms a blended household with Jamie's stepchild.

AD HOC FAMILY

Jamie acknowledges his *ad hoc* family outside Abandawe, where he grasps wife and foster son Young Ian in gratitude for safety. Reviewer Ann Gavin applauds actor John Bell's success as the runaway nephew: "He offered the perfect combination of naivete and brashness with a bit of a wee devil thrown in" (Gavin, 2019). The pledge of love deep-ens before the burning Celtic cross in season five, when Jamie declares Fergus a child of his heart and name. At Wilmington, Jamie and Claire continue providing monetary sup-port and advice. Marsali contributes her own bit of encouragement by asking Murtagh to recruit Fergus for the Regulators. Jamie's dispatch of Fergus to warn Murtagh of a Redcoat trap outside Wilmington further bolsters the spirit of a one-handed fighter, the father of Jamie and Claire's first grandchild and first granddaughter.

The intrusive past harbors more unexpected family ties. For Roger MacKenzie, the placement of his ancestor, the illicit child of Geillis Duncan and Dougal MacKenzie, with

William John and Sarah MacKenzie, confirms a genealogical tie with the MacKenzie clan. Recovering from the death of spitfire pilot Jerry and Marjorie Mackenzie during World War II, Roger acquires a supportive home as well as noted historian the Reverend Reginald Wakefield for a foster dad. In the aftermath of the reverend's death, his foster son learns the lengthy genealogy that links him to the war chief at Castle Leoch and to a survivor of an eighteenth-century witchcraft trial. In helping Claire piece together her multi-century past, Roger finds new hope and love with Brianna, mother of his Scots-American son Jeremiah.

Source

Gavin, Ann. "The Ultimate Ranking of *Outlander* Season 4 Episodes, www.outlandercast.com/2019/03/ranking-outlander-season-4-episodes.html, 13 March 2019.

Solis, Sandi. "Culloden and Wounded Knee: Genocide, Identity and Cultural Survival," *Outlander's Sassenachs: Essays on Gender, Race, Orientation and the Other in the Novels and Television Series.* Jefferson, NC: McFarland, 2016, 17–29.

Fraser, Claire

A classic romantic heroine and quest hero, Claire Beauchamp Randall Fraser merges curiosity and daring with traits of the New Woman. In the words of filmmaker and cinema analyst Courtney A. Hoffman, she serves as a time-traveler "who does not belong to her setting" (Hoffman, 2017, 104). Winner of a 2016 People's Choice Award and double nominee for Golden Globes, star Caitriona Balfe enacts multiple epochs afflicted with conflict, war, and pestilence and scenarios rife with womanizers and rapists, potential drowning, yearning for a lover, abduction, and the stillbirth of a first child.

In late October 1945, the protagonist wrestles with memories of savage spurting wounds from a World War II Allied dressing station revealing shards of bone and sinew. The scenario grips her once more when she prepares to amputate a Redcoat's right arm at Brockton Inn and holds a surgical saw over Jamie's snakebitten right thigh. In the estimation of scholar and feminist author Hannah Herrera, she presents "a complicated woman—a woman not strictly bounded by hegemonic femininity" (Herrera, 2019, 181). Her glimpse of a vase, a personalized Holy Grail, reminds her of unfulfilled desires to express an individualized, homebody self, a preview of her combination of efficiency and wifeliness at Fraser's Ridge.

An amateur botanist and herbalist, according to reviewer Hoffman, the heroine "has room for agency and filmic subjectivity that may reach beyond her body on the screen" (Hoffman, 2017, 104). At the basis of a dolmen at Craigh na Dun, she collects forget-me-nots (*Myosotis scorpioides*), tiny blue wildflowers that reflect honor to the war dead and anticipate the trials and memories of a time traveler. Contributing irony, husband Frank Randall's intelligence work in wartime London weights him with recall of spies who never report back from enemy territory, but it is Claire who battles repeated suspicions and charges of spying for the British. Part of her cover begins with the false identity of Claire Beauchamp, wife of Frank Beauchamp, a fictional Oxford teacher. Of the character's whoosh back 202 years, Balfe declared, "There's a misconception that women were much weaker in those times … they were definitely running the show behind the scenes…. You'll find a strong woman in there somewhere" (Virtue, 2015). For her vigor and daring, Graeme Virtue, a critic for the *Guardian,* forgives her the occasional belt of scotch.

Lost Freedoms

Thrust into healer Davie Beaton's dungeon surgery at Castle Leoch, Claire occupies a below-the-kitchen domain where guest liberties allow a nursing practice. In her element, she does not hesitate to bandy words with Laird Colum MacKenzie about the thin line between guest and prisoner or at interrupting an argument between Colum's brother, War Chief Dougal MacKenzie, and army lieutenant Jeremy Foster. In season one, episode six, Dougal and Lord Oliver Thomas agree that she has a penchant for "ordering men about," an offshoot of experience with Allied soldiers (1:6). At an arranged marriage to save her from villain Black Jack Randall, ethereal in gauze and linen wedding gown, she approaches the chapel in a full-skirted olive-gray concoction that mesmerizes the groom, clad in royal blue uniform with sword, a phallic reminder of male dominance. Claire deflates the fairy-tale altar scene by recoiling from obligatory blood ritual and unfamiliar vows in Gaelic and recalling a mammoth hangover and not much else.

Black Jack's post-nuptial interrogation discloses a weakness in Claire Fraser's ability to lie her way out of danger. In panic at Fort William, she resorts to screaming, an alert to Jamie and her rescuers. The patriarchal aftermath, the larruping of his bride with a belt, drew considerable outcry from critics and female viewers. Critic Yvonne D. Leach posed the issue of wife-beating from Claire's perspective: "The man she is in love with is going to physically harm her because he thinks he has the right to do so" (Leach, 2016, 141). The range of emotions and expressions tested Caitriona Balfe's skill as consummate actor cast in the part of tough-but-love-blinded protagonist who rouses to self-protective mode.

At Jamie's offer of a Highlander's covenant on his cross-shaped dirk—a weapon that conflates a phallic blade with Christianity—Claire appears unmoved by the traditional man-to-man oath and his promise never to harm her again. Clasped in embrace before the bedroom hearth, she wisely satisfies his need for coupling before brandishing a dirk at his throat and threatening him for further breach of civility. The camera stresses her choice of wife on top, a reversal of standard missionary position that she continues to assume at intimate moments throughout their relationship. In a subsequent scene, she relishes cunnilingus, which places Jamie in charge of her satisfaction.

Wife to the Rescue

To cure Jamie of his suicidal urge at Father Anselm's abbey, Claire must jog her mate out of passivity, a submission usually relegated to female characters of romance plots. She treats him with oil of lavender, a name derived from the Latin *lavare* (to cleanse) and declares that death is her only option if he starves himself. Reviewer and author Erica Obey charges the TV series with reenacting Jack's assault of Jamie out of "gratuitous exhibitionism or repressed rage" (Obey, 2002, 160). The Frasers reflect on multiple aspects of forgiveness, a bulwark of their relationship that recurs in season two, episode seven, the gripping post-stillbirth reunion between the couple after his release from the Paris Bastille. Herself a prisoner of ill feelings and doubts, Claire rises above groundless animus to dispel their fears of damage beyond repair to their marital union. Later offers of forgiveness keep the couple balanced in love and tolerance of faults.

Of the contemporaneous nature of the marriage, Caitriona Balfe stated to *New York Times* interviewer Jennifer Vineyard, "Though *Outlander* takes place mostly in the past, it deals with real issues all the time, even if it's the guise of a fantasy and an epic story. It's a safe place" (Vineyard, 2018). Claire adopts a post-military nurse toughness and refers affectionately to Jamie as "soldier" (1:1, 5:6). During macho arguments, she dares separate the squabblers, especially Murtagh Fitzgibbons Fraser and the gypsy Mr. Ward, Jack Randall and Murtagh in Inverness, and, at the Jacobite camp, Murtagh and Fergus. She batters Murtagh over her grief at lost love before discovering that self-absorption blocks appreciation of her terse companion, who suffers unrequited love for Ellen MacKenzie Fraser. An apology strengthens their friendship, which survives to shrouding his corpse at Alamance Creek.

Season two opens on an out-of-sync clip of Claire once more in modern Scotland in 1948 after leaving the Battle of Culloden on April 16, 1746. During rehabilitation at the Rev. Reginald Wakefield's home and comforting words from the housekeeper Mrs. Graham, a camera pan follows an overhead fighter jet, a realistic element of the Cold War and constant sword rattling among superpowers. Despite attempts to suppress sorrow and disillusion, she jerks to attention at the word "flog," which becomes unbearable in light of Jamie's physical torments (2:1). A flashback to Frank's corpse in the hospital morgue views Claire through ribbed glass, a fluctuating trope of emotions splintered by a first love whom she betrayed and unintentionally thwarted.

A WELCOMING FUTURE

The love-starved reunion of the Frasers in 1766 after a two-decade separation pictures a tentative shyness in Claire, who carries from Boston to A. Malcolm's printshop in Edinburgh a host of misgivings. Balfe amplifies the self-doubts of middle age with a breathy delivery of dialogue, à la actor Jane Seymour. The strength of the couple's marital bond unleashes desires Claire has held in check throughout the soulless years with Frank and his fling with mistress Sandy Travers. Claire's smile plumps her cheeks, an authentic show of delight. Inspirited by Jamie's grasp, she resumes the connectivity the pair enjoyed in their first two years as man and wife.

In seasons four and five, Claire demonstrates the helpmeet's support of a frontier farmer/distiller/militia colonel and a mellow regard for daughter and daughter-in-law. Her praise of Marsali Fraser's upbringing swallows years of grievance against Laoghaire for betraying her at a Cranesmuir court for witchcraft. Actor Lauren Lyle presents a strong sense of self and an independent judgment in Marsali that facilitates friendship with a woman she previously called a devil. The two form a surgical team that experiments with homemade penicillin during the Beardsley twins' tonsillectomies. Unfortunately for the series, Sophie Skelton's flaccid assumption of the daughter role achieves impersonal dialogue and limp rapport with actors Balfe and Richard Rankin.

A masterwork, season five, episode seven pictures Claire in two roles. As bedmate, she celebrates Jamie's fiftieth birthday with a tantalizing "Happy Birthday to You," sung in a kittenish Marilyn Monroe enticement of JFK. Still lusty for her man, she contents the colonel on his way to war and adopts an auxiliary post of combat nurse. The arrival of Murtagh's body leaves her sad and humbled by an old friend's death. With the understatement of Mark Antony in William Shakespeare's *Julius Caesar*, she cherishes the fallen Regulator as "my friend" (5:7). Her healing of Jamie's snakebite in episode nine restores health through libido. At his collapse, her caress to his genitals revitalizes and restores him. A tasteful dramatization of desire, the scene illustrates a narrative strength—the fusion of life force with adult sexuality.

Character realities place an arduous toll on Balfe at the finale of season five, when she portrays a menopausal hot flash and endures battery and gang rape before rescue by Jamie and the Rowan County Militia. Just as her face, voice, and posture enact deep pain and sorrow at salvaging Jamie from suicide at the abbey and at her infant's death in 1744, the crushing evil of Lionel Brown's company forces her into hallucinating a bitter Thanksgiving. The dream sequence incorporates elements of trauma, including the orange she snatches from the exploiter Louis XV and Young Ian's enlistment in the U.S. Army. On Jamie's arrival and extermination of Lionel's raiders, she whimpers wordlessly and avoids taking part in vengeful executions of the surviving criminals. The actor's gradual return to sanity at home, in her surgery, and in her bed attests to Balfe's ability to master emotional extremes.

See also Combat Nursing; Jamie Fraser; World War II.

Source

Fusick, Katherine. *Ladies in Rebellion: Women of the 1715 and 1745 Jacobite Risings*. Baltimore: University of Maryland, 2017.

Herrera, Hannah. "Shifting Spaces and Constant Patriarchy: The Characterizations of Offred and Claire in *The Handmaid's Tale* and *Outlander*," *Zeitschrift für Anglistik und Amerikanistik* 67:2 (2019): 181–196.

Hoffman, Courtney A. "How to Be a Woman in the Highlands: A Feminist Portrayal of Scotland in *Outlander*," *The Cinematic Eighteenth Century*. New York: Routledge, 2017, 103–117.

Leach, Yvonne D. "*Outlander* from Book to Screen: Power in Gender," *Outlander's Sassenachs: Essays on Gender, Race, Orientation and the Other in the Novels and Television Series*. Jefferson, NC: McFarland, 2016, 130–152.

Obey, Erica. "Tall, Dark, and a Long Time Dead: Epistemology, Time Travel, and the Bodice-Ripper," *Worlds Enough and Time: Explorations of Time in Science Fiction and Fantasy*. Westport, CT: Greenwood, 2002.

Vineyard, Jennifer. "'Outlander' Takes Manhattan," *New York Times* (2 November   2018).

Virtue, Graeme. "*Outlander*: '*Game of Thrones* Helped Open the Door for Us,'" *Guardian* (21 March 2015).

Fraser, Jamie

In a graphic anti-war narrative, the *Outlander* TV series features a multifaceted hero strong enough to fight for principles, human enough to adore a wife and family, prescient enough to anticipate community needs, and vulnerable enough to twitch his index finger at tense moments. Jamie Fraser overturns the standard objectification of female beauty and sexual allure to manifest an outstanding male physique, macho sensibility, and admission of hubris. In the estimation of essayist Araceli R. Lopez, romance empowers the protagonist for "his desirability—physical beauty, kindness, and self-effacing nature" (Lopez, 2016, 52). To Internet reviewer EllenandJim, Jamie's ethos and exemplary behavior compare favorably with Ross Poldark, central figure in a British historical TV series.

Actor Sam Heughan, a stunning exemplar of maleness, portrays a 22-year-old chivalric warrior whom Graeme Virtue, a screen critic for the *Guardian*, described as "a strapping Scot who is all muck and muscle" (Virtue, 2015). His self-made ideals survive a lashing in October 1739 and, in 1740, mercenary service in Silesia and on the France-Spanish border. No background data explains how he weathers torment in the dungeons of Wentworth Prison or in Paris at the Bastille. No biography justifies why he flourishes at playing chess and whist, captaining a ship, negotiating with royalty and scoundrels, citing Thucydides, crafting a settler's cabin, distilling whisky, and mustering a frontier militia. At a nadir of trust and belief, on May 16, 1771, he loses his godfather, Murtagh Fitzgibbons Fraser, significantly on Jamie's fiftieth birthday. Mourning alone by a small campfire reveals a flaw in his dynamic—separation anxiety, already tested by his parents' deaths and by Claire's twenty-year absence.

COMING OF AGE

Born of an androcentric culture devoted to the Platonic ideal of anatomical splendor and grace, Jamie strives for harmony of strength, honor, and will. He mediates between his father's socially lesser background and the arrogant MacKenzie line represented by Colum, Dougal, Jocasta Cameron, and his mother, Ellen MacKenzie Fraser. To escape the ennui of farming at Lallybroch, he signs on with a paid force, the kind that Roger's folk ballad "Twa Recruitin' Sergeants" denounces for inveigling naive country boys into the military. Becoming a husband rids Jamie of virginity and consumes him with passion for Claire, whom he adores body and soul. An invitation to join Taran MacQuarrie and the Watch tempts him and flatters his ego, but does not convince him to give up marriage and the position of a Highlander laird, a status that suits his sister better than Jamie.

Central to his experiences with the military, a flogging with one hundred lashes at the gate of Lallybroch in southwestern Scotland in October 1739 precedes a second flogging at the Fort William pillory, a focal horror in the *Outlander* series and visual proof of monstrosity in the British Army. After Harry, a Redcoat deserter, gropes Claire at the glade, Jamie accepts blame for failure to heed (a noun that the closed captioning translator misunderstands as "heat") her welfare. Out of range of the British, Jamie's identity varies from Mr. MacTavish, the wanted murderer, to his uncle Dougal's silent Jacobite rallying point. In anger at the war chief for turning him into a sideshow, Jamie claims the right to choose his destiny and, in frustration, pounds a tree with his fist, a foreshadowing of the uselessness of training a Jacobite regiment to engage the British army.

LOVE FOR WOMEN

From the wedding scene onward, Jamie displays romantic heroism as what critic Michelle L. Jones calls *Outlander*'s "central love interest" (Jones, 2016, 72). The loss of Ellen mars his boyhood and produces a restrained mother hunger, forcing him to accept Jenny as a pseudo-mom, a mature role (admirably played by Laura Donnelly) enhanced by her matronly hairstyle, mien, posture, and verbal aggression. Claire, who is five years older than Jamie, introduces him to intimacy with post-coital fellatio, which fills his heart to bursting. In response, he draws from poignant folk balladry the epithet "Mo Nighean Donn, Grádh Mo Chridhe" (My Brown Haired Lass, Love of My Heart, 1:7). Claire slips into the maternal slot with wise advice, forgiveness, and brio that he longs for during their twenty years of separation from 1746 to 1766. During the bathtub scene in the Frasers' cabin, she compliments him on being a son who would please his mother.

For the best scene in the TV series, Jamie applies a Highlander's understanding of maleness to an argument with Claire over a husbandly duty to discipline his woman. In a peaceful mossy setting pocked with ferns, Heughan paces his argument from rage and dominance to the defeat of his notion of virility. The actor remarked to Laura Prudom of *Variety*: "I really got to do some gritty acting…. We sort of tore it out of each other" (Prudom, 2015). The expression of love and acceptance of each other's faults sets the couple on an even relationship, a partnership more in keeping with a twentieth-century wife dedicated to forgiveness. Because she fears she is barren, out of devotion and gallantry, Jamie conceals his disappointment by claiming to be glad she will not suffer a botched delivery, the reason for Ellen's death when he was a boy.

The overturn of the theme of suffering places Jamie in Wentworth Prison under the command of a degenerate, his nemesis, Captain Jonathan "Black Jack" Randall, who forces Jamie into the female role in consensual sex. The extenuated torture, sodomy, and seduction visualize Jamie at the end of his endurance of hurt. With an anguished cry, he visualizes his wife's face and regrets "no more Claire" (1:16). Upon his rescue by wagon to Father Anselm's Benedictine abbey, delirium and trauma obscure his true character and reliance on Claire's healing touch. In mental hell on the infirmary cot, he whimpers like a child the name "Claire," a verbal reminder of the Latin adjective for clear, distinct, bright, pure, like a star or gemstone. To rid himself of shame, he feels the need to vomit, an emesis of humiliation.

A Leading Man

Jamie's tolerance toward peasant ignorance and royal profligacy account for his reputation as a fair leader and proponent of human rights. Reflecting the themes and characters popularized by novelist Sir Walter Scott, he anticipates the soul of the romantic era in *Waverley*. He earns his uncle Colum's regard for avoiding recklessness with others' lives. On arrival at Lallybroch, he ignites harsh words with sister Jenny over the siring of Wee Jamie, whom he fears is illegitimate, and the lodging of Rabbie MacNab, an abused child. In private, Jamie attempts to disprove Claire's criticism of his lordly behavior at their ancestral home, where he grandly occupies his parents' former bedroom and courts respect from tenants.

Perpetuating the theme of forgiveness, in Paris, Jamie plods his way upstairs before apologizing to Claire for breaking a promise, a violation of his ethical code. Intercuttings of mother with infant corpse at l'Hôpital des Anges reprise Claire's emotional turmoil at the dual loss of daughter and husband. The filming does not spell out how much Claire reenacts for Jamie with her singing to Faith a song of the seaside, whether a memory or actual rendering of Claire's parting with the tiny girl. Jamie's proposal—to share mutual sorrow—turns grief into a bonding agent and anticipation of another child if God grants their wish.

A Warrior's Loss

Scholar Marlène Charlier placed the hero at the core of the uprising: "All of what the main character Jamie Fraser does during the first two seasons is about the Jacobite cause. He is in the centre of this event and acts for it" (Charlier, 2019, 8). After Prestonpans on September 21, 1745, Jamie demonstrates a fighting man's savvy. He cleverly promotes Dougal to captain of the Scots dragoons, a method of removing a rogue executioner of the wounded from the bonnie prince's disapproval. On the disappointing retreat north, Jamie assures Lallybroch's men that he will send them safely home, a promise that Murtagh accomplishes. Similarly, his dispatch of Claire to her own time completes a dual protection of wife and unborn child. The recognition of pregnancy reveals consciousness of her menstrual cycle and evidence of a second chance at fatherhood. In season two, episode two, Jamie quashes Jenny's urging that he marry and sire children. His trickle of tears at coupling with Mary MacNab exhibits the grief he bears for losing—and betraying—his soul mate.

In season three, Heughan's pitiable costume at Ardsmuir suits the circumstance of MacDubh, the prison leader restrained in handcuffs and leg irons for treason. Reviewer Yvonne Villarreal of the *Los Angeles Times* elicited a character summation from Heughan: "It's the different stages of grief, really. He goes through anger, sadness … eventually acceptance … but he's still living in the memory of Claire, living in the shadows" (Villarreal, 2018). At a low of fortunes, to feed starving cellmates, Jamie negotiates hunting privileges with prison governor John Grey. A variation of incarceration as an estate groom at Helwater forces him to bed Geneva Dunsany, when he displays courtesy and respect for a snotty, demanding aristocrat. To her question about the nature of love, he differentiates between desire and a lasting passion, a definition he later imparts to Fergus.

New Life

At the Ellesmere birth scene, Heughan indicates by eyes alone Jamie's delight in siring a son, even though the bastard boy remains unacknowledged. Paternal words to the infant in his pram heighten the father's need to shield a child he can't claim. Parting from Willie six years later takes its toll. Superb acting extends Heughan's mastery of emotions in episode six to thorough attention to inking and loading his press and the sudden faint at seeing Claire in the gallery. By segueing to Jamie's concern for removing his pants in front of her, the dialogue lightens the mix of desire and trembling that accompanies the print office tryst.

Dialogue in 1766 indicates Jamie and Claire's fears that mutual desire and physical appeal have withered over two decades of separation. In his garret room, the eye-to-eye caresses dispel worries and precede a long-awaited bedding punctuated by humor and conversation. He betrays anxiety and haste in a nose bump that draws laughter from the lovers and affectionate pillow talk. Distancing himself from a battleground thigh slash by Jack Randall, Jamie reduces explanation of his wound to one word, "Culloden" (3:6). Of the Frasers' intimacy, television critic Kayla Kumari Upadhyaya lapsed into subjectivity: The cozy side of the marriage "makes you feel so lonely in this world because a man like Jamie simply doesn't exist" (Upadhyaya, 2018).

A Man of Worth

In episodes set on the Atlantic crossing to the West Indies, Jamie regresses into petulance and obstinacy because Claire joins the crew of the British man-o'-war *Porpoise* to treat rampant typhoid fever. For *IndieWire,* journalist and reviewer Amber Dowling approved the downturn: "It's actually refreshing to see that this male romantic lead is far from perfect, and it's easy to forgive his shortcomings because they typically tend to happen in the name of love" (Dowling, 2017). On the Carolina frontier, the transformation of Jamie into a colonel in the Rowan County Militia restores his authority and understanding of the risks that lie ahead for the radical Regulators. Actor Heughan observed, "He's not just a man of action, but also a man of intellect, and when the two come together, he's a great, formidable leader" (Radish, 2020).

Following the pacing established in the *Outlander* TV episodes, the one-shot loss of a godfather quickly vanquishes Jamie's earnest lead of the militia. At a climactic point in his North American venture, he loses rationality briefly and demands that Claire revive Murtagh. The death ends Jamie's tiptoeing around Governor William Tryon: he challenges Tryon for martyring North Carolina citizens as an incentive to a bid for governorship of New York. Another fault eats at Jamie as he lies feverish from snakebite: he feels compelled by honor to kill Stephen Bonnet because he helped the pirate escape the gallows.

The finale dramatizes a third catastrophe—rescuing Claire from misogynistic bandits posing as a Committee of Safety. The stress on Jamie wrings a merger of honor and unrelenting vengeance against the marauders who gang-rape his wife. For the gallop into the night, he wears his kilt and wraps Claire in his plaid, a projection of adoration and sanctuary to his wife. The script words a rare statement of principle—he respects her Hippocratic Oath, but takes charge himself of killing her ravagers. Of Scots valor and the Scots-American diaspora, Heughan stated, "I feel honoured to be almost a spokesman for Scotland and to be bringing Scotland to the rest of the world" (Crumlish, 2019).

See also Craigh na Dun; Claire Fraser; Kilt; Honor; Names.

Source

Charlier, Marlène. "La représentation des mythes et légendes dans la série *Outlander*," master's thesis, Université de Franche-Comté, 2019.

Crumlish, Callum. "*Outlander* Season 5: Jamie Fraser Star Sam Heughan Speaks Out on Show Ending 'We'll See,'" *Express* (11 November 2019).

Dowling, Amber. "'Outlander' Review: Tumultuous Waters Rip Claire and Jamie Apart," *IndieWire* (19 November 2017).

Jones, Michelle L. "Linked … through the Body of One Man: Black Jack Randall as a Non-Traditional Romance Villain," *Adoring Outlander: Essays on Fandom, Genre and the Female Audience*. Jefferson, NC: McFarland, 2016, 71–81.

Lopez, Araceli R. "Gazing at Jamie Fraser," *Outlander's Sassenachs: Essays on Gender, Race, Orientation and the Other in the Novels and Television Series*. Jefferson, NC: McFarland, 2016, 44–53.

Prudom, Laura. "'Outlander' Stars Break Down Claire and Jamie's First Fight, That Spanking Scene," *Variety* (5 April 2015).

Radish, Christina. "Sam Heughan Talks 'Outlander' Season 5, What's Next for the Frasers, and His 'Bloodshot' Role," *Collider* (16 February 2020).

Upadhyaya, Kayla Kumari. "*Outlander's* Alchemy Remains Spectacular in Its Hotly Anticipated Return," *AVClub* (4 November 2018).

Villarreal, Yvonne. "As Jamie Fraser in 'Outlander,' Sam Heughan Was Destined to Live in Grief," *Los Angeles Times* (20 March 2018).

Virtue, Graeme. "*Outlander*: '*Game of Thrones* Helped Open the Door for Us,'" *Guardian* (21 March 2015).

Fraser, Murtagh

The fictional role in the *Outlander* TV epic of the taciturn Murtagh Fitzgibbons Fraser falls between primary and secondary character—godfather, companion, indentured servant, guardian, lover, and rabble rouser. On November 1, 1945, he rescues Claire from Captain Black Jack Randall in the woods near Craigh na Dun 202 years in the past and introduces her to War Chief Dougal MacKenzie and his Highland outriders. He also vouches for Claire's character to shield her from accusations of prostitution. At Castle Leoch, his comparison of the flirty Laoghaire to a real woman suggests that Murtagh anticipates a development in Jamie's relationship with Claire. Before the wedding of time traveler and Scots warrior, Jamie relies on advice from Murtagh, his surrogate father, about bedroom intimacy, but rejects the proposal to take Jamie's bride with them to the wild and live off the land.

Wiry and self-sufficient, Murtagh serves as a blend of guardian angel and Jiminy

Cricket. Caustic humor counters his dark visage and verbal snarls. From Claire and housekeeper Glenna "Mrs. Fitz" Fitzgibbons, he gains a reputation for poor personal hygiene. After his pursuing Claire and Jenny from Lallybroch to recover the Watch come his witticisms about their skill at outlawry. By advising Claire on methods of gathering information, he accepts identification as her servant, a pose he assumes at Wentworth Prison. Her vomiting and faint at Father Anselm's Benedictine abbey imply a pregnancy before Jamie learns of it. Just as Murtagh rescued her in the opening episode, he once more carries her to safety and provides the unique plan of retrieving Jamie from his cell amid a cattle stampede.

A Demanding Relationship

In Le Havre, France, Murtagh bridles at receiving only the rudiments of the plot against the Jacobite Rebellion. Weighed against devotion to his godson, he accepts the one-sided proposal to live double lives among luxury-lapping Parisians without knowing the background of Claire's time travel. He aids Jamie in strengthening his mangled left hand and exercising his skills at sword, dirk, and hand-to-hand roughhousing. To the bonnie prince, Murtagh sets parameters for guarding Jamie—"Where he goes, I go" (2:2). The declaration foreshadows tragedy at the separation in season five of a pseudo-stepfather/stepson.

In the aftermath of a street rape in Paris by night, Murtagh must admit his inability to live up to personal ideals, which derive from his commitment to Ellen MacKenzie Fraser. He regrets failing Jamie and carries the vow of vengeance to Sandringham's Belmont mansion a year later, where he beheads the duke with double clouts of an ax. In a recap of the eleventh episode of season two, producer Ronald Moore verified Murtagh's unrelenting vengeance: "Eventually, you're going to run into Murtagh and he's going to cut your head off" (Bucksbaum, 2016). Star Caitriona Balfe added gleefully, "To see Duncan really go at it was hilarious" (*ibid.*).

A man of action in the field and as a highwayman, Murtagh trains Scots volunteers in marching and mastery of sword and dirk, wields the disciplinary lash on recalcitrant sentries, and foments the Regulation movement among North Carolina Scots-Americans. Before the Battle of Prestonpans on September 21, 1745, he fears that his death in combat would have no meaning. The surprising overturn of gruff exterior in season two, episode twelve amplifies his offer to wed Mary Hawkins to spare her widowhood and penury. He words his prospects as poor and propertyless, a testimonial to his humility.

A pop-up question at the execution site after the Battle of Culloden in 1746 predicts Jamie's concern for Murtagh's whereabouts. The survival of the godfather remains doubtful until his reappearance in 1752 at Ardsmuir Prison in dwindling health from hunger, cold, flu, and rat bites. Another poignant parting sends him to the colonies in 1756, while Jamie plods his way to Helwater in northwestern England. The prefix "hel" implies a sentence to limbo for both men.

Devotion to Ellen's Son

As Murtagh's character alters drastically toward radical protest, he gradually recedes from the family scene. Separations grow more ominous at Fraser's Ridge at the wedding of Brianna and Roger MacKenzie in 1770, where Murtagh lurks in the outback and enjoys a rustic rendezvous with Jocasta Cameron. In the wake of Governor William Tryon's demand for the Regulator's head, Jamie frees his godfather from an oath to defend him. Jamie's tears and sink to the ground elevate a sad conclusion to predictor of violence to come. A brief encounter with Bryan Cranna at the Regulators' hideout suggests that Murtagh stays safely out of reach of the British Army. Another small scene, his wedding gift to Jocasta imparts a strong, but doomed love ennobled with a copy of the Fraser crest, a clan emblem that Jocasta sees with her fingertips.

The crux of season five, episode seven results from Hugh Findley's shot to Murtagh's chest that quickly fells him. In his standard guise, he rescues Jamie from Lee Withers's gun and, with his last breath, offers advice on the nature of death. The dialogue characterizes his demise as a life-changing blow to his godson. TV reviewer Alexandria Ingham surmised that, by his mid–70s, Murtagh had lived through drastic spiritual lows and identification with the disenfranchised. He had seized "an opportunity to feel listened to … to take some of the power back after years of not having it" (Ingham, 2020).

The problem for Jamie comes from a lengthy separation from a role model he no longer knows, no longer understands. Star Sam Heughan concluded, "It's a very dense episode…. The repercussions are huge for everyone" (Kosin, 2020). He viewed the death as Jamie's "last real contact with Scotland, the last member of his blood apart from his aunt and daughter … the old world and ways of doing things" (*ibid.*). In salvation amid heartbreak, Murtagh's final words to his *bhalaich* (boy) reassured him that death is not so terrible (5:7). At the big house, Jamie keeps him close with a grave and cairn formed of native stones.

Source

Bucksbaum, Sydney. "'Outlander' Team Breaks Down That Violent Act of Revenge and 'Powerful' Scene Viewers Didn't See," *Hollywood Reporter* (18 June 2016).
Ingham, Alexandria. "Explaining Murtagh's Change of Character in *Outlander* Season 5," *Claire & Jamie* (March 2020).
Kosin, Julie. "Sam Heughan on *Outlander*'s Devastating Double Loss," *Elle* (30 March 2020).
Robinson, Joanna. "*Outlander* Star Sam Heughan on Jamie's Devastating Loss," *Vanity Fair* (30 March 2020).

Fraser Genealogy

The complicated family tree of Jamie Fraser, hero of the Outlander TV saga, outlines segments of the MacKenzie lineage that elevate him to contender for Colum's replacement as laird at Castle Leoch:

Missing from the family tree are links to godfather Murtagh Fitzgibbons Fraser and Cousin Jared Fraser, the French wine merchant. The blending of parents with *ad hoc* children awards Rabbie MacNab to the Murrays, Claire, and Jamie, his rescuers from an abusive father. The brood takes on more pseudo-adoptions with the addition of pickpocket Fergus Claudel Fraser and nephew Young Ian, who fantasizes having Jamie for a father.

Because Brianna Randall is a newcomer to the eighteenth century, she learns bits and pieces about Grandmother Ellen MacKenzie Fraser, whose name she bears. Murtagh recalls Ellen's beautiful eyes and warm smile. Jocasta compares Brianna and Ellen's talent for drawing. Background nuances identify Ellen as the self-determined rebel who refuses beau Malcolm Grant and elopes with the man of her heart, Brian Fraser. To ease Brianna's worries about premarital pregnancy, Jocasta divulges that

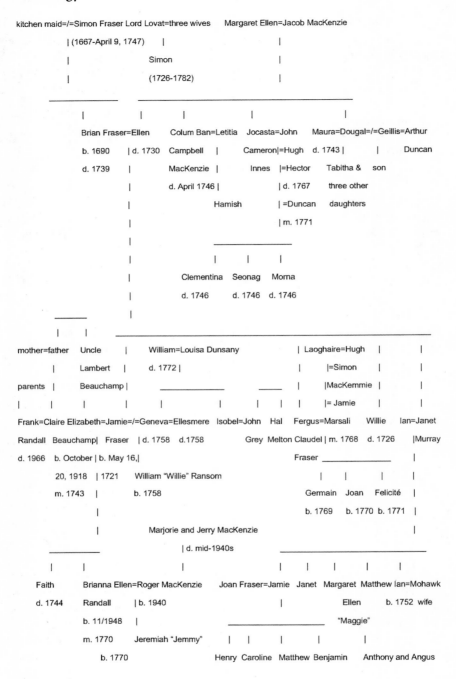

Ellen was "with child" before her marriage (4:11). The woman-to-woman chat depicts a soothing matrilineal talk about family and motherhood. Reviewer Neela Debnath legitimized genealogy for retaining memories of Ellen, who is "never forgotten by the others who hail her for her strength of character and following her heart" (Debnath, 2019).

See also Matrilineage.

Source

Charlier, Marlène. "La représentation des mythes et légendes dans la série *Outlander*," master's thesis, Université de Franche-Comté, 2019.

Debnath, Neela. "*Outlander*: What Happened to Brian Fraser? Tragic Backstory Explained," *Express* (12 November 2019).

_____. "*Outlander*: What Happened to Ellen Fraser? The Tragic Backstory of Jamie's Mother," *Express* (7 November 2019).

Potter, Mary-Anne. "'Everything and Nothing': Liminality in Diana Gabaldon's *Outlander*," *Interdisciplinary Literary Studies* 21:3 (2019): 282–296.

Fraser's Ridge

Set in North Carolina's western piedmont in the foothills of the Blue Ridge after 1768 and filmed in Scotland, the fictional Fraser's Ridge in the TV romance *Outlander* takes shape in virgin forest in sight of Grandfather Mountain, a current scene of Highland gatherings. Scholar Sherri Sutton Davis, a researcher at Fayetteville State University, compared pioneering in the locale to Mircea Eliade's theory of the quest for paradise. The authenticity of Scots émigrés in North America raises complexities. In the purview of Ian Brown, a former drama professor at Kingston University, London, and author of *Performing Scottishness: Enactment and National Identities,* the "significant diaspora" of a home culture yields a "deep-seated, historical bricolage of images, sounds and stories … suffused with sentimentality" (Brown, 246). He urged coverage of "conditions that gave rise to and sustain an emigrant's experience," an allusion to the series views on post–Culloden persecution of Highlanders and taxation by corrupt colonial agents (*ibid.*).

Governor William Tryon identifies the Frasers' acreage as Orange County near Durham, a stretch that the fictional version of George Washington surveyed from 1749 to 1752. The set piece of a view from Fraser land lacks validity, much like supposed glimpses of the Appalachias in the Civil War cinema *Cold Mountain,* which producers filmed in Romania. The couple's discovery of wild strawberries forges a link with the Fraser clan surname, which Jamie credits to Fraselière, a French immigrant to the Highlands whose name derives from the French for strawberry. Just as Jamie falls in love with a view that "spoke" to him, so do his birth children, William Ransom and Brianna Randall (4:4). The shared affection for the spot denotes similar values in offspring who grew up apart from their father and each other.

From Little House to Big House

In a description of the Frasers, *New York Times* TV critic Jennifer Vineyard calls them "accidental immigrants" (Vineyard, 2018). The couple live on venison, jerky, and trout and adapt trees to construction, which Jamie accomplishes with ax, crosscut saw, and adze. The finished cabin, obviously shaped from factory-planed 2" × 8"s, provides hearth, pantry, bookshelves, and bed. Jamie's choice of the winter sunrise as the perfect southeasterly direction prefigures a fulcrum for their life in a new land. Balanced with edgy encounters with Cherokee neighbors, the first months involve friend-making, which Jamie manages with gifts of tobacco and the slaying of a forest monster, the *tskili yona.*

Season five exhibits a startling rise in Fraser fortunes. Set on an outdoor dais, the Randall-MacKenzie wedding aims the nuptials toward a creek, a fluid motif that graces episodes with evidence of plenty and a lineal history that unites First Peoples and frontiersmen. The big house, constructed with the aid of tenants or hirelings, bodes well for the family, leaving the Fraser cabin for occupancy by newlyweds Brianna and Roger MacKenzie. A few of the amenities of the wood frame dwelling built by knowledgeable carpenters consist of an ample fireplace, porch, breezeway, and busy physician's office. Meticulous fretwork and molding suggest supplies from a modern lumberyard. Colonial appointments—pottery, utility baskets, ball fringe curtains, florid wallpaper, a Queen Anne style chest of drawers—imply that the family generates a large disposable income based on rents and farm yield.

COMMUNITY SPIRIT

Good will marks the piedmont lifestyle. Before drawing locals and visitors into drinking and conversation and a front yard reel, Jamie raises a toast to the newlyweds. An affable country gathering on a par with *The Waltons*, the party continues into the night while tenants ignore the ominous redcoated presence of Governor William Tryon. Out of hearing, he threatens to repossess the 10,000-acre compound in recompense for Jamie's failure to capture Murtagh Fitzgibbons Fraser and demobilize the Regulators. Like the difficult decision to support Jacobitism in Scotland, the call-up of the Rowan County Militia once more plunges the Frasers into life-or-death decisions and concern for noncombatants.

Scripting reunites the Frasers and friends periodically, treasuring with guitar music and camerawork their North Carolina sanctuary. Because of Roger's strategy to drive off a locust horde with smudgepots and Claire's shooting of a raging buffalo, the land remains productive and its denizens safe. The threats of local marauders come home to Jamie after Arvin Hodgepile assaults Marsali Fraser, murders Geordie, and abducts Claire. By lighting the fiery cross, Jamie summons help from across Fraser's Ridge. The season five finale dramatizes an uneasy peace—Claire recuperating at home, but the family contemplating Richard Brown's revenge for Lionel's death and the coming American Revolution.

Source

Brown, Ian. *Performing Scottishness: Enactment and National Identities.* London: Palgrave Macmillan, 2020.

Carpenter, Perry. "Why 'Outlander' Season 5 Needs to Include More Steamy Scenes Between Jamie and Claire," *Showbiz Cheatsheet* (7 August 2019).

Davis, Sherri Sutton. "The Heroic Journey in *Outlander*: Tracing the Mythic Path," Ph.D. dissertation, Fayetteville State University, 2005.

Vineyard, Jennifer. "'Outlander' Season 4 Is Nigh. Here's What to Remember," *New York Times* (2 November 2018).

Friendship

Friendships in the TV epic *Outlander* epitomize the ancient Greek concept that dynamic sociability eclipses all other human relations, a belief actuated by Annekje Johansen's gift of a raft to Claire, implied by Ulysses's protection of mistress Jocasta Cameron Innes, shared in "waulking wool" with *ban dhuan* (song woman) Donalda Gilchrest, hoped for in Fiona's coddling of Roger MacKenzie, and corrupted by pirate Stephen Bonnet, who sneaks past Redcoat checkpoints in the name of friend Gavin Hayes (1:5). The kindling of warm and lasting rapport makes myriad beginnings, matching Claire with clinic aide Marsali Fraser, indentured servant Lizzy Wemyss, the flibbertigibbet Louise de Rohan, sister-in-law Jenny Murray, Edinburgh prostitutes, the Cherokee healer Adawehi, and fourteen-year-old sailor Elias Pound. For mercenaries like the elder Ian Murray, years in mercenary service in France, Spain, and Silesia increase his respect for

Jamie Fraser, a boyhood friend at Lallybroch and fellow soldier. The two bond over Ian's battlefield leg amputation, which obligates Jamie to transfer Ian home to sister Jenny's care. During Jamie's six-year self-imposed house arrest after the Battle of Culloden on April 16, 1746, Ian comforts his fellow veteran for losing his heart, Ian's metaphor for Claire.

As brother-in-law, the elder Ian continues his trust and admiration for Jamie and finds a parallel in a relationship with veteran warrior Taran MacQuarrie, head of the Watch. Out of love for Ian, Jamie conceals from Taran that Ian murders Horrocks combat style with a sword thrust through the back. The soldierly fellowship further bonds Jamie to Taran, whom he refuses to abandon at the ambush of the Chisholm rent party. The commitment remains firm at the gallows, where Jamie bids farewell to Taran with the sign of the cross and the expectation of continued friendship in the afterlife, a recompense that Jamie predicts for Rupert MacKenzie on meeting comrade Angus Mohr in heaven.

Gendered Comradery

Mystic woman-to-woman rapport accounts for Claire's offer of a love potion to Laoghaire MacKenzie, comfort for seer Maisri at Beaufort Castle, and treatment in the Castle Leoch kitchen of Glenna "Mrs. Fitz" Fitzgibbons's burned arm. The castle cook renders solace by promising that Claire will soon reunite with Jamie. On a riskier level, Claire states her friendship with Geillis Duncan, a practitioner of Wicca in the ancient Druidic tradition. Claire is safer and more satisfied by a collegiality with Paris apothecary Raymond, who respects her herbal expertise and counsels her on dealings with Le Comte St. Germain. In return, Claire helps the apothecary escape a royal sweep of practitioners of the black arts. A supervisory relationship emerges with mentoring Mary Hawkins and volunteering to aid Mother Hildegarde, who values Claire's clinical skill and altruism. At Claire's bedside in l'Hôpital des Anges, Louise's receipt of Faith's blanket-wrapped corpse from Claire to pass to the mother superior introduces a classic female pairing—a pregnant woman's pity of a new mother's sorrow.

Male bonding takes on similarly varied forms, as in Roger MacKenzie's attempt to counsel Father Alexandre Ferigault on Catholic dogma, Isaiah Morton and John Quincy Myers's loyalty to Colonel Fraser, Josiah Beardsley's search for maggots to cleanse Jamie's infected wound, and Young Ian Murray's alliance with Mohawk Chief Tehwahsehkwe. Before the Battle of Prestonpans on September 21, 1745, Ross and Kincaid swap responsibility for families if either man dies. A dramatic irony pictures Angus, mortally wounded, demanding treatment of a deep saber slash on Rupert's midriff. Angus's comic willing of Scarlett the whore to Rupert lightens the mood of a skirmish that results in Kincaid's death and Angus's unexpected bleed-out from a cannon blast.

Life-and-death situations reinforce the soldierly bond. At the execution of Jacobite traitors by British firing squad after Culloden, Gordon Killick, Jamie, and Rupert realize that escape is impossible. Gordon demonstrates farewell to Jamie by kissing his hand before facing a military execution. The gesture reveals in miniature the comrade's affiliation that continues in scenes of Jamie as MacDubh, the trusted prison intermediary for Ardsmuir dungeon dwellers Gavin Hayes, Lesley, and Murtagh Fitzgibbons Fraser. Before the Battle of Alamance Creek on May 16, 1771, Jamie counsels the Findlay brothers, Hugh and Iain Og, with a bitter truth—war means killing and death.

A Lasting Adoration

The affinity between Jamie and prison governor John Grey at Ardsmuir promotes a mature interchange between heterosexual and homosexual. Although some critics find Grey annoying, Sandi Solis described him as "a welcome, often important and frequently returning friend who, through time and circumstance, comes to have very close ties to Jamie's life and his family" (Solis, 2016, 91). After dispersal of the prison population in 1756, John secures a comfortable spot for Jamie at Helwater, England, as estate groom. During regular professional visits to ensure Jamie's welfare, John continues their partnership at chess games. By promising to foster William "Willie" Ransom, John uses marriage to Isobel Dunsany as a cover for rearing Jamie's illegitimate son. The triad reassures Jamie of his son's fostering while passing on to John the paternity that Jamie craves.

Over time, the trio diversify their complex association. Researcher Brittany Bales noted an improvement in homosexual/heterosexual comradery: "Over the last twenty years, the portrayal of gay, bisexual, and transgendered characters in film and television has evolved with the changing social politics and attitudes about sexuality" (Bales, 2020). Reunions in Jamaica at the governor's reception and at Fraser's Ridge over chess and whisky extend the companionship based on John's pretense to report on Willie's welfare, a sham to conceal an unrequited love of one man for another. The ruse takes on emergency ramifications after John agrees to superintend Brianna during her pregnancy at River Run. He extends his affection for the Frasers with gift books during Roger's recovery from muteness and a lens for Claire's microscope. By presenting a portrait of Willie in his teens, John enables Jamie to reveal the boy's existence to sister Brianna and end secrecy about kinship.

Source

Bales, Brittany, "Viewing History Through a Lens: The Influence of Film on Historical Consciousness," master's thesis, East Tennessee University, May 2020.

Dowling, Amber. "'Outlander' Review: A Season 5 Wedding Sets Up All Kinds of Family Drama," *IndieWire* (14 February 2020).

Ormond, Melissa. "Gender, Fantasy, and Empowerment in Diana Gabaldon's *Outlander*," master's thesis, DePaul University, 2009.

Solis, Sandi. "The Good, the Bad and Lord John Grey: Observations on Desire, Sex, Violence, Lust, and Love," *Adoring Outlander: Essays on Fandom, Genre and the Female Audience.* Jefferson, NC: McFarland, 2016, 82–93.

Gaelic

At crucial points in the *Outlander* TV romance, viewers, like the fictional Claire and Brianna Randall, need to interpret, speak, or write the Celtic tongue, for example, understanding political support in the Highlands for *Charlach* (Prince Charlie, 1:5), writing a note to Jamie from Sandringham's Belmont mansion, and discussing the Gaelic/English translation of the nickname "Bree" (4:9). The minority language of Ireland and much of Scotland and the Outer Hebrides supports a vigorous oral culture maintained by storytellers, historians, folklorists, mythographers, and harpers the quality of Gwyllyn the Bard and raconteurs Rupert MacKenzie and War Chief Dougal MacKenzie. Scots historians claim early medieval sire Goidel Glas as the common Gaelic ancestor and the fifth-century CE. British slave Patrick as their Christianizer. Conflicts with the English began in the twelfth century and initiated the anti–Gael movement, the impetus to Jacobitism.

When fictional time traveler Claire Randall arrives outside Inverness on

November 1, 1743, she encounters the underpinnings of the fourth and last Jacobite rising, a political impasse that the title figure in *Dr. Quinn, Medicine Women* encounters among nineteenth-century Cheyenne. Upon Claire's rescue from Captain Black Jack Randall by Murtagh Fitzgibbons Fraser, she realizes that language becomes a deliberate social divider among Dougal's band of outriders—the men alternate between English and vernacular Gaelic when excluding her. In private, the band thrashes out the possibility that she infiltrates their coterie as an English prostitute and spy. Her confrontations with suspicious males generates what author Coinneach Maclean of the University of Glasgow calls "the commoditisation of Gaelic culture in the image of the Highland Warrior" (Maclean, 2014).

At Castle Leoch, where residents speak, sing, and live Gaelic, even court ritual and entertainment lie beyond Claire's comprehension. At Laird Colum MacKenzie's evening gathering for staff and guests, Jamie translates for her the authentic ballads of Welsh harper Gwyllyn the Bard, a paid performer familiar with antique Gaelic lore. To a rapt audience of superstitious Highlanders, he sings of other time travelers passing through the Druidic stones at Craigh na Dun to different historical eras. The fact that past voyagers returned home from the time slip gives her hope of escaping Castle Leoch, where she is simultaneously a physical and language prisoner.

A Muted Culture

Luckily for the TV series cast, tutor Àdhamh Ó Broin aids actors in their lines, which reverence the sufferings of Highlanders after the Battle of Culloden on April 16, 1746. He explained to Paige Albiniak, an interviewer for *New York Post,* that British suppression of the ancient Highland tongue silenced Scots culture:

> My grandmother thought it was an injustice, and that someone in the family should learn it and bring it back…. If you want to destroy a people, destroy their language. It contains their entire history and their way of looking at the world [Albiniak, 2014].

Vernacular Gaelic speech returned to strategic use during World War II when Scots speakers duped the Nazis into believing that Highlanders were conversing in Russian.

From careful listening, the fictional Claire begins to recognize common words, particularly *Craigh na Dun* (rock fort), *sassenach* (outsider, especially English), *dinna fash* (don't worry), *laird* (chief), and *slàinte*, the everyday toast wishing good health for drinkers. During rent collection for Colum, the phrase *Guma fada beò Stiùbhart* (long live the Stuart) imparts duality in the two funds—one for rent and one for restoring King James III to Britain's throne (1:5). After Claire's wedding to Jamie, he honors her with the phrase *mo nighean donn* (my brown-haired lass, 1:9), a blandishment that returns in subsequent seasons along with *mo cridhe* (my heart, 5:11). Thus, dialogue interlaces episodes with essential native terms, a proof of authenticity.

Claire finds variant uses for Gaelic. In season one, episode fourteen, she enlarges on dual languages while singing a bawdy ditty to audiences that incorporates the patois of seduction. In confinement at Belmont, the mansion of the Duke of Sandringham, Claire pens a note to Jamie in make-do Gaelic that misspells "help" (2:11). The choice of language, a handy device for concealing her location, stymies Redcoats who might intercept the message. The attempt at communicating in indigenous dialect signals her sympathies with Highlanders and their mission to rid Britain of anti–Catholic Hanoverian monarch George II.

Jamie's continual speaking in English, French, Latin, and Gaelic leaves his wife out of his private thoughts, particularly two winsome prayers for her welfare and that of her *bairn* (baby, 1:3, 1:12). After meeting tenants at Lallybroch on quarter day, he mutters drunkenly in Gaelic and urges her to learn the language, an element of her union with a Scot and rise to the role of Lady Broch Tuarach. After the Battle of Culloden on April 16, 1746, on parting with Rupert MacKenzie for execution before the Redcoat firing squad, Jamie whispers his farewell in their home language, *Slàn leat, Ràibeirt* (Farewell, Rupert, 3:1). The musket shots that pierce Rupert echo the suppression of Scots culture, including the teaching of Gaelic in schools. A link to the past, Jamie's prison nickname Mac-Dubh (son of the dark) at Ardsmuir connects him to a dark time for surviving traitors to the Hanoverian crown.

WORDS OF HOME

The most gripping Gaelic exchange occurs in the sixteenth episode of season one, "To Ransom a Man's Soul." While Jamie struggles with shame and guilt at Father Anselm's Benedictine abbey and longs to die, he demands friend Willie's dirk. Jamie begs godfather Murtagh Fitzgibbons Fraser to end the torment: *Leig leam falbh* (Let me go die, 1:16). Because the patient pleads for release from suffering, Murtagh accuses him of *tha do cheann sa bhrochan* (sticking his head in the porridge), a jovial way of upbraiding and cajoling his godson for wanting to turn Claire into a widow. Murtagh continues relying on Gaelic in France by proposing slitting the throat of the bonnie prince, who speaks only English and French.

As the action moves from Scotland and France toward the Caribbean and Georgia, Gaelic seems less necessary for characters. The comfort of Scots Celtic returns at the opening of season four in which Gavin Hayes bravely accepts execution on the Wilmington gallows for killing an irate husband. When survivors gather in the tavern to hold a *caithris* (wake), best buddy Lesley begins a solo of *Eisd Ris* (Hear him, 4:1), a Gaelic lament for a man who died too young. The chorus draws Jamie, Claire, and Scots patrons into the lament, an upbeat salute to Gavin punctuated by tankard raps on the table. The compelling scene depicts "Eisd Ris" echoing in a city street, a testimonial to the influence of Highlands culture on coastal North Carolina.

Television reviewer Ann Gavin considered Gaelic an impediment for Scots-Americans like Hector and Jocasta Cameron and the Frasers. She remarked on language comprehension among "the struggles of learning a new culture in a new land" (Gavin, 2019). On parting from Young Ian at Shadow Lake, New York, in season four, episode 13, Jamie promises his nephew *cuimhnich* (remembrance, 4:13), the unfailing tie to kinship and the past. At the height of pre-combat tension in "The Ballad of Roger Mac," Jamie performs a watery ritual in Gaelic honoring Dougal's training in war readiness. Jamie's shock at Murtagh's death elicits one word, *ghoistidh* (godfather, 5:7), a plaintive statement of separation from his primary Gaelic interlocutor.

See also Highlanders; Language; Music.

Source

Albiniak, Paige. "House of Tutor: Dialect Coach Brings Gaelic Authenticity to *Outlander*," *New York Post* (22 August 2014).

Cruickshank, Janet and Robert McColl Millar, eds. *Before the Storm*. Aberdeen, Scotland: *Forum for Research on the Languages of Scotland and Ulster Triennial Meeting, Ayr*, 2017.

Gavin, Ann. "The Ultimate Ranking of Outlander Season 4 Episodes, www.outlandercast.com/2019/03/ranking-outlander-season-4-episodes.html, 13 March 2019.

Maclean, Coinneach. "The 'Tourist Gaze' on Gaelic Scotland," PhD thesis, University of Glasgow, 2014.

Gothic

The *Outlander* TV series incorporates an arresting number of Gothic images, paranormal motifs, and conventions, such as Ian's drinking of truth tea concocted by a witch doctor, flocks of birds departing the aura of Aaron Beardsley's trading post and escaping Arvin Hodgepile's raid on the big house, the appearance of Frank Randall's ghost to his daughter, a tax agent's corpse in a cask of crème de menthe, and Geillis's attendance at the burning of Granny Joan MacClellan at the stake in Cranesmuir. Examples stir immediacy:

- a dog harrying a bloodied boy's remains near Rose Hall
- the filling of a snake head with penicillin
- an episode of the Gothic TV soap *Dark Shadows*
- black beetles cleaning flesh from the goat Arabella's skull
- Marley's death from a stake through the throat
- Foret's use of hangman's grease as a salve
- Claire's whimpers while Jamie surveys the damage of gang rape.

The more graphic, unexplained, and disconcerting the Gothic element, like the birth of a deformed child in the film *Hawaii* and the murder from car exhaust in *House of Cards,* the more it increases psychic ambivalence and involves the viewer in suspenseful choices, intimate fears of enforced confinement and sexual violation, and forbidding consequences.

Standard situations from mid-nineteenth century classics envision Claire Fraser struggling for autonomy while immured by dominant males in a locus of evil—a dungeon laboratory stocked with outdated remedies in grubby bottles. In the open air, two of War Chief Dougal MacKenzie's guards trail her and question every move. After her arrest by Redcoats and marriage to Jamie Fraser, her new husband shinnies from fortress walls by rope and, with empty pistol and bare hands, saves her from a fiend. In Errol Flynn mode, the hero leaps with his damsel into deep water and swims to safety, a plunge similar to Sully's rescue of the title figure from a cliff in the TV series *Dr. Quinn, Medicine Woman.* Such recapitulation of time-tested platforms invests the production with daring and fervid attachment between lovers, the foundations of *Outlander* popularity.

THE FEMALE RESCUER

Inversions of typical scenarios increase the appeal of a central theme—liberation from turgid attitudes toward male and female. Before their wedding, Jamie admits his virginity and hopes that Claire will understand how to deflower a male, a postmodern regeneration of the sexually experienced hero. Upon his capture at the ambush of the Chisholm rent party, she gallops after him and cross-dresses for stage performances of a coded song, much like the troubadour Blondel who signaled Richard the Lionheart with an original couplet during his imprisonment at Dürnstein Castle near Vienna in late December 1192. Upon locating Jamie in the sub-levels of Wentworth Prison, Claire negotiates a mythic rescue deep in the dark cellblock, a feminist resetting of the Greek hero Theseus flushing out the Minotaur from a Cretan labyrinth.

In season one, the director risked losing impact in the fifteenth episode through chiaroscuro—limiting light on a bestial struggle. The grappling of Captain Black Jack Randall, Jamie, and the inarticulate guard Marley flickers in and out of focus, as does

Claire's attempt to unlock the rear entrance to Wentworth Prison, a parallel of Jack's aim to sodomize Jamie. The discovery of her husband creates a paradox—his reunion with a beloved wife, whom he must send away to avoid Jack's raping her. The standoff, however bedimmed in shadow, convinces Jamie to yield to a pervert, who ramps up the Gothic torture with a second blow to Jamie's left hand, impaling him to a table, an echo of Christ-like sufferings and a nullification of agency.

Photographing the Body

Much of the series relies on less obvious Gothic artifice that includes frequent camera pans of ordeals epitomized by the stitching of Jamie's mangled middle finger, lashing of inattentive Jacobite sentries in 1744, and Dougal's twisting a blade in the belly of Jeremy Foster, a British prisoner of war. By opening the first episode on Claire's treatment of torn bone and tendon in a World War II Allied field station in France, the anti-war theme resonates with stark anatomical studies of Geordie's gut and thigh wounds from a charging wild boar and, after the Battle of Prestonpans, Angus's mouth gurgling blood into his beard from the brunt of a cannon ball. At the height of Claire's delivery of stillborn daughter Faith at l'Hôpital des Anges in Paris, an overhead camera shot dramatizes legs splayed as Monsieur Foret, the royal executioner and volunteer surgeon, extracts the lifeless fetus, a trope for the Frasers' doomed hopes to impede the Jacobite rebellion.

In season three on board the English man-o'-war *Porpoise*, the villain is microbial. Claire advances from traveler to physician amid green-tinged faces and pockmarked torsos of seamen infected with typhoid fever, a bacterial scourge. With clear directions issued STAT, she directs the crew to upgrade sanitation by mopping up vomit and directing fresh air into the septic ward. The fight for sailors' lives does not halt frequent deaths, epitomized by the stitching of remains in canvas sacks. Elias Pound's insistence on forcing the final stitch through the corpse's nose offsets a common Gothic fear, the possibility of burying living people.

From the microcosm of a naval vessel, the action segues to another form of death-in-life, the struggles of African slaves. When the man-o'-war reaches Kingston, the series dramatizes unbearably hot Jamaican atmosphere, black children in cages, and slaves branded like cattle. Juxtaposed to people sold from bamboo crates, the voodoo rite of masked Maroons around a fire transfixes the Frasers with the enterprise of runaways. With costumed dance and gyrations, they intend to root out colonial evil, the indefensible British domination of island blacks in the name of agrarian profit and institutional promotions, the reason for John Grey's rise to Jamaica's governor.

Beasts by Dark

In the Carolinas in season four, costume Gothic in the wild dramatizes imitation shapeshifting similar in menace to Robert Montgomery's 1837 frontier horror novel *Nick of the Woods; or, The Jibbenainesay*. The colonial element exposes its menace in *Tskili Yona*, a sociopath masquerading as a hybrid wilderness monster on a par with Sasquatch, Nessie, and Yeti. In the darkness, an exiled Cherokee rapist and deranged bear-man mauls Jamie's horse Finley. Clad in ursine hide and claws, the mad shapeshifter threatens mountain man John Quincy Myers, whose midline laceration viewed at close range needs Claire's intervention against arterial bleeding and infection to skin and muscle.

On the loose by night, the bear-man, played by Flint Eagle, inserts what reviewers

EllenandJim term an "over-the-top St. George and the Dragon archetype" (Ellenand-Jim, 2019). In tenebrous environs similar to Theseus's groping for the minotaur on Crete, the phantasm threatens Jamie with hand-to-hand combat, an edgy wilderness resistance to white settlement. A stake through the abdomen impales the exile by directing his momentum against himself, a basic tactic of martial arts ensuring a quick kill. The grappling of man and beast foreshadows the erasure of wild animals and Appalachian tribes from their home ground as well as the rise of the Scots hero to *Yona Dihi* (bear killer, 4:4).

The fifth season enacts Gothicism during the Rowan County Militia's search for the Regulators who repay tax agent corruption with tar and feathering. To aid Josiah and Kezzie Beardsley, Claire and Jamie's scan of Indian trader Aaron and Fanny Beardsley's property heightens suspense and assaults the senses with gloom and foreboding. Among shadowy nooks and malodorous attic, Aaron lies moribund from stroke and torture. The worsening civil situation discloses a somber side of Jamie's conscience. The impromptu murder of Lieutenant Hamilton Knox frees Jamie from hanging for sedition in a site clouded with fireplace smoke, a symbol of the nebulous state of loyalties in Rowan County, North Carolina. Jamie retreats from savagery by rescuing a gray kitten named Adso, a reference to a tenth-century CE Benedictine monk who warned Christians of the anti–Christ.

See also Culloden; Grotesque; Star Chamber; Violent Deaths.

Source

EllenandJim. "Outlander, Season 4, from *Drums of Autumn*: The Colonialist American Past, a Book of Fathers & Ghosts," *EllenandJim* (10 February 2019).

Frankel, Valerie Estelle, ed. *Adoring Outlander: Essays on Fandom, Genre and the Female Audience.* Jefferson, NC: McFarland, 2016.

Modleski, Tania. *Loving with a Vengeance: Mass Produced Fantasies.* New York: Routledge, 1982.

Grotesque

Skillful dialogue and cinematography in the *Outlander* TV series twine Gothic conventions and scenarios with grotesque excess. Examples are as distorted and graphic as the open torso teaching Marsali Fraser anatomy, as repugnant as Marley sniffing his fingers after groping Claire's genitals, and as terrifying as Cherokees riddling the Muellers with flaming arrows. One scenario, Jamie's examination of a corrupt government agent's chest burned with hot tar, allows him an occluded reflection on his own flaying by cat-'-o-nine-tails, scarring his self-image. Editors Mary Harrod, a French professor at the University of Warwick, and Katarzyna Paskiewicz, an English philologist at the University of Barcelona, identify such melodrama with the standard paradigm—"overt villainy, persecution of the good, and final reward of virtue; … dark plottings, suspense, breathtaking peripety," an apt description of the lopping of Father Alexandre Ferigault's ear and his burning at the stake with Johiehon, his Mohawk lover (Harrod and Paskiewicz, 2017).

Visual horrors raise the viewer response to war and civil injustice. Because of "structural multiplicity and refusal of closure," critic Jorie Lagerwey, a media expert at University College Dublin, declared that *Outlander* "defies easy generic classification" (Lagerwey, 2017, 199, 198). She concluded that variant motifs produced an erotic romance, "an historical epic, a war show, a time-travel fantasy, and any number of other genres," all of which accommodate the grotesque (*ibid.,* 204). Among tourniquets, amputations, eye surgery, throat cautery, and other medical procedures, Claire's rescue of Ghanian slave Rufus at River Run from a massive iron hook through the left torso reflects extreme slave punishment and genocidal atrocity in the plantation South. In season five, the suffocation of a severely burned Dutch girl depicts the no-choice situation of finding her alive in agony after arson at the family cabin. Makeup leaves no doubt that she cannot survive the suffering and destruction of her skin. For the twelfth episode, a riveting view of Marsali injecting serum of water hemlock root into Lionel Brown's neck settles the issue of who will kill a vicious felon and how.

ANATOMICAL DESTRUCTION

In a setting of period injustice similar to Shirley Jackson's "The Lottery," Jamie's survival of two sessions of one hundred lashes each by dragoon Captain Black Jack Randall illustrates another grotesque form of bondage and dehumanization in English colonialism. To heighten the near-slaughter of an eighteen-year-old Scots prisoner, superb makeup intersperses a grid of crisscrossed stripes with pieces of flesh held by slivers of skin, the scraps of out-of-control British colonialism and anti–Scots genocide. Jamie accepts compassion from viewers of the scars—Claire Randall, Geneva Dunsany, Jacobites, renters on MacKenzie land. For a relative, Jared Fraser, the disfigurement establishes Jamie's reason for loathing the English.

Other depravity takes broad embodiments, from the nailing of the tanner's boy Novelli's ear to a Cranesmuir pillory to the shooting of Isaiah Morton in the back during the Battle of Alamance Creek, executing youths for treason at Culloden, and the slashing of an adversary's eyes by gambler and smuggler Stephen Bonnet. Author Lucie Armitt, a English professor at the University of Lincoln, justifies the "juxtaposition of competing worlds" in fantasy by emphasizing the "strange, fabulous or grotesque" (Armitt, 2020, 3). During rent collection, War Chief Dougal MacKenzie's company stands transfixed at sight of two Scots spread-eagled and crucified. Before the Jacobites honor them with Christian burial, the rotting remains, carved on the chest with T for treason, loll in mockery of St. Andrew's execution. The grisly position prefigures British disrespect to the Jacobite flag, which reduces Andrew's plight to a white × on a blue background.

MAN'S INHUMANITY

Sadism tends to afflict the vulnerable—Claire with Captain Jack Randall's knife raised to slice her nipples, Kezzie deafened by multiple blows to the ears, and Brianna with Bonnet's fist to the nose. Child abuse in the woods pits turncoat Corporal MacGregor against Fergus, a boy pinned under a saber that shears his left hand. The camera arouses pity and disgust by accentuating a spurting wrist and severed palm. The close-up anticipates worse scenarios in season five—Jamie preparing Aaron Beardsley for mercy killing to spare amputation of his charred foot and a snakebite turning gangrenous in Jamie's right thigh. The startling of viewers with the abhorrent allows cinematography to extend moral affronts with memorable pictures.

After-effects of atrocities spare the viewer unsavory scenes of cruelty, particularly the death of a white captive of the Mohawk from exhaustion and thirst, priestly exorcism of a demon from Tammas Baxter, Archibald Campbell's sundering by Jamaican Maroons, Greg Edgars's immolation, and, in season five, Fanny's burning of husband Aaron Beadsley's feet as recompense for beating her, two indentured servants, and four previous wives. In Claire's search of the slave quarters at Rose Hall, Jamaica, she locates the corpse of a young boy, the victim of kidnap and a slit throat. A target of Arabs, Hugh

Munro displays the scars of boiling oil poured on his legs by Islamic proselyters, a cultural malevolence like the slaughter of prisoners of war at Gallipoli in *The Water Diviner*. More disgusting, the root of Hugh's tongue is all that's left of slicing by Algerian Muslims. Similarly, the ghost of Otter Tooth presents his scalped head cleft down the center. The dehumanization of casualties recurs in season five with the hanging of Captain Roger MacKenzie, the wrong man in the wrong time and place, a faulty locus that he shares with the protagonist of Ambrose Bierce's Civil War story "An Occurrence at Owl Creek Bridge." An on-scene tracheotomy spares Roger's life, but cannot relieve months of muteness, dysphonia, and a monstrous dread—anticipation of death in the noose.

   See also Gothic.

Source

Armitt, Lucie. *Fantasy*. New York: Routledge, 2020.

Harrod, Mary, and Katarzyna Paszkiewicz. *Women Do Genre in Film and Television*. New York: Routledge, 2017.

Hobby, Blake, ed. *The Grotesque*. New York: Infobase, 2009.

Lagerwey, Jorie. "The Feminist *Game of Thrones*: *Outlander* and Gendered Discourses of TV Genre," *Women Do Genre in Film and Television*. London: Routledge, 2017, 198–212.

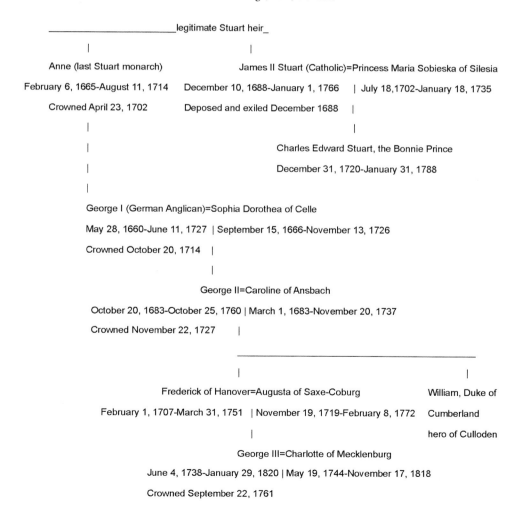

Hanover Dynasty

The installation of Britain's German monarchy made a vast impact on world history, particularly Anglicanism, colonialism, and the dominance of English. In an article for the *Journal of Military History,* Ciro Paoletti at Rome's State University La Sapienza described the Hanoverian victory over Stuart pretenders as the eventual assurance of an independent North America, freedom of religion, and English as the official language.

The rise of the German Hanovers in 1685 boded ill for the 317-year-old Stuart dynasty. A bloodless coup on November 11, 1688, ousted James II of England/James VII of Scotland to exile in Italy and replaced the Stuart dynasty with the House of Orange. The overthrow aroused the Jacobites, who adopted the Latinized name of James as a moniker for their exiled monarch, legitimized by the divine right to rule. The Scots efforts to dethrone an Anglican king ended in defeat at the Battle of Culloden on April 16, 1746.

Source

Holder, Geoff. *The Jacobites and the Supernatural.* Stroud, UK: Amberley, 2010.
Paoletti, Ciro. "The Battle of Culloden: A Pivotal Moment in World History," *Journal of Military History* 81:1 (2017).

Healing

Devaluation of a female healer reveals the eighteenth-century censure of women in ancillary roles, which Claire Fraser obscures under the print alias Dr. Rawlings. Forced into medical mode in the opening episodes of the TV chronicle *Outlander*, she faces unexpected nursing duties, including post-therapy care of a dislocated shoulder and bullet wound. Despite her looks and feistiness, according to Margaret McAllister at Queensland University and Donna Lee Brien at Central Queensland University: "She is also feared because she had access to health care knowledge that is completely foreign to the people of this time" (McAllister and Brien, 2020, 36). As a result, Scots treat her as a dark other for her expertise, especially knowledge of female reproduction, an influence that arouses the wrath of wife abuser Lionel Brown.

Throughout Claire's tenure in Scotland and the New World, combat training and herb research leads her to prisons, an epidemic-ridden British brig, childbirths, and deathbeds. For Margaret Campbell, a badgered fortuneteller, Claire combines the anti-migraine powers of tansy oil in mistletoe tea for seizure and valerian for sleep. At an Edinburgh brothel, she accepts advice from prostitutes on soaking sore genitals in herbal water and using vinegar or wine as a spermicide. The conversation about vaginal cleansing and contraception prefigures a friendship with Cherokee healer Adawehi in season four, when Claire studies native herbalism for pregnant women.

The Experienced Nurse

In the opening episode, to prevent broken bones from amateurish first aid, Claire volunteers to realign Jamie's right arm with the shoulder, a manipulation she repeats in Geordie in season five, episode eleven. Her assertive style annoys War Chief Dougal MacKenzie's outriders, whom she orders to provide a belt or cloth for a sling and disinfectant for a wound to Jamie's right shoulder. Male Highlanders detest her brusque manner, blasphemy, and swearing. They are more accustomed to the ministrations of Davie Beaton, a deceased charmer, apothecary, leech, or healer in the medieval Celtic tradition established on the isle of Islay in 1300. Until the mid–1700s, the Beatons or MacBethads maintained a Celtic healing service based on the manuscripts of Hippocrates, Avicenna, and Averroes and collected testimonials from healed Scots kings and the Frasers of Lovat.

Claire wisely claims no expertise beyond agency. At the rape scene engineered by Harry in the glade seven weeks into her time travel, she sensibly diagnoses her own symptoms of shock and sits to calm herself. For Laoghaire MacKenzie, she prescribes a love charm to spur Jamie's libido and, at a Brockton tavern, prepares a wounded British soldier's right arm for amputation. Other cases receive similar wise treatment:

ailment	patient	treatment	healer
aching stump (1:12)	Ian Murray	guelder rose; water pepper	Claire Fraser
alcoholic hysteria (1:10)	Dougal	sedative	Claire Fraser
alcohol poisoning (3:10)	Johansen	sleep it off	Claire Fraser
amputation (1:5)	English private	tourniquet	Claire Fraser
amputation (3:2)	Fergus Fraser	tourniquet, whisky	Jamie Fraser
anisomelia (5:10)	Eppie	a shoe lift to equalize leg length	Claire Fraser
ant bites (3:11)	Claire Fraser	salve	Mamacita
appendicitis/peritonitis (5:2)	Leith Farrish	calomel, bloodletting, mercury	Mrs. Farrish
assisted suicide (2:12, 2:13)	Colum	yellow jasmine	Claire Fraser
bayonet wound (4:1)	Stephen Bonnet	alcohol disinfectant, bandage	Claire Fraser
bed sores (5:3)	Aaron Beardsley	debriding with maggots	Fanny Beardsley
belly pain, gas (1:10)	Arthur Duncan	fennel	Claire Fraser
broken wrist (5:11)	Rose Brown	balm of Gilead, splint	Claire Fraser
bruised kidney (2:10)	Jamie Fraser	test urine for blood	Claire Fraser
bullet wound (1:1, 1:2)	Jamie Fraser	alcohol, dressing, comfrey, cherry bark	Claire Fraser
bullet wound (2:11)	Rupert	disinfect with whisky, surgery	Claire Fraser
burn (1:16)	Jamie Fraser	lavender oil	Jack Randall
burn (5:2)	Thomas	honey, antimony powder	Mrs. McGillivray
burn (5:3)	Aaron Beardsley	debriding	Claire Fraser
childlessness (1:13)	Claire Fraser	rosehip and raspberry leaf tea; egg beaten into lady's mantle	Jenny, Granny MacNab
chronic cough (2:2)	Alex Randall	*althea officinalis*	Claire Fraser
chronic cough (2:12)	Alex Randall	ginger, chamomile, arsenic, laudanum, milk thistle	Mary Hawkins
chronic cough (2:12)	Alex Randall	poultice, thornapple, coltsfoot	Claire Fraser
combat wound on left leg (5:7, 5:11)	Lionel Brown	rebandaging	Claire Fraser

ailment	patient	treatment	healer
contraception (2:3)	Suzette	mugwort	Master Raymond
cough from asthma (1:5)	Ned Gowan	thornapple smoke	Claire Fraser
crushed fingers (1:16)	Jamie Fraser	laudanum, massage, exercise	Claire, Brother Paul
cut forearm (3:11)	Claire Fraser	stitching, disinfect with alcohol	Yi Tien Cho, Jamie Fraser
despair (1:16)	Jamie Fraser	lavender oil	Claire Fraser
dislocated shoulder (1:1)	Jamie Fraser	alignment, sling, compresses	Claire Fraser
dislocated shoulder (5:11)	Geordie	alignment	Claire Fraser
ear removal (4:12)	Father Ferigault	washing	Roger MacKenzie
euthanasia (4:2)	Rufus	yellow jasmine	Claire Fraser
exposure, exhaustion (3:11)	Claire Fraser	rehydration, rest	Mamacita, Father Fogden
fake smallpox (2:6)	warehousemen	diagnosis	Le Havre doctors
fever (1:16)	Jamie Fraser	icy water	Brother Paul
fever (3:8)	Jamie Fraser	penicillin	Claire Fraser
gallstones (5:5)	Graham Menzies	penicillin	Claire Fraser
gangrene (5:3)	Aaron Beardsley	amputation	Claire Fraser
gashed arm (1:6)	Redcoat	opium, amputation	Redcoat surgeon
gashed leg (1:4)	boar hunter	binding and stitching	Claire Fraser
gashed thigh and belly (1:4)	Geordie	tourniquet	Claire Fraser
gashed left torso (1:10)	Jamie Fraser	stitching	Claire Fraser
gunshot to right upper arm (5:4)	Alicia Brown	disinfect with whisky	Claire Fraser
gunshot to right upper chest (5:7)	Isaiah Morton	bandage	Claire Fraser
hanging (5:8)	Roger	tracheotomy	Claire Fraser
head wound (3:9)	Manzetti	peppermint oil	Claire Fraser
hook in the side (4:2)	Rufus	laudanum, surgical removal	Claire Fraser
inguinal hernia (4:8)	Edmund Fanning	alcohol, surgical repair	Claire Fraser
malaria (4:9)	Lizzy Wemyss	Jesuit bark	Claire Fraser
mental agitation (3:7)	Margaret	mistletoe, valerian, tansy	Claire Fraser
morning sickness (4:1)	Marsali Fraser	peppermint, frequent small meals	Claire Fraser
murder (2:3)	clients	monkshood	Master Raymond
nightmares (2:2)	Jamie Fraser	Nepeta cataria	Claire Fraser
nightmares (2:2)	Jamie Fraser	Valeriana officinalis, humulus lupulus	Master Raymond
nightmares (2:7)	Fergus Fraser	counsel	Claire Fraser
poisoning (1:3)	Tammas Baxter	belladonna	Claire Fraser

ailment	patient	treatment	healer
poisoning (1:10)	Arthur Duncan	relieve choking	Claire Fraser
poisoning (2:4)	Claire Fraser	bitter cascara	Claire, Jamie Fraser
poisoning (2:7)	St. Germain	unknown substance	Master Raymond
pregnancy (2:4)	Louise de Rohan	abortion with barberry and hellebore	Claire Fraser
rape, shock (1:8)	Claire Fraser	rest	Claire Fraser
rape, shock (2:4)	Mary Hawkins	poppy syrup, herbal compress	Claire Fraser
rat bite (3:3)	Murtagh	milk thistle	Jamie Fraser
revenge (2:3)	enemies	bitter cascara	Master Raymond
scurvy (2:13)	Prince Charles	tea	Claire Fraser
scurvy (3:3)	prisoners	watercress	Jamie Fraser
seasickness (3:9)	Jamie Fraser	ginger tea	Claire Fraser
seasickness (3:9)	Jamie Fraser	acupuncture	Yi Tien Cho
shame, despair (2:4)	Mary Hawkins	counsel, soothing herbs	Claire Fraser
sleeplessness (1:3)	Arthur Duncan	valerian root	Geillis Duncan
smallpox (2:1)	two crewmen	diagnosis	Claire Fraser
snakebite (5:9)	Jamie Fraser	cut fang holes, suck out venom	Roger
snakebite (5:9)	Jamie Fraser	onion poultice, maggots, penicillin	Claire Fraser
splinter removal (2:11)	Ross	disinfect with whisky	Claire Fraser
sprained ankle (4:7)	Brianna	icy water	Brianna
tonsillitis (5:1, 5:5)	Josiah	surgery	Claire Fraser
tonsillitis (5:5)	Kezzie	penicillin, surgery	Claire Fraser
typhoid fever (3:9)	crewmen	fluids, cleanliness	Claire Fraser
typhoid fever carrier (3:9)	Howard	isolation	Claire Fraser
tooth removal (2:11)	woman	pull with tweezers	Claire Fraser
withered legs (1:3)	Colum	massage	Claire Fraser

Claire silently assesses Colum's withered legs, a crippling syndrome likely to shorten his life as it did nineteenth-century artist Henri de Toulouse-Lautrec. Her manipulation of Colum's lower back eases chronic pain with the only treatment available for a terminal condition. At the MacKenzie gathering, the wild boar hunt demands skilled treatment of goring by tusks, which maims one stalker's leg, leaving him with a limp, and kills Geordie from blood loss to belly and thigh. Claire's skill with patients eases him during his final moments through storytelling reminding him of home.

Patients in Need

Conception, pregnancy, and birthing recur in the series, introduced by Geillis Duncan's dance to the Earth Mother by firelight and the flaunting of her rounded belly to summon the Celtic deity. Claire's discovery of a dead infant on the fairy hill intro-duces the barbarism of the changeling, a staple fantasy of Celtic lore. At Lallybroch, the pre-birth manipulation and breech delivery of Margaret Ellen "Maggie" Murray deepens the trust and respect that Claire and Jenny have for each other. To hasten motherhood for Claire, Jenny quotes Scots folklore from Granny MacNab—drink rosehip and raspberry leaf tea and raw egg beaten into lady's mantle under a crescent moon. In subsequent epi-sodes, Claire battles ignorance based on superstition and astrology, particularly blood-letting and doses of mercury, by which Mrs. Farrish hastens her husband Leith's demise from appendicitis and peritonitis.

Because "nurse" carries a mixed meaning, Claire accepts "healer" or "guérisseuse" as a professional identification. On the gallop northwest to find Jamie, posing as an itiner-ant healer, she draws his attention by doctoring the results of accidents and illnesses. The motif prefigures her insistent treatment at Father Anselm's abbey of her husband's men-tal trauma, fever, and crushed left hand. The mangled fingers and palm require comfort and the setting of nine bones in a crude splint of twigs, wire, and linen followed by exer-cise and massage. Rehabilitation at the abbey involves Brother Paul, an efficient sickroom aid and supplier of cold stream water, bandages, and bowls of broth, the sources of nutri-tion that Jamie rejects.

With Brother Paul's encouragement, Claire supplies spiritual grounding to retrieve her mate's psyche from the ritual death of his honor and heterosexuality. Under her guidance, Jamie adapts society's norm to accommodate a spirit broken by the fiendish Captain Black Jack Randall. Jamie later weeps at failing to protect Fergus, the couple's foster son, against Corporal MacGregor's saber blow to the left wrist. By breaking barriers within the masculine ideal, Jamie outgrows a rigid knight's code to express a love and intimacy more enduring than he had felt before Randall victimized him.

Public Health

Upon diagnosing two cases of smallpox and subsequent deaths in Le Havre, Claire uses knowledge and experience to stop an epidemic at the French port before it inundates Paris. At Master Raymond's suggestion, the former nurse redirects her military train-ing and experience to a charity outreach and feeding station, the fictional l'Hôpital des Anges. The Catholic assistance to the poor during a famine dates to 651 CE and the open-ing of l'Hôtel-Dieu de Paris, the historic medical center near Notre Dame Cathedral. By liquidating personal property and holy vessels, St. Landry the Confessor, the bishop of Paris, operated the medical facility and soup kitchen for a decade with the aid of fifty Knights Hospitallers and one hundred Augustinian nuns. It served Parisians through the Renaissance.

Marriage poses an obstacle to Claire's fictional dedication to medicine. In a sulk, Jamie broods over her volunteerism, a proof to him of female self-indulgence. He fails to assess her career ambition and spirits revived from opportunities to treat the sick. The cinematography enhances noble labors with shots of stately columns and vaulted ceil-ing overshadowing patient cots and Claire's collection of urine. Jamie expects marriage to HIM to fill her day, along with her activities at the card and tea tables of leisured rich women. The disconnect adds a twentieth-century fault to a self-centered husband still rooted in 1744.

Dramatic Encounters

In addition to bedside care, Claire's skill at psychological counsel heals characters who come to her for advice and comfort. She exerts compassion for son-in-law Roger MacKenzie for nearly dying in a noose, to Alicia Brown for attempted suicide, to marital abuse victims Fanny Beardsley and Rose Brown, and to rape victims Mary Hawkins, Fergus, Jamie, and Bree. Of the nurse's importance to Mary, producer Meril Davis described her as a "mentor [whose] confidence and empowerment have rubbed off" (Vineyard, 2016). To rid Fergus of nightmares, Claire evokes details of child sodomy. Just as she reassures Mary of her blamelessness for rape, Claire solaces Fergus for his shame and guilt for the duel that incriminates Jamie and sends him to the Bastille.

The TV series stresses the parenting that draws Fergus and, to some degree, Mary into an *ad hoc* Fraser nuclear family under Claire's guidance. Imitating Claire's agency, Mary assumes control of purchasing medicines and dispensing them at McGillivrey's boarding house to ease chronic respiratory distress in her lover, Alex Randall. In Wilmington, Claire becomes gentle stepmother and adviser to Marsali Fraser's pregnancy by suggesting chewing peppermint and eating small meals as cures for morning sickness, an ailment that previously assailed Claire from the fishy smells of a French harbor at Le Havre.

Claire involves helpers in surgery, including Yi Tien Cho, Brother Paul, Brianna, Marsali, Governor William Tryon, Mr. and Mrs. Bug, Jamie, and Young Ian. The firing of bird shot at Lallybroch into Jamie's left shoulder jars Claire into surgical mode. The scene interrupts her furious departure from the eighteenth-century marriage and replaces anger at Jamie's concealed second wedlock with removal of five shot, one of which endangers an artery in his left underarm. Stitching and tending the wound and monitoring fever ease the tension, giving Jamie a chance to explain why he deceived Claire about marrying Laoghaire. The scene exonerates Claire for stealing a hypodermic syringe and penicillin from a Boston hospital, her fallback treatment for fever and the beginning of a pharmaceutical lab at Fraser's Ridge.

Because of her knowledge of typhoid fever and 1838 research by Englishman William Budd, Claire intervenes in a shipboard epidemic on the English ship *Porpoise*, a 74-gun man-o'-war already stripped of officers and operating on 75 percent crew strength. The newness of the treatment for a salmonella bacterium angers sailors, especially the cook, who charges Claire with an hysterical—read: female—response to the outbreak. Because more men fall sick and die during the 6- to 30-day incubation period, he distrusts her methods of cleanliness, sterilizing water, and a liquid diet. The episode creates respect for her maintenance of antisepsis protocols that Joseph Lister introduced in 1865.

A Demanding Career

In Wilmington, the series borrows from *Dr. Quinn, Medicine Woman* the motif of an emergency hernia operation on Edmund Fanning in front of gawking witnesses in the theater lobby and another intervention in season five, episode eight with a tracheotomy to relieve Roger's near asphyxiation by a noose. Equipped with a medical kit outfitted with a microscope, Claire commandeers helpers to collect knife, needle, and thread and involves Governor William Tryon as surgical assistant. On the frontier, she treats John Quincy Myers for bear clawing on his torso and delivers Petronella Mueller's baby daughter, named Clara in the midwife's honor. At the big house on Fraser's Ridge, she serves patients waiting on the porch, including Josiah Beardsley, a hunter who suffers chronic tonsillitis. In casual conversation with other women, she encourages the use of raw honey as a topical ointment on burns.

In the field with the Rowan County Militia at Brownsville, Claire lacks appropriate equipment and penicillin for killing bacteria, which Jamie dubs "wee beasties" (5:1). Author Stephen J. Greenberg notes in an essay for the *Journal of the Medical Library Association* that Claire "benefits from the fact that she has had the full series of vaccinations that any modern soldier and most civilians would have had as a matter of course but which would have been almost magical in the past" (Greenberg, 2020, 311). Experience with twentieth-century healing frustrates her as she applies period herbalism in place of more sophisticated pharmaceuticals.

LEARNED ASSISTANTS

Another echo of *Dr. Quinn,* Claire's training of Marsali Fraser in anatomy produces an assistant for the surgical theater just as frontier physician Michaela Quinn trained stepdaughter Kathleen and taught her to recognize malaria. Marsali also monitors the growth of bread mold into penicillium, which she and Claire observe under the microscope. For the double tonsillectomies of the Beardsley twins, a demanding regimen calls for Marsali as surgical nurse to supply scalpel and cork. Claire also needs the aid of Mr. Bug and Lizzy, who drape the patients and steady the lantern. In later collaborations, Claire discusses with Marsali the missing water hemlock roots, a cure for migraine that could also result in suicide.

A surprise touch of magical thinking amid realistic pioneer medicine, before the amputation of Jamie's leg, Brianna's transformation of a snake head into a hypodermic syringe enables Claire to treat his infected wound with penicillin. In commentary, Kayti Burt, a reviewer for *Den of Geek,* mused "on the mortality of this man who has survived wars, but is merely mortal and living in pre–Revolutionary North Carolina where a broken needle can mean the difference between life or death" (Burt, 2020). To replace the syringe that Lionel Brown deliberately smashes, Claire draws a barrel for a glassblower to replace. Greenberg characterizes her ingenuity as "imaginative to the point of the incredulous, but still entirely feasible, every time" (Greenberg, 2020, 313).

In the season five finale, a misogynist retaliates against Claire for empowering women. Of abductor Lionel Brown, TV critic Jennifer Still stated, "The level of arrogance Lionel possessed likely kept him from thinking too deeply on his grand plan to drag Claire to Brownsville to 'repent' for spreading her modern medical knowledge" (Still, 2020). A dramatic irony ends his bluster after Claire refuses to seek vengeance under strictures of the Hippocratic Oath. Marsali, who took no oath, energetically stabs him in the neck with a syringe of water hemlock poison, a rapid demise for a woman-hating fiend. In reference to Lionel's anti-woman rancor, Still added, "How disgusting it is that crimes like these still go on today" (*ibid.*).

See also Acupuncture/Acupressure; Childbirth; Combat Nursing; Euthanasia; Prophecy.

Source

Burt, Kayti. "*Outlander*: Does Jamie Die in the Books?," *Den of Geek* (20 April 2020).

Gehring, Abigail. *The Illustrated Encyclopedia of Natural Remedies.* New York: Skyhorse, 2020.

Greenberg, Stephen J. "Claire Fraser, RN, MD, OMG: History of Medicine in the *Outlander* Novels and Series," *Journal of the Medical Library Association* 108:2 (April 2020): 310–313.

McAllister, Margaret, and Donna Lee Brien. *Paradoxes in Nurses' Identity, Culture and Image: The Shadow Side of Nursing.* Abingdon, UK: Routledge, 2020.

"The Physicians of the Western Islands," *British Medical Journal* (19 May 1906): 1178.

Ross, Anne. *Folklore of the Scottish Highlands.* Stroud, UK: History Press, 2000.

Still, Jennifer. "'Outlander' Season 5 Finale Recap: 'Never My Love,'" *Decider* (11 May 2020).

Vineyard, Jennifer. "How *Outlander*'s Revenge Scene Came Together," *Vulture* (19 June 2016).

Heirlooms

Clan loyalties and family history endear keepsakes to *Outlander* characters as devoted as Murtagh Fitzgibbons Fraser to his tartan scrap and crest, Claire to the dragonfly in amber, and Jamie to his sword, which he wills to grandson Jemmy MacKenzie. From the past, the list includes Brian Fraser's five-lobed Viking blade and ruby ring, the Rev. Reginald Wakefield's Stuart wall banner, the bonnie prince's travel canteen, and John Grey's sapphire pendant, a dual reminder of shared history with Jamie in prison and of Grey's passion for a heterosexual male. Combat elevates items to family relics. Over two centuries, the engraved handle of Frank Randall's razor passes down from Captain Black Jack Randall, an iconic blade wielded by a sociopath.

From war memories, the chronicle glimpses regrets. Roger MacKenzie's reclaiming of a toy two-seater spitfire from the attic introduces a late-in-life keepsake. He handles the plane as though reliving incidents in his orphaning during World War II, which took his father Jerry, a spitfire pilot. In a post–Culloden period, when the British harass Jacobites, Jamie reviles Redcoat vandalism of the wall-mounted Fraser crest. The diagonal slash nudges him to end six years of hiding and surrender to protect Lallybroch from more serious incursion.

Integral to the plot, Jamie's carved snake, marked with "Sawny," a child's pronunciation of Alexander, summons memories of Willie Fraser, an older brother who died in 1726. The disappearance of Sawny in Paris instigates a household search and Jamie's apprehension of Fergus, the brothel pickpocket at La Maison de Madame Elise. Jamie's carving of a similar snake in 1764 for his son William "Willie" Ransom epitomizes a love for a six-year-old offspring. In a female version of heirlooms, Jenny's gift of bracelets made from a wild boar's tusks passes on family affections—Murtagh for Ellen Fraser, Ellen for daughter Jenny, and Jenny for her English sister-in-law Claire. For Murtagh, recovery of the bracelets prompts him to confess unrequited love for Jamie's mother.

Ellen's Scots pearls, a post-nuptial gift to Claire from Jamie, derive from Scottish Travellers, a Highlands name for Gypsies who harvest rare rose-pink spheres from freshwater mussels in the River Tay. The necklace passes to Claire with a touch of melancholy at Ellen's death in 1730 during childbirth. Suggesting Jamie's mother hunger, the ache in the groom's voice recognizes Claire's femininity and a possible demise like Ellen's. At the climax of Jamie's rescue from Wentworth Prison, the epic employs coincidence tying Marcus MacRannach with Ellen's wedding day and his gift of a pearl necklace. Remaining in Claire's possession, the strand eventually follows the matrilineage from ownership by Ellen to Claire, from Claire to Mrs. Graham, willed to Fiona, back to Claire, and on to Brianna for adorning her wedding dress.

Sacred Spoons

Jamie's presentation of treasured silverware further bonds Claire with the Frasers. The apostles' spoons depict Jesus's twelve followers at the Last Supper, a touchstone of the sacramental eucharist. Initiated in the early 1300s in Husting, England, the late medieval baptismal gift honored Jesus or the Virgin Mary or St. Paul with a thirteenth spoon. In England, Lithuania, Italy, Spain, France, Finland, and Germany during the Tudor era and Reformation, a nimbus topped each figure. In 1913, expert H.D. Ellis observed, "This halo I take to be, if not the primitive and original form in which the sanctity of the Apostle was expressed, at all events the most ancient now known" (Ellis, 1913, 284).

Emblems identified each apostle—Andrew with a cross, Bartholomew and his butcher knife, James the Greater holding walking stick and book, James the Lesser grasping a laundry bat, John raising a chalice, Judas Iscariot clutching a moneybag, Jude Thaddeus equipped with a carpentry rule or T square, Matthew bearing a wallet or bladed weapon, Philip gripping a staff or loaves of bread, Simon clutching a saw or club, Simon Peter carrying a fish or key, Thomas lofting a spear, and Christ lifting the globe topped by a cross. Where Judas Iscariot gave place to St. Matthias, the latter bore an axe. Other alterations in the standard twelve apostles commemorated gospel authors Luke and Mark with scroll and wings.

SIGNIFICANT BELONGINGS

Season four awards Brianna an engraved bracelet and heart-shaped charm, a lover's gift. The jingle inscribed on the inside reprises an ambiguous French rhyme that ponders degrees of affection from passionate to nonexistent. Although she rejects Roger's marriage proposal at the clan gathering on Grandfather Mountain, she continues wearing the bauble and uses its gemstone to ensure her passage through the stones at Craigh na Dun. When the romance progresses to handfasting, the couple substitute the bracelet for a ring. Dramatic irony follows an amorous embrace, argument, and Roger's departure in anger. Brianna, on her way to the inn, discovers Claire's precious wedding ring and incites Stephen Bonnet, a thief, smuggler, murderer, and rapist. The heirlooms generate marital problems, primarily Brianna's uncertainty about which male sired her son Jemmy, a plight that continues in season five, episode nine with Bonnet's alleged rights to River Run, Jemmy's inheritance.

For the opening of season five, Governor William Tryon pressures Jamie into retreating into Highlander persona. Jamie turns to his chest of Scots mementos for identity. The leather-covered lid, outlined in nail heads, stows kilt, plaid, and blade, vestiges of a military career. In Jacobite uniform, Jamie retrieves some of the confidence lost from Tryon's scolding that the Regulators and leader Murtagh Fitzgibbons Fraser still roam free. The tokens, for all their symbolism and nostalgia, close the past in Jamie's history after he accepts a British army tunic at the Battle of Alamance Creek on May 16, 1771. The brief uniforming in red commits him to New World honors as colonel of the Rowan County Militia and fighter for American independence.

HURTFUL MEMORIES

The backstory revealed in season five, episode six divulges a horrendous loss to Hector and Jocasta Cameron. As they flee the Highlands after the Battle of Culloden on April 16, 1746, a Redcoat patrol discovers their transport of French gold from Louis XV toward the coast. In the melee that follows, two dragoons die; Hector inadvertently shoots Morna. Hysterical beyond comfort, as the carriage hurries away, Jocasta clutches her daughter's blue hair ribbon. In 1771 before union with Duncan Innes, her fourth husband, Jocasta reveals a sorrow that gnaws for a quarter century. The gold bars that purchased River Run intimate ill-gotten wealth and the abandonment of Jocasta's third and last daughter on the moor. Flight from Scotland validates the family's split with the past and affirms their destiny as investors in a New World plantation manned by African slaves.

The episode fills in details that a dazed wanderer, tacksman Duncan Kerr, mutters to Jamie at Ardsmuir Prison. Duncan correctly identifies the gold as cursed and the seeker as a white witch, a reference to Geillis Duncan and her hunt for War Chief Dougal Mackenzie's treasure box. Ironically, Duncan Innes presents Jocasta a pre-wedding gift—a lavender pillow embroidered with *Luceo non Uro* (I shine not burn), the MacKenzie motto, evidence of clan and family pride. At a significant scene mourning Murtagh's combat death, Jocasta wears the Fraser crest that he gave her before her wedding. Claire's retrieval of the crest from Murtagh's corpse indicates the family's love and admiration for Jamie's godfather.

See also Coincidence; Matrilineage; Treasure; Unrequited Love.

Source

Ellis, H.D. "Some Steps in the Evolution of the Apostle Spoon," *Burlington Magazine for Connoisseurs* 23:125 (August 1913): 283–285, 287.

Peck, Ashlee. "*Outlander*'s Scottish History," *FamilyTree*, www.familytreemagazine.com/entertainment/26578/#.

Radford, Mona A., and Edwin Radford. *Encyclopaedia of Superstitions*. New York: Home Farm Books, 2013.

Vineyard, Jennifer. "What to Remember before the 'Outlander' Season 3 Premiere," *New York Times* (8 September 2017).

Helwater

At the aristocratic Helwater estate in northwestern England in 1756 among privileged British adversaries that Jamie fought at Culloden a decade earlier, he begins a life incognito as an ex-con from Ardsmuir Prison. Filming places the fictional Lake District manor at Gosford House, a three-story neoclassic country estate in East Lothian on the Firth of Forth, a setting for the film *The House of Mirth*. The design features a two-story gate, colonnades, a marble hall and dual staircase, Palladian windows, pyramidal mausoleum, and symmetrical pavilions. Riding trails penetrate thick forests and encircle ponds, a waterfall, boathouse, and lavish stables. Architect Robert Adam built the mansion on 5,000 wooded acres in 1781 for Janet Charteris and James Wemyss, the Earl of Wemyss, and for their second son Francis Charteris and wife Catherine Gordon. Janet and James's Jacobite son, David Wemyss claimed to be a scion of the prestigious Sinclairs, Douglases, and Malcolm I dating to 943. David served on the staff of Bonnie Prince Charlie and, in 1746, fled to France, forfeiting his claim on Gosford House.

An understanding between fictional Major John Grey and Lord William Dunsany enables Jamie, a former traitor, to assume a semi-normal task as indentured groom in upscale stables where horses share his captivity. However, othering among the English demeans his Highlander heritage and red hair. Deceptions mount with his name change to Alexander "Mac" MacKenzie. The artifice conceals from Louisa Dunsany that he fought in the Battle of Prestonpans on September 21, 1745, when her son, Captain Gordon Dunsany, died in combat against the victorious Jacobites.

SIRING A SON

Attendance on the Dunsanys reduces the fictional protagonist to a new form of incarceration, this time in tailored uniform and obsequious manners. While attending to carriage upkeep and the equestrian needs of sisters Isobel and Geneva Dunsany, Jamie identifies Geneva's connivance as blackmail while he hauls and dumps manure, a symbol of her deceit. At the time of her betrothal to the elderly Earl of Ellesmere, she coerces "Red Jamie" into ending her virginity, a coition that he at first resists as unfitting for people of markedly different castes (3:4).

Another in a string of *Outlander* TV series rapes, Geneva's sexual coercion takes place behind locked doors in a posh boudoir engulfed in florid wallpaper. Before entering her four-poster bed, Jamie respects Geneva's modesty and slowly disrobes for her inspection. With a haughty air, she allows him to touch her skin and remove a frothy peignoir before puncturing her maidenhead. The ending of her virginity perpetuates one of Hollywood's favorite myths—that a single bedding results in instant conception.

The overbearing estates of Helwater and Ellesmere, both filmed at Gosford House, foreground Jamie's first glimpse of son William "Willie" Ransom in 1758. The groom rescues his bastard son from Ellesmere's blade within hours of the boy's birth and Geneva's death from hemorrhage. With a pistol shot to the head, Jamie fells the jealous husband and embraces the swaddled orphan. In a brief fatherly comment to the baby in his pram, Jamie declares himself nearby. He implies protection and affection, but wills himself to tolerate another form of bondage and silencing for the next six years.

FATHERING A LORD

While six-year-old Willie practices riding in 1764, people notice his resemblance to the looks and posture of Mac, his riding coach. The paradox of a birth father trying to discipline a spoiled son while calling him milord and catering to his mischief worsens the situation for Jamie, who must return to Scotland to avoid a scandal. Before leaving, he christens Willie in a secret Roman Catholic sacrament and renames him William James, a folk baptism with the father's first name. Departure from Helwater reduces Jamie to tears. Music director Bear McCreary pairs the separation with the apocalyptic lyrics of "A Hard Rain Is Gonna Fall," composer Bob Dylan's anti-war anthem.

The song proves prophetic. Jamie leaves behind a twisted tale of unrequited love: Lord John Grey's lust for Jamie and marriage to Isobel Dunsany, who nurtures a crush on her noble soldier boy. After testing his bisexuality in London, John agrees to foster Willie as stepfather. Cinematography highlights a ponderous estate and presumes that John and Isobel can flourish as man and wife and as parents to a wealthy son, the 9th Earl of Ellesmere. In a later reunion with Jamie, the boy displays aristocratic pretensions groomed at Helwater to maintain a patrician profile. In fall 1772 at age fourteen, William begins his preparation for replacing his father, Lord Dunsany, and becoming an earl.

See also Names; Unrequited Love.

Source

Cliffe, Nicole. "*Outlander* Recap: Indecent Proposal," *Vulture* (1 October 2017).

Gordon, Diane. "'Outlander' Recap: 'Of Lost Things' Introduces the Dunsanys, Another Child for Jamie and a New Love Story," *Variety* (1 October 2017).

"Gosford House," www.thecastlesofscotland.co.uk/the-best-castles/stately-homes-and-mansions/gosford-house/.

Highlanders

Through script and cinematography, the *Outlander* TV romance introduces the uniqueness of fictionalized Scots at the height of their culture, when British army posters featured iron-jawed Highlanders as recruiting icons. The pictorial figure flourishes in romanticized re-creations, the focus of Sir Walter Scott's novels, Rudyard Kipling's poems and short stories, and current gatherings of the clans in Halifax, Nova Scotia, and Grandfather Mountain, North Carolina. In season one, stress on the foul odors of rescuer Murtagh Fitzgibbons Fraser enhances the stereotype of a feral race of hard-eyed, sensual men capable of defending Scotland's far north and testing Claire Beauchamp's virtue. At the arrival of War Chief Dougal MacKenzie with his outriders to the courtyard of Castle Leoch, housekeeper Glenna "Mrs. Fitz" Fitzgibbons rushes from the kitchen to welcome them, offer breakfast, and tease Murtagh about smelling like sheep dung, the essence of an agrarian society.

Cinema critic Courtney A. Hoffman remarked that "The Highlands, though deeply entwined with England in terms of history, [are] a nearly blank canvas for filmic portrayal," especially the northern Scots as victims of English imperialism (Hoffman, 2017, 106). The first episode situates in semi-darkness an unknown Highlander in tam, tartan, and kilt watching Claire from an Inverness street on Samhain Eve, 1945. The pose suggests anticipation, as though a lover awaits an eventual union with the time traveler through Craigh na Dun. The fictional circle of magic stones, a carryover from the ritualized past, exemplifies Celtic architecture featuring menhirs like the historic Callanish circle, dating to 2900 BCE on Lewis island in the Outer Hebrides.

A British imperial legacy, Scots pride in ethnic dress invigorated traditional highland fling and sword dance, ceilidhs and bouts of drinking, manly posturing, and military might, which contributed to the notion that all Highlanders were drunken and uncivil, even brutal or murderous. Fictional Laird Colum Ban Campbell MacKenzie sets an example of pride and authority by threatening a tailor for trying to cover his withered legs with a long coat. He chastises brother Dougal, nephew Jamie, and attorney Ned Gowan for soliciting funds to restore King James III to the throne. At Beaufort Castle, "Himself" debates nephew Jamie and brother-in-law Lord Simon Lovat until reaching a neutrality pact banning the Frasers and MacKenzies from the Jacobite uprising of 1745.

Dramatization differentiates between the kilted, feather-bonneted wedge attacks set to the skirl of bagpipes and controlled enfilade of the uniformed British army that Jamie masters in France during the continental wars. Season two depicts Dougal, a more vigorous, less rational character, as leader of the infamous "highland charge" (2:10). The skirmish tactic sends sprinting combatants camouflaged in mud down a declivity while wielding claymores. Bare-chested, they shriek battle cries, a foreshadowing of the antebellum South's rebel yell. Historically, lowlanders and Redcoats tended to avoid such military displays as violations of sane combat principles. For the sake of humor, the *Outlander* cast questions the fighting fervor of Angus Mohr, a small-framed soldier who prefers knifing opponents with the *sgian dubh* to battling with his sword. At his death from a cannon blast, he leaves to his pal, Rupert MacKenzie, a weapon seldom— or never—used.

Dougal disagrees with nephew Jamie on the need for indoctrination in European methods and abandoning the tumultuous raids that brought Highlanders fame/infamy.

Among the fictional Scots-Americans in North Carolina, Governor William Tryon regards Jamie as a natural leader of Highlanders. Tryon's opinion voices the romanticized United Kingdom ideology of "martial races ... men who are biologically or culturally predisposed to the arts of war," a stereotype that prevailed into the nineteenth century (Danilova and Purnell, 2019, 4). Prejudice favoring the macho Scot heightened the legend of the battle-crazed, fearless, professional warrior who out-performed disciplined recruits from the British colonies, a fabrication that prevails in the films *Highlander, Braveheart,* and *Outlaw King* and in museum displays of the Seaforth, Cameroonians, Black Watch, Royal Regiment of Scotland, Gordon Highlanders, and Royal Highlander Fusiliers.

See also Celtic Beliefs; Kilts; Scots Culture.

Source

Danilova, Nataliya, and Kandida Purnell. "The 'Museumification' of the Scottish Soldier and the Meaning-making of Britain's wars," *Critical Military Studies* 5:2 (2019): 1–19.

Gold, John R., and Margaret M. Gold. "The Graves of the Gallant Highlanders," *History & Memory* 19:1 (Spring/Summer 2007): 5–38.

Hoffman, Courtney A. "How to Be a Woman in the Highlands: A Feminist Portrayal of Scotland in *Outlander,*" *The Cinematic Eighteenth Century.* New York: Routledge, 2017, 103–117.

Strachan, Hew. "Scotland's Military Identity," *Scottish Historical Review* 85:2 (2007): 315–332.

Homosexuality

The theme of homosexuality invests much of the *Outlander* TV narrative, in which romantic melodrama endorses equality in desire, sexual relations, and marriage. Jamie identifies at age sixteen his appeal to Clarence Marylebone, the Duke of Sandringham, a flashy aristocrat secretly allied with Captain Jonathan "Black Jack" Randall, an infamous pervert. Sandringham's characterization undermines scenes that present him as a player in royal politics. By tricking him out in overdone suit, wig, stylized demeanor, and Hollywoodized "faggy" voice proclaiming "poppycock" and "libelous falsities," the series demeans him into a caricature based on outworn notions of queerness (2:2). His overt lust for Jamie moves the plot along, but at a cost to realism. The clownish decapitation scene restores dignity and worth to Murtagh Fitzgibbons Fraser, his executioner, and relegates Sandringham to the growing bone pile. The episode does nothing to further LGBTQ dignity.

Variance between the effete Sandringham and monstrous Jack Randall poses extreme views of the homosexual male, particularly prison authorities who exploit inmate control. Jamie, lacking experience, debates whether to accept Jack's deal of "buggery" in exchange for release from a second flogging (1:12). Significant to the decision, his father's unconcern for sexual union with Jack highlights Brian's more pressing opposition to yielding to the British. Jack's pursuit of Jamie reaches its height near the end of season one with anal rape. Bargaining over means of death offers the prisoner a favor, an insignificant bargaining chip in a sickening incarceration.

Perhaps the most controversial of elements, the lengthy intercutting of scenes between Jack and Jamie caresses overlong actor Sam Heughan's musculature. Critics question intercalary versions in episodes fifteen and sixteen, which account for the prisoner's post-traumatic stress syndrome. Puzzling in its psychological drama, Jack's seduction of Jamie with kisses, groping his crotch, and admiring his physique creates a paradox of ruined, bloody left hand, vicious anal penetration, and threats to retrieve

Claire from safety. Jack follows up sodomy with mind games ending in Jamie's branding himself with the JR seal, an extension of the Redcoat carving T for treason in crucified Jacobites.

The plot overlooks how a nurse as thorough as Claire does not find the burned-on circle during her initial examination of Jamie's hurts beneath a tabard hospital gown. By posing as the absent wife, Jack brings his victim to climax and deeper despair. Jamie's horror at his response to anal lovemaking disgusts the warrior, who views his persona in terms of solid masculinity. By concluding season one with the conception of Faith— ostensibly at Lallybroch—the series reduces psychic stress and rewards the viewer with hope for a normal future for the Frasers.

Season three depicts John Grey confessing love for a deceased soldier, an opening for an overture to MacDubh, Jamie's prison moniker. By touching Jamie's hand, John elicits a death threat, an overreaction that recurs after Phillip Wylie manhandles Claire. John's tears foretell encounters at the governor's mansion in Kingston, Jamaica; in the North Carolina wilderness with a heterosexual man he longs to possess; and during polite minuets and sarabandes at River Run, where John's widowerhood appeals to young women. His high-minded refusal to accept Jamie's body honors Wille's need for a foster father. In noble exchanges, John refutes the dynamics of Black Jack Randall, ostensibly courteous on the surface, but seething with vicious lusts underneath.

See also Jack Randall; Rape.

Source

Donelan, Carol. "'Sing Me a Song of a Lass That Is Gone': Myth and Meaning in the Starz Original Series Outlander," *Quarterly Review of Film and Video* 35:1 (2018): 31–53.

Frankel, Valerie Estelle, ed. *Outlander's Sassenachs: Essays on Gender, Race, Orientation and the Other in the Novels and Television Series*. Jefferson, NC: McFarland, 2016.

Honor

At highs and lows in Jamie Fraser's televised story, he represents the Scots paragon of conditioned soldier, outlaw, polished intellectual, and frontier colonel. *Town & Country* journalist Caroline Hallemann characterizes his ethos as a family trait "explicit and ingrained from the cradle" (Hallemann, 2020). After delivering Lionel Brown's body to brother Richard, Jamie nods respectfully and resists any urge to broaden antagonisms. When he falls short of ideal chivalry, reprehensible behavior wounds his soul (*ibid.*). His commitment to right thinking reveres his parents, Brian and Ellen MacKenzie Fraser, but mostly Claire. In the season five finale, he recognizes her value to his better traits: "A man's life springs from his woman's bones and in her blood is his honor christened" (5:12).

From a first encounter with Claire in the *Outlander* TV epic, Jamie pledges gentlemanly behavior as well as protection from less scrupulous residents at Castle Leoch. The promise warns that lone women, especially English outlanders, are fair game. In his late teens, rebellion against Captain Black Jack Randall's Redcoat squad fails to protect sister Jenny from humiliation and potential assault. Out of obligation to a female relative, Jamie prefers having his throat slit than give up Jenny to a sexual opportunist. For taking Laoghaire's punishment for disobedience, Jamie suffers battery, then bows to his uncles Colum and Dougal, Laoghaire's father, and Rupert MacKenzie, a gesture of obeisance to clan tradition. Under Claire's medical treatment once more, Jamie justifies rescuing Laoghaire's reputation, an abstract that he values for himself and others.

The Victim

For Jamie's public image, he hesitates to display a scarred back, in part because of dignity and personal pride. He chooses not to show Auld Alec, the stable manager, the results of a double flogging lest Alec think him a pitiable victim of two hundred strokes with the cat o' nine tails. The elder Ian Murray has similar reservations about people recoiling from his amputated right leg and reducing him from fighting man to useless cripple. Into adulthood, both Ian and Jamie retain the code of manhood developed during their youthful military forays in Silesia, France, and Spain.

For Jamie, even negotiations with his Redcoat harasser at Fort William call for fealty to one's word and a refusal to feed Jack's obsession with his handiwork with a cat-'o-nine-tails. When Jack lies unconscious on the chamber floor, Jamie is not tempted to murder a defenseless opponent, even one who dishonored Jenny and allegedly sired her first child, Jamie's namesake. With the same principle, he pledges integrity to Jack at Wentworth Prison and respects a covenant that Jack will not harm Claire. The battery of his principles dogs Jamie during recuperation at the Benedictine Abbey, where he struggles to salvage his former self as husband and lover.

Political Criteria

In season two, the Frasers' deceptions to end Jacobite treason leave the couple with a hollow feeling of disgracing a chivalric code. They repeat their mantra of the greater good to the survival of Highland culture, which will lose rights and stature in Culloden's aftermath. On the fateful morning of April 16, 1746, Jamie saves Claire from the battle by ushering her to Craigh na Dun, but he rejects flight for himself. He remains with the Jacobites with the intent of dying on the field. Out of individual conscience and love of the fatherland, he returns to the fray and joins godfather Murtagh Fitzgibbons Fraser in combat to the last of their strength. Given the opportunity to die before a firing squad, Jamie longs to end the struggle and expire immediately, a military death shared with youngsters Giles MacMartin and Frederick MacBean and comrades Gordon Killick and Rupert MacKenzie.

While godfather and godson survive in cells at Ardsmuir Prison, Jamie manifests familial devotion to his pseudo-parent and returns from a short escape to the Selkie Island to mediate for fellow Jacobites as MacDubh. He assures prison governor John Grey that he keeps his word, a phrase that returns frequently to the dialogue as a mark of personal standards. Hasty promises, one of Jamie's most painful faults, sometimes bind him into untenable positions, such as lifelong upkeep for his second wife and her two girls. Reviewer Nicole M. DuPlessis at Texas A&M University remarked on Jamie's application of ideals to sex: "[His] sense of honor renders him capable of periodic (in his case, long-term) abstinence" (DuPlessis, 2016, 94). The loss of intimacy burdens him with a sour, pessimistic disposition, but preserves his ideals.

At a tenuous moment before Jamie flees the fire in Carfax Close that destroys his Edinburgh printshop, his trustworthiness to friends continues in season three with payment of smuggling profits to Yi Tien Cho, Young Ian, Fergus, Lesley, and Gavin Hayes. At Lallybroch, Jamie claims his defects by apologizing for lying about Young Ian's involvement in bootlegging and for concealing the boy's whereabouts. On board the French brig *Artemis,* Jamie respects Claire's steadfast allegiance to medicine, which he compares to his devotion to marital vows. Of his love and purpose, series originator Diana Gabaldon declared him "the head of his family, in the most traditional eighteenth century ways: he protects them, feeds them, leads them and loves them. He knows that's his job; it always has been" (Cohn, 2020).

A LIFELONG ADHERENCE

Decency and decorum accompany Jamie to the West Indies, where his example encourages Yi Tien Cho to atone for roasting Arabella, Father Fogden's pet goat, and teaches Young Ian to admit to Geillis Duncan Abernethy that he is not chaste. In America, Jamie forecasts colonial suppression and land theft among first peoples. At Fraser's Ridge, he makes a show of dropping his knife and introducing himself to the Cherokee, his neighbors. The series rewards the hero with a frontier name, *Yona Dihi* (Bear Killer), a sobriquet identifying a noble act protecting his wilderness home and community (4:4). With the respect earned by Daniel Boone in history and on movie and TV screens, the fictional Jamie continues to comport himself with dignity, especially after the wrongful beating of Roger MacKenzie. The two wrangle in person, with Jamie taking blows without retaliating, due penance for his hasty judgment.

In the opening episode of the fifth season, loyalties test Jamie's rigid notion of honor. In an interview with Caroline Hallemann, a journalist for *Town & Country,* Sam Heughan rationalizes the protagonist's choice to lead the Rowan County Militia: "He needs to do it for his family and for his tenants. He has to secure this land and make it a safe place for them, so he goes in league with the British," who further blot his standards by awarding him a Redcoat uniform (Hallemann, 2020). In the second episode, a formal separation from Murtagh causes Jamie to equivocate radical extremes: he validates needs of the poor and hungry while rebuking Regulators for tar-and-feathering tax agents. The violations of civil warfare on both sides underscore a truism about combat—heated anger, revenge, and divided loyalties cause people to commit atrocities they would repudiate in peacetime.

In season five, episode nine, sparring over matters of conscience returns Jamie to life-or-death choices. Infection from a venomous snakebite saps his strength and slows his heart rate, causing him to founder toward death. Facing amputation, he wars with Claire and himself about living his last years as a one-legged man. Bristly with pride, he rejects the surgery until his nephew reminds him of two examples—the elder Ian Murray and Fergus Fraser, both amputees. The dilemma brings out Claire's mystic quality. Star Sam Heughan summarized, "She has this healing ability in her hands and in her body. I think it's her love and her presence that certainly brings him back from the edge" (LeSavage, 2020). A last minute *deus ex machina* moots the discussion and results in healing. The episode leaves unsettled the matter of honor and its frequent collisions with pride.

The season finale highlights honor in both Frasers. Finding Claire abducted from the surgery, Marsali beaten, and Geordie stabbed to death, Jamie summons the militia by lighting the Celtic cross, a flaming message of dependence on his comrades. At sight of Lionel Brown's gang subdued on the ground, Jamie words the difference between his honor and Claire's—she adheres to the Hippocratic oath; he kills her enemies for her. On return home to snuggle her in bed, he rewards her with safety, the gift of a chivalric warrior to his lady.

See also Deception; Jamie Fraser; Highlands.

Source

Cohn, Paulette. "Jamie Faces Death in This Week's *Outlander*—Diana Gabaldon Discusses the Episode's Symbolic Role Reversals," *Parade* (19 April 2020).
DuPlessis, Nicole M. "Men, Women and Birth Control in the Early *Outlander* Books," *Outlander's Sassenachs: Essays on Gender, Race, Orientation and the Other in the Novels and Television Series.* Jefferson, NC: McFarland, 2016, 82–96.
Hallemann, Caroline. "Everything We Know So Far about *Outlander* Season 5," *Town & Country* (2 January 2020).
_____. "How *Outlander* Created a Whole New Breed of Superfan," *Town & Country* (7 February 2020).
LeSavage, Halie. "Sam Heughan Explains Jamie and Claire's 'Most Intimate' *Outlander* Moment Yet," *Glamour* (20 April 2020).

l'Hôpital des Anges

Claire's devotion to volunteer medical work originates from Master Raymond's suggestion that she abandon shallow bourgeois pursuits in Paris and treat charity patients at l'Hôpital des Anges. The fictional clinic, spiritual center, and feeding station provides the *Outlander* TV series with a female view of socioeconomic conditions for the lowest caste. The hospital receives hungry peasants on the front steps for meals and admits the sick and injured to a large inner space crammed with cots and examining tables. Nuns from the Couvent des Anges distribute food and care for patients suffering from diabetes, scrofula, burns, pregnancy, and broken bones. Amid soaring arches, a few curtains separate cots, but give no privacy to patients warehoused in one ward.

Episodes placing the heroine in a hospital setting in 1744, according to Diane Bénédic-Meyer, "d'intensifier la narration pour mieux donner à voir les facettes du personnage" (intensify the narration to offer a better view of facets of her character, Bénédic-Meyer, 2019). Claire impresses Mother Hildegarde, the supervisor, by sipping urine to determine that "sugar sickness" (diabetes) causes the patient's constant thirst and hunger (2:3). Claire states the prognosis—death in a few weeks. From collecting bedpan contents, she advances to treating problem cases that involve simple surgery, emergency care, and preparation of a corpse for burial.

Varied tasks stress willingness to tackle necessary nursing, which she manages with the aid of nuns, Fergus, and Mary Hawkins. A touch of whimsy coordinates the mother superior's work with the investigative skills of Bouton, a small terrier who sniffs out infection. Claire becomes a patient during and after Monsieur Foret's difficult delivery of her first child, Faith Fraser. Close camerawork follows the crash of a Virgin Mary statue, a blue-cloaked figure whose myth fails to comfort Claire.

The *Outlander* series bases scenarios on the outreach of l'Hôpital de la Charité, a Christian concept of shelter and treatment of the poor founded south of the Seine River in 1606 by Marie de Médecis and furthered by Louis XIV. At a decisive time in anatomical knowledge, the city developed other general hospitals, hospices, and emergency clinics receiving the indigent, mentally unstable, travelers, immigrants, prostitutes, and foundlings and orphans. Eighteenth-century physicians introduced treatment innovations by training medical students to diagnose symptoms rather than follow the medieval notion of body humors, the focus of the Hôtel-Dieu de Paris, the world's oldest hospital. Operated across from Notre Dame Cathedral on L'Île de la Cité in 651 by Augustinian nuns, the crowded facility tripled use of 1,200 beds by assigning up to six adults and eight children per cot.

Source

Bénédic-Meyer, Diane. "La construction d'un tissage émotionnel au féminin dans la série *Outlander*," *TV/Series* 15 (2019).
Jones, Trahern, and Lindsay Jones. "A Tour of Old Parisian Hospitals," *Student Hospitalist* (March 2012).

Humor

To balance atmosphere and tone, comic expressions and badinage interweave serious, violent situations in the *Outlander* TV dialogue. Examples joke about Auld Alec's selection of Brimstone for Claire to ride at the wild boar hunt, Rupert MacKenzie's pretense of a wink with his good eye, hand amputation changing Fergus into a man of leisure, and Ulysses's smirk at the expense of clumsy bridegroom Duncan Innes. During the search for documents in the Wakefield attic, Roger MacKenzie amuses Brianna with a rat satire, a Scots banishment of vermin described in 1885 in Alexander Stewart's compendium *'Twixt Ben Nevis and Glencoe*. At difficult moments, Claire reverts to a World War II anachronism with "Jesus H. Roosevelt Christ," her response to seeing Jamie in a British uniform and at his collapse from snakebite.

Juxtaposition dims jests to black humor with ties to death, particularly Lizzy Wemyss's comment on a "good day for dyeing," a pun on soaking clothes in indigo solution and on Jamie's brush with snake venom (5:9). In a husbandly scene, Arthur Duncan, the procurator fiscal for Cranesmuir, states his thanks for his attentive wife Geillis, who later poisons him with white arsenic and cyanide. The grievous loss of soldiers Rupert and Angus Mohr as narrative comic relief calls for replacement by Lesley and Gavin Hayes, former prisoners at Ardsmuir. The two ex-cons lighten atmosphere and mood with sarcasm until they expire in North America by grisly deaths—slashed throat and hanging, obvious methods of silencing. At the Wentworth gibbet, Taran MacQuarrie's gallows humor turns to the likelihood that hanging in a noose will cause him to ejaculate his "juice," a comment intended to amuse Jamie, who is next in line for execution (2:15).

MALE COMEDY

Because of constant "man talk," much of the imagery is penile—wedding night smirks, Angus's gag about his "wee man," Rupert's clowning over which woman to swive first, and his joke about his dirk being too long and too heavy for his women (1:5). In camp during rent collection, War Chief Dougal MacKenzie entertains the entourage with a dialogue joke featuring a lustful man and Granny Mary, his elderly wife, whom he's aged with sexual attentions. Although Jamie gallantly refers to marital relationship with Claire as "touching," he takes part in crotch humor with his groping of Claire's bare "honeypot" and his charge against Isaiah Morton's cock for dishonoring Alicia Brown (5:11, 2:2). At the finale of season five, Lionel Brown words his disregard for women by telling nephew Cuddy the location of Claire's vagina between "wind and water" (anus and urethra, 5:12). Lionel's diminution of females nets a suitable end from Marsali's injection of poison in his neck.

The series wrings occluded humor on out-of-the-way puns, for example, heretic/hair tick in season five and the conniving of "Sally (quick sortie)," the alias of a grifter in a trio of waylayers whom Frank Randall trounces in an Inverness alley (5:1, 1:8). A conversation between Claire and Jamie debates the Black Kirk's rumored harborage of demons. Incongruously, the ruined abbey once belonged to Benedictines, the

Catholic brotherhood dedicated to hospitality and welcome. In another satirical twist, Dougal's comment on poison being a female weapon belies Claire's aid to Colum MacKenzie's suicide and assistance to Jamie in knifing his uncle in the gut. The stabbing ends discussion of poisoning the bonnie prince with yellow jasmine (strychnine) in his tea.

Urination makes its share of witticisms, including childhood capers at the Black Kirk and pissing on the stones. While wetting a wall at Castle Leoch, Murtagh and Jamie debate riding off into the wild. A replay of teenager William John Grey attacking Jamie with a knife to the throat at the Corrieyairack military camp interrupts Jamie in mid-stream. After the 1745 Battle of Prestonpans in season two, Jamie proves his kidney uninjured by a horse's hoof and takes a Redcoat's sixpence bet that he can direct urine to a distant flask. The male jokes about relieving themselves return at a Rowan County Militia campsite because the cold causes their privates to shrink. Jamie declares that he tried to "pish" but couldn't find it, a muted penis joke that gets a laugh from Claire (5:6).

BALANCING TONE

Jamie's glib tongue and gift for sarcasm lightens serious dialogue, for example, his witty description of eating grass to relieve famine, a proposal of a boot in the hindquarters for Geneva Dunsany, and regret at transport to prison in a wagonload of chickens. In a sterner scene involving Colum's punishing Laoghaire for disobedience to her father, Jamie's untranslated Gaelic comment about ending the evening with entertainment manages to stir laughter in the audience before he takes a severe beating from Rupert's fists. Claire uses impromptu humor for the same purpose—to riposte Colum's questions about demons in Oxfordshire by identifying them as Scots. Although low key, the one-liner illustrates an ongoing antagonism between ethnicities.

Dramatic irony heightens less comic scenes, for example, Lord Ellesmere's comment on drowning any infant born with red hair, an oblique prediction of his threat with a knife to baby Willie Ransom for being illegitimate. In a subsequent scene, Jamie is shoveling horse manure when Geneva blackmails "Red Jamie" to take her virginity or else face a return to prison (3:4). The testy scene precedes forced fornication that rewards the hero with a son. A mixed tone and atmosphere in Jamie's controlling a willful six-year-old results by insulting the boy as a "wee bastard," unfortunately, a truth known only to Jamie and Isobel (*ibid.*). The droll scene suggests that siring a child is only the beginning of a parent's obligations.

PACING COMEDY

Irony settles the definition of sadist, an anachronism to Jamie that typifies his relationship with rogue and villain Captain Black Jack Randall. While the new husband delights in thrashing Claire with his belt, he acts out sadism with apparent glee decades before the coining of "sadist." Claire's understanding of male libido returns control to the bride, who denies the groom access to her bed. Jamie's capitulation to twentieth-century feminism underscores her command of the situation, which concludes with coitus in the wife-on-top position. At Lallybroch, a clichéd drunk-husband-and-annoyed-wife scene segues from Jamie's pride in beating Ronald MacNab for battering young Rabbie to curiosity about Claire's experience with elephants. The hangover scene that follows pictures her accepting his discomfort as normal, not worth a scolding. He rounds out the contretemps with a quip about the family serving bannocks at his wake.

Claire lightens a tense survey of Redcoats holding Jamie prisoner following the Watch's Chisholm rent robbery. To Jenny's belief that Jamie is too smart to tackle ten adversaries, Claire raises her eyebrows, a subtle suggestion that his tactics can be haphazard. The extension of mild humor in Claire's fortunetelling discloses a disgruntled Scots wife who endures a fat and lazy husband. Claire relieves the wife's discontent by predicting a long life for the woman and a short one for her mate. At a pub near Wentworth Prison, a quick turnover of setting depicts Angus and Rupert, jesters-in-chief, as less heartless than slick at engaging two guards in a losing dice game.

The all-male humor incorporates frequent anal comments laced with scatology, notably, complaints of ass-kissers, Roger's step into buffalo feces, wondering whether Voltaire ever dug a latrine, "shat his pants," thistles up the ass, and Rupert's observation that Jamie farts and snores in his sleep (2:10). In one of many significant motifs, Jamie captures John Grey in mid-urination, a parallel to John's attempt to kill Jamie while he pissed on a wall at Corrieyairack. In a late-in-life conversation over a game of chess, Jamie chaffs John about "shitting himself" while tied to a tree (3:3). Jamie's solution to the constipation of Louis XV fails on several levels, notably, a visual gag in a tasteless setting. The series does a better job at teasing Murtagh for bedding the maid Suzette. By gradual revelation of her bedmate, the scene discloses Claire's annoyance at Murtagh, a companion she holds in perhaps too high regard.

Jocular Mates

Discussion of a name for the Fraser baby suggests "Lambert," which Jamie discards as too English. Over Claire's honorarium to her archeologist uncle, Jamie proposes "Dalhousie," a choice that Claire compares to a sneeze, a gibe perhaps derived from a name-taunting scene in the film *Comes a Horseman*. The Christian name Dalhousie derives from the clan castle of William Ramsay de Dalwolsey, a descendant of a German pirate who helped boost David I to the throne of Scotland. Founded in Midlothian south of Edinburgh the South Esk River after 1140, the landmark featured a medieval keep, bottle dungeon, moat, and drawbridge operated by a counterbalance. The historic site saw the early struggles of William Ramsay and Robert the Bruce to rid themselves of Tudor control under Edward II at the Battle of Bannockburn in 1314 and at Nisbet Moor in 1355, an appropriate reminder of Scots obduracy and perhaps a reason for naming the child Dalhousie Fraser.

On a cheery note, Jamie returns happily to Claire's bed in their Paris quarters with a bite on his thigh. The conversation tangles into an impasse as he tries to explain his lust for a prostitute during a session of *soixante-neuf*, mutual oral sex that he hesitates to translate into English for his refined wife. The more he accounts for his fervor, the angrier he makes Claire, who is love-starved and resentful of bearing pregnancy and morning sickness without his sympathy. Although comic in its miscommunications, the situation precedes Jamie's testimonial of personal trauma at Wentworth Prison. Exercising forgiveness between mates, Claire awakens him in his separate sleeping area and arouses him to love. Pacing of the scene jogs back to comedy with the treatment of the bonnie prince's love bite from Louise de Rohan's monkey Colette.

Source

Hughes, Roxanne. "*Outlander*: Diana Gabaldon Shocks Fans with ALARMING Jamie Fraser Reveal," *Express* (18 September 2019).

Stewart. Alexander. *'Twixt Ben Nevis and Glencoe: The Natural History, Legends, and Folk-Lore of the West Highlands*. Edinburgh: William Paterson, 1885.

Indenturing

The concept of indenturing in the *Outlander* TV chronicle, a variation on slavery and imprisonment, accounts for the use of poor European immigrants and former felons as cheap labor in North America. Contract work began in 1000 CE with agreements between land owner and laborer. An English law from June 1349 required that all unskilled males and females under age sixty serve a master under the Ordinance of Labourers. After the first white indenturee with the Virginia Company of London reached Jamestown aboard the tall ships *Discovery*, *Godspeed*, and *Susan Constant* on May 14, 1607, bonded laborers and tobacco farmers rose in population to a half million menials in the thirteen colonies. As opposed to lifetime enslavement, indenturing bound two-thirds of white immigrants to servitude for five to seven years in payment for their transoceanic passage, clothing, and upkeep.

The British used hirelings as a cost-effective means of housing felons in distant colonies. In September 1696, indenturing punished colonists guilty of fornication, illegitimate pregnancy, swearing, and drunkenness. In 1756 from Ardsmuir Prison after its closure, the fictional ex-con Murtagh Fitzgibbons Fraser, along with Gavin Hayes, travels by sea to unknown locations in North Carolina. At Woolam's Creek, the contract system allots Murtagh a valuable skill in blacksmithing, which he advances to silversmithy and ownership of a forge bought from his owner's widow. He allies with Quaker yeoman Herman Husband, the historical founder of the Regulators, who backs poor settlers against corrupt sheriffs and tax collectors.

The Vulnerable

Success like Murtagh's seems more assured to the able and astute. Gavin Hayes's less propitious experience engenders fear of the dark, ghosts, and sea voyages, which terrify him with the unknown. Played by James Allenby-Kirk, the indentured servant, a poor shambler, bears an incongruous first name derived from Gawain, a knight of the Round Table and nephew of King Arthur. Shipmates harass him for a Jonah to the point of suicide, but friends reverence his passing in a Wilmington gibbet. Fellow ex-con Lesley leads the singing of "Eisd Ris" (Hear him) at a wake and joins in interring him in hallowed ground. The furtive burial by night fittingly robs a greedy church minister who demands a bribe to accept a lowly soul like Gavin in consecrated ground.

The worst of domestic scenarios disempowers twin two-year-olds, Josiah and Keziah Beardsley, for thirty years after their parents and four sisters die of disease on a transatlantic voyage. Reared like feral Roman founders Romulus and Remus, the boys earn no wages, receive no education, wear rags, and steal cheese to supplement a skimpy diet. Under vicious trader Aaron Beardsley, who pays the cost of their transportation, they sleep in a cold barn and endure beatings that puncture Kezzie's eardrums, causing profound deafness. The boys profit from tonsillectomies, improved nutrition and clothing, and Jamie's kindness in declaring their age fourteen, too young for military service in the Rowan County Militia. The twins repay kindness by helping Jamie recover Claire from abductors.

KIND MASTERS

In the fictional saga, other indenturees fare better by luck. Brianna Randall agrees to take Lizzy Wemyss from Scotland to North Carolina as maidservant. Lizzy risks separation from her father in a colony where the punishment for running away could reach 21 lashes. Upon departure by the vessel *Phillip Alonzo* in 1768, Brianna gains a mystic okay from the ghost of Frank Randall, who approves of her charity to a young girl trapped in an unsuitable arrangement with a potential sex enslaver.

The girls' relationship warms from mutual care—Brianna during recovery from rape and Lizzy during recuperation from malaria, which Brianna's mother Claire treats with rest and Jesuit bark. Lizzy gains the best of bonded servitude—a kind household and education in practical nursing from Claire and training from Brianna in cookery, dyeing, and childcare of Jemmy. The emotional separation from the MacKenzies in season five illustrates the value of indenturing to an endangered female.

Source

Stewart, Bruce E. *Redemption from Tyranny: Herman Husband's American Revolution.* Charlottesville: University of Virginia Press, 2020.

Watson, Alan D. "A Consideration of European Indentured Servitude in Colonial North Carolina," *North Carolina Historical Review* 91:4 (October 2014): 381–406.

Jacobites

A period of disgruntlement at the rise of George I over the Stuart dynasty in 1714 fomented socio-economic warfare between agrarian and privileged classes. A proto-nationalist political revolt, Jacobitism drew law-abiding Catholic Scots into sedition in defiance of the Church of England, Dutch monarch William of Orange, and George I, an Anglican king from Hanover, Germany. Their number included anti–Williamites and anti–Hanoverians, Catholics and Episcopalians, divine rights supporters, Highlanders, and Tories. The movement fueled alliances and risings in 1689 and 1708. Because of installation of George I on August 1, 1714, rebels led three more revolts—September–November 1715, June 1719, and 1745 following the arrival of the bonnie prince to the Isle of Eriskay on July 23. During a period of British military involvement in the War of Austrian Succession, the last rising brought the bonnie prince from exile in Rome to rouse the fourth and final Jacobite revolt against the British army of George II and to escape the disastrous aftermath.

Similar to the allegorical political terrorism during the Troubles in Northern Ireland as portrayed on *Star Trek: The Next Generation,* the *Outlander* TV epic sympathizes with the pro–Stuart faction, in part because of Claire Randall's time slip perspective. Zoë Shacklock at the University of Warwick mused that the heroine's voiceover support of Highlander passion and their blue and white flag could transfer approval for "the Yes (i.e., pro-independence) campaign in the Scottish independence referendum" (Shacklock, 2016, 316). According to her essay for *Visual Culture in Britain,* Sky Atlantic TV asserted that contemporary media typically ignores local political movements and avoids electronic suppression as "not only backwards but entirely bizarre" (*ibid.,* 316). Otherwise, programming could regress into a reactionary form of surveillance and censorship.

Men like the fictional Murtagh Fitzgibbons Fraser, War Chief Dougal MacKenzie, and Jamie Fraser promoted the divine right of kings and echoed the ill will of historical Jacobite pirate Stede Bonnet, who chucked a promising future in sugar planting to protest the German figurehead. On the morning of April 16, 1746, Jamie wisely departs from his wife and unborn child at Craigh Na Dun with a simple explanation—the times are dangerous and violent, no place for his family. The Scots supporting the iffy Stuart cause risk lives, property, and the entire Highland culture, which the British demolish through the Disarming Acts, Heritable Jurisdictions Act, Act of Proscription, and Dress Act of August 1, 1746. From the persecutions grew a feminist myth of Flora MacDonald, the rescuer who guided the bonnie prince at night from Benbecula in the Outer Hebrides to the Isle of Skye and who survived imprisonment for treason until June 1747 at the Tower of London.

Treason placed Scots in precarious position. The anti–Jacobite sentiment of fictional Laird Colum MacKenzie and, to a lesser extent, of historical Lord Simon Lovat, expresses a wait-and-see approach over hasty alliance with rebels who may die on the gallows or chopping block. In 1746, the men hesitate to gamble on a social order that would follow an idealistic unseating of an entire dynasty. Because of three past risings and their failures, the older men speak from concerns for clan and property. Nonetheless, at Kingussie, Jamie and Murtagh begin training raw Highlanders, who cluster under the familiar blue flag.

Crossed corner-to-corner with the white execution gibbet of St. Andrew, the banner bore the white saltire from 1385 symbolizing a long, proud heritage. For farmers unused to marching or weaponry, Jamie introduces them to pride in ethnicity and vigor in a difficult fight. Cinematography acknowledges the risk with a sweep of the post-battle conditions and the fading and inert forms surrounding Jamie at Culloden. Into the mid–1900s, the Rev. Reginald Wakefield honors a framed Jacobite flag on his foyer wall while Gillian Edgars rouses a new generation of Jacobites to restore Scotland's pride and independence.

See also Stephen Bonnet; Bonnie Prince; British Army; Culloden; Highlands.

Source

Crawford, Amy. "The Gentleman Pirate," *Smithsonian* (31 July 2007).

Deanie, Marc. "Referendum Riddle Over Hit Series UK No-Show," *The* (London) *Sun* (14 August 2014).

Martinelli, Marissa. "How *Outlander* Keeps Getting Tangled Up in Real-Life U.K. Politics," *Browbeat* (14 July 2016).

Shacklock, Zoë. "On (Not) Watching *Outlander* in the United Kingdom," *Visual Culture in Britain* 17:3 (2016): 311–328.

Jamaica

In a burst of history, coincidence, and Gothicism, the producers of the *Outlander* TV chronicle attempted too much in the brief character docking in Jamaica. An English possession from 1670 until 1962, the Caribbean island advanced from a former Spanish landfall to a British colony in 1707. Part of the area's rise to power, the indenturing of fictional Lizzy Wemyss and of Scots Jacobites Lesley, Gavin Hayes, Murtagh Fitzgibbons Fraser, and others transferred from Ardsmuir Prison in 1756 supplied plantations with laborers serving time for treason against the Hanoverian king George II. Kingston became the busiest destination for the French brig *Artemis,* Portuguese pirate frigate *Bruja,* and other ships approaching the colonial Americas.

A source of black bondsmen, West African abductees arrived regularly to Jamaican holding pens, where dealers marketed, processed and branded, and resold one third of England's kidnapped Africans, more than half taken from the Bight of Benin. Abductees of pirates like the fictional crew of the *Bruja* also satisfied demand for sex slaves, especially shapely, virginal youths like Henry, Abeeku, Robbie, and Young Ian Murray. The boys appeal to the sybaritic appetites of Geillis Duncan Abernethy, a wealthy Scots widow turned villain whose fervor for a Stuart king runs afoul of Claire and daughter Brianna. In a review for *IndieWire,* Amber Dowling noted, "If Black Jack Randall is Jamie's biggest adversary, Geillis Duncan (Lotte Verbeek) is Claire's" (Dowling, 2017).

A CORRUPT ENVIRONMENT

The choice of Jamaica as the locale for historical fiction and costume drama reflects what editor Katherine Byrne describes as "piracy, royalty, colonialism, and region"—topics that "resonate politically, culturally or economically with the interests of contemporary audiences" (Byrne, 2018, 2). Star Sam Heughan observed to journalist Jennifer Vineyard, "The journey becomes more interesting than the destination" (Vineyard, 2017). The episode "The Bakra," filmed in South Africa, delineates a West Indian caste system structured around privilege and subjugation. Enslavers deliver fresh, young workers to a Kingston sales force for the perusal and purchase by bureaucrats and upper-class whites, the profiteers on Caribbean agriculture and trade in sugar and rum.

Immense wealth for British settlers derives from sugar plantations, the enrichers of Geillis Abernethy's deceased husband. Compared to the English of the motherland, Anglo-Jamaicans earned fifty times the profits acquired in their homeland and exhibited their affluence at a fictional reception for Governor John Grey, where liveried staff serve champagne and brandy. Essential to fashion, English style periwigs, embroidered vests, jewels, and ruffled dresses flaunt expendable cash. However, the oppressive heat and infection of English newcomers to a tropical climate tends to kill off the weak from fever, including John Grey's wife Isobel Dunsany and newly arrived planters like Abernethy.

SLAVES AND MAROONS

The elegance and indolence of Caribbean life contrasts the island's evil underside. During the Frasers' sojourn in Kingston in 1767, they view African slave pens for the first time and attend an auction where a market manager brands a slave woman's arm with a cattle iron. Claire, folding her ladylike parasol, whacks an auctioneer fondling the penis of slave Temeraire to attest to his virility and value as a breeder. The purchase of Temeraire discloses to Claire that even free blacks face the danger of re-enslavement if they have no proof of ownership. The double bind explains why whites hold the upper hand in economic and legal disputes.

At an evening entertainment for the new governor, Jamie disapproves of Governor Grey's investment in slaves from the *Bruja* for official domestic staff. Jamie dispatches Temeraire on a reconnaissance mission to locate a recently purchased white servant—his nephew, Ian Murray—and to scope out a possible haven for Temeraire with island Maroons, free and refugee blacks who reside in the Blue Mountains. In the background, a voodoo ritual draws West Africans into masking, dance, chanting, and animal sacrifice on a par with TV fantasy shows from the 1950s. Of the Gothic elements, editor Gemma Goodman and Rachel Moseley explained that *Outlander* and other fantasies "attempt to solve the mystery of the past, to impose modern moral values upon it, and bring order and stability to the chaos of history" (Byrne, 2018, 6). Unfortunately for the narrative, the effort achieves no believable result.

See also Maroons; Rose Hall; Slavery.

Source

Burnard, Trevor, and Kenneth Morgan. "The Dynamics of the Slave Market and Slave Purchasing Patterns in Jamaica, 1655–1788," *William and Mary Quarterly* 58:1 (January 2001): 205–228.

Byrne, Katherine, Julie Ann Taddeo, and James Leggott, eds. *Conflicting Masculinities: Men in Television Period Drama.* New York: Bloomsbury, 2018.

Dowling, Amber. "'Outlander' Review: Claire and Jamie Rush Through Jamaica in a Semi-Repetitive Storyline," *IndieWire* (3 December 2017).

Galle, Jillian E., Elizabeth Bollwerk, and Fraser D. Neiman. "The Digital Archaeological Archive of Comparative Slavery," *Monticello Department of Archaeology*, 2007.

Goodman, Gemma, and Rachel Moseley. "*Outlander*: Body as Contested Territory," *Conflicting Masculinities: Men in Television Period Drama.* New York: Bloomsbury, 2018.

Gordon, Diane. "'Outlander' Recap: Claire Encounters a Face from the Past in 'The Bakra,'" *Variety* (3 December 2017).

Vineyard, Jennifer. "How *Outlander* Made Those Sea Journeys Feel So Incredibly Real," *Elle* (28 November 2017).

Kilts

For accuracy, the Scots outfit for the *Outlander* TV costume drama reflects historic drawings and ethnic description of kilts and their accouterments. As far back as the 1500s, outdoorsy Gaels wore their native outfit as daily attire for traversing boggy moors. Acknowledging the fetching male Highlander tradition, series originator Diana Gabaldon stated, "There's nothing better than the image of a man in a kilt" (Derakhshani, 2014, C5). A forerunner appeared in 230 CE in a plain check woven of unbleached white and brown. Either in Celtic Gaul or Ireland after 300 CE, Picts chose the *léine* (tunic) and three-to-four-yard *brat* (shoulder wrap) as a cheap, unsewn traditional drape. In 1097, Norse historian King Magnus Barefoot emulated the Hebridean short tunic over his bare legs. Ruggedly sexualized, the folkloric dress established masculinity standards among Highlanders and earned the originators a reputation for paganism, lawlessness, and savagery.

By 1400, the Highlander, a descendent of the Irish *Scoti*, wore a mantle and shirt above the thigh and left the lower leg uncovered. Advances in extracting dyes from local lichens and birch and oak bark yielded earthy colors in some 8,000 varied setts or patterns that resulted in overlapping browns and grays in the Fraser and MacKenzie tartans. The sixteenth-century kilt required from seven to nine uncut yards of 45-inch wide tartan wool or linsey-woolsey for the hip covering and back drape. Fitting began with pleating from the center back outward and separated a drape for crossing the left shoulder. A wide leather strip or drawstring held the *breacan an fheile* (belted plaid blanket) in folds or pleats at the waist beneath a fur or leather sporran, a pouch to hold necessities. David Hesse cited in *Warrior Dreams: Playing Scotsmen in Mainland Europe* a primordial appeal from a swagger "which makes the hips and the sporran swing just right … like pubic hair" (Hesse, 2014, 71). A detailed fit of the heavy twill *felie-mbor* (great kilt) or plaid assigned six or seven box pleats to the back, apron to the front, and finished length at mid-knee with fringe on the right side.

NATIONAL COSTUME

Essential in the films *Highlander, Rob Roy,* and *Braveheart,* according to fashion expert Brennan A. Barks, the Scots outfit became "an instantly recognizable visual representation of their culture and their heritage" (Barks, 2018, 373). The Scots diaspora introduced kilts around the world, particularly in the British colonies and to .007 in the James

Bond film *On His Majesty's Secret Service*. By 1600, imported indigo enhanced plainer colors. Researcher Lisa Hix explained that the British army began regimenting highland dress for Scots recruits in 1739 according to identifiable tartans. When separated into the *feileach-beag* (little kilt) and upper cloak, the loose fold spread over the musket lock to ward off wind and inclement weather. The wearer ensured footing by lacing light slippers over knee hose at arch and ankle.

Mercenaries like Jamie Fraser and the elder Ian Murray earned recognition for their unique untailored plaids and belted mantles in muted browns and greens. They slept in tartans and may have gathered them over linen shirt and cravat before arising. In 1578, John Lesley, the Bishop of Ross and author of *History of Scotland,* declared the kilt battle dress for all classes rather than formal wear exclusive to the wealthy and royalty. Three years later, historian and humanist George Buchanan of Killearn named camo brown as the soldier's choice for lurking in heather or resting from combat. In proof that monarchs could afford the best, the bonnie prince chose an overstated red plaid edged in gold lace, which relied on cochineal dye imported from the American tropics at a price sometimes sixty times that of sugar ($342.72 per pound today). Costume expert Peter Eslea Mac-Donald added, "Red was the *de rigueur* color across Europe at that time because it was so expensive" (Hix, 2017).

In reference to the uniquely gendered uniform from a masculine perspective, actor Graham McTavish, who plays War Chief Dougal MacKenzie, told *New York Times* journalist Bruce Fretts, "It's a totally freeing experience wearing a kilt. It represents something from the past that has style and elegance—you're not going out dressed in sweatpants, sneakers and a baseball cap" (Fretts, 2015, 18). During the great Edinburgh bubonic plague of 1644, restrictions forced citizens to the north and west to abandon the kilt, which could cover symptoms of the black death. Highland women expressed political opinions in the 1730s by creating the *earasaid* (shawl), a female adaptation of the male plaid that Claire Fraser wears on her first trip to Lallybroch. The original Scots kilt disappeared with the suppression of the highland culture after the disaster at Culloden on April 16, 1746, and the decline in kilted regiments and fife and drum tattoos after 1790. Punishment for public display of the Highland outfit required six months jailing.

Outlander Authenticity

Outlander illustrates the intricacies of kilt wearing, even for Fergus, who mimics Jamie's shoulder plaid. An introduction to season one, episode nine of the TV series pictures Jamie Fraser donning his utilitarian kilt by lying on the plaid for folding and concluding with pinning his brooch at the shoulder to display Fraser clan crest and motto—*Je suis prest* (I am ready). Cuffed leather boots with thin sole over gartered stockings complete the outfit. For a visit to Versailles in season two, the second episode, he scolds Murtagh for failing to scrub his knees, an essential part of Scots evening hygiene.

Throughout battles at Prestonpans and Culloden in 1743 and 1746, according to analyst Sarah Moxey, "The kilt is the integral part, keeping the focus on the highlands of Scotland and this perceived tradition of a martial warrior persona" (Moxey, 2018). Before plunging into battle, Jamie sweeps aside the plaid length that covers his head against the morning mist, a signal to his followers. Members of the Scots diaspora who fled post-war vengeance spread Celtic traditions around the globe. After the retribution of English law against Jacobites, in season three, Murtagh demonstrates the sorrow of a Highlander for his plaid, which survives in a scrap he tucks into a cell wall at Ardsmuir Prison. The tartan solaces him during post–Culloden despair and declining health from hunger, cold, flu, and rat bites.

In colonial North Carolina in season four, the emblematic *Outlander* costume takes on new vigor. Murtagh, the leader of the Regulators, maintains his tradition with a scrap of plaid, tam, and skirted leather over high boots. At Jamie's forced recruitment as Rowan County Militia colonel, he counters Government William Tryon's bluster in the debut of season five by giving him "a Scot" (5:1). To display Highland roots, Jamie retrieves from a leather-covered foot locker the entire high-low outfit plus *bidag* (dirk), sporran, and crest with motto. Striding across the big house lawn to call fellow Scots-Americans to arms, he halts at the flaming Celtic cross and begins mustering fighters, less like a laird than a general. The season ends with Jamie treasuring Murtagh's scrap of kilt dress. In the finale, he dons Scots uniform and rallies the militia for the recovery of his abducted wife, whom he wraps in the Fraser colors.

See also Celtic Beliefs; Scots Culture.

Source

Barks, Brenna A. "From Waverley to Outlander: How Scottish Dress Became Everyone's Dress," *Fashion, Style & Popular Culture* 5:3 (2018): 373–388.

Coventry, Laura. "*Outlander* Costumes—Jamie's Jacobite Style," *Scots Magazine* (1 March 2019).

Derakhshani, Tirdad. "'Outlander' Highland Fling," *Philadelphia Inquirer* (17 August 2014): C5.

Fretts, Bruce. "Behind 'Outlander,' on Starz, True Hearts in the Highlands," *New York Times* (16 April 2015): 18.

Hesse, David. *Warrior Dreams: Playing Scotsmen in Mainland Europe.* Manchester, UK: Manchester University Press, 2014.

Hix, Lisa. "True Kilts: Debunking the Myths about Highlanders and Clan Tartans," *Collectors Weekly* (15 November 2017).

Moxey, Sarah. "Review: A Global Force," *Scottish Affairs* 27:2 (2018): 262–265.

Terrero, Nina. "'Outlander' Costume Designer Dishes on Those Dazzling Clothes," *Entertainment Weekly* (2 April 2015).

La Dame Blanche

The introduction of La Dame Blanche in the second season, episode five of the *Outlander* TV romance reprises a form of pan-European Gothic wisewomen or specters. Traditional stories incorporate the supernatural female in medieval Irish banshee verse, French folklore in Brittany and Normandy, the Mexican child abductor La Llorona, Slavic Baba Yaga, and Walter Scott's night hags and crones in the novels *Guy Mannering, The Abbot,* and *The Monastery.* The name "La Dame Blanche" returned to use among a spy ring in World War I Belgium that monitored German troop movements at railroad depots. The fictional concept of a maleficent death harbinger alarms Claire, bringing back memories of a witch trial in Cranesmuir and a stake surrounded with kindling. In Paris, the fear stirred in street thugs by the white lady indicates that citified French share the superstitions of Highland Scots.

Perhaps because Uncle Lambert, a field archeologist, reared Claire, she scoffs at the notion of a supernatural female, who has no credence in her intellectual and religious background. On a visit to Beaufort Castle, home of Lord Simon Lovat, Jamie perceives that mention of la Dame Blanche piques his suggestible grandsire, who appears rueful for his wrongs against women. Jamie hounds Simon with a testimonial to a woman who blights male genitals like gelid apples. According to TV reviewer Ellie Walker-Arnott, the visionary female "sees to the centre of a man, and can turn his soul to ashes, if evil be found there" (Walker-Arnott, 2016). By having Claire act out a vision of Simon's historic beheading, Jamie overpowers and manipulates an impressionable grandfather.

In season two, a mirage comforts Jamie on the Culloden battlefield, a shining angelic fantasy out of place among bloodied casualties. The white costume and gentle words reprise Claire's work as a combat nurse. Evidence of belief in a white witch crops up in 1752 in the rambling last words of tacksman Duncan Kerr, a wandering elder. At Ardsmuir, Jamie reveals the significance of the *ban-druidh* (white lady) to prison governor John Grey as proof of Claire's residence in the outlying islands (3:3). In the eighth episode, Jamie narrates his swim to Selkie Island and his disappointment in finding no white lady, a phantasm of reuniting with Claire. The powers of La Dame Blanche to curse the superstitious recurs in the season five finale when Claire stokes her abductors' belief in sorcery with threats and glares.

See also Star Chamber; Superstition; Witchcraft.

Source

Ross, Anne. *Folklore of the Scottish Highlands.* Stroud, UK: History Press, 2000.
Walker-Arnott, Ellie. "*Outlander* Season Two: Who Is La Dame Blanche?," *Radio Times* (1 May 2016).
Wilkinson, Amy. "*Outlander* Recap: La Dame Blanche," *Entertainment Weekly* (30 April 2016).

Lallybroch

A fictional setting for a portion of the Fraser clan, Lallybroch emerges from cinema magic reshaping Midhope Castle, a tower house constructed in 1582 outside Linlithgow for habitation and defense against invasion along the Firth of Forth. The Fraser homeplace with its crested front door bears a name fused from the Gaelic for "plaything" and "tower." The farm suits classical romance for its tight socio-economic community and agrarian values, sources of strength for Jamie after his wounding at Culloden on April 16, 1746. Overlooked by Broch Tuarach, a round tower and one of the repeated circles and phallic obelisks in saga themes, the residence lacks the crenellations, ramparts, and watch towers of larger castles. Its most aristocratic element, the laird's office, contains the books, globe, and accouterments of an educated man as well as account ledgers. Bucolic camera shots of the structure feature columns of smoke from both ends suggesting warmth and welcome.

During Claire and Jamie's residence on the Fraser estate after their marriage in 1743, she begins to feel at home. The couple sleep in the laird's quarters, a symbolic promotion that displaces the Murrays from authority and control. Claire learns more about the old laird's love story and the deaths of both parents and of older brother Willie in 1726 from smallpox. Lacking his father, mother, and male sibling, Jamie assumes a new importance among farm folk as laird, but he remains the outsider, the mercenary returned to farming.

Jamie annoys Claire with trumped-up superiority over his sister, Janet "Jenny" Murray, the previous manager and decision maker. The brother-and-sister relationship seesaws, according to TV reviewer Amy Wilkinson, into "bickering yet adoring siblings," who love and annoy each other (Wilkinson, 2015). The narrative develops a dispute at the family cemetery that discloses Jamie's faults and the unsettled grief of brother and sister for their father, Brian Fraser. They both lament his ignoble death at the steps of the Fort William whipping post. The mossy headstones exemplify a lengthy tradition of occupancy by the Fraser clan.

Homeward Bound

Claire and Jamie's arrival on Fraser land incorporates shots of verdant rolling meadows and granite outcrops set against Jamie's memory of arrest by Captain Jack Randall and a flogging at the front arch, a representation of endurance and pride. For balance, close-ups of the mansion share space with chickens and goat pens, evidence of an unassuming farmyard that caused the boredom that Jamie fled in his teens. A serious obstacle—the paternity of Wee Jamie Murray—elicits a dark, grousing side of his uncle, who demands details of Randall's mistreatment and Wee Jamie's conception. Gnawing at Jamie's amiable disposition, the naming of the boy after him requires clarification as well as proof that Jenny's unborn child is not a second Randall bastard. Jenny's reliving of sexual abuse elevates her importance to Fraser family history as a heroine in dangerous times, which she survives by ridiculing Randall's impotence.

Episodes enhance inherent problems with farm management—pebbly bannocks because of a non-functioning mill wheel, farm worker Ronald MacNab's abuse of his son Rabbie, Jamie's hangover, and a year of low yield. The combination rent collection on Quarter Day and celebration of the laird's homecoming acknowledges a unity in Lallybroch tenants and the controlling family. Significant to the occasion, Jamie stands during the settling of accounts and chats jovially while Ian sits to keep accounts. The new laird expresses an undeserved grandeur by refusing advice from his sister, a mere female. He scolds Jenny a second time for paying the Watch to protect Lallybroch from Redcoats. It takes Claire's tumbling Jamie from bed to defy his lordly posturing and create an equitable family member deserving the title Laird of Lallybroch.

SETTLING HOME DISPUTES

On departure from France after the stillbirth of daughter Faith in 1744, the Frasers nestle in the family home along with Ian and Jenny, a prolific couple who anticipate another birth. Interior shots of Jenny's bedroom characterize majestic period taste in leafy wallpaper in shades of blue and white. Temporarily content in the tapestry-draped great hall, the Frasers set out on a mission to gain support from Lord Simon Lovat, Jamie's fractious, womanizing grandsire. After dispatching Fergus to transfer title to Wee Jamie and sending Murtagh Fitzgibbons Fraser to escort Lallybroch soldiers from the Battle of Culloden in 1746, Jamie mutters feverishly in the hay wagon that transports him to Jenny and Ian. Murmuring "Lallybroch" in delirium, he slowly recovers from a moribund state in a nurturing home environment.

In season three, the Frasers' flight from the Edinburgh fire to Lallybroch in 1766 provokes a confrontation and uncomfortable cohabitation with the Murrays. *Variety* reviewer Laura Prudom classified Jamie's mulishness as a necessary coming of age: He's "a little bit of a brat … a guy that needs to grow up … he has pride and stubbornness and things he has to get over" (Prudom, 2015). Because Jenny issues no welcome, the Frasers ponder how to revive their marriage at a less hostile locale, possibly on the western edge of the property, a hint at their eventual emigration to North Carolina. The proposal to settle in the colonies draws humor from Jamie, who cannot imagine a diaspora of all his relatives and tenants. In future time, Claire visits Lallybroch and finds a derelict building left untended in the twentieth century.

See also Architecture; Fraser Genealogy; Heirlooms.

Source

Prudom, Laura. "'Outlander' Postmortem: The Past Catches Up to Jamie at Lallybroch," *Variety* (25 April 2015).

Wilkinson, Amy. "'Outlander' Recap: 'Lallybroch,'" *Entertainment Weekly* (26 April 2015).

Land Grants

To encourage frontier expansion and the production of taxable income, from July 1765 to June 1771, North Carolina's Governor William Tryon issued land patents to individuals, a paternalism that Emma Dibdin, a critic for *Town & Country,* viewed as a vulture—"this kind of brooding menace of the British empire" (Dibdin, 2020). The system of Crown grants, begun by Charles II in 1663, continued until the American Revolution, when the North Carolina general assembly authorized patents for vacant property. Just as Claire predicts, tories—loyalists to the British king—lost property to confiscation and resettlement by patriots.

Fictional Jamie Fraser allows himself to be seduced by land ownership. TV reviewer Kayti Burt declares that he and Claire bargain with "their status as white Europeans with friends they can convince to come settle and an aunt, Jamie's Aunt Jocasta, in a position of power" (Burt, 2018). Burt added that the grant involved "his loyalty to the crown and the promise that he will encourage more white Europeans like himself to come over," a spur to the Scots-Irish diaspora (*Ibid.*). In 1768, the couple establish Fraser's Ridge on 10,000 acres of west central North Carolina to recruit tenants on 100-acre plots of lands. Season three pictures the signing of the grant and Jamie's receipt of a plat map of the area, for which his renters owe annual quitrents of ½ cent per acre, paid in sterling. Thus, a 100-acre lot cost the tenant 50 pence per year, the equivalent of $88.84 today.

During 1752–1763, the period that Jamie serves at Ardsmuir Prison and Helwater, England, the Wilmington port already streamed with immigrants encouraged by shippers and merchants. Some 10,000 Scots Highlanders included skilled settlers like fictional Jamie, Young Ian Murray, Marsali Fraser, Murtagh Fitzgibbons Fraser, Hector and Jocasta Cameron, silversmith Graham MacNeil, and trail guide John Quincy Myers and unskilled laborers such as Fergus Fraser, Lizzy Wemyss, Gavin Hayes, Lesley, engineer Brianna Randall, and Roger MacKenzie, an out-of-work history professor. Historic frontiersmen tended to choose lands near Cross Creek (Fayetteville) along the Upper Cape Fear and rivers to the northwest. Waterways offered sources of transportation and commerce that also appealed to German newcomers like Gerhard and Rosewitha Mueller and their widowed daughter-in-law Petronella. Letters from first-generation settlers to family members proposed grist mills, stores, taverns, and lumberyards and stated living costs cheaper than Scotland, especially around Hillsborough.

The core of the fictional *Outlander* TV epic dramatizes a period of civil war between issuers of land grants and taxpaying frontiersmen. A year before Jamie's arrival, Tryon reported that the colony was the fastest growing in North America. After the election of militant Regulators like fictional Murtagh, Lee Withers, Ethan MacKinnon, and Bryan Cranna to the lower house in November 1769, Tryon directed the Rowan County Militia personally to the granted properties in 1771, placing him and his Redcoats at the fictional wedding of Brianna and Roger. Because the tax protestors refuse to disband and accept a gubernatorial pardon, Tryon and the Redcoats fire cannon and swivel guns on two thousand poorly armed Regulators at the Battle of Alamance Creek on May 16, 1771.

The unintentional lynching of Roger prompts Tryon to offer restitution in the form of a land grant for 5,000 acres. With Young Ian's help, Roger stakes out his property. On the attempted return to the twentieth century in 1772 through the stones at Shadow Lake, New York, Roger leaves the grant to Ian. The historical land allotment process ended at the start of the American Revolution on April 19, 1775. Authorities didn't revive a system of property allocation until 1777.

    See also Fraser's Ridge; Governor Tryon.

Source

Burt, Kayti. "*Outlander* Season 4 Episode 1 Review: America the Beautiful," *Den of Geek* (5 November 2018).

Dibdin, Emma. "*Outlander's* Governor Tryon Was a Very Real Person Set on Stopping the Regulator Movement," *Town & Country* (17 February 2020).

Merrens, Harry Roy. *Colonial North Carolina in the Eighteenth Century: A Study in Historical Geography.* Chapel Hill: University of North Carolina Press, 1964.

Tise, Larry E., and Jeffrey J. Crow. *New Voyages to Carolina: Reinterpreting North Carolina History.* Chapel Hill: University of North Carolina Press, 2017.

Language

One of the more frustrating aspects of the fictional *Outlander* TV series, untranslated Gaelic sets Claire Randall apart from Highlanders during the first encounter with the Scots outback on November 1, 1743. Speech bears melody, urgency, and emotion, but closed captioning on Netflix and Starz obscures Gaelic meaning. On the positive side, she absorbs the romantic intensity of ballads by Welsh poet Gwyllyn the Bard, which he sings to harp strums. Sound without meaning places the viewer in Claire's position amid speakers who choose Gaelic over English, particularly the tavern brawlers battling War Chief Dougal MacKenzie's rent collectors after defaming Claire as a slut. The unexplained words of foreign languages continue with ecclesiastical Latin from Father Bain, Chinese from Yi Tien Cho, Mamacita's Spanish, Fergus Fraser's French, Portuguese from sailors, Cherokee and German at Fraser's Ridge, and Mohawk on the long trek to Shadow Lake, New York.

The extended use of Gaelic for important speeches cloaks good and bad: Laird Colum MacKenzie's welcome to clan members at the MacKenzie gathering, potential sexual assault of Claire by guests in Castle Leoch, and Dougal's propaganda to tenants favoring the Stuart pretender, the bonnie prince. For impact, the term "sassenach" recurs in title, dialogue, and epithet (1:1). At choice moments in Jamie's arguments with his new wife, he mutters in unintelligible Gaelic, a suggestion of retreat into native views on manhood, romance, and matrimony. The closed captioning translator misunderstands one common term, "sha" ('tis so), a common interjection introducing a remark. The translation appears as "sure" or "show" (1:8, 2:1, 2:2). Other errors in captioning misconstrues debt/death, reive/reave, lad/laird, nighean donn/laying down, and fash/fuss.

Shaping Character

Early on, the series reveals Claire's favorite swear interjection, "Jesus H. Roosevelt Christ," a slangy contrast to the mystic language intoned by Druid leader Mrs. Graham and her ten sister dancers at Craigh na Dun. In company with Dougal's paternalistic outriders, Claire shocks them by swearing vigorously, a suggestion of macho epithets acquired under Uncle Lamb's parentage and among Allied soldiers during World War II. She further blasphemes by disdaining anti-woman scriptural injunctions from St. Paul, who preferred female silence to verbal aggression in the command "Let your women keep silence in the churches" (I Corinthians 14:34). Her verbal aggression introduces a feminist slant that precedes outbursts to Frank Randall on adultery and divorce and to

Jamie on spousal abuse and Lady Broch Tuarach's authority. In both marriages, Claire refuses to yield to silencing or minimizing.

Throughout the series, language shapes characters and their intent, as with Jamie's withdrawal of "wee bastard" as an admonition to William "Willie" Ransom for disobedience, Marsali Fraser's command that Fergus stay with her in the woods during labor and delivery of Felicité, and Roger MacKenzie's ungentlemanly retort of "cram it up yer hole" to Jocasta Cameron (3:4; 5:1). Claire's pose of gentlewoman requires precise British elocution, especially while convincing Sir Fletcher Gordon at Wentworth Prison of her Christian piety. At the pinnacle of Murtagh's dialogue about suffering with Jamie at the abbey clinic, viewers have only expression, gesture, and verbal exchange to interpret the meaning of a Gaelic debate. Because the conversation precedes discussion of suicide and Claire's collapse in a faint, the information that Jamie relays advances the plot and the events of season two, which reveal Claire's first pregnancy.

THE PRECISE ANGLO

In the style of Lord Thomas, Jeremy Foster, Hal Melton, and Louis XV, the prim language from Lord William John Grey overshoots the demands of a career soldier with what TV reviewer EllenandJim call "a plumy English accent" (EllenandJim, 2019). A bit prissy for vernacular use, John's consolation to Brianna at River Run identifies her malaise as "you are to be a mother," a flowery euphuism for "pregnant" (4:11). He follows with euphemistic claims to have met "husbandly duties" with his former wife Isobel Dunsany, a roundabout way of saying "marital intercourse" (*ibid.*). His debate with Claire about their mutual love for Jamie retains a respectful distancing that recurs in John's departure to England from Fraser's Ridge and the man he yearns for.

The introduction of North Carolina Governor William Tryon yields another overly precise British speaker who guards his public comments much more than does his wife Margaret. He admits in private to Jamie that colonial law varies from actual negotiations between settlers and tax agents. At Brianna and Roger's wedding, Tryon continues to imply rather than state his demands. Only on the field at the Battle of Alamance Creek on May 16, 1771, does he risk verbal battle with his opponent. At the Redcoat victory, Jamie retreats into gentlemanly parlance by charging Tryon with aiming artillery at aggrieved citizens. The charge justifies radical patriot brainstorming an invasion of the British cargo vessel *Dartmouth* at the Boston Tea Party on December 16, 1773, and before the battles of Lexington and Concord on April 19, 1775, the onset of the American Revolution.

See also Gaelic; Humor; Literature; Names; Storytelling.

Source

Dossena, Marina. "The Prince and the Sassenach," *Reference and Identity in Public Discourses* 306 (2019): 43–66.

EllenandJim. "Outlander, Season 4, from *Drums of Autumn*: The Colonialist American Past, a Book of Fathers & Ghosts," *EllenandJim* (10 February 2019).

Law

Much of the drama of the *Outlander* TV series hinges on the choices and motivations of Jamie Fraser, a fictional Scots mercenary and outlaw from his late teens. Despite functioning outside English statutes, he bases his personal philosophy on honor, Catholic dogma, and human rights. His revulsion at scourging and other barbarous government punishments incites anger that Captain Black Jack Randall lashed Jamie's back two hundred times in October 1739. Jamie intercedes for Josiah and Kezzie Beardsley, who labor under a 30-year indenture contract with a child abuser, and scorns a North Carolina sheriff who branded Josiah with a T for thief after the boy stole a cheese. The extremes rank alongside hunger and disease among inmates at Ardsmuir Prison and Randall's sodomizing of a small boy, which goads Jamie into dueling with Randall.

At Castle Leoch, English attorney Edward "Ned" Gowan, the Scots-trained arbiter of contractual offenses in the United Kingdom, superintends a legal dodge—Claire Randall's marriage to Jamie. To ensure legalities, he explains the need for both wedding ritual and physical consummation within one day's time to transform her from an Englishwoman to a Scot. The stratagem nullifies Randall's demands on Claire as a British subject and cancels any future interrogation at Redcoat headquarters in Fort William for allegedly spying for the English. Legally, the ploy rests on ongoing questions of British occupation authority over clan property, to which Laird Colum MacKenzie holds full control.

While the Frasers reside in France in 1744, legal questions dog their political enterprise. Claire's diagnoses of two sailors alert the harbormaster at Le Havre to deaths of sailors from *le petit variole* (smallpox, 2:2). To prevent an epidemic, the disease requires quarantine and the burning of the *Patagonia,* Le Comte St. Germain's cargo vessel. The rampant androcentrism common to the era introduces additional questions of wedlock and women's rights in Europe. For good reason, Louise de Rohan worries about managing an illicit pregnancy sired by the bonnie prince. She fears her husband, Jules de Rohan, may charge her with adultery or have her remanded to a convent, an all-female house arrest similar in circumstance to Jamie's imprisonment in the Bastille without trial.

Prison and Second Marriage

In the third season, during Jamie's four-year incarceration at Ardsmuir from 1752 to 1756 and indenture at Helwater, England, he serves a stern royal sentence imposed on a traitor. Meanwhile, in Scotland, Highlanders face obstructions of civil liberties and clearances of clan land. After the Battle of Culloden, weapons ownership defies the 1746 English disarmament order in the Highlands. Because a pistol hidden in the Lallybroch dovecote fascinates Fergus, Wee Jamie Murray, and Rabbie MacNab, Fergus discharges it at a crow to satisfy an old superstition that the bird could threaten death to Jenny's newborn son, Wee Ian. Mary MacNab blames herself for the crow shooting and gains mercy from the Redcoat investigator for her simple candor. The act of clemency contrasts previous forays by British search squads on Fraser property, where a soldier defaces a patriotic wall hanging, an expression of personal beliefs.

In spousal abuse against Jamie, a pistol in Laoghaire's hands threatens him with serious bleeding from five bird shot wounds, one at an artery under his left shoulder. During the marital contretemps at Lallybroch, Ned arrives to interpret legalities of Jamie's remarriage and to arrange alimony and upkeep for a former spouse and two daughters, a long-lived domestic law dating to Hammurabi's legal code from 1754 BCE. According to British jurisprudence, her crime is punishable by transportation to colonial Virginia, a sentence that equates her with thieves, burglars, prostitutes, political rebels, and frauds. Ironically, she eludes arrest and removal at the same time that Claire, Jamie, and Young

Ian migrate to the West Indies and the Carolinas in pursuit of Portuguese child traffickers. Fortunately, in North Carolina, gun and knife ownership for the pioneers is a frontier necessity.

New World Law

When the action moves to Jamaica, Jamie needs the intervention of Governor John Grey to squelch a warrant for a murder he didn't commit. At the governor's Kingston mansion, John advises Lieutenant Thomas Leonard that he lacks paperwork to arrest Jamie and that naval rule on the English man-o'-war *Porpoise* ends at the water's edge. Another set of legalities in North Carolina dissuades Jamie from manumitting River Run's slaves and shielding Rufus, a wronged bondsman, from retribution by Byrnes, a vicious white overseer. In a history of Rowan County, author Sam Ervin, Jr., explained criminal execution of a guilty slave: "There were a score of crimes which bore the death penalty … the judges did not scruple to put these laws into effect. The blow of the law fell swiftly upon the guilty" (Ervin, 1917, 35). To spare Rufus from lynching, Claire euthanizes him with poison, a violation of her Hippocratic Oath, but not a felony. In a haze of clouded human rights, the Frasers choose to abandon Jocasta Cameron's gift of River Run and press on west out of range of colonial laws governing slavery.

The importation of English parliamentary law initiates colonial North Carolina jurisprudence. Before William Tryon assumes the governorship of New York, passage of the Riot Act of January 15, 1771, threatens the Regulators, who intend to disrupt the state assembly at New Bern. A standard British Army rule condemns Lieutenant Hamilton Knox's stabbing death of Ethan MacKinnon, a jailed, unarmed Regulator untried by the court system. The killing resides on contested ground governing prisoner rights and the military code. In season five, episode five, Tryon issues pardons for all Regulators except Murtagh Fitzgibbons Fraser, who must hang for fomenting rebellion against the Crown. New pressures on Jamie cause him to asphyxiate Lieutenant Knox and conceal the murder as smoke inhalation, the result of a malfunctioning flue. The murder is a stopgap measure to prevent Murtagh's apprehension and execution.

In contrast to the statute that would charge Claire with murder for defending herself against sneak thief and rapist John Barton in Madame Jeanne's Edinburgh brothel, the twentieth-century directives of divorce could force her testimony to Frank's adultery with former graduate student Sandy Travers. Other North American provisions allow counties to determine whether to halt the sale of alcohol, the source of Barton's crime and the livelihood of Jamie and smuggler Stephen Bonnet. Bonnet also maintains a veneer of gentility while frequenting gambling on women's fistfights and victimizing other gamblers.

On May 16, 1771, the Battle of Alamance Creek places the Frasers on the side of colonial law, but against the human rights of settlers. Jamie's disburdenment of his Redcoat uniform settles the matter with an outright revolt against Tryon's pronouncements. Series originator Diana Gabaldon stated to *Parade* reviewer Paulette Cohn, "This is the turning point for Jamie; the place where he definitively severs his connection (however unwilling) with the Crown and becomes in his own soul a Rebel" (Cohn, 2020). In the aftermath of tories vs. patriots, backcountry settlers relied on committees of safety and vigilantism to protect them from criminals.

See also Deception; Disarming Acts; Land Grants; Witchcraft.

Source

Cohn, Paulette. "Author Diana Gabaldon Reveals Why the Death on Tonight's *Outlander* Is a 'Turning Point' for Jamie," *Parade* (29 March 2020).

Donelan, Carol. "'Sing Me a Song of a Lass That Is Gone': Myth and Meaning in the Starz Original Series *Outlander*," *Quarterly Review of Film and Video* 35:1 (2018): 31–53.

Ervin, Samuel James, Jr. *A Colonial History of Rowan County, North Carolina.* Chapel Hill: University of North Carolina, 1917.

Robertson, Calum. "Celebrating a Scottish Past: Construction, Contestation and the Role of Government," *World Archaeology* 50:1 (2018): 337–346.

Literature

The *Outlander* TV narrative frames Scots and New World history through a romantic merger of historical fiction, scripture, drama, folksay, and film. Citations from various sources reflect learning, as with Jamie's recitation of St. Patrick's Celtic prayer for the dying, the child Brianna's love of Dr. Seuss, Ethan MacKinnon's emulation of the Spartacus legend with "I am Murtagh Fitzgibbons," Joe Abernethy's reference to Lady Jane from D.H. Lawrence's novel *Lady Chatterley's Lover,* and Captain Jack Randall's "Mrs. Beauchamp among the Savages," a snide jest based on the autobiography of a female missionary (5:2, 1:6). From common aphorism comes the episode titles "A Man of Worth," adapted from the writings of Confucius and Marcus Aurelius, and the Scots proverb "If Not for Hope," concluding "the heart would break." An extended fairy tale motif pictures Claire in the hands of Randall at Fort William and Brianna locked at Balriggan in the cottage of Laoghaire MacKenzie MacKimmie, a feminist overthrow of male-centered folklore furthered by Joanie's rescue.

- Scripture impacts dialogue with wisdom and lyricism, as in the titles "Better to Marry Than Burn" (I Corinthians 7:9), "Vengeance Is Mine" (Romans 12:19), "Through a Glass, Darkly" (I Corinthians 13:12), "Mercy Shall Follow Me" (Psalm 23:6), and "Of Lost Things," a prayer to St. Anthony. On December 24, 1968, Claire listens to a recitation of Genesis 1:1–10 from astronauts Bill Anders, Jim Lovell, and Frank Borman aboard Apollo 8. The pairing of characters with biblical elements asserts the sacred upbringing of Scots and other Christian characters: Claire's comparison of the bloody inn doorway to Yahweh's slaying of Pharaoh's firstborn (Exodus 13:15)
- Claire's "Stranger in a strange land" (Exodus 2:22)
- Rupert's scolding "let a woman be silent" (I Timothy 2:11)
- the Cranesmuir courts mantra "Thou shalt not suffer a witch to live" (Exodus 22:18)
- Father Bain's reference to the Whore of Babylon (Revelation 17:5)
- Louis XV's judgment of suspects by handling serpents (Mark 16:18)
- the bonnie prince's comparison of Jamie to doubting Thomas (John 20:24–29)
- Alice McMurdo's recitation of Psalm 91 for strength
- seamen's search for an unlucky "Jonah" (Jonah 1:8–12)
- Thomas Leonard's recitation of "De Morte" from the Book of Common Prayer followed by leading his crew in the Lord's Prayer (Matthew 6:9–13 and Luke 11:2–4)
- Father Fogden's recitation of Psalm 100
- Murtagh's attempt at "Bear ye one another's burdens" (Galatians 6:2)
- Jamie's correction of Roger's citing Matthew 18:6

- Marsali's cry of "Deliver us from evil" (Matthew 6:13 and Luke 11:4)
- Lionel's ironic hint at his own demise with "high and mighty" (II Samuel 1:19)
- Richard Brown's accusation of Lionel for reaping what he sowed (Galatians 6:7).

While Claire labors to make penicillium, office assistant Murdina Bug compares her bread baking with Christ feeding the multitudes "loaves and fishes" (Matthew 14:17; Luke 6:9). Notably, at a dire moment in season five, episode nine, Roger Mackenzie intones the *De Profundis,* a plea for rescue and mercy from Psalm 130 for Jamie's recovery from snakebite.

Memorization weaves dialogue with pertinent passages, for example, the episode title "The Deep Heart's Core" from Irishman William Butler Years's poem "The Rose." For pleasure, Claire cites "Present in Absence," John Donne's metaphysical meditation on time travel issued posthumously in 1633. Willie Mackenzie's debate with a chapel priest over the date of Claire and Jamie's wedding involves quotations from Timothy and Hebrews, which Willie learned from catechist Father Bain. At a tense confrontation in season five, a Regulator inverts "swords into plowshares" into "plowshares into swords," a revision explaining how North Carolina farmers become radical protesters (Isaiah 2:4; 5:2).

LITERARY CLARIFICATIONS

The application of citations tends to simplify confusions. To Laoghaire's legal charges against Jamie for bigamy, attorney Ned Gowan recites, "Nor Hell a Fury, like a Woman scorn'd," a favorite aphorism from Act III, Scene 2, of William Congreve's 1697 tragedy *The Mourning Bride.* At Jamie's healing of the rift with Claire over beating her for disobedience, he repeats a line from Chapter 13 of Charles Dickens's *Nicholas Nickleby*—"You are my home," a declaration of belonging that recurs at the mini-wedding on Claire's departure through Craigh na Dun. With respect for additional Victorian literature, the Rev. Reginald Wakefield elucidates Scots writer Arthur Conan Doyle's belief in simple explanations, which Sherlock Holmes stated in the story "A Scandal in Bohemia." Nineteenth-century literature recurs in the Randalls' nostalgic Christmas readings of Dickens's *A Christmas Carol,* a literary classic that differentiates in tone and gravity from the 1968 TV cartoon tradition of "A Charlie Brown Christmas."

The *Outlander* TV narrative situates citations for dramatic intensity, as epitomized by Brianna's recitation in season five of Robert Frost's poem "The Road Not Taken." Scripting introduces a female holocaust in the tenth episode with a citation from William Shakespeare's *Macbeth*: "By the Pricking of My Thumbs," a reference to supernatural intuition (IV, i, 44). Claire admits dire consequences of the witch trial by citing 21-year-old American Revolution martyr Nathan Hale's regret in 1776 that he had only one life to give for his country. At a parody of King Arthur's struggles, Jack Randall quotes Sir Thomas Malory's "Le Morte D'arthur" (1485): "Whoso pulleth out this sword of this stone and anvil, is rightwise king born of all England," a mockery of Jamie's attempts to break free of his bolted chains in Wentworth Prison.

The second season foreshadows unpredictable outcomes in Claire's citation in episode eight from Scots poet Robert Burns's ode "To a Mouse":

> The best laid schemes o' Mice an' Men
>   Gang aft agley,
> An' lea'e us nought but grief an' pain,
>   For promis'd joy!

In the background, the digging up of potatoes hints at the destitution and crushing of the clans after the 1746 Battle of Culloden and at the Irish potato famine of 1845. A strong economic significance attaches to Robert Burns's tagline "Freedom an' whisky gang the-gither," the conclusion to the 34-stanza "The Author's Earnest Cry and Prayer" (Gavin, 2017). In season three, the poetic protest of the 1786 restrictions on distilleries provided a title for *Outlander*'s episode five, which anticipates Jamie's dependence on bootlegging for a living.

WISDOM LITERATURE

The Frasers prove adept at applying literature to serious situations, especially Jamie's lending of Samuel Richardson's novel *Pamela* to Ulysses at his hideout and a citation from Thucydides's *The History of the Peloponnesian War* (431 BCE) about courage in the face of known dangers. To substantiate treatment of a typhoid fever epidemic in season three, episode nine, Claire bandies lines from Shakespeare's *Hamlet* with Captain Raines, who questions her beliefs about marine superstition. She and Jamie share a flashback in 1768 by reciting a translation of Roman erotic poet Catullus's "Vivamus atque Amemus" (Let us live and let us love, commonly called "Counting Kisses") by Richard Crashaw, an early seventeenth-century English metaphysical poet (3:4). The passionate ode, composed around 60 BCE, urges a lover to express affection with myriad kisses, counted in the hundreds and thousands. To further romance, the unidentified speaker ignores gossips who disapprove of passion. The English version foreshadows Jamie's commissioning of a silver wedding ring inscribed in the original "Da mi basia mille" (Give me a thousand kisses), which he recites in the episode "Blood of My Blood" (4:6). Reviewers EllanandJim term the graceful line "fantasy romance material," an anticipation of the flowing Italian by Renaissance sonneteer Francesco Petrarch (EllenandJim, 2019).

Historic ties to literature in North Carolina incorporate storytelling, song, and drama including Brianna MacKenzie's summation of Captain Ahab's pursuit of the mythic white whale in Herman Melville's *Moby Dick*. At the Wilmington theater, players perform a real five-act blank verse tragedy, *The Prince of Parthia* by Thomas Godfrey, who died of sunstroke and fever in Wilmington on August 3, 1763, at age 26. He did not live to see his neoclassic landmark staged in Philadelphia's New Theatre on April 24, 1767, colonial America's first professional stage play. The governor's wife, Margaret Wake Tryon, points out to Claire heiress Martha Dandridge Custis Washington in the lobby and quotes playwright Christopher Marlowe's famous line from *Dr. Faustus*, "the face that launched a thousand ships," a salute to Helen of Troy (4:8). In reference to a trap to catch the Regulators, Tryon cites "All the world's a stage," the beginning of Jaques's monologue in William Shakespeare's comedy *As You Like It* (II, vii, 1). For the fictional production, seating protocol separates men from women, a quaint custom unknown to Shakespeare.

See also Deception; Music.

Source

Catullus. "Vivamus atque Amemus," https://en.wikibooks.org/wiki/The_Poetry_of_Gaius_Valerius_Catullus/5.

Fletcher, LuAnn McCracken. "'Scott-land' and *Outlander*: Inventing Scotland for Armchair Tourists," *Literary Tourism and the British Isles: History, Imagination, and the Politics of Place*. Lanham, MD: Lexington Books, 2019, 191–220.

Gavin, Anne. "Freedom & Whisky—The Real Story behind *Outlander*'s Episode 3.05 Title," *Outlander Cast* (10 October 2017).
Godfrey, Thomas. *The Prince of Parthia*. Boston: Little, Brown, 1917.
Kobatchnik, Amnon. *Blood on the Stage, 1600 to 1800*. Lanham, MD: Rowman & Littlefield, 2017.

MacKenzie, Brianna Randall

The "200-year-old baby" of prophecy in the *Outlander* TV character pedigree, Brianna Ellen Randall Fraser MacKenzie exhibits propensities of both the MacKenzies and Frasers (3:12). Unlike her poised mother Claire, the daughter possesses an outspoken 1960s feminism that wields independence at the expense of gentility and grace. Reared in a fractious household, she admires her mother's devotion and intellect, yet senses that Claire maintains a sham relationship with Frank Randall, Brianna's adored stepfather. His sudden death in 1966 and Claire's revelation of a Scots birth father, James Fraser, traumatize at a time when the daughter needs to grieve for her dad. Sense imagery depicts her handling and sniffing his pipe, a symbol of fragrance, male comfort, and warmth.

Before Brianna's arrival through the stones at Craigh na Dun in 1968, three portents mark her passage from Boston to Scotland to Wilmington. Adawehi, the Cherokee healer, foresees her presence near Fraser's Ridge. While Claire chats with Adawehi about herbs for motherhood, a rabbit hops into view, a lively omen that dates to Jamie's survival of the Battle of Culloden in 1746 and Brianna's favorite childhood toy in 1948–1949. Jamie, who has never seen his Anglo-Scots daughter, dreams of a birthmark under her left ear—a diamond that predicts her value to him, as revealed in his Gaelic endearments in "The Birds and the Bees" (4:9). Nuanced discussion of beehive robbing implies the sweetness of a father-daughter relationship and Jamie's hope that she will acclimate to an eighteenth-century home in North Carolina.

Time Traveling

Disappointing on first appearance, Brianna (Sophie Skelton) portrays too bumptious, defiant, and spoiled a personality—the smart-mouthed college dropout. In helping Frank through a hangover, she parallels a scene in season one in which Claire gives Jamie "hair of the dog" to ease his morning after Quarter Day (1:12). Unfortunately, continuity lags because the viewer knows too little about Brianna before she becomes Roger MacKenzie's handfast wife and pirate Stephen Bonnet's rape victim. Genevieve Valentine, a reviewer for the *New York Times,* commented on the gap that raises corrosive memories and frustrating flashbacks of battery and sexual abuse: "This is the sort of story moment that needs as much character specificity behind it as possible to avoid being exploitative, and we just don't have that background for Brianna" (Valentine, 2018).

In a reasoned dialogue with Roger at Harvard, Brianna questions the false bases of history. The humanistic discipline deviates from her reliance on architectural and engineering truths from her major at Massachusetts Institute of Technology. She regains some mature presence in demands for "no more lies," a precept that Claire and Jamie respect (3:5). On embarking from Scotland for North Carolina to warn her parents that a newspaper clipping divulges how they will die in a cabin fire, Brianna shares a sweet nod with Frank's ghost, who approves her kindness to indentured servant Lizzy Wemyss. Ironically, the dire prophecy of a fiery death comforts Jamie because he assumes he cannot die from snake venom or combat at Alamance Creek.

A Test of Mettle

Critic Valentine noted that the Brianna-Roger subplot emerges from character faults and painful errors in judgment, particularly Roger's callous demands on Brianna, a "good Catholic girl" whose hopes for romance go up in smoke like the wicker deer at the clan gathering on Grandfather Mountain (4:3). Brutalizing by Bonnet further confuses her outlook, causing her to suppress nightmares and private tears and to channel post-rape anguish into ghoulish drawings. Like Jamie, Brianna responds to violence with violence, some directed at herself for not fighting the assailant hard enough. At Fraser's Ridge, she whacks her birth father in the face and wishes him hell-bound for assaulting Roger. Savage charcoal drawings at River Run and in her cabin at Fraser's Ridge direct rage onto images she burns in the fireplace.

Season five at the MacKenzie cabin pictures Brianna in the role of hovering parent tending baby Jemmy through a cold. As a loving wife, she encourages a silent husband with the gift of a paper airplane, a symbol of creativity and loft. Episodes resurrect a mature investment in family after she recalls the outcome of the Battle of Alamance Creek on May 16, 1771, when Redcoats overwhelm the Regulators with cavalry, swivel guns, and cannon. A female Paul Revere, she rides to Jamie and Roger to warn them that fate favors the Redcoats. Her dispassionate view of three captives hanged from a tree proves her the wrong actor for the job.

Juxtaposition against scenes with Marsali Fraser illustrate Brianna's impersonal responses. She gains some appeal by luring a loping buffalo away from Jemmy and by devising a hypodermic syringe out of a snakehead to save Jamie from infection. Critic Amber Dowling offered sympathy with the character after the family males plot Bonnet's murder: "It's the ultimate victimization of a woman whose actions indicate that she may actually consider herself a survivor" (Dowling, 2020). A *deus ex machina* sparing Bonnet from drowning, she again offers too little motivation as to why she shot a rapist and kidnapper. Her humanity reaches greater heights in season five, episode eleven, when she bids farewell before returning through the Shadow Lake stones. On return to her ravaged mother, Brianna applies gentle washing by the fireplace to bruised skin, but her offer of hand and ear lack conviction that she can guide Claire through emotional trauma.

Source

Dowling, Amber. "'Outlander' Review: A Female Character Stays Afloat in a Sea of Masculine Energy in Episode 10," *IndieWire* (26 April 2020).

Robinson, Joanna. "*Outlander* Continues to Struggle with Its Biggest Challenge in Season 4," *Vanity Fair* (14 January 2019).

Upadhyaya, Kayla Kumari. "*Outlander* Peddles a White Savior Narrative in Jamaica," *AVClub* (3 December 2017).

Valentine, Genevieve. "'Outlander,' Season 4, Episode 3 Recap: Mysterious Encounters," *New York Times* (18 November 2018).

_____. "'Outlander' Season 4, Episode 9: Fraser Hospitality," *New York Times* (31 December 2018).

MacKenzie Genealogy

Overall obeisance to Laird Colum and his brother, War Chief Dougal, indicates that clan MacKenzie enjoys a sincere unity and group pride. Their unity models the Greek concept of φιλία (*philia*) meaning brotherly oneness, group amity, or a sense of belonging.

Jacob MacKenzie
|

Brian=Ellen   Colum Ban=Letitia=/=Dougal=Maura=/=Geillis=Arthur Duncan   Murtagh=/=Jocasta=John Cameron

Fraser | d.1730   Campbell | | | =Greg Edgars   Fitzgibbons |=Hugh Cameron

d. 1739 | MacKenzie   Hamish   Tabitha &   son   d. 1968   Fraser |=Hector Cameron

| d. 1746   three more   reared =Abernethy | d. 1767

| daughters   by William | =Duncan Innes

| and Sarah | m. 1771

| MacKenzie

| Clementina   Seonag   Morna

| d. 1746   d. 1746 d. 1746

|

| Glenna Fitzgibbons

| _____   grandmother

| | | |

| parents   Uncle Lambert   father

| Beauchamp |

Willie   Ian=Janet "Jenny" Ellesmere=Geneva=/=Jamie Fraser=Claire Elizabeth=Frank Randall |

d. 1726 Murray   m, 1757   Dunsany| b. May 16, | Beauchamp   d. 1966 |

| d. 1758   d. 1758 | 1721 | b. October 20,   Laoghaire =Hugh

| | m. 1743 | 1918   MacKenzie |=Simon

| | | MacKimme |=Jamie

| William "Willie" Ransom | |

| b. 1758 | |

| 9th Earl of Ellesmere | |

Jamie Matthew Ian Janet Margaret Faith   Brianna=Roger MacKenzie   Fergus=Marsali MacKimmie   Joanie
Murray   b. 1752 Ellen d. 1744 Ellen | Wakefield   Claudel | m. 1768

| "Maggie"   Randall | b. 1940   Fraser |

| _____ | b. 1948 | m. 1770   _____

| | | | _____ | | | |

Henry Caroline Matthew Benjamin | | Jeremiah "Jemmy"   Germain   Joan   Felicité

                              Angus   Anthony   b. 1770   b. 1769   b. 1770 b. 1771

Colum displays wisdom lacking in Dougal by weighing the best of Jamie's advice concerning a fourth Jacobite rising. The wait-and-see method enables "the MacKenzie" to soothe Dougal without capitulating to treason against the Crown.

The genocidal post-war Clearances in spring 1746 force historic Stuart loyalist Hector Cameron to flee Scotland with fictional wife Jocasta, admirably played by Maria Doyle Kennedy. With French gold filched from the Jacobites, they begin a new life at River Run on North Carolina's Cape Fear River, where, in widowhood, she gracefully manages a planter's career subsidized by human bondage. She recognizes MacKenzie traits in niece Brianna, who charms Lord John Grey into a faux-marriage proposal. Auntie Jo herself, whom reviewer Ann Gavin calls "the lady-boss of River Run," excels at clan manipulation after Brianna's wedding to Roger (Gavin, 2019). As a way to authenticate Jemmy's fatherhood, Jocasta tricks Roger into displaying family honor by rejecting inheritance of a slave-operated plantation. A Machiavellian to the end, she grips a quill pen and blindly outlines her signature on a will naming Jemmy the heir to River Run.

The revelation of Hector's rash departure from Scotland, leaving behind dead daughters Clementina, Seonag, and Morna, establishes an unforeseen trait in Jocasta. Her memories raw from leaving Morna's corpse in the mud motivate a need for a quiet life with a safe, nonviolent mate. The choice of Duncan Innes over Murtagh Fitzgibbons Fraser rends her heart, an on-camera meltdown convincing in its controlled sorrow, guilt, and regret, all focused on one blue hair ribbon. In an interview with Lynette Rice, TV review for *Entertainment,* actor Maria Doyle Kennedy interpreted the devastating choice: "She will always come second to his cause. And she just can't go through it again. That constant danger" (Rice, 2020).

See also Prophecy.

Source

EllenandJim. "*Outlander*, Season 4, from *Drums of Autumn*: The Colonialist American Past, a Book of Fathers & Ghosts," *EllenandJim* (10 February 2019).

Gavin, Ann. "The Ultimate Ranking of *Outlander* Season 4 Episodes, www.outlandercast.com/2019/03/ranking-outlander-season-4-episodes.html, 13 March 2019.

Rice, Lynette. "Maria Doyle Kennedy on Jocasta rejecting Murtagh on *Outlander*: 'Devastating,'" *Entertainment Weekly* (22 March 2020).

Makeup

The makeup and hair of actors for the *Outlander* TV episodes draw on skill and psychology. The results authenticate an array of character action—horseback riding, dance, toil, malaise, sports, criminal assault, and lovemaking, the endeavor in which rake Phillip Wylie loses his patched mole, a mark of the eighteenth-century peacock. At a height of expertise, body markings and colorations on star Caitriona Balfe authenticate a gang rape that concludes season five. The effect on rescuers and on Brianna and Marsali cause a standstill of action. Jamie admits that viewing her cuts and contusions drives him to murderous extremes. In contrast, Lionel Brown, who survives until the next day with fewer visible lesions, deserves the execution that ends his evil life.

Cosmetics impart passage of time, as with the advance of Claire's pregnancy with Faith in Paris in 1744 and the growth of Jamie's bushy red beard during imprisonment at the Bastille. Careful choice of coloring stirs emotion, especially Claire's velvety complexion and rosy cheeks against her *robe rouge*, hovering camera shots of Jamie's livid snakebite, and the gouts of blood from Angus Mohr's grizzled jaws as he gasps from internal bleeding. For authenticity, Jamie's blackened nails give a professional touch to his work at the printshop. The aging of Murtagh Fitzgibbons Fraser's complexion accounts for post-prison indenturing at a North Carolina forge at Woolam's Creek and the outlawry of a rabble rouser 70-odd years old.

LASTING SCARS

Much like the distorted shapes of physiognomies in the films *The Elephant Man, Spartacus, Legends of the Fall,* and *Mask,* facial colorants and additives create realistic welts on Jamie's back and damage to his pierced left palm, branded torso, and snakebitten right thigh. Before modeling a scourging during War Chief Dougal MacKenzie's canvassing for donations to the Jacobites, Jamie reveals his scars to Claire, whom he barely knows. In France in 1744, cousin Jared Fraser grows silent at a first glance of Jamie's disfigurement, which validates his hatred of Redcoats. The stripping of Jamie's shirt in Wentworth Prison reduces him to tears at Captain Black Jack Randall's delight in the mangled skin, obscured by dungeon murk. The stark alteration of hope and health after the Battle of Culloden on April 16, 1746, one of the most moving character shifts in the series, convinces the viewer of Jamie's pain from a saber slash to his left thigh and his moribund condition during a jouncing wagon ride home to Lallybroch.

Other scenarios gain traction from bold opticals. A witty visual jest at the opening of season two, episode eleven pictures the puffing of powdered whitener on a full-bottomed peruke that topples to the floor from its stand. The imagery prefigures the justified beheading of Clarence Marylebone, the duplicitous Duke of Sandringham, in recompense for sending rapists for Mary Hawkins and his numerous other double-dealings. Brandishing the gory skull hacked from a noble "slippery fish," Murtagh Fitzgibbons Fraser exults in reclaiming his honor as Jamie's security guard (Bucksbaum, 2016). The cinematography of a decapitated torso further rewards Mary a comeuppance to a pompous lowlife.

MURDEROUS STRIPES

A shocking display of illness and suffering in "Free Will" concentrates on Indian trader Aaron Beardsley, a serial abuser of five wives and two indentured boys. He deserves the burns that fifth wife Fanny inflicts on his feet and the puncture wounds in his right leg, which maggots debride. Severely wizened by stroke, he incurs facial paralysis along with discolored eyes and skin mottled with bedsores. A monstrosity cooped up in the attic, he survives long enough for Jamie to end his misery with a bullet to the head, a scene that TV cameras conceal from the viewer. The concept of a merciful death returns in episode eleven, in which Roger suffocates a Dutch girl to end her suffering from distressing burns.

A few colorants fail at realism, notably the overly pink cheeks of housekeeper Glenna "Mrs. Fitz" Fitzgibbons and Young Simon of Lovat, who resembles a Kewpie doll. Less unsettling are views of Jamie's lip tint, which often appears magenta rather than a normal mouth tone, and the overemphasis of his eye makeup in "The Devil's Mark." At its least convincing, makeup results in the ghoulish globs and frazzled wig on William "Buck" MacKenzie, played by Graham McTavish in Halloweenish disguise. Much of the finery of "The Bakra" episode appears faintly ridiculous, perhaps purposely depicting Jamie in lifeless white periwig and unnatural skin tone. The leftovers of Geillis Duncan Abernethy's lopped head and remains lack any touch of reality, whether makeup or costume.

See also Costumes.

Source

Avina, Alyssa. "*Outlander*: 10 Behind-the-Scenes Secrets You Never Knew about the Makeup," *ScreenRant* (7 October 2017).

EllenandJim. "Outlander, Season 4, from *Drums of Autumn*: The Colonialist American Past, a Book of Fathers & Ghosts," *EllenandJim* (10 February 2019).

Snodgrass, Mary Ellen. *World Clothing and Fashion*. New York: Routledge, 2015.

Maroons

Maroons—black castaways or fugitives from bondage depicted in the TV historical fiction *Outlander*—joined aboriginal West Indian Arawak and Taino in a bid for independence from British colonialism. Named from the Spanish *cimarrón* (wild), around 1655, they formed isolated clans and villages in east Jamaica's Blue Mountains and inhabited similar enclaves and farms in Cuba, St. Vincent, Dominica, Puerto Rico, St. Lucia, and Haiti. Mainlanders clustered in Belize, Florida, French Guiana, Guatemala, Honduras, Nicaragua, Panama, and Suriname. Theft of food stores, tools, and herd animals increased their notoriety among white European landowners. Via creolized language and drumming, supernatural liturgy, and herbal medical care, Maroons revived ancient African traditions that united blacks from Akan, Fante, Ashanti, Coromantee, and Congolese backgrounds.

The resistance of creole runaways in Jamaica's Maroon War began in 1728 and continued until the treaty with England on April 20, 1740. A suppression of Tacky's Revolt in May 1760 concluded with display in Spanish Town of the rebel's head on a pike. Because of the value of sugar plantations and rum to British Jamaica in the 1700s, the purchase of abducted black Africans like Claire and Jamie's rescue of Temeraire from the auction block in 1768 increased the nonwhite population of Jamaica to 99.5 percent. The cost to Jamie—£20—equals two years' wages for Scots or $43,413.24 in current evaluations.

At secret places in mountain communities of eastern Jamaica, worshippers like the fictionalized fugitives who extricate Yi Tien Cho and fortuneteller Margaret Campbell and murder Archibald Campbell syncretize Central and West African cults. They sympathize with the oppressed, regardless of ethnicity. Spirituality takes a unique form of Obeah or Voodoo and features sacred oaths. Around a central fire, they perform the Kromanti play, a metaphorical Ghanian enactment of mythic heroes and battles involving the Akan from the Gold Coast.

The TV series illustrates how the sacred circle ritual, like the Druidic dance at Craigh na Dun and aboriginal ritual from prehistory, invokes ancestral identity and eases worries about security, white insurgents, and spirit possession. Similar in drama to Maori haka poses, the Maroons' choreography features warlike posturing, animal imitations, holy drumming, signal horns, and victory cries. From sunset to dawn, a seer or healer guides the troubled through herbal remedy, supernatural pantomime, masking, and animal sacrifice. The exhausting evening has a mesmerizing effect on participants, who exemplify the Greek philosopher Aristotle's concept of willing suspension of disbelief.

With guerrilla skirmishes in the forests and mountains until the Second Maroon War of August 1795, Maroons continued to revolt against colonial flogging, maiming, and chaining. The revolution climaxed with a surrender to British militia and a subsequent Maroon diaspora. After three ships deported six hundred exiles on July 21, 1796, from Cudjoe's Town, Jamaica, to Maroon Town (Trelawny), Nova Scotia, cold winters and unfamiliar flora caused survivors to repatriate to black Africa. On May 31, 1800, they settled on the Sierra Leone coast at Freetown.

    See also Jamaica; Slavery.

Source

Bilby, Kenneth. *True-Born Maroons.* Gainesville, FL: University Press of Florida, 2008.
Chopra, Ruma. *Almost Home: Maroons between Slavery and Freedom in Jamaica, Nova Scotia, and Sierra Leone.* New Haven, CT: Yale University Press, 2018.
Leigh, Devin. "The Origins of a Source: Edward Long, Coromantee Slave Revolts and the History of Jamaica," *Slavery & Abolition* 40:2 (2019): 295–320.

Marriage

Betrothals, seductions, and marriages supply much of *Outlander* TV drama and themes of intimacy and soul connection. In *The Greatest Cult Television Shows of All Time,* compilers Christopher J. Olson and CarrieLynn D. Reinhard examined the series, in part because of its mature survey of romantic love, courtship, and sex. A range of model relationships covers the breathless young love of Fergus and Marsali MacKimmie, the troubled courtship of Roger Wakefield and Brianna Randall, Isaiah Morton's faulty arranged marriage, and the late-in-life union of Duncan Innes with Jocasta Cameron, the thrice-widowed owner of River Run plantation. For a touch of humor, before the Battle of Prestonpans, after Kincaid bequeaths to Ross his wife Marina and six children if he should die in battle, Angus Mohr leaves Scarlett, his favorite prostitute, to comrade Rupert MacKenzie. Rupert doubts that willing a working girl to a friend equates with Kincaid's gesture of protection for his family. The humor turns into noir humor after Angus and Kincaid die from combat wounds.

According to Carol Donelan, a cinema expert at Carleton College in Northfield, Minnesota, eighteenth-century marriage in Scotland like that of Marsali, Brianna, and Marina Kincaid "subsumed a wife's identity into that of her husband" (Donelan, 2018, 31). At the altar, under common law and church dogma, the bride abandoned rights and personhood to become a wife, the fate of Morag MacKenzie, mate of the abusive William "Buck" MacKenzie. Because a transaction in *Outlander's* season one allies two males—War Chief Dougal MacKenzie with his nephew Jamie Fraser—Claire Elizabeth Beauchamp becomes a negotiable entity—a parcel delivered to a man willing to rescue her from the sociopathic Captain Black Jack Randall. Donelan posits that, out of vengeance for a legal trick that makes Claire a Scot, Jack pursues Jamie beyond two floggings to a prison cell rape, torture, and branding, a homoerotic version of slave markings.

A String of Pearls

In preparation for the impromptu pairing of Claire with Jamie Fraser, the TV episodes introduce the city hall union of Claire and Frank Randall, a civil coupling devoid of religious traditions. In a flashback to their tour of Castle Leoch, she deliberately omits undergarments, an overt gesture of sexual appetite. The couple attempt to repair their oneness after Claire's disappearance and return and derive an open marriage arrangement in Boston based on co-parenting Brianna, Jamie's daughter. Actor Tobias Menzies described the twenty-year evolution as an untenable sacrifice for Frank that progresses from "rage, disappointment, hurt, and anger and then settles into something more resigned … a love with a lot of scar tissue" (Vineyard, 2017).

After wedding Jamie, Claire's thoughts turn to pearls loosed from a string and the scattering of images of the past, spheres of female individuality before wedlock. Clad in a dazzling gauze and linen gown speckled with a shower of silver leaves, she appears to cast her lot with a Highlander soldier. Before taking vows, she steps out of sunlight into a dark chapel, an image of the unknown future for eighteenth-century brides under the control of husbands. At the groom's pledge of protection by clan, name, and physical safeguard, Claire learns that he agrees to wed to shield her from harm. Their wedding night, in the description of critic Graeme Virtue, culminates in "a relishable but relatable mixture of nerves, desire, and animal passion" (Virtue, 2015).

In the opinion of analyst Valerie Estelle Frankel, the Fraser union constitutes "a true romance—sometimes classic, other times gender-flipped and filled with surprises" (Frankel, 2016, 1). Roger MacKenzie's brief mention of the cuckoo hints at the root word of cuckoldry, the sexual alliance that turns Claire into a bigamist and taints her first love. Jamie outpaces Frank as soul mate by seeking total union with Claire, who completes him emotionally. To compound the romantic idyll, repeated copulations adopt the Hollywood notion of simultaneous orgasm.

Jamie excels at keeping their passion vital. He kisses Claire's fingers, nuzzles her hair, and lip-nibbles from throat to breasts. In 1771, he pleads for her touch as he nears death from snakebite. Romance author Penelope Williamson explained, "Sex is not enough; he must possess her heart and soul, even while he in turn becomes possessed" (Williamson, 1992, 130). A subsequent description of her ring as the key to Lallybroch ameliorates the wife-as-chattel motif by making her titular half owner of the clan estate. Paradoxically, even as laird and lady, the newlyweds find Jenny Fraser Murray still in control of the family property.

LOVE IN THE TIME OF WAR

The security of shared affection and physical union collapses as the newlyweds face impending war with the British and the post-war foundering of Highland society. In one of the most impassioned scenes of the *Outlander* narrative, Jamie says goodbye to wife and unborn child in the only way he can express earnest regret—he couples with Claire within the stone ring that brought her into his life. As though confessing before God, he admits a lifetime of crimes, but thanks the Almighty for a rare mate, a fervent speech similar to the ardent final lines that Mel Ferrer speaks in Edmond Rostand's *Cyrano de Bergerac*. The elegant farewell, similar in pain to the bitter moments as Claire parts from her stillborn daughter Faith and considers amputating Jamie's right leg, illustrates essayist Hannah Herrera's claim that *Outlander* "[complicates] and, to great effect, [denies] the assumption that the future is always better than the past" (Herrera, 2019, 194).

Season two, episode nine mocks anti-marriage sentiment in Willie's departure from Dougal's band to wed an Irish girl and resettle in the colonies, a dramatic foreshadowing of the future in North Carolina awaiting the Frasers and the rest of the Scots-Irish diaspora. A disconcerting nuptial three episodes later unites Mary Hawkins with Black Jack Randall, a British army captain who can sustain her and Alex Randall's unborn child with funds and a reputable name, even after his predicted death at Culloden the next day. The exchange of vows, set against Alex's death rattle, bodes ill for Mary, who has no knowledge that Jack will soon die in battle, leaving her a double widow with a pension.

The Aggressive Female

The frustrated masturbation scene in season three, episode two incorporates Claire's fantasies of Jamie in beefcake pose, an inverse of the hackneyed woman-as-eye-candy motif. A poor substitute, her awakening of a drowsy Frank for middle-of-the-night sex places her once more in the superior pose, evidence of her continued maneuvering of the men in her life. The ploy fails with a fireplace seduction that Claire initiates. To interviewer Neela Debnath, actor Tobias Menzies quotes from the script: "That line in front of the fire, when he goes, 'When I'm with you, I'm with you. You're with him.' That's as close as he gets to addressing, directly, this other person," who lives on in Claire's mind (Debnath, 2019). Too late, she realizes that Frank intuits her need to fantasize lovemaking with Jamie, a mental escape from an inert marriage in twentieth-century Boston. In similar straits, Jamie accepts a tryst with Mary MacNab, a domestic at Lallybroch, but weeps at reviving desire for a stranger. The couple's dialogue in an austere cave recognizes that both parties, like Offred in *The Handmaid's Tale,* need replenishing from a sexual drought.

At difficult passes in the *Outlander* TV series, definitions of marriage examine different angles of affection, desire, and commitment, notably, Fergus's delivery of baby Felicité in the forest, Ellesmere's arranged nuptials with Geneva Dunsany, Lionel Brown's abuse of wife Rose, and Young Ian's loss of his Mohawk mate. Jamie informs Jenny that losing his wife before Culloden was too painful to discuss. To Joanie, her stepfather defines a lasting union as a bond, a connection that he once had with his first wife, but lacks with Laoghaire, who never recovers from the physical abuse imposed by husband Simon MacKimmie before his imprisonment. To Fergus, Jamie expands on the totality of feeling he has for Claire, a consuming passion beyond the power of words. In the finale, Claire scrubs at her silver wedding ring as though scraping away the damage done by Lionel and his raiders.

See also Couples; Craigh na Dun.

Source

Debnath, Neela. "*Outlander*: Did Frank Randall Believe Claire's Time Travel Story?" *Express* (30 October 2019).

Donelan, Carol. "'Sing Me a Song of a Lass That Is Gone': Myth and Meaning in the Starz Original Series *Outlander,*" *Quarterly Review of Film and Video* 35:1 (2018): 31–53.

Frankel, Valerie Estelle, ed. *Outlander's Sassenachs: Essays on Gender, Race, Orientation and the Other in the Novels and Television Series.* Jefferson, NC: McFarland, 2016.

Herrera, Hannah. "Shifting Spaces and Constant Patriarchy: The Characterizations of Offred and Claire in *The Handmaid's Tale* and *Outlander,*" *Zeitschrift für Anglistik und Amerikanistik* 67:2 (2019): 181–196.

Olson, Christopher J, and CarrieLynn D. Reinhard. *The Greatest Cult Television Shows of All Time.* Lanham, MD: Rowman & Littlefield, 2020.

Vineyard, Jennifer. "Actor Tobias Menzies on the 'Outlander' Death We All Knew Was Coming," *New York Times* (25 September 2017).

Williamson, Penelope. "By Honor Bound: The Heroine as Hero," *Dangerous Men & Adventurous Women.* Philadelphia: University of Pennsylvania Press, 1992, 125–132.

Matrilineage

The channeling of female-to-female inheritance in the *Outlander* TV narrative surveys beliefs, lore, and instincts not inherent in male bloodlines. Relayed by storytelling, ballads, and examples, time travel via touching the monolith at Craigh na Dun consolidates a women's society that nurtures Celtic veneration of the Earth Mother. Unlike males, who exert energies in weaponry and war, Inverness women revere the antique spiritual traditions of Samhain and a night ritual by lamplight. In Mrs. Graham's tutelage of Frank Randall on Druidic marvels, she authenticates twentieth-century information from four generations of grandmothers, all of whom understand how earth's powers focused on the central stone. When Roger MacKenzie learns more about Claire's disappearance through the stones into the past, he receives the same freely given assumptions from Fiona that Mrs. Graham, her grandmother, imparted to Frank—a gift of peace and mystic possibilities that women bestow.

Females appear more trusting of nature and supernatural strengths than the male dependence on targes, claymores, daggers, and dirks. Ellen MacKenzie Fraser, an unconventional member of the MacKenzie clan, sanctions a long-lived matrilineal strand, an unusual emergence of the outspoken warrior woman in a patriarchal society. Although she never appears in the TV series, the core character charges multiple scenes with a metaphysical spark. Two surviving children remember her with a melancholy devotion and grief that she died in childbirth along with her fourth baby, a womanly death as predictable as the demise of soldiers in war. For Jenny, the regal, statuesque figure centers memories of Ellen and recurs in sister-in-law Claire's height and shape. Into the future, precedents set by the intangible matriarch of Lallybroch retain force and eminence, even in the New World.

The Matriarch

Through the intimacy of wedlock, Claire confers special female gifts on her husband. Before his wedding day, Jamie speaks adoringly, longingly of his mother to godfather Murtagh and compares her qualities to Claire's. Athena Bellas, a lecturer at the University of Melbourne, typified a "carnal dimension" in cinematic "techniques like high contrast lighting, caressing gestures, extended shot duration, heavy use of extreme close-ups, slow panning camera-work, and a rich, warm colour palette" (Bellas, 2019, 507). A few maternal heirlooms remain—a string of Scots pearls and a pair of bracelets made from wild boar tusks, silver-capped relics of elemental nature that epitomize a feminine glow, memory, and stalwart self-determination. Critic Valerie Estelle Frankel, a teacher at San Jose City College, identified the wedding night gift of pearls to Claire as "a cosmic and social symbol of ties and bonds," a mythic link to the Greek concept of ἔρως (eros) and to sexual satisfaction in the marital example of Brian and Ellen (Frankel, 2015, 35).

An intimate scene with Murtagh Fitzgibbons Fraser in season five, episode one accounts for Jamie's reliance on a companionable and protective godfather who takes Ellen's place at her death. To Claire, Murtagh reveals unrequited love for Ellen, who passed over him as a possible husband in favor of Brian Fraser of Lallybroch. Another suitor, Marcus MacRannoch of Eldridge Manor, confides that he gave Ellen the pearls as a wedding gift. The motif of idealistic men pursuing the elusive Ellen reenacts the courtship of Helen of Troy in Homer's *Iliad*. The losers promise to continue shielding their lady love, a semi-divine daughter of Zeus whose Greek name prefigures "Ellen," meaning "shining one." In the opening of season five, the motif of protection and devotion seals Murtagh's vow to remain true to his orphaned godson.

A Fount of Positive Values

For Jamie, Ellen becomes a role model for romance, compassion, and enduring adoration. The name survives in Claire's christening their daughter Brianna Ellen Randall for both Fraser grandparents and a great-grandmother, Margaret Ellen. At a serious low in Brianna's confidence, Ellen's younger sister, Jocasta MacKenzie Cameron, narrates events in Ellen's girlhood, when she defied her father, Jacob MacKenzie, and her brothers Colum and Dougal and eloped from Castle Leoch with the man of her choice. Jamie's storytelling animates Ellen's *joie de vivre* and wedlock to Brian after they conceive a first child, a tale of premarital oneness that recurs in Brianna's handfasting with Roger MacKenzie. Claire expresses reverence for the MacKenzie-Fraser matrilineage by passing on the family pearls, which Jamie clasps around Brianna's neck before her wedding to Roger, father of their son Jemmy.

In the third generation, Brianna identifies in her Scots grandmother a strain of twentieth-century feminism—an independence and rebuff of social constraints not common to Ellen's time. The trait passes to Jenny Fraser Murray, a tough-minded pseudo-laird of Lallybroch who nettles, spoils, and tends her scampish brother and who immodestly seduces future husband Ian Murray. Because of blindness, Aunt Jocasta trusts memory to guide her admiration for Ellen, especially the artistic talent that produces a self-portrait hanging at Lallybroch. The skill passes to Brianna, enabling her to vent anger at a rapist and to capture the beauty of her baby son and Phaedra, a slave at River Run. The portraits exemplify aspects of mother love alongside respect for female pluck.

See also Feminism.

Source

Bellas, Athena. "*Outlander*'s Tactile Caress: A Multisensory Romance," *Continuum* 33:5 (2019): 507–524.
Debnath, Neela. "*Outlander*: What happened to Ellen Fraser? The Tragic Backstory of Jamie's Mother," *Express* (7 November 2019).
Frankel, Valerie Estelle, ed. *The Symbolism and Sources of Outlander.* Jefferson, NC: McFarland, 2015.

Mercenaries

A backstory that peeks through the plot of the *Outlander* TV epic indicates that Jamie Fraser gains the rudiments of fighting and self-defense from his uncle, War Chief Dougal MacKenzie. In his late teens in 1740, Jamie broadens his skill at soldiery while serving a foreign army in France, Spain, and Silesia. He joins Scots mercenaries for money rather than political ideals, a form of profiteering approved by his cousin Jared Fraser. During Jamie's observation of the British army, he and other Scots gain an education in highly disciplined and regimented European infantry tactics, which rely on hirelings of independent military contractors during and after the Thirty Years' War. The training serves Jamie in Scotland after he forms amateurs into a Jacobite regiment in 1743 to support Bonnie Prince Charlie.

Paired with boyhood friend and comrade Ian Murray (played by Steven Cree), Jamie has adventures in fictional combat in France and during recuperation in a French brothel. In a romance with the flirty Annalise de Marillac, he fights a duel with her future husband. During Continental wars, Ian suffers a shot to his lower right leg. Jamie ensures his return home, where Ian accustoms himself to amputation and a wooden leg with the help of Jamie's sister Jenny. Of the limb that encumbers him in the TV series, Cree stated, "It took a lot of getting used to. It was really painful at first" (Debnath, 2019).

By the end of the French Revolution, more national armies in Great Britain, France,

Prussia, and America relied on citizen soldiers rather than outsider recruits like Ian and Jamie, who fight for cash and youthful exploits. In season five, Captain Roger MacKenzie sings "Twa Recruitin' Sergeants," a pre–1745 cautionary ballad warning farm youth like Jamie and Ian of the mercenary recruiter's false lures. One explanation from military historian Sarah Percy at the University of Queensland credited the shift to "patriotic motivation," which produced troop cohesion in state forces (Percy, 2007, 96). She stated that, after 1740, the fielding of skirmishers and light squads as harassers of enemy armies required trustworthy men who could rely on their own initiative and forage for supplies. Overall, "Commanders had to trust that these troops would not desert while operating far from the main body of the army" (*ibid.*).

More information about the fighting in Europe in season one, episode thirteen clarifies the past lives of fictional soldiers of fortune. In exchange for warding off Redcoat patrols and invading clans, the Murray household pays extortion money to the Watch, whom TV critic Amy Wilkinson calls "a group of ruthless scoundrels intent on robbing and pillaging" (Wilkinson, 2015). The French battle cry *Jamais pris vivant* (Never be taken alive) illustrates the spirit that infuses young dogs of war, who expect no rescue if they become prisoners of the enemy (1:13). Basing their philosophy on ideals of total freedom, leader Taran MacQuarrie opts for easy gallops under the sky and a quick death.

For his jaunty outlook, Taran is easy to like. Ian acclaims him a buddy because they share a soldierly background and respect wounded veterans. The *esprit de corps* of men in arms heartens Ian, who plunges his sword through Horrocks, a blackmailer and British deserter. The close ties between veterans results in a plan to bury Horrocks and reclaim the blackmail money. Jamie's admission of murdering Horrocks and his agreement to ride with the Watch indicates the appeal of outlawry, a greater risk than warring as a youthful rent-a-soldier.

Source

Debnath, Neela. "*Outlander*: How Did Ian Murray Lose His Leg? The Heartbreaking Story," *Express* (5 November 2019).

Percy, Sarah. *Mercenaries: The History of a Norm in International Relations.* New York: Oxford University Press, 2007.

Stratton, Curtis H. *War Coin: A Brief History of Mercenaries and Their Impact on World History.* Privately published, 2019.

Wilkinson, Amy. "'Outlander' Recap: 'The Watch,'" *Entertainment Weekly* (3 May 2015).

Militias

To supplement the British army in a war against the rebellious Regulators, fictional Colonel James Fraser recruits farmers and smallholders for the Rowan County Militia, a non-professional regiment assembled only during times of threat. Drawn from the oversized county in piedmont North Carolina, the fighting brotherhood of Fraser's Ridge citizens aged sixteen to sixty requires town-by-town canvassing to fill enlistment rolls. The pay equals 40 shillings (approximately £2 or $388.70 in current value) on enlistment and two shillings (25 pence or $48.59) per day during service. In an assessment of the episode "America the Beautiful," TV reviewer Kayti Burt held out slim hope that a militia could quell lawbreakers. She predicted, "Jamie and Claire are going to have to get a lot more radical if they want to make a difference as white landowners in Colonial-era North Carolina" (Burt, 2018).

The task, imposed by Governor William Tryon at Fraser's Ridge after the 1770 wedding of Brianna Randall and Roger MacKenzie, illustrates the intent of the ambitious resident of Tryon's Palace to suppress local anti–Redcoat reprisals and strengthen his hold on the New York governorship. A militaristic episode in season four takes on a ritual air after Jamie lights the fiery cross Celtic style and begins summoning kin and neighbors along the Catawba, Deep, Haw, Neuse, Tar, and Yadkin rivers. By selecting non-professional riflemen, on May 16, 1771, he musters Scots-American irregulars to suppress the fractious Regulators of the Appalachian lowlands. To illustrate the inexperience of boy soldiers, the TV script depicts brothers Hugh and Iain Og Findlay and fourteen-year-old twins Josiah and Keziah Beardsley, whom Jamie rejects as too young to risk their lives.

Season five, episode four depicts the varied field methods of Jamie and his son-in-law and foster son, Captain Roger MacKenzie and aide Fergus Fraser, who arrive in Brownsville in the midst of a shooting feud. Lacking a military background, Roger employs free whisky and an evening of folk music and dance. The lyrics to "Bonnie Laddie, Highland Laddie" and "Twa Recruitin' Sergeants" prefigure the naiveté and zeal of young recruits, one of whom shoots and kills Murtagh Fitzgibbons Fraser. The entertainment and drink subdue the Browns in a skirmish against Isaiah Morton, who admits seducing Alicia Brown in late 1770. Their troubled romance, on a par with the Celtic tale of Tristan and Isolde, becomes more tangled with Isaiah's acknowledgment of a wife and Alicia's revelation of pregnancy. Her father, Lionel Brown, declares Isaiah an outlaw and threatens to kill him on sight for thwarting an engagement to Elijah Ford, a prosperous tobacco farmer. The complex animosities disrupt militia enlistment, slow the pre-battle muster, and muddle post-skirmish issues after Claire charges Lionel with shooting Isaiah in the back.

Non-standard recruitment threatens disorder. When Jamie arrives in Brownsville, he disapproves of Roger's methods, which cause two militiamen to withdraw from service in disgust. Jamie frees Isaiah from rope manacles and joins in militia merriment by dancing a highland fling, a rare evidence of his musical talent. After helping Isaiah and Alicia escape on horseback, Jamie refocuses on the recruitment of more soldiers. The mobilization culminates in an alliance of Rowan County volunteers with professional British troops. C.L. Hunter's *Sketches of Western North Carolina* (1877) regretted that "true patriots, who did not comprehend the magnitude of [Regulator] grievances, fought against … the *disciples of liberty* in the west" (Hunter, 1877, 11).

Armed with swivel guns and cannon, in "The Ballad of Roger Mac," Redcoats easily overpower the Regulators, bullyrag prisoners of war, and martyr three perpetrators with an impromptu hanging. According to Hunter, the Battle of Alamance Creek produced "the *first blood shed* for freedom in the American colonies" (*ibid.*). Governor Tryon, before departing for New York on May 30, began "committing acts of revenge, cruelty, and barbarity succeeding the Alamance battle" (*ibid.*, 12). The hard-handed attack dissuades Jamie from allying with Tryon, who shows no mercy to citizens protesting government corruption and tax gouging. The issues become central themes of the American Revolution. The symbolic removal of a British uniform jacket anticipates Jamie's switch of fealty from the militia to the patriot army.

See also American Revolution; Regulators; Governor Tryon.

Source

Bassett, John Spencer. *The Regulators of North Carolina (1765–1771)*. Washington, DC: Government Printing Office, 1895, 141–212.
Burt, Kayti. "*Outlander* Season 4 Episode 1 Review: America the Beautiful," *Den of Geek* (5 November 2018).
Ervin, Samuel James, Jr. *A Colonial History of Rowan County, North Carolina*. Chapel Hill: University of North Carolina, 1917.

Hunter, C.L. *Sketches of Western North Carolina.* Raleigh, NC: Raleigh News, 1877.

Reiher, Andrea. "'Outlander' Recap: 'The Company We Keep' Finds Jamie and Claire Caught in Brown Family Drama," *Variety* (8 March 2020).

Murray Genealogy

The Murray household, permanent residents of the Fraser estate, preserves clan land with a farm family's diligence. Goodwill salvages Lallybroch in 1740 after Jamie Fraser returns fellow mercenary Ian Murray from the continental wars. A combat amputee, Ian revives a childhood friendship with former playmate Jenny Fraser, who proposes their impromptu marriage. To save their home from thieves and Redcoats, the Murrays pay extortion fees to the Watch.

The birth of Jamie Fraser Murray produces a firm androcentric basis for the Fraser-Murray estate. Because his uncle, Jamie Fraser, anticipates dying at the Battle of Culloden, on the morning of April 16, 1746, he dispatches Fergus with a deed of sasine ensuring that young Jamie has a secure claim to clan property. Otherwise, the Crown could seize the land from a traitor like Jamie. In Claire's twentieth-century research at the Edinburgh archives, she traces ownership of Lallybroch to a series of Murray descendants before the abandoned residence sinks into disrepair.

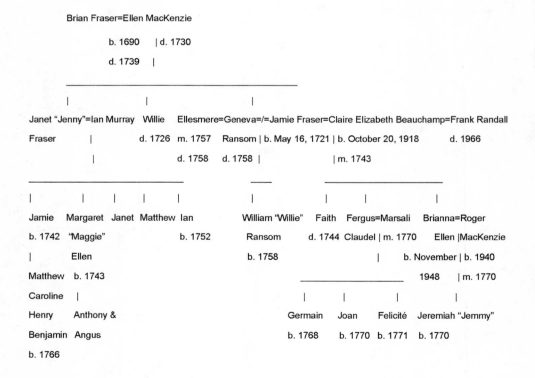

Source

Donnelly, Laura. "The Disappearing of Clan Murray," *Outlander Locations* (11 September 2019).

Prudom, Laura. "'Outlander' Postmortem: The Past Catches Up to Jamie at Lallybroch," *Variety* (25 April 2015).

Wilkinson, Amy. "'Outlander' Recap: 'Lallybroch,'" *Entertainment Weekly* (26 April 2015).

Music

Music sets atmosphere and theme in the fictional *Outlander* TV series, especially the introspective woodwind phrase that denotes mutual desire in the Frasers and Claire's humming "Three Blind Mice" to her three-month-old. Individual scenarios profit from a military tattoo of drums from Captain Leonard's squad at the governor's ball in Kingston; Roger MacKenzie singing "Bonnie Laddie, Highland Laddie" and "Twa Recruitin' Sergeants" to the hot-blooded Browns at Brownsville; and fiddles, flute, jugs, and banjos harmonizing on the backwoods tunes of Appalachia. At a celebration of wellness, sailors on the English man-o'-war *Porpoise* join in "Nancy Dawson," a popular eighteenth-century pan-British hornpipe extolling an historic dancer at Sadler's Wells. To men at sea for long spells, she seems the ideal woman. To survivors of epidemic typhoid fever, a romantic air concludes terror with positive memories.

At the series opener, the background music blends the pensive "Skye Boat Song" with an austere Celtic soloist and varied melodies on harp, penny whistle, uilleann bagpipes, and fiddle. The musical possibilities expand in season five with a choral arrangement. Of his purpose, composer Bear McCreary stated, "I have bent and adapted this song into many different styles I could never have foreseen…. With each permutation, the integrity and soul of the song remains clear" (Donvito, 2020). The occluded pun on "lass" refers to Claire's time travel and hints at the bonnie prince's escape in the guise of a servant, Betty Burke.

The theme song's opening line describes the traditional engulfing of Scots females into an overwhelmingly patrilineal culture. In a first major battle with Jamie over paternalism, Claire demands the right to be an individual free of his dominance rather than the submissive Scots lass of folksong and verse. More alterations in season two add French lyrics sung to viola de gamba, season three West Indian beat, bluegrass from the Appalachias, *a cappella* at Fraser's Ridge, and background strains of 1940s swing and big band recordings. TV critic McKenzie Jean-Philippe, an editor at *Oprah Magazine,* described the strains as "sensual and romantic, earthy and mystical" (Jean-Philippe, 2020).

Other *Outlander* melodies opt for ribald fun rather than melancholy. Male choristers rely on indecent texts, as with "The Lobster Song," a seagoing shanty that revels in smutty language. For travel during the rent collection, War Chief Dougal MacKenzie and his men sing "The Maid Went to the Mill," a bawdy seduction air that suggests the miller's forced sex on a female mill customer. After the birth of a son, the maid informs her parents that the child resulted from "getting her corn ground" free of charge (1:5). For diversity, the episode introduces "Mo Nighean Donn" (My Brown-Haired Girl), Donalda Gilchrest's wooing song for waulking wool. The energetic call and response rhythm accompanies pounding fresh hot urine into the weaving to set the dye. The blandishment recurs in Jamie's frequent endearments to Claire.

Music for Setting

Fictional shifts in centuries require musical dividers, as with the separation of Claire from two worlds in Joni Mitchell's title "Both Sides Now" and in Frank Randall's loss of Claire in season one, episode eight, when a muted trumpet phrase identifies the post–World War II milieu with her longing to escape. The feasting at Castle Leoch in episode ten demands bold bagpipe phrases, followed by a fiddle playing "Comin' Thru the Rye," a cliché melody for Scots and Scotland. Season five ends with a citation from the Fifth Dimension's "Never My Love," a promise of unending devotion.

For Claire's stage performances, Murtagh Fitzgibbons Fraser replaces her choice of "The Boogie Woogie Bugle Boy" with a seduction tune, "The Reels o' Bogie," in which sexual innuendo compares a river valley to female genitalia. In an ironic shift of tone and atmosphere, an official fife and drum tattoo at Wentworth Prison obscures the rumble of shaggy Scots cattle breaking down a dungeon door. The reunion of Claire and Frank Randall on April 16, 1948, jars the viewer with a radio blast of "Milkman Keep Those Bottles Quiet," Ella Mae Morse's swing tune artistically out of pace with a poignant dialogue. The lyrics echo Claire's complaint that the twentieth century is too noisy.

Musical advice smooths the discord between husband and wife in Paris in 1744. Jamie at first sneers at Claire's volunteer job nursing the sick at l'Hôpital des Anges because it places career above her commitment to him. His disapproval declines because he needs a musician who reads German, a search that puts him in touch with the no-nonsense Mother Hildegarde. The decoded keys of Johann Sebastian Bach's harpsichord inventions give Jamie specifics of the Jacobite canvass for funds. At the same time, progress in derailing the bonnie prince's intent harmonizes the Frasers, ending the animosity caused by Jamie's spying and Claire's self-rescue in volunteering to aid the poor.

Song and Nationalism

The musical backdrop maintains a check on atmosphere. To the scree of bagpipes that accompany training Jacobite volunteers at Kingussie, plaintive Scots songs hint at grim outlooks and casualties to come. At the decisive march to join the bonnie prince, an authentic solo of "Moch Sa Mhadainn's Mi Dùsgadh" (Early as I Awaken) lightens soldiers' hearts with praise for the prince's nobility. The lyrics applaud the fealty of Donald Cameron of Lochiel, a central figure in the uprising who suffers grievous wounds at Culloden. Written in 1745 by Alexander McDonald, the uplifting quatrains confirm Highlander faith in the Stuart dynasty.

Traditional Gaelic singer Griogair Labhruidh of Ballachulish extolled the paean to Prince Charles Stuart for surviving an era in which teachers beat school children for voicing their native dialect or wearing Highland plaids. The soloist saluted the marching song for modeling "the free flowing, ornamented and non–Western rhythms of the natural Gaelic music of Scotland" marked by percussion and bagpipe drone to "strong intervallic leaps and a simple, repetitive structure" (McCreary, 2016). On the training of the Rowan County Militia to Highlands war tactics in season five, the repeat of "Moch Sa Mhadainn's Mi Dùsgadh" unites disparate scenes as Jamie once more prepares himself for violence.

Following the Battle of Prestonpans on September 21, 1745, Ross the Smith and Rupert MacKenzie mourn in song the loss of fellow combatants Kincaid, a Lallybroch craftsman, and Angus Mohr, one of Dougal's outriders. Robert Dyer's vernacular Cavalier drinking ditty from the late 1600s, "Down among the Dead Men" refers to empty booze bottles under a table, where sodden drinkers collapse. By extension, the lugubrious text, thumping out repeats of "down, down," calls for a blackout of sorrow and memory (2:10). In place of horrific losses, the drinkers choose swilling and wenching while they still live, a sybaritic motif common to military existentialism as old as seventh-century BCE Greek poet Archilochus.

In the post–Culloden misfortunes, Bear McCreary had a prime opportunity to represent Jamie's longing for Claire in the Hebridean song "The Eriskay Love Lilt" or Mary MacInnes's original version "Gradh Geal Mo Chridh" (Fair Love of My Heart). Oddly, preceding Claire's approach to Carfax Close and Jamie's printshop in 1766, the musician chose to repeat "Comin' Thru the Rye." The tune is an anachronistic reprise of Robert Burns's 1782 poem about Jenny, who gets her skirt wet while crossing the Rye River southwest of Glasgow. Women's clothing circles back to prominence in Young Ian's drunken off-key rendition of "Hap Me wi' Thy Petticoat" in flirtation with Brighid, a willing tavern wench.

North American Tunes

The opening of season four presents an Appalachian folk tribute in the Southern bluegrass twang marking the Frasers' first four months in North America. Murtagh's brief whistling of "The Boogie Woogie Bugle Boy" reprises a perky image of Claire on the rural stage in male attire. Ray Charles's version of Katharine Lee Bates's "America the Beautiful" bitterly satirizes actual conditions in Wilmington, North Carolina, which *Variety* reviewer Andrea Reiher terms "the not-so-beautiful America" (Reiher, 2018). Gavin Hayes's execution on the gibbet calls for Lesley's Gaelic lament, *Eisd Ris* (hear him), a dirge that unites Scots tavern drinkers. The solo anticipates Lesley's demise in a grisly battle of sleeping passengers against the criminals who sully America's promise.

Visually and musically, dissonance plays a prophetic role in *Outlander* TV scripts. The background lyrics of "America the Beautiful" belie the actual safety of immigrants Jamie, Claire, Young Ian, and Lesley on their way west. Of the musical backdrop, Genevieve Valentine, a reviewer for the *New York Times,* remarked, "Pairing a robbing, beating, assault, and murder with the tune of 'America the Beautiful' is one of the more heavy-handed musical cues this show (or any show, ever) has given us" (Valentine, 2018). Maureen Lee Lenker, a reviewer for *Entertainment Weekly,* summarized the paradox: "America is both beautiful and ugly, a land of opportunity and horrors, a place that giveth with one hand and taketh away with the other," an allusion to Job 1:21 that captures Lesley's burial on the riverbank after Bonnet slices his throat (Lenker, 2018). Despite multiple crimes on the way west, the Frasers' resolve to settle on the frontier illustrates New World optimism.

In a salute to community oneness, a choral version of the familiar theme song, performed with additional polish and elocution, opens season five in style. Anachronistic Scots hymnody—"Abide with Me" at Leith Farrish's graveside—diverges from Roger's wedding night rendition of "L-O-V-E" and "Jeremiah Was a Bullfrog," a 1970s tune to entertain a toddler. Roger's ominous "O My Darlin' Clementine" introduces the singer's apprehensions about dying in combat, the fate of his parents, spitfire pilot Jerry and Marjorie MacKenzie, during World War II, and the destiny of the United States in Vietnam. The song contributes a female name meaning "merciful" in episode eight as Roger struggles to recover his voice after a near lynching. In his nightmares, the British show no mercy in Governor William Tryon's offhand choice of three captives for hanging.

Simultaneous with Roger's attempt to overcome trauma, Jocasta Innes sings "The Flowers of the Forrest" at the cairn of her lover, Murtagh Fitzgibbons Fraser. The six stanzas of a female dirge, alike in tone to "Where Have All the Flowers Gone," mourn Scots soldiers killed by the English in 1513 at the Flodden border war. The anti-war lyrics suit victims at the Battle of Culloden on April 16, 1746, as well as the Battle of Alamance Creek on May 16, 1771. A standard Canadian and British commemorative at funerals of soldiers killed in Afghanistan, "Flowers" also marked the passing of Queen Victoria. To set the season five finale in memory of the late 1960s, Claire hallucinates a family nightmare to the lyrics of "Never My Love," a classic by the Association. The words reiterate the theme of unwavering love between Fraser couples.

See also Gaelic; Language.

Source

Donelan, Carol. "'Sing Me a Song of a Lass That Is Gone': Myth and Meaning in the Starz Original Series Out-lander," *Quarterly Review of Film and Video* 35:1 (2018): 31–53.

Donvito, Tina. "Obsessed with the *Outlander* Theme Song? Here's Why It's So Special, Especially Season 5's Version," *Parade* (23 March 2020).

Gregory, E. David. *The Late Victorian Folksong Revival.* Lanham, MD: Rowman & Littlefield, 2010.

Jean-Philippe, McKenzie. "*Outlander*'s Theme Song 'The Skye Boat Song' Was Changed Again for Season 5," *Oprah Magazine (*18 February 2020).

Lenker, Maureen Lee. "*Outlander* Recap: Is It the American Dream or Nightmare?," *Entertainment Weekly* (4 November 2018).

McCreary, Bear. "*Outlander*: Return to Scotland," https://www.bearmccreary.com/#blog/blog/outlander-return-to-scotland/, July 19, 2016.

Reiher, Andrea. "*Outlander* Season 4 Premiere Recap: Jamie and Claire Meet 'America the Beautiful,'" *Variety* (4 November 2018).

Salto, Cattia. "*Outlander*: Wool Waulking Songs," *Terre Celtiche* (11 April 2018).

Valentine, Genevieve. "'Outlander' Season 4 Premiere Recap: No Good Deed Unpunished," *New York Times* (4 November 2018).

Names

The *Outlander* TV narrative makes multiple use of names as characterization, allusion, allegory, and theme, for example, the nickname Roger Mac, which implies "Roger son," a positive relationship between the orphaned war baby and his sometimes gruff father-in-law. Season one opens on the word "sassenach," a term for "foreigner" that attaches to Claire Randall as an aspersion and hint at spying and, later, as a pet name (1:1). Her maiden name—Claire Elizabeth Beauchamp—reflects a bright, unsullied personality and a birth family bearing the French surname "fair field." The middle name "Elizabeth" allies her with England's Renaissance queen and defeater in August 1588 of the Spanish Armada.

Claire's marriage to Frank Randall before World War II gains meaning from Viking connections of Randall to the Nordic Randulf (wolf shield). The significance recurs at Lallybroch, where Claire Fraser, the newly declared Lady Broch Tuarach, identifies an heirloom Viking sword with five-lobed pommel, the Carolingian blade of choice during the rise of Norse raiders in the high Middle Ages. Significant to the theme of wedlock, the sword remains under the laird's bed as a token of masculinity and protection for his family. The Norse connection returns in Claire's journalistic pseudonym Dr. Rawlings, derived from the Norse "famous wolf." Late in season five, Germain dubs her "Grand-mama," giving it a French pronunciation.

Just as the script distinguishes Claire, it makes much of Jamie Fraser's traits. He, too, acquires stature from linkage to monarchy: James I (James VI of Scotland), Alexander (Alexander the Great, Alexander MacMalcolm I of Scotland), and Malcolm (Malcolm III Canmore the Fierce), one of four Scots rulers bearing that cognomen. The surnames MacKenzie and Fraser identify two strands of clan kinship after Ellen MacKenzie's marriage to Brian Fraser, a less prestigious figure by birthright than his wife. Over time,

Jamie's last name passes through a cycle of alterations, beginning with Young Jamie Mac-Tavish, his alias and acquired clan at Castle Leoch to prevent betrayal to the Redcoats. At marriage, he proudly proclaims himself the husband of Claire Fraser, a status change that elates both parties.

More Jamies

War and sedition force Jamie into subsequent appellations that suit a troubled military career. His explosive censure of Wee Jamie derives from a false rumor that the infant was sired on his sister Jenny by Captain Black Jack Randall, a Redcoat officer and sexual opportunist. A notorious warrior at the Battle of Prestonpans on September 21, 1745, later pictured on wanted posters, Jamie acquires the alias "Red Jamie" for his thatch of red hair and a connotation of ferocity and bloodshed. By concealing his ginger top in 1746 with a brown tam, he gains a new alias, "Dunbonnet," a "brown hat" disguise on the run originated in Sir Walter Scott's novel *Waverley* (3:2). Among Jacobite followers in Ardsmuir Prison on the Atlantic Coast of northeastern Scotland in 1752, he becomes MacDubh, literally "son of the dark," a suitable Gaelic designation for a grieved, disheartened widower (3:3).

In 1756, Jamie's transfer to Helwater, an English estate in the Lake District named possibly for "heal" (healing) water or "helio" (sun) water, demands a new name. He hides past allegiance to the bonnie prince from the mansion mistress, Louise Dunsany, an anti–Jacobite. As a stable groom, Alexander "Alex" MacKenzie, he encourages his illegitimate son, Willie Ransom, to call him the nickname "Mac." At Willie's informal baptism as a fellow "stinking papist," a scorned Scots faith, he accepts "William James" as a secret link to his equestrian trainer (3:4). By the time that Jamie reconnects with his son, Willie has given up his boyhood name in favor of the more manly "William," a common coming-of-age alteration (4:6).

A new concealment of identity in Edinburgh appends Alexander and Alex to Malcolm, thus again replacing Jamie's first name and patronym. The subterfuge proves wise after Harry Tompkins, a tax snoop, seizes seditious documents from Jamie's printshop stash. The fire that burns the place of business and evidence of sedition also engulfs his Edinburgh identity, conveniently ridding him of notoriety. The name recurs on the man-o'-war *Porpoise* after Tompkins reveals Jamie's alias and crimes against the Crown, an example of past criminality that haunts him across the Atlantic Ocean to the West Indies.

In the New World, where Jamie stands before Cherokee neighbors and proclaims himself James Fraser, he gains a relief from the swirl of appellations. The discovery of wild strawberries corroborates the choice of a North Carolina home by a red-haired member of the Fraser clan, which takes its name for the French *fraiser* (strawberry). At a high point of tension with Cherokee neighbors, he wins respect by killing the *Tskili Yona*, a marauding bear-man. In a gesture of honor, the Indians dub Jamie *Yona Dihi* (Bear Killer), a renaming ritual common to Native Americans after a life-changing event or heroic deed. By season five, he advances to Germain's grandpère, Jemmy's Grand'Da, and Colonel Fraser. With a touch of Scots charm, Jamie dubs the abandoned Beardsley infant "Wee Bonnie" and proposes adopting her into the household (5:3). Fergus names his third child Felicité (good fortune), who arrives in the wild as her grandfather recovers from snakebite.

SECONDARY ROLES

Nuance freights secondary character names with significance, as with Frank Randall, an astute scholar known for candor; Adso the cat, named for a tenth-century French saint and battler of the anti–Christ; and immigrant Yi Tien Cho, Chinese for "leans against heaven" (3:6). A long roll call of characters identifies biblical names—Elijah Ford, Mary Hawkins, Stephen Bonnet, Isaiah Morton, Jonathan Randall, Jeremiah MacKenzie, James Fraser, Aaron Beardsley, Keziah and Josiah Beardsley, Samuel Lewis, Thomas Leonard, Abner Brown, Simon MacKimmie, Lord Thomas, and Abigail, a slave suitably identified by a synonym for "lady's maid." Other identities suggest behaviors and personality traits:

- Jonathan Wolverton Randall (wolflike), who gains infamy from preying on men, women, and children
- The Rev. Reginald Wakefield (regimented, watchful), who alerts Frank to evil in Inverness
- Laoghaire (Leery), an untrustworthy domestic at Castle Leoch
- Father Bain (destroyer), a dour disciplinarian
- Jeremy Foster (guardian), a Redcoat lieutenant concerned for Claire's welfare
- Minou (kitty), a diminutive for Sandringham's hectored secretary
- Ronald MacNab (grabber), the abuser of son Rabbie
- Horrocks (debris), deserter and blackmailer
- Taran MacQuarrie (prey), a local Watch leader wanted for thievery
- Colonel Quarry (prey), prison warden at Ardsmuir
- Mr. Ward (guardian), a gypsy who aids Claire's search for Jamie
- Marley (forest animal), a lurking, witless guard at Wentworth Prison
- Master Raymond (wise protection), a Paris apothecary and healer
- Sister Angelique (angelic), a nun treating patients at l'Hôpital des Anges
- Magnus (great), the majordomo who transports Claire to the hospital during labor
- Father Anselm (godly protection), named for a saint who revered welcome and hospitality
- Ransom (payoff), Earl of Ellesmere, an appropriate name for an elderly husband who uses his wealth to bargain for a young bride
- Dr. Thorne (barb), one of a group of educated males who belittle women
- Duncan Kerr (cur), a ragtag moor wanderer
- Jerry and Millie Nelson, named for the TV couple Ozzie and Harriet Nelson
- Sandy Travers (crossing over), the mistress Frank Randall intends to marry
- Percival Turner (twister), a tax agent who takes bribes from smugglers
- Father Fogden (pun on "fogged in"), a mad priest on Hispaniola who converses with a coconut
- Ermenegilda (treasure), the beloved Cuban mate of Father Fogden
- Giduhwa (motherland), the original Cherokee home
- Adawehi (religious leader), a fitting name for a Cherokee healer
- Gerhard (brave spear), a crazed German settler who scalps Adawehi
- Gerald (rule of the spear) Forbes, the attorney who overpowers Jocasta
- Leith Farrish (man force), a reference to the cadaver that Marsali studies
- Lionel Brown, a feral appellation for an abductor and rapist

- Morna (mourned) Cameron, a daughter who dies during her family's flight from Scotland to North Carolina
- Phillip Wylie (wily), an opportunist, gambler, and womanizer
- My Darlin' Clementine (merciful), an ironic name that echoes through season five, episode eight
- Felicité (good fortune), a newborn named after her grandpère's recovery from snakebite
- Tebbe (brave), a Germanic name suited to Claire's comforter
- Hodgepile (rural hog), a suitable surname for a murderer and rapist.

On the Cape Fear River in the plantation South, owners typically identify slaves by classical terms—Atlas, Eutroclus, Phaedra, and Ulysses—fitting accompaniments to the Greek names Hector and Jocasta Cameron at River Run and Hercules, Geillis Duncan's henchman at Rose Hall, Jamaica. For the Frasers' sojourn in a baroque Parisian milieu, Jamie changes Claudel's name to Fergus, replacing an effete first name with a manly Gaelic sound and history of kings and lords and the Scots missionary St. Fergus. At Fergus's wedding to Jamie's stepdaughter, Marsali MacKimmie, Jamie formally distinguishes his foster son as "Fergus Claudel Fraser." For the mustering of the Rowan County Militia, the colonel proclaims a fatherly relationship with the "son of my name and of my heart" (5:1).

Roll call after the collection of prisoners of war from Culloden on April 16, 1746, produces full names of the condemned, who struggle with emotions as they await a rifle bullet. Most touching, the answers of youths Giles MacMartin and Frederick MacBean bear the dignity and courage they acquire from adult role models Gordon Killick, Rupert Thomas Alexander MacKenzie, and James Alexander Malcolm MacKenzie Fraser. One inexplicable result of character identities, the repetition of cognomens such as Alexander/Alex appears to have no plan or reason beyond repeated family names Alicia, Jamie, Janet, Joan, Jeremiah, and Ian. The series contains four Johns, four Williams, three Willies, three Geordies, two Jemmys, two Harrys, two Marys, two Josephs, two Duncans, two Franceses, and two Abernethys. Some names pair human with beast or place: two Findlays and a Finley (a horse named "righteous one"), Josiah Beardsley and John Grey's Virginia home on fictional Mt. Josiah, and Clarence Marylebone, the Duke of Sandringham, whose given name also serves the Frasers' abrasive mule. Lallybroch dog Lucas (dazzling) shares a name with Phillip Wylie's Arabian horse. Also puzzling is the repeat of Germain as the Christian name of Marsali and Fergus Fraser's first child and the patronym of the vengeful Parisian Comte St. Germain, linked with a fifth-century CE Gallic bishop of Auxerre and healer of demonic possession.

See also Allegory.

Source

Bangley, Bernard. *Butler's Lives of the Saints.* Brewster, MA: Paraclete, 2005.
Black, George F. *Surnames of Scotland.* Brighton, UK: Churchill & Dunn, 2015.
Lansky, Bruce. *100,000+ Baby Names.* New York: Da Capo, 2019.

Native Americans

Outlander, a televised cultural epic, incorporates indigenous actors as proof of authenticity. At the opening of season four, a barefoot company of aborigines clad in skins and adorned with rattling seashells stacks rocks into a monolithic circle. In obeisance to pagan astronomy, they thrum in a counter-clockwise ring dance venerating the heavens. A poorly dramatized view of Iron Age anthropology, the set piece depicts humankind as shaky, ghoulishly made up, and visually unfocused. The setting recurs without dancers after Roger MacKenzie, in flight from his Mohawk captors, flees to the stones. A blip of time indicates his return to the twentieth century until the grimace of his captor in a steamy bathroom mirror interrupts the passage.

To ease an ethnic shift from Scotland and France to North America, TV producer Maril Davis chose cast members from First Peoples. To avoid union interference, she "flew a group of First Nation actors from Canada and also consulted with a Cherokee leader in North Carolina about the tribe's culture and concerns about onscreen portrayals" (Vineyard, 2018). Veteran performers include Tom Jackson (Tehwahsehkwe), a featured Cree player in *Skinwalkers* and *Cold Pursuit;* Trevor Carroll (Otter Tooth, Ta'wineonawira), a Canadian director, producer, and writer of *Common Chord;* and Cree actor Tantoo Cardinal (Adawehi), an intuitive native character on *Dr. Quinn, Medicine Woman, Dances with Wolves, Legends of the Fall,* and *Longmire.* A grandmotherly clairvoyant, Adawehi practices herbalism and forms a professional bond with Claire by exchanging information on birthing protocols, a positive interest in the survival of the next generation.

A Genuine View

Authenticity burdens the scripts with obvious conflicts. For costumes, out of "an obligation to do it right," designer Terry Dresbach conferred with native cast: "That is your toughest audience, and that's who you want to feel that you respected and honored their traditions" (Hallemann, 2018). On encountering North Carolina aborigines, the fictional Frasers must legitimize their claim on native land. Genevieve Valentine, a TV critic for the *New York Times,* stressed the obvious: "Jamie, who spent years trying to defeat the English occupiers on his family's ancestral lands, begins planning his homestead in Cherokee territory and there's no sign the show notices this cognitive dissonance" (Valentine, 2018).

Valentine commented on the significance of a time traveler's perspective, the only one "who has the historical context to understand the scale of the American genocide" (*ibid.*). The resonance between Claire and Otter Tooth's ghost derives from the burden of knowing the destiny of First Peoples. The arrival of Brianna Randall and Roger MacKenzie compounds the impact of history. Paradoxically, it is Young Ian, born in the eighteenth century, who commiserates with the native population and defends them from scurrilous charges of burning a Dutch cabin and shooting a resident with an arrow. In the season five finale, Claire meets Wendigo Donner, an abductor who bears the name of an Algonquian cannibal monster and the last name of an 87-member Donner expedition that floundered in deep snow while crossing California's Sierra Nevada in spring 1846. Their reliance on human remains for food connects the 48 survivors with cannibalism.

Animosities

At a telling moment in the fictional confrontation between whites and Cherokee, the *Outlander* TV epic fills German immigrant Gerhard Mueller with a misguided antagonism against a mounted party that stops by his creek to water their horses. He misinterprets the blessing of waters with tobacco as a curse and blames the tribe for measles that kills daughter-in-law Petronella and infant granddaughter Clara. Ironically, he and wife Rosewitha brought the contagion from Cross Creek. Television analyst Kayla Kumari Upadhyaya called his requital against an elderly woman "horrifying evidence of his monstrosity" (Upadhyaya, 2018). Incorporating a white man's scalping of Adawehi, the episode blames Europeans for an inhumanity that legend and fiction typically foists on Indians. An unstated connection between Germans like Mueller and World War II reflects ethnic animosity in the combat that opens *Outlander*.

On Young Ian Murray's return to Fraser's Ridge in 1771, his austere expression and Mohawk feathers, braid, and outfit suggest a young outlander deeply altered by adopting the Native American language and culture. His sheathed knife centers a wool jacket marked by hard wear; over his shoulder, he bears bow and quiver. While adults refrain from prying into his experience at Shadow Lake, New York, two-year-old Germain Fraser is the only resident to comment on Ian's Mohawk haircut and the eight dots tattooed under his eyes. Most telling of wardrobe elements, the purple and white wampum bracelet betokens an heirloom of his lost wife, a bicultural tragedy that he can't convey to his Uncle Jamie. On joining the Rowan County Militia in retrieving Claire from abductors, Ian first shaves the sides of his head and sweeps blood across his forehead. In action against the bandits, he throws his tomahawk into Arvin Hodgepile's chest and wields his war club against the remaining white desperados.

See also Dance; Piracy; Prophecy; Racism.

Source

Hallemann, Caroline. "*Outlander*'s Terry Dresbach on the 'Terrifying' Challenge of Designing This Season's Native American Costumes," *Town & Country* (25 November 2018).
Reynolds, William R. *The Cherokee Struggle to Maintain Identity in the 17th and 18th Centuries.* Jefferson, NC: McFarland, 2015.
Robinson, Joanna. "*Outlander*'s Thanksgiving Episode Gives the Book's Native Americans a Much-Needed Update," *Vanity Fair* (26 November 2018).
Upadhyaya, Kayla Kumari. "*Outlander* Bungles the Conflict in 'Savages,'" *AVClub* (2 December 2018).
Valentine, Genevieve. "'Outlander,' Season 4, Episode 3 Recap: Mysterious Encounters," *New York Times* (18 November 2018).
_____. "'Outlander' Season 4 Premiere Recap: No Good Deed Unpunished," *New York Times* (4 November 2018).
Vineyard, Jennifer. "'Outlander' Takes Manhattan," *New York Times* (2 November 2018).
Weaver, Nicole. "Why 'Outlander' Doesn't Have Americans Playing Cherokee and Mohawk Characters," *Showbiz CheatSheet* (6 October 2018).

Parallels

Unity in the expansive *Outlander* TV production depends in part on narrative symmetry, unexpected regularity, or scenes that reflect or predict future action. Parallels resonate in parents who lose their children—Claire, Jamie, Shona MacNeill, Geillis Duncan, Dougal MacKenzie, Louise and William Dunsany, Lucinda and Hiram Brown, Hector and Jocasta Cameron—and those who foster waifs—Claire, Jamie, Reginald Wakefield, Ian and Jenny Murray, William John and Sarah MacKenzie, and Lucinda and Hiram Brown. In season two, episode 7, Captain Black Jack Randall's child abuse introduces a series of motifs and details that begins with raping Fergus. The exploitation reprises threats, sodomy, and carnal felonies committed against Claire and Jamie Fraser. Like Jamie, Fergus endures forced anal penetration, an assault that troubles his sleep with unspeakable flashbacks. Suitably, both males profit from Claire's counsel to rid them of shame and guilt.

The irony of Claire's abduction and gang rape in 1773 by backcountry outlaws enables Jamie to enact acceptance, pity, and love for his badly mauled wife.

The retrieval of Jamie from Wentworth Prison ends his torment by a sodomite with the collaboration of Claire and Murtagh Fitzgibbons Fraser, who herds nineteen shaggy highland cattle to the back door that Claire leaves open. The clamor and mooing disguise sounds of rescue while the British Army struts its might with a military tattoo. At a tense moment in season five, Jamie recycles the ploy of animal intervention to help lovers escape an angry father. While Isaiah Morton and Alicia Brown gallop up an empty road, Jamie scatters Brownsville's horses in the opposite direction and blames a goat for meddling, a clever end to an explosive showdown that could have cost Isaiah's life and left Alicia to bear a fatherless child. The dual scenes base script logic on reuniting separated lovers, an age-old romantic motif that infuses both comedy and tragedy.

On Claire's return home from l'Hôpital des Anges, Fergus presents her a bouquet of blue cineraria (*Cineraria pericallis*), a funereal token of remembrance. The color echoes the forget-me-nots she examined at Craigh na Dun and the blue wings that prophesy healing and a connection with the Virgin Mary, the blue-robed mother of Jesus who also grieves for a dead child. (The heron wings create an unintended pun on child delivery by stork.) As in the case of rape for Mary Hawkins, Brianna, and Fergus, Claire's counsel eases Jamie's pain. At Father Anselm's abbey, she assures Jamie that their love can weather the assault on his dignity and manhood. In jolting him out of his funk, she resorts to slapping her patient, a method she learned from brother-in-law Ian Murray, who apparently directs it toward his stubborn wife Jenny. Claire's resolute words illustrate her skill at consoling a troubled mate.

Nurse and Healer

Key to Claire's professional demeanor lie scenes of diagnosing, prescribing herbal therapies, treating wounds and broken bones, compounding remedies, and tending the dying and their survivors. Season one of the TV narrative opens on Allied combat nursing in World War II at a field dressing station, where she clamps a femoral artery to save an injured soldier from bleeding to death. Post-time travel shows Claire grieving over a dead changeling infant left in a tree for the fairies and treating gored wild boar hunters and Tammas Baxter, a child poisoned by lily of the valley berries. Her cuddling and sorrow predict the loss of stillborn daughter Faith, whom she clasps all day. The prefatory scene anticipates an innate longing for motherhood and unbearable sadness at preventable harm to the defenseless.

The motif expands as Claire's Harvard medical education enables chancy surgeries, inquests, quarantine, and births—delivering Petronella Mueller and Fanny Beardsley's daughters, boring into the skull of housebreaker John Barton to relieve pressure, treating Isaiah Morton's gunshot wound to the right lung, removing tonsils from the Beardsley twins, and setting sanitation standards on the British man-o'-war *Porpoise* during a typhoid fever outbreak. While conducting an autopsy on Leith Farrish to determine that a burst appendix and peritonitis killed him, she discovers bloodletting from his arm and dosing with mercury pills. Faulty home care foments Claire's outrage at ignorance and prompts an essay to educate the eighteenth-century mind beyond superstition and folklore. The publication of ghost-written advice surprises her with a new professional identity, Dr. Rawlings.

VIEWS ON HUMAN RIGHTS

Action in seasons three and four introduces human rights violations from multiple perspectives. In Jamaica, Jamie purchases an African from a Kingston slave market to prevent the auctioneer's public humiliation of the boy by demonstrating his genital prowess. Named Temeraire (bold), the Ghanian remains with the Frasers until they can release him safely among Maroons, a community of escaped slaves living outside Rose Hall. On arrival in the North Carolina foothills, Claire foregrounds the destiny of Native Americans with memories of Highland losses after the Battle of Culloden on April 16, 1746, when Redcoats persecuted traitors with death, indenturing, and divestment of property and clan powers. The narrative stresses that the Cherokee, Mohawk, and other first nations risk losing traditional lands to greedy English imperialists and investors, the same people who kidnap and trade Africans for profit.

Other scenes anticipate or echo choices and moral decisions that imbue North American history. After the British ambush Taran MacQuarrie and the Watch, Jenny burns a Redcoat messenger's feet to gain information about her brother's capture. "Free Will," an episode in season five, reprises the messenger's terror by close inspection of Aaron Beardsley's hot-foot torture. Fanny wants her husband to stay alive to suffer more agony for murdering four former wives and mistreating two indentured servant boys, Josiah and Keziah. Both episodes end the torment with murder—Murtagh Fitzgibbons Fraser garroting the British courier and Jamie euthanizing Beardsley with a bullet to the head. However, the justification for the two killings differs: Murtagh obliterates an eyewitness to the search for Jamie while Jamie ends Beardsley's misery from a paralytic stroke, maggot-ridden bed sores, and a gangrenous foot.

A poignant pair of actions, the parting of Alex and Jack Randall and of the MacKenzie brothers amplifies love and antipathy in blood relations. For Laird Colum MacKenzie, a pre-suicidal wrangle with Dougal airs jealousy and mistrust. Without faith in Dougal, the true sire of Hamish, Colum opts to leave his heir and clan rule to Jamie, a MacKenzie nephew in the Fraser clan. At Colum's demise from drinking yellow jasmine poison, Dougal weeps and embraces him in a welter of regret and unfinished business. For the Randalls, a pathologic Jack offers to support Alex's unborn child and future widow Mary until Alex insists on a marriage of the two. Under the watch of a dying brother, Jack grudgingly pledges wedding vows that govern the relationship one more day until Jack's death at the battle of Culloden on April 16, 1746. The mortal circumstances of two sets of brothers leaves to an unpredictable future the chiefdom of Hamish MacKenzie and the survival of Mary Randall and her baby.

See also Foreshadowing.

Source

Donelan, Carol. "'Sing Me a Song of a Lass That Is Gone': Myth and Meaning in the Starz Original Series Outlander," *Quarterly Review of Film and Video* 35:1 (2018): 31–53.

Harrod, Mary, and Katarzyna Paszkiewicz. *Women Do Genre in Film and Television*. New York: Routledge, 2017.

Martinelli, Marissa. "How *Outlander* Keeps Getting Tangled Up in Real-Life U.K. Politics," *Browbeat* (14 July 2016).

Parenting

The care and protection of children occupy serious places in the lives of Claire and Jamie Fraser while they tend Willie Ransom and Brianna and foster Fergus, Marsali and

Joanie MacKimmie, Wee Bonnie Beardsley, and Young Ian Murray and, to some degree, Elias Pound on the naval brig *Porpoise*. In Paris, the Frasers accept Fergus, a nameless pickpocket reared at Madame Elise's brothel, as an employee in a mail theft cabal against the bonnie prince. Jamie indulges the boy and thanks him for guarding Claire the night of the brawl that ends with arrests by gendarmes. The question of rearing foster children affects other lives, even the bonnie prince. During a private consultation, Claire counsels Louise de Rohan, Prince Charlie's lover, on bearing his child and mothering it with her husband Jules. The triad precedes John Grey and Isobel Dunsany's care for her nephew Willie and of Claire and Frank Randall's two decades of rearing Brianna. To Claire's late-term worrying in 1744 that she lacks mothering skills because of her mother's death, Jamie comforts her with promises to learn what they don't know about raising bairns.

On relocating to Lallybroch, Fergus settles securely into the role of son and greets his fostering parents at Kingussie, the training camp for the Jacobite army. On Jamie's command to take the Lallybroch deed to the Murrays, he embraces the boy and calls him *mon fils* (my son, 2:12). Affection deepens at Marsali MacKimmie's marriage to Fergus, where Jamie officially names him Fergus Claudel Fraser. The fatherhood role recurs in season five, episode one, in which the colonel summons Fergus to the Rowan County Militia with the blandishment "son of my name," a hearty affirmation of a waif he rescued from early training in crime (5:1).

PARENTAL CONCERNS

In the letdown after the Battle of Culloden on April 16, 1746, Jamie, in a cave hideout for six years, encounters Fergus's pre-teen accusations that his paternal ideal has given up on a fifth rebellion. Jamie's grief at the Redcoat Corporal MacGregor's amputation of Fergus's hand demonstrates a father's remorse for his child, whom he had previously promised to protect and support. Jamie restates the initial bargain to offer masses for a year if Fergus should die in his service. Blaming himself for the boy's handicap, Jamie himself becomes the orphan in need of security. He crumples into Jenny's arms, a collapse assuaging the mother hunger he has suffered since boyhood and in the six years that Claire has been gone. Gladly, Jenny tends to Fergus's needs with ample whisky and words what comfort she can to Jamie. Their relationship implies that Jenny replaces Ellen Fraser as surrogate parent.

At River Run, Jocasta, the charming widow Cameron, abuses a mothering role with niece Brianna by manipulating her loyalty to Roger MacKenzie, a captive of the Mohawk. Auntie Jo predicts that the handfasted couple will never reunite. To heighten family prestige, she gathers four prominent colonials and coerces Bree to marry one of them to parent her unborn child and spare the family shame. At the impromptu engagement of Bree and John Grey, Jocasta rewards her with a self-congratulatory MacKenzie honorarium for capturing a titled lord, the most aristocratic of a field of five eligible men. To Bree's questions about love, Jocasta brushes off the suggestion that she must find romance before delivering her fatherless baby.

NEEDY CHILDREN

Perhaps the best evidence of Jamie's dedication to wife and family occurs in season five, episodes three and four with comfort to Josiah and Keziah Beardsley, who live in indentured servitude from age two. In rescuing the boys from horror, the Frasers encounter a sadist suffering his wife Fanny's vengeance for beating her and the two servant boys.

After identifying "Wee Bonnie" Beardsley's ethnicity in 1771, Jamie sees Claire absorbed in the needs of a biracial infant, whom Fanny abandons. He cares so deeply for Claire's need to nurture that, in season five, he suggests adopting Wee Bonnie. Because Claire is menopausal, he offers to share the experience they didn't get with Brianna and Willie without the suffering caused by Faith's birth. The proposal reveals new depths in Jamie as the couple reaches middle age.

At Brownsville, multiple aspects of adoption turn Claire from her own yearning to the needs of Lucinda Brown, her breast still engorged after losing a newborn. The episode depicts Claire's urge to comfort the wetnurse who feeds the biracial newborn. Because Hiram and Lucinda have lost a premature child, Claire convinces Jamie to leave Wee Bonnie with a loving couple, a choice based on the best future for an African American girl who is likely to incur prejudice and rejection. At the same time, Jamie's beneficence nurtures their loving commitment, a part of wedlock that overcomes the ill-fortune of never being a typical nuclear family.

See also Frank Randall.

Source

Cohn, Paulette. "*Outlander*'s Jamie and Claire Just Rejected Their Last Chance to Raise a Child Together— Diana Gabaldon Explains Why," *Parade* (8 March 2020).

Donelan, Carol. "'Sing Me a Song of a Lass That Is Gone': Myth and Meaning in the Starz Original Series Outlander," *Quarterly Review of Film and Video* 35:1 (2018): 31–53.

Keen, Suzanne. "Probable Impossibilities: Historical Romance Readers Talk Back," *Style* 52:1 (2018): 127–132.

Paris

The gilt-edged decadence of Paris in 1744 shifts the fictional *Outlander* TV historical fiction from a rugged Scots outback and long gallops over the moors to baroque salons, costumes, carriages, and mannered dialogue. Production designer Jon Gary Steele justified the move for stylistic reasons: "Eighteenth-century Paris is the most magnificent period in terms of design for architecture, art, fashion, and landscape" (Desowitz, 2016). The smartly dressed king Louis XV hosts entertainment at Versailles and flaunts his orangerie and cups of chocolate, a fad introduced from Central America. A morning regimen admits males to view his dressing for the day, a diversion for elite guests curious about the royal lifestyle.

Featuring the bonnie prince in an opulent bordello backdrop, season two separates the Frasers night and day and costs them sleep in their borrowed residence. Conflicts depict Claire coping with early pregnancy by walking along the docks to stifle morning sickness and managing the well-trained staff of cousin Jared Fraser's upscale townhouse. Meanwhile Jamie runs a wine business and spends late nights monitoring the monarchic blather of a would-be Stuart king. Actually filmed in Prague, tree-lined boulevards and Jared's walled courtyard contrast a back alley where roving companies of Les Disciples search for virgins to deflower.

Amusements and Poverty

Drollery accents the coupling of Murtagh Fitzgibbons Fraser with the maid Suzette, house domestics removing the wreckage of a dinner party, and the employment of Fergus, the household pickpocket, as postal thief. In the background, the bonnie prince claims to receive funding for a Jacobite war from the Duke of Sandringham, Le Comte

St. Germain, and Louis XV. For a balanced view of European social status, cinematography grips viewers with a female patient dying of diabetes, Mother Hildegarde playing a Bach invention at the pianoforte, Claire in chic crimson décolleté hobnobbing with over-dressed aristocrats, diners critiquing a Lully opera, the smallpox-ridden merchant-man *Patagonia* burning in the harbor, and Jamie dueling with his nemesis at the Bois de Boulogne to requite child sodomy. In the background, Jamie contends with himself over nightmares and flashbacks that limit his intimacy with Claire.

The socioeconomic backstory juxtaposes Parisians in varied castes—one begging for alms on the steps of the charity dispensary, the fictional l'Hôpital des Anges near the historic Notre Dame Cathedral, and another hoisting foam-encircled nipples at Murtagh Fitzgibbons Fraser in a Versailles salon. A-list card games, a chess match, and Louise de Rohan's coddling of pet monkey Colette attest to ample leisure time and disposable income. Louise's tea klatches picture daft females in conversation about the love lives of domestics and ways to rid Paris streets of the unsightly poor. Unlike nobles who fraternize and name-drop at Versailles and dally by trellises in the primly hedged gardens, Claire spends her days analyzing urine and treating wounds, scrofula, burns, broken bones, and mysterious infections, in part with the aid of an in-house terrier named Bouton. The time traveler's inner thoughts ponder the mere 46 years that separate a sybaritic society from the 1789 French Revolution and the beheading of the next Louis, who won't be born for another decade.

CONFLICTS IN THE CITY

The dissimulations of the second season cause Claire and Jamie, both cradle Catholics, to wonder about their culpability for stealing St. Germain's wine shipment and faking smallpox among his warehouse workers. Star Caitriona Balfe described the alteration of couple dynamics as "duplicitous roles, befriending people and using that information. Their honeymoon is over" (Hahn, 2016). Claire takes advice from Master Raymond, an occultist apothecary blessed with a gentle, reassuring manner: he knows how to prohibit pregnancies, fake murder, and soothe nightmares of well-heeled clients. She appears to match him herb for herb in diagnostic experience and spares him execution at the French Star Chamber with a sleight-of-hand trick. A memorable character for his demeanor and captivating exotica, Raymond eases her pressing concern for the Randall genealogy and the possibility that Frank will never exist, a time-traveler's puzzler.

Disordered family life and insecure wedlock regain their marital buttress from mutual afflictions—Jamie's arrest for dueling and the harrowing birth and death of Faith Fraser, delivered by the royal executioner, Monsieur Foret. After Claire's recovery from puerperal sepsis, the prime killer of parturient women into the nineteenth century, Jamie's return from the Bastille on the Seine River clears the air of the couple's accusations, score-keeping, and regrets. The TV production closes the Paris chapter at a burial site in the convent garden on a touching farewell to Faith, a word-play indicating the couple's renewed faith in each other. For the sake of their sanity, they flee Paris and return to Scotland.

See also Altruism; Bonnie Prince Charlie; Costumes; Dueling; Execution; Star Chamber; Versailles.

Source

Desowitz, Bill. "'Outlander' Season 2: How Designers Nailed the Glam 18th Century Paris Look (Emmy Watch)," *IndieWire* (22 April 2016).

Hahn, Kate. "How *Outlander* Is Taking the Art of Love (and War) to Paris in Season 2," *TV Insider* (29 March 2016).
Jones, Trahern, and Lindsay Jones. "A Tour of Old Parisian Hospitals," *Student Hospitalist* (March 2012).
Kline, Wendy. *Coming Home: How Midwives Changed Birth.* Oxford, UK: Oxford University Press, 2019.
Prudom, Laura. "'Outlander' Stars on 'Surprising' Season 2 Twists, Parisian Politics and Changing History," *Variety* (8 January 2016).

Pioneering

Historical fiction in the *Outlander* TV epic details the progression west from River Run to Fraser's Ridge, which takes the Frasers ten days. Historian John Preston Arthur, compiler of *Western North Carolina: A History* (1914), summarized pioneer journeys through heavy wilderness: "Behind the axmen went a mixed procession of women, children, dogs, cows and pack-horses loaded with kettles and beds" (Arthur, 1914, 74). Immediate needs for the newcomers involve camping, erecting brush shelters, watching for Indians, and tying meat sacks in trees to protect food supplies. Hunting and gathering include stacking firewood, hauling water, picking wild garlic, and netting and cleaning trout for roasting on a spit. Young Ian repairs holes in fishnets. For a short deer hunt in "Blood of My Blood," Jamie packs simple herbal cures and foods and raises a blanket over bedding near the campfire to shelter son Willie, a privileged boy unaccustomed to roughing it.

With the aplomb of rancher Clara Allen in Larry McMurtry's *Lonesome Dove* and pioneer Caroline Ingalls in the *Little House* TV series, Claire, devoid of corset, bum roll, and frothy outfits, accomplishes whatever needs doing. Home building finds her locating a runaway mule, dragging felled tree trunks to the cabin site, and chopping short limbs with a hatchet. Her kitchen prowess wins no awards, but she knows how to cure meat into jerky, dry herbs for seasonings and remedies, and tend and stitch emergency wounds. For self-protection, she practices target shooting with a rifle, dropping a buffalo in its tracks with one shot. Director Denise Di Novi justified the effort: "Claire is a tough woman and she can protect herself to a certain degree, more so than most women in this time" (Bennett, 2019, 153). The skills are necessary "because so much of the story takes place with her alone, waiting for possible danger" (*ibid.*).

THE EXPANDED FAMILY

Jamie and Young Ian labor at dislodging rocks from the cabin foundation and planing trunks with an adz to create four-sided building timbers for the one-room cabin, smokehouse, outhouse, and medical shed. In the plans, a rock chimney sets the stage for a hearth blessing, a group reverence to God and the family's future. Much of their provisioning in Rowan County results from herding milk goats, raising a pig, planting a vegetable bed, stringing up gourds for martin houses, and foraging for maggots to clean a wound. Murtagh Fitzgibbons Fraser imports barrels from Charleston for aging whisky, which Jamie and Ian distill from rye and barley for drinking, sanitizing, and trading. Shared labor strengthens unity in the family and among neighbors.

While adapting to fathering a grown daughter, Jamie teaches Brianna about bee stealing, a means of relocating honeycomb closer to the cabin. He discovers that she is already a crack shot with a rifle and a willing hand at washing and drying laundry. Claire learns to knit, layers a rabbit skin vest with her ever-present shawl, and travels to Gerhard and Rosewitha Mueller's cabin to deliver their granddaughter Clara. Because frontier wardrobes merge old with new, costumer Nina Ayres added, "We looked at mountain men and fur traders and the Native Americans … at how we could change the silhouette of men by using moccasins and leggings that the Native Americans wore and then mixing that with European and Western costume" (Zemler, 2018).

THE FRASER COLONY

At the big house, pioneering burdens lessen with a roomier dwelling, growing tenancy, and assistance with baking brick before a fire, painting walls, gardening, sewing, and carpentry on the foundation and front porch. Claire sews a creamy linen wedding dress for Brianna and embroiders Scots thistles at the hem and neckline. Jamie hires Josiah Beardsley to hunt for the family's meat while Claire treats patients and bakes and moistens bread in glass cloches to mold into penicillium. For finished meat, Marsali Fraser hacks pork into serving portions and saves blood and offal for other uses. Secretly, she studies Leith Farrish's cadaver and practices wound repair by stitching pig tissue.

Female settlers' skills in the North Carolina wilds range from beating laundry by a stream and straining indigo for dye to dipping wicks into wax for candles and grinding apples for cider. Claire and Jamie investigate less prosperous conditions at Aaron Beardsley's trading post, a decrepit wood barn and cabin stocked with goats, crates, barrels, and bundles of hides and furs. Their compassion ends with a home burial for Aaron and rescue of Fanny Beardsley's infant, a tempting opportunity to add childrearing to their lives. Of her pioneer life, Claire prefers to continue housework and a medical practice at the big house, where she saves Jamie from infection by using a crude homemade syringe that Brianna crafts from a snakehead. On return from abduction in season five, Claire relishes an ordinary day.

See also Fraser's Ridge.

Source

Arthur, John Preston. *Western North Carolina: A History.* Raleigh, NC: Edwards & Broughton, 1914.
Bennett, Tara. *The Making of Outlander: The Series.* New York: Random House, 2019.
Rumple, Jethro. *A History of Rowan County, North Carolina.* Salisbury, NC: J.J. Bruner, 1881.
Zemler, Emily. "How *Outlander*'s Costume Designers Took Jamie and Claire into the New World," *Elle* (10 December 2018).

Piracy

Film pirates date to early cinema history—to the appeal of Long John Silver, Captain Hook, Sea Hawk, Jack Sparrow, and Captain Blood, a 1935 swashbuckler played by Hollywood heartthrob Errol Flynn. In *The Cinematic Eighteenth Century,* editors Srividhya Swaminathan of Long Island University and Steven W. Thomas at New York's Wagner College refer directly to the lure of pirates in screen iconography, particularly *Crossbones* and *Black Sails.* They note that the "criss-crossing narratives" merge sea adventures with "slavery and sexual taboos, as well as royal families, colonial encounters, and revolutionary movements," all motifs of the *Outlander* TV narrative (Swaminathan and Thomas, 2017, 5). Encounters with the three-masted frigate *Bruja* in season three, episode twelve, introduce the fictional Frasers to human trafficking, a possible explanation for the impromptu kidnap of nephew Young Ian by Portuguese buccaneers off Scotland's Selkie Island, typical of the remote and solitary spots that sea brigands plunder.

Swaminathan and Thomas summarized the glamour of a global buccaneer who "circumvents reason, morality, and international politics" (*ibid.,* 130). In direct competition with Spain, seafaring theft derived from the success of Sir Francis Drake in 1563 on the galleon *Golden Hind* at enriching the treasury of Elizabeth I with Spanish gold. Her successor, James I, plotted to turn England into a trading emporium headed by the East India Company and backed in 1611 by the spoils of the *Pearl,* the king's 150- to 200-ton privateer. The author of "Buccaneer Ethnography," Anna Neill at Kansas University identified such court-sponsored raiding as "historically central to English colonization of the New World as well as to the growth of English maritime power [that] helped to reshape the language of imperialism" (Neill, 2000, 165).

FILMING FREEBOOTERS

Fictional images of pirates imprisoning Young Ian in the *Bruja's* hold and in the Jamaican mansion Rose Hall amid a cluster of boys stolen for the sexual delight of Geillis Duncan preface the auctioneer's genital demonstration of Temeraire, the Ghanian whom Jamie buys at the Kingston slave market for £20 ($3,715.29 at the current value). In both instances, coercion and sexual exploitation await young males from buyers and traffickers. At the Frasers' intervention, Temeraire has a better chance of liberation among Maroons than Young Ian, Henry, and Abeeku from Geillis's keepers at Abandawe. The boys become prey of the *Bakra* (white woman) and her murderous staff, who slit the throats of Robbie and three other virgins after their sexual appeal ends with copulation.

The drama of season three enacts real aspects of the Atlantic slave trade, perpetrated after 1600 by Arab, Berber, British, Dutch, French, Genoan, Maltese, Portuguese, Scandinavian, Spanish, Turk, Venetian, and West African profiteers. The Portuguese and Spanish advanced from impounding Native American laborers in the style of Christopher Columbus to a systematic commerce in blacks, who could survive brute drudgery and tropical heat longer than Indians. Throughout the 1700s, the white planter's production of sugar cane and rum made British Jamaica a prime investment choice.

BUILDING FORTUNES

The abduction of laborers to serve as sugar workers, domestics, and breeders continued until 1869 in Portuguese colonies in Brazil, Malacca, India, Bahrain, Macau, and the Philippines. To connect Rufus, a North Carolina slave on the Cafe Fear River at River Run, with the involvement of Africans, the series identifies his sister as Abena, a suggestion of the nation of Benin. Described in the film *Band of Angels,* the Dahomey of Benin, Ashanti of Ghana, Yoruba of Nigeria, and other West African tribes filled their treasuries by engaging in human bondage from 1600 to 1800. Slavers boldly anchored offshore on the Bight of Benin to arrange with Chief Tegbesu human transport from the Gulf of Guinea to bondage markets in the Western Hemisphere.

West Indian pirates like the historical Stede Bonnet bought letters of marque allowing them to seize and plunder Spanish sea traffic as privateers for the British crown. On September 5, 1717, George I decreed a one-year's grace to any pirate surrendering to a colonial governor, an amnesty that appealed to Blackbeard and Bonnet. In season five, the fictional Stephen Bonnet expands his territory from waylaying barges on the Cape Fear River to gambling, smuggling luxuries and whisky, and white slavery, illustrated by the sale of Brianna MacKenzie to Captain Howard. In the estimation of TV critic Kayti Burt, the *Outlander* episodes established that "the misuse of power is not something specific to the English or to Europe or even to institutions. It can be anywhere, even in this new land of hope" (Burt, 2018).

See also Stephen Bonnet; Maroons; Smuggling.

Source

Burt, Kayti. "*Outlander* Season 4 Episode 1 Review: America the Beautiful," *Den of Geek* (5 November 2018).
Neill, Anna. "Buccaneer Ethnography: Nature, Culture, and Nation in the Journals of William Dampier," *Eighteenth-Century Studies* 33:2 (Winter 2000): 165–180.
Nwaubani, Adobe Tricia. "When the Slave Traders Were African," *Wall Street Journal* (20 September 2019).
Swaminathan, Srividhya, and Steven W. Thomas. *The Cinematic Eighteenth Century*. New York: Routledge, 2017.

Prestonpans

East of Edinburgh at the eleventh-century coastal saltworks known as "Priest Town Pans," the battleground of Prestonpans on the Firth of Forth situated the first major triumph of the 1743 Jacobite rebellion. A lopsided victory, the historic skirmish cost the British 500 casualties and 600 prisoners of war, more than ten times the Scots losses. Filming for the fictional *Outlander* TV narrative opens on a decaying Highlander killed in the woods, a one-man proof of the slaughter to come after Jacobite victories at Perth and Edinburgh. The lead-up to combat assimilates Claire Fraser's careful preparation of a medical ward and her encouragement of female volunteers. The script offsets female cooperation with squabbles among two historical figures—Commander George Murray and Irish quartermaster John O'Sullivan—and the fictional Jamie, a result of the political undercurrent to unseating the Hanoverians. In a book review for the *British Journal for Military History,* historian Arran Johnston classed their victory as "only temporarily decisive" (Pittock, 2019, 74).

On September 21, 1745, fortune brings the fictional troops of exiled Prince Charles Edward Stuart and Lord George Murray to victory over General John Cope. At first, the boggy ground at Prestonpans impedes cavalry and represents the speculative coming together of pro and anti–Stuart factions after months of negotiations in Paris. A farm boy, Richard Anderson, based on a real Scot from Whitburgh, voluntarily leads Jamie's Jacobite regiment over a concealed trail before dawn, a serendipity that speeds the aggressive Scots into play before British sentries awaken. The approaching regiment steals through heavy fog, a suggestion of unclear Jacobite outlooks and anticipations. To enhance confusion and the cooperation of nature, the filming took place in a smoky tent.

After a half-hour conflict results in a British rout of some 1,000 men and the capture of 600 more, Jamie claims the day for his troops. Their Highlands charge, a Scots specialty, proves War Chief Dougal MacKenzie right about traditional battlefield methods. The episode dramatizes the ups and downs of military heroism in the prince's salute to Dougal for testing the swamp within musket range of the enemy. The prince condemns his murder of imprisoned and wounded Redcoats. Two poignant deaths lessen joy in victory—the loss of Ross's pal Kincaid and the unforeseen internal hemorrhage of Angus Mohr, the irrepressible jester of troops, convincingly played by Stephen Walters. Star Sam Heughan relished the acting of Jamie and godfather Murtagh "when it hits them what they've achieved, but also what they've lost" (Prudom, 2016).

The episode amplifies war strain by picturing the boy Fergus fresh from a kill with the dazed expression of a first-time knife fighter. Exhausted and disillusioned, he receives Claire's mothering, a service lacking after the Battle of Culloden to condemned teen prisoners Frederick MacBean and Giles MacMartin and to the Findlay brothers, Hugh and Iain Og, after the Battle of Alamance Creek. Away from safe medical treatment for Redcoats at Tranent, Dougal extends the slaughter by knifing the courteous Lieutenant Jeremy Foster and other survivors among captured British. His mania typifies the crazed battle obsessions that turn dedicated warriors into butchers.

In later episodes, character reflection alters memories following combat. To impress Wee Jamie and Rabbie, Fergus treats as evidence of maturity his stabbing of a British adversary, a hand-to-body experience more thrilling than shooting with a pistol or musket. The losses haunt Jamie at Helwater, England, where William Dunsany and his wife Louisa grieve the Jacobite slaying of their son, Captain Gordon Dunsany. Jamie mitigates the difficult recall of Gordon's death with his own heartache at losing two children. The admission causes Dunsany to re-envision his stableman as a father rather than a Prestonpans victor and former enemy of the Crown.

See also Bonnie Prince Charlie; Helwater.

Source

Pittock, Murray. "Arran Johnston, 'On Gladsmuir Shall the Battle Be! The Battle of Prestonpans 1745,'" *British Journal for Military History* 5:1 (2019): 73–75.
Prudom, Laura. "'Outlander' Recap: Sam Heughan Breaks Down the Victories and Losses of 'Prestonpans,'" *Variety* (11 June 2016).
Riding, Jacqueline. *Jacobites: A New History of the '45.* London: Bloomsbury, 2016.
Tomasson, Katherine, and Francis Buist. *Battles of the '45.* Rakuten, Japan: Pickle Partners Publishing, 2017.

Prophecy

Auguries recur in the *Outlander* TV series with foreshadowing and portents of fictional events to come, the contribution of Tebbe to the season five finale. As in the days of the prophetess Pythia at Delphi's Temple of Apollo in 1400 BCE, verbal prognostication omits the how and why, particularly pirate Stephen Bonnet's anticipation of dying in water. In the beginning of season one, Mrs. Graham, the Rev. Reginald Wakefield's housekeeper, combines oolong tea and palm reading in a casual view of Claire Randall's future. The kitchen discussion parallels the minister's perusal of Frank's genealogy, a graph of the past. Paradoxically, the Randall family tree becomes Claire's present after she tumbles into Celtic stones at Craigh na Dun outside Inverness on November 1, 1743, and encounters eighteenth-century Scotland. For a time traveler, prognostication takes on a puzzling mystique of history lessons and on-site revelations.

Mrs. Graham's prescience foreshadows Claire's galloping north to find Jamie in the thirteenth episode as well as her instructing Jenny on British persecution of Scots and famine over the two years following the defeat at Culloden on April 16, 1746. On her brother's word, Jenny accepts her sister-in-law's prediction without question, even though Claire is a suspect Englishwoman. The prophecy enables the Lallybroch family to survive on potatoes, a crop with a better yield and longer shelf life than wheat. Meanwhile, on the road with Murtagh Fitzgibbons Fraser, Claire turns fortunetelling into humor by reading the palm of a dissatisfied Highland woman eager to escape marriage to a lazy lout and flee with a tall, red-haired Scot.

In "The Fox's Lair," professional forecasting aids the Frasers' mission to Beaufort Castle. Seer Maisri (played by Maureen Beattie) and her hard life illustrate the ambiguous status of a clairvoyant in a tyrant's employ. Her vision depicting a victim on the headsman's block peeves Lord Simon Lovat, the chief of the Beauly Frasers, a clan dating to the twelfth century. At a political confab among Jamie, Simon, and Colum MacKenzie, Claire intrudes and playacts Maisri's revelation. The oracle substantiates Simon's historical jailing at the Tower of London and the laird's decapitation at Tower Hill on April 9, 1747, at age eighty. Claire's fictional repeat of the prophecy inflates Lovat's terror of the occult. After his historic week-long trial at Westminster Hall in March 1747, George II commuted the execution from drawing and quartering to beheading.

Men of Insight

Fiction broadens styles of foresight in 1744 in a Paris apothecary. In a shop full of exotica, Claire witnesses an ancient form of conjury and pinpoints Master Raymond's divination method. In girlhood, she and Uncle Lambert had observed the South African Zulu casting chicken bones to descry the future. To answer her question about Frank Randall's destiny, Raymond scatters four sheep knuckles on a zebra hide, a visual proof of the master's interest in curiosities. The bones verify that Claire will meet Frank again. After Raymond treats her for puerperal fever at l'Hôpital des Anges, he promises to see her once more, a prediction that elevates her to judge at a royal trial in Louis XV's Star Chamber. She rescues Raymond with an unexplained poisoning of Le Comte St. Germain, a bit of razzle-dazzle ending the apothecary's collaborations with Claire.

"All Debts Paid" in season three introduces a befuddled seer, MacKenzie tacksman Duncan Kerr, an itinerant diviner on the moors near Ardsmuir Prison who rambles like the apostles of early Christian lore in Asia Minor. In an inscrutable deathbed speech, he fuses Gaelic and French with English, an amalgam that Jamie interprets. Kerr's regret at the loss of Dougal, Colum, and Ellen MacKenzie legitimizes his role in clan history. He hints at Geillis Duncan's grief for her lost love, whom she exalts to hero of the Battle of Culloden even though the war chief was already dead. Without a clear reference point, Duncan foresees that a *ban-druidh* (white witch) will come for Jamie, a hero with MacKenzie blood. A mystic plot closure, the chaotic details forecast the Frasers' adventures in Kingston, Jamaica, and the addled fortunetelling of Margaret Campbell (played by Alison Pargeter).

Oracular Results

Subsequent portents are more puzzling than illuminating. More elements of Kerr's divination recur in season five, episode six when Jocasta Cameron relives her family's flight from Scotland with the "cursed" French gold that later buys River Run in North Carolina, a plantation corrupted by black slavery (3:3). Likewise unclear, Margaret's references to tree toads and blood in Jamaica warn Claire of murder in Abandawe, a time slip portal. Claire's identification of Geillis's neck injury in Joe Abernethy's office suggests a similar proof of skeletal perceptions on Fraser's Ridge, where Claire connects a skull with Otter Tooth's ghost and his glittering opal. The stone warns the Cherokee that white settlers threaten First Peoples. Of the spectral prophet, Genevieve Valentine, a reviewer for the *New York Times,* complained of an aura of unreality: "In moments like these that you can feel things straining at the seams" (Valentine, 2018).

Prophecy recurs in season four during Claire's meeting with Giduhwa and her husband's grandmother, Adawehi. Bearing a Cherokee name meaning "religious healer," Adawehi foretells inescapable death—her own—and a future for Claire rich in wisdom and healing expertise. The dreamscape omits Gerhard Mueller's gift of Adawehi's scalp, a confirmation of his barbarity and racism. In a casual setting, Adawehi intuits that Brianna Randall has arrived in North America. The setting conveys vulnerability visualized by a rabbit, a recurring icon of fragility in the *Outlander* series. An insightful dream alerts Jamie to his daughter's diamond-shaped birthmark behind her left ear. The shape forecasts a precious father-daughter relationship.

In the fifth season, Roger MacKenzie's three-month recovery from near lynching involves family members in conversation and distractions from trauma. When flashbacks reprise his final moments, Marsali Fraser deals tarot cards, a form of divination dating to 1400, when Europeans imported Egyptian occultism. Played for amusement, the packs of cards took on prophetic interpretations in the late eighteenth century. Readings depicted the universe through arrangements of the fool, temperance, Satan, tower, moon, sun, earth, star, judgment, justice, hermit, strength, chariot, lovers, emperor and empress, priestess, pope, magician, and hanged man. Because repeated distribution relates Roger to the gibbet victim, he perceives his identify changed forever.

See also Brianna Randall Mackenzie; Names; Treasure.

Source

Gurung, Regina. "'Outlander' Season 4 Episode 4: Alarming Prophecy Suggests a Vulnerable Character May Soon Die," *Entertainment Weekly* (27 November 2018).
Mackenzie, Alexander. *History of the Frasers of Lovat.* Inverness, Scot.: A. & W. Mackenzie, 1896.
Valentine, Genevieve. "'Outlander,' Season 4, Episode 3 Recap: Mysterious Encounters," *New York Times* (18 November 2018).

Racism

The *Outlander* TV series integrates various forms of "other" as fictional icons of displacement, genocide, and need, the status of Mamacita, the grieving Cuban mother of Ermenegilda; Eutroclus, the freedman Cape Fear River pilot; Rufus, a tortured field slave from Adjumako, Ghana; Tebbe, a mulatto outlaw; and Annekje Johansen, a belabored Scandinavian goatherd who enables Claire to flee the British man-o'-war *Porpoise*. The saga also calls attention to anti–Gypsy prejudice and beliefs that Mr. Ward's itinerant Rom lie and deceive. Claire reclaims the gypsy's honor by kissing Ward for reporting promising news and calling herself a fellow gypsy. His name suggests a guardian who shields Claire from despair at the loss of Jamie to the Redcoats.

Harmony crops up in unusual places in season two. On reuniting with Jamie in 1766 in his Edinburgh printshop, Claire delights that her husband has rescued Yi Tien Cho, a literary Chinaman who remains bitter at his sexual negation by white women, even trollops. Although Cho saves the crew of the French brig *Artemis* from mutiny during "The Doldrums" by reciting his life story, Jamie turns his companion into a commodity among the elite in Jamaica. TV critic Kayla Kumari Upadhyaya charges that the hero "wants to benefit from Yi Tien Cho's suffering. Because make no mistake: The ogling and interrogation that Yi Tien Cho experiences at the party is nothing short of suffering" (Upadhyaya, 2017). The reviewer charges script authors with struggling to record colonialism and racism by picturing Cho's alliance with Maroon dancers and his affection for Margaret Campbell, a Scots fortuneteller.

Viewing Bondage

When the Frasers make their way inland on the Cape Fear River in season four, slavery is undeniable, both agricultural and in-house. At River Run estate, Jocasta Cameron accosts Claire for refusing Jamie's inheritance of the plantation, a business maintained through human bondage. Television critic Genevieve Valentine, a journalist for the *New York Times*, characterizes the dilemma as frustrating for "putting Jamie and Claire in a no-win scenario … a catalyst for character development, showing us the choices they make and how they're affected by failure" (Valentine, 2018). Even though they are "well-meaning white people," the answer to America's original sin overwhelms their capabilities, much as it stymied the Quakers and other abolitionists (*ibid.*).

In contrast to Claire's twentieth-century views and intent to retrieve Rufus from a vicious overseer and adamant mob, Jocasta exonerates herself for dehumanizing black Africans. Critic Valentin notes, "Those who consider themselves good people can quickly become complicit in terrible things," an inkling that fictional cop Dave Robicheaux learns from General John Bell Hood during time travel in the film *In the Electric Mist with the Confederate Dead* (*ibid.*). "Auntie Jo" considers her dealings benevolent because she purchases slaves in family groups, a chilling rationalization of dehumanizing bondage. According to *New York Times* reviewer Jennifer Vineyard, the Frasers are guiltless: "At the same time, the characters have learned in previous seasons that they can't change history, no matter how outraged they (and we) might be about it" (Vineyard, 2018). The harsh lesson takes Gothic shape upriver, where Claire encounters Otter Tooth, another time traveler tormented and murdered for trying to change the Native American future.

BRIEF TAKES ON EQUALITY

A second twentieth-century time traveler compounds the variance in opinion with the antebellum plantation mistress. At Jocasta's special dinner for her niece at River Run, Mistress Alerdyce expresses shock that a genteel girl like Brianna Randall devotes artistic talent to a portrait of Phaedra, a beautiful black domestic and seamstress. Of the saga's dramatizing of eighteenth-century prejudice, critic Princess Weekes charges, "*Outlander* zigzags, because it doesn't take the time to truly break down the historical nuances it wants to have" (Weekes, 2018). Rather than solve the human rights issues of a Cape Fear community, the Frasers move on to the wilderness.

At Fraser's Ridge in the North Carolina piedmont, the family meets a new challenge—white usurpation of traditional Cherokee lands, which the Cherokee previously stole from the Tuscarora. The transition suggests that Americans of whatever race cannot escape the mélange of attitudes among ethnicities who settle the Caribbean and North American colonies. The harboring of Ulysses adds another dimension—shielding a former slave who murders a white man. In halting Gerald Forbes from suffocating Jocasta, Ulysses easily snaps the attorney's neck, at the same time revealing a repressed love for his white mistress. Through the intervention of John Grey, Ulysses escapes an anti-black backdrop and gains instant freedom in English custody, a perturbing contrast of the imperialist state and its New World satellites.

See also Colonialism; Maroons; Native Americans; Prophecy; River Run; Slavery.

Source

Upadhyaya, Kayla Kumari. "*Outlander* Bungles the Conflict in 'Savages,'" *AVClub* (2 December 2018).
_____. "Outlander Peddles a White Savior Narrative in Jamaica," *AVClub* (3 December 2017).
Valentine, Genevieve. "'Outlander' Season 4, Episode 2 Recap: Southern Hospitality," *New York Times* (11 November 2018).
Vineyard, Jennifer. "'Outlander' Takes Manhattan," *New York Times* (2 November 2018).
Weekes, Princess. "The Problem of *Outlander*'s Historical Narrative," *The Mary Sue* (8 October 2018).

Randall, Frank

For the *Outlander* TV narrative, character development involves a stark juxtaposition of husbands for protagonist Claire Elizabeth Beauchamp Randall Fraser. The first, Frank Randall, an Oxford historian and veteran British intelligence officer rapt in patrilineal research, presents the clichéd scholar who lives and dies tragically. He studies documents that elucidate his link to British army captain Jonathan Wolverton "Black Jack" Randall, an infamous eighteenth-century ancestor and ravager of the Highlands in service to the Crown. At a second honeymoon in late October 1945, Claire shares with Frank the emotional residue of five years of combat nursing, which he proudly reveals to Harvard professors. He appears to suppress personal traumas by immersing himself in past minutia while she peruses the future through a cryptic reading of oolong tea leaves and palmistry.

During field work at Inverness, Scotland, a series of eerie Samhain events on October 31, 1945, mars Frank's revival of romance with his wife. After five years essentially apart during the war, at a reunion with Claire, a competent army veteran, he appears nervous and unsure of his role as lover and husband. She undresses Frank just as she takes over the initiation of coitus with her second husband. An aggressive libido attests to the spirit of the New Woman, the emergent post–World War II female imbued with agency and self-reliance. Perhaps out of doubts about their relationship following a long separation, Frank implies that she may have had a fling with a wounded Highlander. Long before Frank seeks a divorce, the query about a Scot looking up at her in a hotel window reveals faults in the Randalls' relationship.

THE SUDDEN LOSS

In the estimation of critic David Hesse, compiler of *Warrior Dreams: Playing Scotsmen in Mainland Europe,* the *Outlander* theme derives from "female discontent with contemporary masculinity," the jittery manhood lodged in a meticulous Harvard professor. Claire's abrupt disappearance stuns Frank, who paces Craigh na Dun and insists that police find his wife. While she maneuvers among strangers in early November 1743 at Castle Leoch, Frank experiences an emotional meltdown mitigated only slightly by the Christian principles of the Rev. Reginald Wakefield. At the Inverness police station, Frank bridles at an officer's rude statement that a gulled husband is a fool for not recognizing the phantom Highlander as Claire's lover. Later interpretations speculate that the unidentified ghost is Claire's Scots husband.

Dialogue extends sympathy for Frank as he absorbs the truth of Claire's two-year and five-month marriage to Jamie and the conception of their two daughters. In an interview with TV reviewer Neela Debnath, a writer for *Express,* actor Tobias Menzies relayed Frank's doubts about reuniting with Claire: "As the rationalist and academic, I'm not sure how he can entirely. It's just part of the burden he'll have to carry when he takes her back" (Debnath, 2019). Frank's flare-up in a storage shed suggests the violation of stored memories, which no longer define his marriage. Joy at impending fatherhood routed by fury resurrects Frank's private hell—a medical test proving him sterile. At Harvard, he learns the particulars of a spring seminar on the Wars of the Roses, a politically murky historical era guaranteed to further separate the sorrowing husband from domestic reality.

A Fractured Reunion

A player of dual characters, actor Tobias Menzies performs an extraordinary change of persona from the role of Jack to Frank, his descendent. Reviewer EllenandJim pities Frank's modern role of "loving, tired, suffering father and yes betrayed husband" (EllenandJim, 2019). He sets the norm for daughter Brianna's view of male authority figures by taking her camping and teaching her to shoot. While sulking in his Harvard office, Frank soaks up liquor and avoids his daughter's astute questions about his dissatisfaction with research. To rescue him from disquiet, she serves hangover relief—a cream tea with scones, a reflection of Frank's love of England and its traditions.

After Frank's bitter fight with his wife, an unforeseen traffic accident kills him while he mulls over returning to Oxford with Brianna. The sudden death lops short his plan to divorce Claire and marry Sandy Travers but appears to do little damage to his body. A silent reunion with Bree as she boards the ship *Phillip Alonzo* for America graces Frank's ghost with a fatherly blessing on his daughter, whose kindness to waif Lizzy Wemyss expresses an altruism that makes him proud. His gentle childrearing confuses her as she tries to accommodate a new daughter/father relationship with Jamie. She continues to dredge up memories of Frank's parenting and guiltily agrees to replace "Daddy" with "Da."

Source

Debnath, Neela. "*Outlander*: Did Frank Randall Believe Claire's Time Travel Story?" *Express* (30 October 2019).

Donelan, Carol. "'Sing Me a Song of a Lass That Is Gone': Myth and Meaning in the Starz Original Series *Outlander*," *Quarterly Review of Film and Video* 35:1 (2018): 31–53.

EllenandJim. "*Outlander*, Season 4, from *Drums of Autumn*: The Colonialist American Past, a Book of Fathers & Ghosts," (10 February 2019).

Hesse, David. *Warrior Dreams: Playing Scotsmen in Mainland Europe*. Manchester, UK: Manchester University Press, 2014.

Randall, Jack

By weighing the personae of Frank and Captain Black Jack Randall, both impeccably acted by Tobias Menzies, the *Outlander* TV series juxtaposes a scholarly historian with a vicious sociopath/career officer in the British army's historic 8th Dragoons, a light cavalry regiment. Ironically, both characters share experiences in military intelligence. For Jack, control of the vulnerable brings out a sadomasochistic urge to molest, whether male or female, child or adult. He lodges an ingenuous complaint that one hundred lashes against Jamie in October 1739 fatigued his arm and, at Madame Elise's brothel, makes do with the child Fergus, even though he requested a different brothel worker.

Jack speaks proudly of his home tutoring to rid him of a Sussex accent. He displays knowledge of French with a rude comment to Claire about the demimonde and continues to strut his talents with an arch, mean-eyed likeness of her face that he sketches in rough pencil on a table napkin. In the role of deranged tormentor, he admits that darkness consumes his soul. To *Variety* interviewer Maureen Ryan, producer Ron Moore depicted a split in Jack's motivations: "He embraces the darkness and hates himself for doing it all at the same time" (Ryan, 2016).

Jack and the Frasers

Language and gesture dramatize Jack's potential for torture and slaughter in what analyst Michelle L. Jones, a graduate student at the University of Regina, Saskatchewan, calls "a bisexual love triangle" (Jones, 2016, 72). Unlike Jamie's chivalric conscience, Captain Randall masks his smarminess beneath a facade of English courtesies and military correctness. In private, he heaps crude epithets on Claire while undermining Jamie's heterosexual confidence in satisfying her. At Wentworth Prison, the dreary setting gives the deranged jailer complete control of his victim, who yanks at ankle chains to escape a monster, an English equivalent of the Greek Minotaur, a sexual miscreant.

In a transgender performance, Jack perfumes his long hair and pretends to be Claire, a pose of rapist and wife in Jamie's mind that defiles the Frasers' future intimacy. Jack gently proposes carnal privileges to Jamie's body, "taking Claire's sexual prize from her" (*ibid., 76*). His merger of passion with hate goads him into caressing the scars on Jamie's back, admiring his handiwork with the cat o' nine tails. His mockery of the victim's honor and probity shreds the English model of gentlemanly fortitude. He swathes his exterior in civility and social polish to conceal an abomination to the military code.

A DOOMED FUTURE

Before Louis XV and a smirking entourage at Versailles in 1744, Jack bows and scrapes with practiced finesse that conceals the loathsome lechery with which he menaced both Jenny and Claire. Hitches in posture indicate back pain from the shaggy highland cattle stampede at the Wentworth dungeon, the site of his plunder of Jamie and the collapse of a wood door on Jack. After a stiffly polite encounter with the Frasers, Jack accepts Jamie's challenge to duel in the Bois de Boulogne. From a distance, Claire views the final sword and saber thrusts and Jack's collapse from a jab to the crotch, which he survives after transfer to medical care in England. The wound implies that he can never sire children.

"The Hail Mary" episode depicts Claire's coming-to-knowledge about time travel and altering history. A forced wedding at the bedside of Alex Randall places Jack in the unwanted role of father/uncle to Mary Hawkins's unborn child. Mania causes Jack to pummel his brother's corpse, shocking Mary and Claire with its *volte-face* from loving brother. In reflection on the scene, star Caitriona Balfe stated, "When Alex dies and Black Jack starts wailing on him, oh my God, it was some crazy stuff" (Bucksbaum, 2016). The face-off at Culloden maintains stasis between toned, athletic warriors before disclosing Jack's corpse atop Jamie's maimed body. By keeping the competition equal, the drama heightens viewer fear that Jamie may eventually fall to his nemesis.

Source

Bucksbaum, Sydney. "'Outlander' Team Talks Black Jack's 'Chilling' Moment of Rage, Mary's Loss and Claire's Redemption," *Hollywood Reporter* (25 June 2016).

Jones, Michelle L. "Linked … through the Body of One Ma': Black Jack Randall as a Non-Traditional Romance Villain," *Adoring Outlander: Essays on Fandom, Genre and the Female Audience*. Jefferson, NC: McFarland, 2016, 71–81.

Nagouse, Emma. "To Ransom a Man's Soul': Male Rape and Gender Identity in *Outlander* and 'The Suffering Man' of Lamentations 3," *Rape Culture, Gender Violence, and Religion*. London: Palgrave Macmillan, 2018, 143–158.

Ormond, Melissa. "Gender, Fantasy, and Empowerment in Diana Gabaldon's *Outlander*," master's thesis, DePaul University, 2009.

Ryan, Maureen. "'Outlander' Boss Ron Moore on Eliciting Emotional Response, Season 2 and Surprising Storytelling," *Variety* (3 May 2016).

Randall Genealogy

Unfortunately for the Randall family tree, the perversities of army captain Jonathan Wolverton "Black Jack" Randall dominate the first half of the *Outlander* TV series and the life of twentieth-century descendant Frank Randall, an Oxford history professor who later thrives at Harvard. Of Jack's twisted mentality, critic Zoë Shacklock, on staff at the University of St. Andrews in Fife, Scotland, describes him as "a sadistic rapist with a love for torture" (Shacklock, 2016, 315–316). TV reviewer Neela Debnath, a critic for *Express,* accounts for the nickname "Black Jack" because of "the darkness of his soul which isn't hard to believe from the acts he's committed," including sodomizing a child (Debnath, 2019).

As a devotee of history, Frank devotes part of his second honeymoon in late October 1945 to researching the Randall genealogy, especially kinship with Jack and his influence on the residents of Castle Leoch:

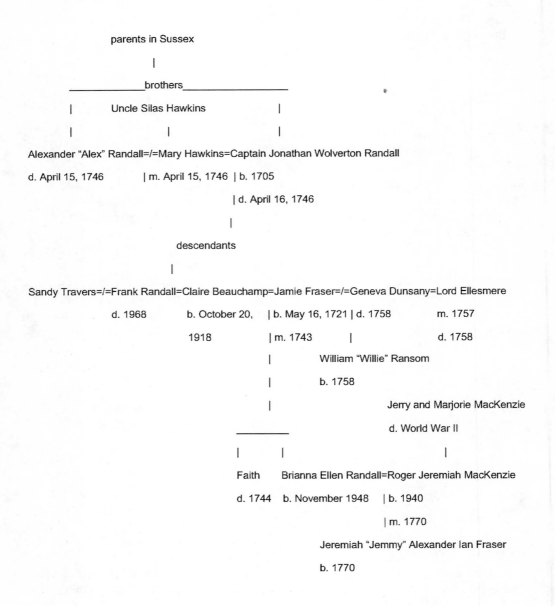

```
                        parents in Sussex

                               |

_____brothers_____          •

        |           Uncle Silas Hawkins            |

        |                   |                       |

Alexander "Alex" Randall=/=Mary Hawkins=Captain Jonathan Wolverton Randall

d. April 15, 1746      | m. April 15, 1746 | b. 1705

                                 | d. April 16, 1746

                                 |

                  descendants

                       |

Sandy Travers=/=Frank Randall=Claire Beauchamp=Jamie Fraser=/=Geneva Dunsany=Lord Ellesmere

        d. 1968        b. October 20,  | b. May 16, 1721 | d. 1758      m. 1757

                       1918           | m. 1743         |             d. 1758

                                      |        William "Willie" Ransom

                                      |              b. 1758

                                      |                      Jerry and Marjorie MacKenzie

                                      |                      d. World War II

                       _____

        |          |                              |

        Faith      Brianna Ellen Randall=Roger Jeremiah MacKenzie

        d. 1744    b. November 1948   | b. 1940

                                      | m. 1770

                   Jeremiah "Jemmy" Alexander Ian Fraser

                              b. 1770
```

Debnath believes that the eighteenth-century Randalls "continue to have an impact on the series" for two centuries (*ibid.*). Contributing to the down side of an entire extended sept, pirate Stephen Bonnet's rape of Brianna Randall the night of her hand-fasting further clouds the lineage with a psychopath's claim on her son Jeremiah "Jemmy" MacKenzie, the heir to the River Run plantation.

Source

Debnath, Neela. "*Outlander*: How Are Frank Randall and Black Jack Related?," *Express* (19 November 2019).
Hill, Libby. "'Outlander' Recap: Claire and Jamie Play God, Poorly," *Los Angeles Times* (7 May 2016).
Shacklock, Zoë. "On (Not) Watching *Outlander* in the United Kingdom," *Visual Culture in Britain* 17:3 (2016): 311–328.

Rape

From episode one, the first season of the *Outlander* TV epic, like *Game of Thrones,* sets a predatory atmosphere with threats and acts of rape that extend into the season five finale. As described by Jennifer Still, a TV reviewer for *Decider,* Claire Fraser lives through a horror—"gang-raped and left for dead while tied to a tree in the middle of the woods" (Still, 2020). Reviewer Ann Gavin refuted media assault on the series for sexual violence: "The truth is what is depicted in the book and the show is very typical for the times. The book was not written to adhere to modern-day sensibilities when it comes to sex, power, and rape" (Gavin, 2019). Claire's tumble into the eighteenth century immediately threatens her with sexual assault by Captain Black Jack Randall and subsequent other males, both known and unknown. The risk dramatizes an era not conducive to women living or traveling alone. TV critic Kayti Burt applauds the realistic view of danger: "The show takes sexual violence seriously and doesn't fall into lazy, damaging tropes" (Burt, 2016).

To wrest the emotional horror out of a face-to-face view of an assailant, the filming of "Both Sides Now" slows and broadens camera angles to depict Claire priming herself to stab Harry, a Redcoat deserter who seizes her from Jamie. Of the predations to Claire and Jenny Fraser, scholar Mary Heath located the source of danger "in places where violent men are in power and able to control their surroundings" (Heath, 2019, 44). Producer Ronald D. Moore legitimized the motif and its value: "Rape is a pretty serious thing we deal with in the show, and we wanted to treat it right" (Vineyard, 2016). The theme takes an ethnic turn into season four with the punishment of a Cherokee warrior for rape, a crime that leads to exile and insanity. Symbolically, he mentally shapeshifts into the *tskili yona* (evil bear), a beast beyond the bounds of conscience.

Building on Vulnerability

Developing the assault theme with Jack Randall's ongoing abuse, the series villain blames Jamie for his own humiliation and continues to jeopardize Claire. Critics Caroline Blyth and Jane Davidson-Ladd of the University of Auckland explain his rationale: "The victorious combatants 'invade' … women's bodies, treating them as foreign territory upon which they can stamp their military and masculine prowess" (Blyth and Davidson-Ladd, 2018, 156). The conquests equate with capture, subjugation, and colonization of enemy females. Surprisingly, critical commentary finds Jamie's ravishing more revolting than threats against Claire. Analysts Blyth and Davidson-Ladd surmise that "female rape has become 'enduring and inevitable' within dominant discourses of gender and sexuality … it is simply 'expected'" (*ibid.*, 155). Aliraza Javaid, on staff at the University of East London, explains in terms of society's expectations: "In a culture that emphasizes male superiority, power and control, subordination or powerlessness are unacceptable" (Javaid, 2016, 288).

Scenarios picture variety—Claire's verbal jousting with war chief Dougal MacKenzie, an overt womanizer incited by drink, and an under-the-skirt tussle with Marley, a bestial jailer at Wentworth Prison. A droll side note, Claire's impromptu confrontation of Jamie in sight of teen-aged would-be assassin William John Grey at a barn in Corrieyairack in the central highlands playacts the Jacobite's coarse groping under Claire's skirts and brazen kissing and threats of ravishing. In adulthood, Grey realizes that the couple spoofed a lusty attack by Red Jamie on an Englishwoman who turns out to be Mrs. Red Jamie. The delayed thanks from Jamie for Grey's attempt to protect an innocent female trapped in a war camp prompts a lifelong friendship based on mutual respect for female honor.

In a scene that develops Claire's sympathy with rape victims, close camerawork on Danton's molestation of Mary Hawkins in a Paris alley identifies the attacker and his cohorts as *Les Disciples*, an organized street gang led by a birthmarked man, a suggestion of the biblical mark of Cain. Under the vile machinations of the Duke of Sandringham, the thugs value virginity as a reward for thuggery and group pride. In the long run, the sexual assault by the duke's hireling deranges Mary, a naive English girl who experiences hallucinations from a poppy sedative. In retrospect, she feels altered for life—a person soiled, damaged beyond recovery. She shares with Brianna Randall and her maid Lizzy Wemyss a distaste for a violated body. In retrospect after Mary knifes Danton in the chest, star Caitriona Balfe delighted at the workings of justice: "She truly deserved to get that peace of mind" (Bucksbaum, 2016).

Male Rape

The resonance of rape encompasses the epic and inspires Claire to press two false indictments of violation. As proofs of female potency, one charge sends Jack Randall temporarily to the Bastille and another inveighs against Mr. Cosworth, the cook on the English man-o'-war *Porpoise,* a misogynist who dislikes Claire for meddling in the captain's log. Jamie, too, bears a mental burden of loneliness and guilt "worse than death," a motif that empowered the aftershock of male rape in *The Kite Runner* (2:6). Visualizing the residue of homosexual degradation, he sees himself naked, helpless in the shadow of a grass blade, an existential image fraught with depletion and debility. Claire's experience counseling soldiers in World War II guides her wisdom in freeing Jamie's mind of undeserved taint. Jennifer Vineyard, a journalist with the *New York Times,* concluded that the show is "therapeutic for those who have suffered sexual assault, because it focuses on the recovery" (Vineyard, 2018).

The protagonist's outrage at Black Jack's sodomizing of Fergus, a boy incapable of fighting back, burgeons into a capital crime. Child abuse so scandalizes Jamie that he fights Jack in an illegal duel set in the Bois de Boulogne, the dark underside of Paris gentility. Dismayed by Fergus's hesitant recounting of nightmares about the attack, Claire amends her anger at Jamie and forgives him for requiting an assault too abhorrent for either foster parent to tolerate. A recompense for Jamie at Culloden on April 16, 1746, the death of Jack in battle from a sword thrust to the torso and the strangulation of a Redcoat with a handful of Scots turf repay interlopers for mayhem against Highlanders.

Escaping Memories

In the past of the Fraser lineage, Jamie's grandsire, Lord Simon Lovat, bears a reputation for debauching and misusing females. At Beaufort Castle, his threat to send rapists against Claire launches a dramatic response from Jamie. By laughing at his strutting grandfather and intimidating him with a white witch's reprisal, Jamie arouses fear in a superstitious elder. Jamie's lengthy description of a sorceress capable of genital blight and blasted souls ends with smashing a whisky bottle in Lovat's fireplace. The effective whoosh of blazing alcohol encourages the Frasers to enact fearful mischief. In place of the specter of rape, Claire instills an image of Lovat's historical beheading on April 9, 1747, in London by a Stuart executioner amid a spread of white roses, a clever metaphoric conclusion to a made-up vision. Jacobites celebrated the white blossom on "White Rose Day," June 10, the birth dates of James III and VIII.

The theme of sexual ravaging recurs on the Frasers' arrival in Jamaica to locate nephew Ian Murray at a Kingston flesh market. A victim of human trafficking by Portuguese pirates, he falls prey to Geillis Duncan Abernethy at her island retreat, Rose Hill. The naked femme fatale soaked in goat's blood drugs and molests him. The memory later invades his thinking while he digs a grave for Gavin Hayes. Jamie's confession of post-rape trauma in season four solaces Young Ian, the victim of Geillis's lust for immature boys.

Reviewer Kayla Kumari Upadhyaya commended star Sam Heughan for a stirring, honest dialogue with actor John Bell. Her TV critique described the scene as a raw "compassionate conversation between two male survivors of sexual assault—something I've never seen on television before" (Upadhyaya, 2018). Because of Uncle Jamie's counsel, the boy accepts titillation by Geillis as a normal physical reaction, a welcome relief of guilt that he can bury alongside Gavin's corpse. A less defined rape on the frontier imperils Cherokee ethos and results in the exile of a native wife abuser who shapeshifts into an ursine mauler, a poorly defined crazy-making that reviewer EllenandJim termed anachronistic.

The horror that grips Claire in season five, episode twelve pictures her engulfed with hallucinations and inert with sorrow at an attack and betrayal she cannot escape. Excellent makeup recreates serious bruising and a slice across her right breast, but cinematography obscures multiple penetrations by her abductors. Retribution by the Rowan County Militia occurs offsides, yet reserves for her the execution of part of the criminal party. Because Jamie acknowledges her fealty to the Hippocratic Oath, she leaves to his men to kill the remaining stalkers. The detention of Lionel Brown in her surgery turns her stomach. For comfort, she enjoys an ordinary day and comfort from a snuggle with Jamie. The series leaves open how trauma will affect her in season six. Producer Matt Roberts concluded, "Every attack like this is individual and how people deal with it is individual, there's no right way or wrong way" (Reiher, 2020).

See also Jamie Fraser; Jack Randall.

Source

Blyth, Caroline, and Jane Davidson-Ladd. "To Ransom a Man's Soul: Male Rape and Gender Identity in *Outlander* and 'The Suffering Man' of Lamentations 3," *Rape Culture, Gender Violence, and Religion* (2018): 143–158.

Bucksbaum, Sydney. "'Outlander' Team Breaks Down That Violent Act of Revenge and 'Powerful' Scene Viewers Didn't See," *Hollywood Reporter* (18 June 2016).

Burt, Kayti. "*Outlander*: La Dame Blanche Review," *Den of Geek* (1 May 2016).

Byrne, Katherine, and Julie Anne Taddeo. "Calling #TimesUp on the TV Period Drama Rape Narrative," *Critical Studies in Television* 14:3 (September 2019): 379–398.

EllenandJim. "Outlander, Season 4, from *Drums of Autumn*: The Colonialist American Past, a Book of Fathers & Ghosts," *EllenandJim* (10 February 2019).

Gavin, Ann. "The Ultimate Ranking of *Outlander* Season 4 Episodes," www.outlandercast.com/2019/03/ranking-outlander-season-4-episodes.html, 13 March 2019.

Heath, Mary. "Villains and Heroes: An Analysis of *Outlander*'s Portrayal of Sexual Violence," master's thesis, Arizona State University, 2019.

Javaid, Aliraza. "Feminism, Masculinity and Male Rape: Bringing Male Rape 'Out of the Closet,'" *Journal of Gender Studies* 25:3 (2016): 283–293.

Nagouse, Emma. "'To Ransom a Man's Soul': Male Rape and Gender Identity in *Outlander* and 'The Suffering Man' of Lamentations 3," *Rape Culture, Gender Violence, and Religion*. London: Palgrave Macmillan, 2018, 143–158.

Reiher, Andrea. "'Outlander' EPs Break Down Claire's 'Survival Mechanism' in Season 5 Finale," *Variety* (10 May 2020).

Still, Jennifer. "'Outlander' Season 5 Finale Recap: 'Never My Love,'" *Decider* (11 May 2020).

Upadhyaya, Kayla Kumari. "*Outlander*'s Alchemy Remains Spectacular in Its Hotly Anticipated Return," *AVClub* (4 November 2018).

Vineyard, Jennifer. "How *Outlander*'s Revenge Scene Came Together," *Vulture* (19 June 2016).

_____. "'Outlander' Takes Manhattan," *New York Times* (2 November 2018).

Regulators

A pre-democracy birth pang dramatized in seasons four and five of the *Outlander* TV series, the Regulation movement (1768–1771) became an outlet for disgruntlement among settlers of the North Carolina piedmont in Anson, Orange, and Rowan counties. In a history of Rowan County, author Sam Ervin, Jr., summarized complaints "of the injustice of the officials, of extortion, of corrupt courts, and of being compelled to pay taxes in money, of which there was a scarcity in circulation" (Ervin, 1917, 35). Protesters, emulators of Wilmington's Sons of Liberty, received no sympathy from Governor William Tryon and little redress from his colonial assembly.

In 1882, John Dalton Whitford, a columnist for the *New Berne Weekly Journal,* summarized the governor's shortsightedness: "Tryon did not then know the world was rapidly changing and men were rising up that would never acquiesce in principles and acts that would degrade them—make them abject slaves" (Whitford, 1882). Mostly farmers, the back country pioneers resisted vindication of corrupt, exploitative New Bern officials. A fictional rallying cry arises from Murtagh Fitzgibbons Fraser, Bryan Cranna, Lee Withers, Ethan MacKinnon, and other former Jacobites familiar with British antipathy toward Highlanders. Oblivious to the rising tide of revolt, Tryon "continued active and faithful only in what he conceived would rebound to the interest of his Sovereign and himself and add wealth and glory to England" (*ibid.*).

The Revolutionaries

Historic North Carolina immigrants, refugees escaping high credit costs in Connecticut, fled to promising land along the Catawba, Deep, Haw, Neuse, Tar, and Yadkin rivers. In lieu of cash, they lived by a back country barter system devoid of coins and luxury. They contented themselves with crude housing similar to Jamie and Claire Fraser's branch shelter and Gerhard and Rosewitha Mueller's log cabin. To support themselves, they traded homemade tax-free whisky, a labor of Jamie, Young Ian, and Murtagh to produce a salable or swappable commodity.

By 1766, two thousand citizens had defaulted on state taxes. Jethro Rumple, author of *A History of Rowan County, North Carolina* (1916), called the Regulator Movement "a good cause, prematurely, rashly and violently conducted" (Rumple, 1916, 125). Historian C.L. Hunter's *Sketches of Western North Carolina* (1877) noted an emerging tragedy— western rebels fought "evils scarcely known in the eastern counties, and misunderstood when reported there" (Hunter, 1877, 12). He saluted the colonial forerunners of the Sons of Liberty and other revolutionary organizations because "The spirit of liberty which animated the Regulators was the true spirit which subsequently led to our freedom from foreign oppression" (*ibid.*).

A Tax Revolt

The historic Regulators followed the advice of Quaker pamphleteer Herman Husband of Randolph County, a radical but pacifist disciple of Benjamin Franklin. Dissenters from Morganton to Raleigh resisted fiscal inequality nonviolently by refusing for three years to pay extortionate fees and taxes collected by dishonest agents and colluding sheriffs. Governor William Tryon, a colonial profiteer and defender of the divine right of kings, labeled the Regulation Movement a form of sedition, a hint at the Scots-American connection with the Jacobites of the mid–1740s. In April 1768, Edmund Fanning, a Yale- and Harvard-educated embezzler from New York, pressed Tryon to enlist militiamen and declare war in eight counties, including Rowan.

About the time that the fictional Fraser household emigrates to North Carolina, proto-democracy presses Regulators and their leader, Herman Husband, toward freeing themselves from an unscrupulous royal government. In early spring 1768, a peasant mob assaulted the ruling class in Hillsborough. Their crimes began with attacking the steeple of the newly completed Anglican church of St. Martin's Parish. In the spirit that fueled the Boston Massacre the previous March 5, North Carolina rioters destroyed Hillsborough shops and offices on September 25, 1770, spit on magistrates, and beat Fanning, who called the insurgents rabid dogs.

The crimes worsened on October 3, 1770, with threats to 27-year-old Judge Richard Henderson and dragging attorney William Hooper through the streets. The next day, assailants fired bullets into the West King Street home of Fanning, an arrogant attorney, judge, and sheriff and the focus of their rancor. Regulators added arson to vandalism by ripping bedding and upholstery and torching his house, furnishings, clothes, and papers and threatening to burn the governor's mansion at New Bern. In 1895, state historian John Spencer Bassett described Fanning as "a full-fledged office-holding bird of prey" deserving of ill treatment (Bassett, 1895, 159). Television critic Maggie Fremont added that the fictional Fanning "has his hands in all the tax shenanigans as well as the militia— he seems extremely shady" (Fremont, 2018). After mob violence, he comes under Claire Fraser's surgical care in the lobby of a Wilmington theater for hernia repair, a fitting gut injury for a double crosser.

Suppressing Rebels

As described in season five, episode six, tax petitions and the state assembly's passage of the Riot Act of 1771 kept the Regulators' issues before official eyes. Pioneer recalcitrance aroused Governor Tryon to send General Hugh Waddell west from Hillsborough with 1,200 troops to launch the Battle of Alamance Creek, a preface to the American Revolution. North of Concord, Regulators in Indian guise and blackface seized two wagonloads of Waddell's stock of ammunition en route from Charleston and dynamited them, diversionary strategy enacted in the series by Murtagh Fitzgibbons Fraser and his men.

On May 16, 1771, at the Haw River south of Burlington, North Carolina, the protesters awaited their fate. Historian Rumple recorded eyewitness accounts that "many of them [were] unarmed and seemed to be rather spectators than soldiers, and the rest were armed with their hunting pieces, with enough ammunition for a day's sport in the woods" (Rumple, 1916, 122–123). The real and fictional Tryon rebuffed overtures from the Rev. David Caldwell, who attempted a peaceful parlay. After the withdrawal of British fomenter Fanning and rebel adviser Husband, Redcoats launched the attack. They encountered fictional Jamie Fraser's adaptation of standard European strategy—the Highland style of breaking ranks and native American methods of hiding behind trees and bushes. Lack of ammunition forced the Regulators to rout and flee the battleground.

Tryon sealed Regulator fate by burning the woods. Within the hour, his 1,100 troops and the hated villain Fanning fired three cannon to trounce 2,000 poorly armed farmers and smallholders. Leader Husband escaped arrest, but Tryon retaliated by torching his home in Sandy Creek, Orange County. TV critic Julie Kosin, a journalist for *Elle,* characterized the lopsided combat as "a federal government turning on its own people in a time of crisis" (Kosin, 2020). Star Sam Heughan reduced the two-hour battle in the woods to "muskets and guerrilla warfare" (*Ibid.*). Of the twelve captives, half received pardons. Six faced capital punishment for treason and went to the gallows on June 9, 1771. The remaining six pledged allegiance to the crown. Their rebel vitality inspired formation of the Fayetteville Sons of Liberty and stimulated the Revolutionary War against George III.

See also Execution; Murtagh Fraser; William Tryon; Tryon's Palace.

Source

Bassett, John Spencer. *The Regulators of North Carolina (1765–1771).* Washington, DC: Government Printing Office, 1895, 141–212.
Ervin, Samuel James, Jr. *A Colonial History of Rowan County, North Carolina.* Chapel Hill: University of North Carolina, 1917.
Fremont, Maggie. "*Outlander* Recap: Operating Theater," *Vulture* (23 December 2018).
Hunter, C.L. *Sketches of Western North Carolina.* Raleigh, NC: Raleigh News, 1877.
Kosin, Julie. "Sam Heughan on *Outlander*'s Devastating Double Loss," *Elle* (30 March 2020).
Rumple, Jethro. *A History of Rowan County, North Carolina.* Salisbury, NC: J.J. Bruner, 1881.
Snodgrass, Mary Ellen. *Civil Disobedience: An Encyclopedic History of Dissidence in the United States.* New York: Routledge, 2009.
Whitford, James Dalton. "Rambles about Town: Tryon's Palace," *New Berne Weekly Journal* (3 December 1882).

Rescue

For Gothic fiction and romance novels, last minute salvation is a given, whether for Jamie in Jamaica in season three of the *Outlander* TV series from a charge of murder, for Temeraire from auction at a Kingston slave market, for Claire from drowning or molestation by Phillip Wylie, or for Jocasta Cameron Innes, whose slave Ulysses kills Gerald Forbes, her attacker. In 1743, Jamie's first rescue of Claire from Captain Black Jack Randall's clutches at Fort William interrupts rape and possible breast disfigurement with a knife. A second swoop in the last moments of the Cranesmuir witch trial further allies husband and wife, both of whom have suffered the lash. Jamie's first aid to her stripes reverses the past nursing of Jamie's hurts from dislocated shoulder and gunshot above the right clavicle. In a loving scenario, he hears her story of time travel and offers the reward she most needs—acceptance.

The least believable of rescue scenes, Jack Randall's hurried gallop to retrieve Jamie from the gallows at Wentworth Prison poses questions about the inscrutable look on actor Tobias Menzies's face. The lengthy episode concludes with the driving of nineteen shaggy cattle through a back gate and Murtagh Fitzgibbons Fraser's rush to Jamie's dungeon cell. Gently swaddling his godson in a plaid, the elder man carries him out of danger to a waiting wagon. The watch-and-wait at Father Anselm's Benedictine abbey forces Murtagh to accept an unspeakable choice—euthanize Jamie rather than let him starve himself to death. Similar to Gabriel Oak's desertion of Bathsheba Everdene in Thomas Hardy's *Far from the Madding Crowd,* Claire's tough love approach rescues her husband once more with a sharp whack for his obstinacy. She rewards him with the acceptance he once bestowed on her.

THE JACOBITE RISING

Close companions offer succor in violent times. After Claire's removal of a musket ball from Rupert's eye at an abandoned church in season two, she employs a ruse by shouting to Redcoats for release from a Scots band. Abetted by Fergus and Dougal MacKenzie, she slumps in a fake swoon that fools British officers. Her relocation to Belmont, the imposing manse of the Duke of Sandringham, renews peril and requires complex plotting by Jamie, Murtagh, and Hugh Munro. The narrative uses the episode to debate the odious Sandringham's loyalties and to settle past mysteries about how and under whose order a ravager attacked Mary Hawkins in a Paris alley. Further endangerment of Mary and Claire results in the murders of the duke and his henchman Danton, a satisfying redress of a raid orchestrated by Le Comte St. Germain.

A short, but heroic role for actor Grant O'Rourke, Rupert's retrieval of Jamie from the killing fields of Culloden Moor on April 16, 1746, pictures a rescuer divided by love and hate. The cleanup of corpses places both men in danger of Redcoats thrusting bayonets into Jacobite survivors. With Jamie safely bedded in a strawed stall, Rupert makes his peace with the murderer of Dougal, the Mackenzie war chief. Dignified in the face of his own execution by Redcoat musket, Rupert marches stoically to the wall, a departure replete with admiration and sorrow at the ignoble execution of Jacobites.

FAMILY FIRST

In carrying Young Ian from the burning Edinburgh printshop in season three, Jamie equates the beloved nephew with son Willie Ransom in importance. Saving the child's portrait from the mantel, Jamie illustrates the significance of natural and foster children to his life. For "The Bakra" at Governor John Grey's ball in Kingston, multiple rescues muddle images of true humanity. TV critic Kayla Kumani Upadhyaya described the episode as weak in racial parity for the Frasers' use of Yi Tien Cho as a party curiosity and the slave Temeraire for surveillance. Upadhyaya supports Kumani's argument with sense: "Jamie refers to [Temeraire] as his 'servant' although there is no discussion had about salary—only the promise of future freedom" (Upadhyaya, 2017).

Jamie's struggle to preserve loved ones heightens in season three, episode thirteen, in the location of Claire under a storm-tossed sea. Where his wife is concerned, Jamie frequently turns into superhero. The staking of the shapeshifting man-bear outside the cabin at Fraser's Ridge, comforting her from sorrow over Adawehi's murder and scalping, and shielding his wife from womanizer Phillip Wylie extend Jamie's service to his mate. At a nadir of the Battle of Alamance Creek on May 16, 1771, however, she is unable to relieve his grief for godfather Murtagh Fitzgibbons Fraser, who dies of a bullet wound to the chest.

Claire's devotion to Jamie pairs with Roger MacKenzie's effort to drag his father-in-law out of the woods for treatment of snakebite. The TV drama pictures Roger as a Presbyterian incapable of offering Roman Catholic last rites, but determined to save Jamie from death through prayer for the sick and reunion with a search party. As Claire stands ready with saw to remove Jamie's infected right leg, the rescue passes to Brianna, a third party who improvises a hypodermic syringe at the last minute before surgery. The unified effort, including Young Ian's apology for insulting Jamie's courage, supports the theme of family effort to sustain a frontier community.

All reunite in rescuing Claire at the season five finale from Lionel Brown's outlaw company. Within the band, Tebbe, a mulatto played by Alexis Rodney, gives hope of rescue, but leaves her to the cruelties of merciless raiders. Characters appear so shocked by her bruising and lacerations from gang rape that they stare transfixed until Jamie lifts her from the ground. They perform essential duty at the big house by treating the next morning as an ordinary day, the deliverance she needs to combat the night's terrors.

See also Combat Nursing.

Source

Bucksbaum, Sydney. "'Outlander' Team Breaks Down That Violent Act of Revenge and 'Powerful' Scene Viewers Didn't See," *Hollywood Reporter* (18 June 2016).
Upadhyaya, Kayla Kumari. "*Outlander* Peddles a White Savior Narrative in Jamaica," *AVClub* (3 December 2017).
Vineyard, Jennifer. "How *Outlander*'s Revenge Scene Came Together," *Vulture* (19 June 2016).

Ritual

A mystic strand in folk literature, ritual draws ethnic groups into traditional actions, songs, dances, reverence, and liturgy that pledge anew belonging to a people and faith. Examples involve the abandonment of a sick infant to the fairies, Claire's confession of bigamy to Father Anselm at the abbey chapel, Geillis Duncan's summoning of the Earth Mother by moonlight, and the Presbyterian baptism of Jeremiah Fraser MacKenzie, grandson of a staunch Roman Catholic. The Randalls' celebration of Samhain on October 31, 1945, at Inverness and the secret viewing of a circle dance by lamplight among the stones of Craigh na Dun link the *Outlander* TV tale to time travel in eighteenth-century Scotland.

Frank introduces Scots rites with an historian's pronouncement: "There's no place on earth with more magic and more superstition mixed into its daily life than the Scottish Highlands" (Gavin, 2016). In her first view of cockerel's blood on doorways, Claire compares the symbol to the Passover, the night around 1250 BCE when the Israelites escaped the worst of the plagues of Egypt by smearing lamb's blood on home entrances (Gavin, 2016). Post-Samhain formalities at the Castle Leoch great hall in November 1743 involve prayers, vows, and recitations, beginning with clan pledges of loyalty to Laird Colum MacKenzie over a loving cup and a solemn Catholic wedding performed by a chapel priest to unite a Scots warrior with a sassenach. At the cost of two decades of separation, the initiation transforms Claire into the treasured wife of a Highlander and the mother of their two daughters.

Time slip imprints the series with archetypal transformation. For mythic agency,

Jamie claims that the old ones motivated Claire's breach of the time barrier, an obstacle that releases the Celtic mother goddess's powers into a concentrated spot on Craigh na Dun. The deity's constancy offers the Inverness Druidesses a dependable form of worship expressed in chant and ring procession by lantern light. To epitomize his soulful union with Claire, Jamie gives her a ring formed from his key to Lallybroch, a home he hopes to share with her as laird and lady. The iron ring, an iconic heirloom, passes through blessing, theft, and reclamation, costing their daughter Brianna a brutal rape, the temporary sacrifice of her mate, and months of terror and nightmares of her assailant, pirate Stephen Bonnet. Completing the Frasers' altar ceremony, a sharing of blood and a pledge of unified bone and blood bypass Christian dogma with a pagan oath sealed by a dirk.

Mystic Rites

Season three introduces shipboard ritual that forces the superstitious to touch an iron horseshoe, a cryptic mariners' regimen unknown to Claire. Questions of compliance threaten the life of Gavin Hayes, who offers to sacrifice himself to the sea until his friend Jamie dissuades him. On a sighting of the British man-o'-war *Porpoise*, Claire's Hippocratic Oath forces her onto the ship, where she treats patients afflicted by epidemic typhoid fever. She observes and assists ceremonial bundling of the dead in canvas shrouds. The final stitch passes through the nose of the corpse, a pragmatic proof that the unflinching body is really dead. To assert gratitude to each sailor, the burial crew tops bundles with the Union Jack, a segment of burial at sea that impresses the men with duty and pride.

The season forces the Frasers through ordeals that include Jamie's first jailing in a floating cell and Claire's leap onto a homemade raft in the Atlantic Ocean off Grand Turk. The sequence ends a lengthy action with West African voodoo, a ritual Jamaican worship service that begins with black devotees humming during their advance to a gathering of Maroons near Rose Hall. Bare feet maintain contact with earth, the source of pagan divinity. Drumming and chant draw the Frasers to an intense all-African tread around a fire. Costuming illustrates a red-turbaned priest, white outfits topped with masks, an alligator head, and the female tignon, a slave era headdress and mark of dignity for black women.

The syncretism of voodoo with fortuneteller Margaret Campbell's gift for foresight alludes to better times after abolition of slavery. A rooster decapitation and savage expressions and gestures precede the Maroons' pummeling of Archibald Campbell, whom Margaret calls "the monster" (3:13). Visceral drama reveals heroism in Yi Tien Cho and his love for Margaret and lauds Jamie's promise not to lose his second daughter as the couple lost the first, an occluded pun on faith/Faith. The episode ends in the cave at Abandawe with Claire beheading Geillis Duncan Abernethy, the crazed Jacobite stalker who threatens death to Brianna, the portentous 200-year-old baby. Geillis suffers recompense for murdering and immolating her husband, Greg Edgars, as a means of subverting Scots history. Her distortion of time travel ritual exposes a wicked streak that threatens the extended Fraser family and the future of Scotland.

Immigrant Rituals

Righteousness and pledges extend the Fraser household to a diasporic Scots-American community in piedmont North Carolina. To spare friend Gavin Hayes from burial outside hallowed ground in Wilmington, Jamie and his family place the hanged man in an inviolable cemetery, a theft of sacred ground from a disreputable minister. On Roger MacKenzie's pilgrimage to join his beloved Brianna at Fraser's Ridge, he cuts ties with his adoptive family, the Rev. Reginald Wakefield, who took him in after his parents, Jerry and Marjorie MacKenzie, died in World War II. Roger performs a sanguine house blessing on his childhood home at Inverness with salt, champagne, and good wishes for harmony in the marriage of Fiona Graham to Ernie Buchan. An invitation to sing at a Scots gathering on Grandfather Mountain, North Carolina, assimilates Roger into a calling of the clans and the burning of the stag, a prehistoric sacrificial beast replaced in modern times with a wicker statue representing solidarity and prosperity.

A house blessing, which embodies wholeness and probity, hallows the New World cabin of James and Claire on the edge of a region shared with the Cherokee. At the union of Brianna and Roger, neighbors and kin dance traditional reels and celebrate Roger's heroic return from a near-death experience with Mohawks at Shadow Lake, New York. To welcome his son Jeremiah into the family, Roger slices his thumb and marks the baby pagan style with blood on the forehead and a formal naming—Jeremiah Alexander Ian Fraser MacKenzie—after the seventh century BCE prophet Jeremiah, who warned of idolatry and the recompense of sin.

Formal Farewells

A dramatic ritual marks an unavoidable rift with colonial government. Military service beckons Jamie once more to the warrior role, for which he dresses in traditional kilt, brooch, dirk, and plaid, clothing that restores the essence of manhood and devotion to heritage. By igniting a Celtic cross and swearing himself and his militia to tenants' protect, he converts the allegiance he bore to Scotland at the Battle of Culloden a quarter century earlier in 1746 to fealty to his immigrant community. As demonstrated by the philosophical split in season five, episode two, the fine demarcation between Highlander and loyal North Carolinian heightens dramatic strain on himself and his kin. Before the Battle of Alamance on May 16, 1771, Jamie wades into a stream for a blood sacrament communing with the spirit of Dougal MacKenzie, the war chief who taught his nephew combat craft.

Ignorance and ritual mark the community of Fraser's Ridge with prosperity and loss, causing death to Leith Farrish from a burst appendicitis after his wife administers folk physic—bloodletting and mercury pills. A Christian funeral rite incorporates earthly interment with Roger's singing of "Abide with Me," a graveside request that the Almighty remain close to the wilderness dwellers. The burial precedes the mounding of stones into a cairn over Murtagh Fitzgibbons Fraser. His lover, Jocasta Innes, sings "The Flowers of the Forrest" and regrets that she never wed Murtagh. Since the Battle of Flodden on September 9, 1513, her folk lament served somber Scots, British, Canadians, and Australians as a dirge, bagpipe march, and war memorial. In a dissociative state apart from her captors, Claire dreams of Thanksgiving, a uniquely American family ritual, and chooses from the living and dead her table guests, including Jocasta and Murtagh.

See also Burial at Sea; Christianity; Clergy; Dance; Fire and Heat; Kilt; Music.

Source

Gavin, Anne. "Fairies, Folklore, Witchcraft & Waterhorses—The Symbolism & Superstitions of *Outlander*," *Outlander Cast* (25 October 2016).

Gopaldas, Reshma. "*Outlander* Season 5 Finale Recap: In 'Never My Love' Claire Struggles to Survive and *Outlander* Breaks Us," *sheknows* (10 May 2020).

Noorda, Rachel. "From *Waverley* to *Outlander*: Reinforcing Scottish Diasporic Identity through Book Consumption," *National Identities* 20:4 (2018): 361–377.

Reiher, Andrea. "'Outlander' EPs Break Down Claire's 'Survival Mechanism' in Season 5 Finale," *Variety* (10 May 2020).

River Run

A restful two-story mansion with attic dormers, the fictional colonial home of Jocasta Mackenzie Cameron Innes, thrice-widowed sister of Colum, Dougal, and Ellen MacKenzie Fraser, projects welcome and relaxed grandeur. In Bladen County southeast of Fayetteville on the lower Cape Fear River, the arrivals—Jamie, Claire, Ian, and Rollo—step off a barge at Jocasta's landing in 1768 and enter the illusion of peace and easy money in the American South. In violation of Deep South standards, Claire immediately alarms the majordomo, Ulysses, by urging maids Mary and Phaedra to use her first name. Always attuned to medical needs, she investigates the herb bed for possible additions to her pharmacopeia while Jamie and his "Auntie Jo" discuss agriculture, the monetary focus of North Carolina.

Because of their mutual love for Ellen, Jamie, Brianna, and Murtagh Fitzgibbons Fraser have reason to feel comfortable at River Run with the sister who most resembles Ellen. The mistress of a sizable property, Jocasta survives retribution against three Cameron husbands for joining the MacDonalds in leading Highlanders against George II. One of many Scots who fled English vengeance after the rising of April 16, 1746, she chose a pun on escaping certain death as the name for her colonial home. She flourished at growing tobacco and grain and at selecting wines and decor for a splendid environment. During a formal introduction to Jocasta's great niece, Brianna Fraser, aristocratic guests enjoy wine service in the foyer and parlor, dinner menus featuring corn and other Southern vegetables, and luxurious guest rooms papered and draped in silk and fringe.

PLANTATION GLORY

The grand structure reflects the elegance of an historic landmark—Orton Plantation house, a Greek revival mansion built by Roger Moore in 1735 on 10,000 acres of low country wetlands. The location reiterates the fictional Jamie's choice of River Run for future rice terracing and the use of historic architect Kenneth McKenzie Murchison's slate-roofed wood structure as a movie backdrop for *Divine Secrets of the Ya-Ya Sisterhood* and *Dawson's Creek*. Details—fluted Doric columns of the facade, ball-finial roof parapet, twenty acres of garden esplanades and fountains, cemeteries, axial walkway, sundial, gatehouses, live oak allée, bridges, and pond—enhance the palatial views of antebellum affluence, made possible by the work of hundreds of slaves. Flanked by a kitchen house, temple-style chapel with octagonal belfry, belvedere, camphor grove, laborers' quarters, vegetable beds, and hunters' camp, the layout projects genteel tastes, dynastic wealth, and grueling labor.

The flaw in the fictional River Run, human bondage, sickens Claire for its casual insensitivity towards butler Ulysses, maids Mary and Phaedra, and columns of nameless field hands harvesting tobacco and hoeing a flat expanse for the next crop. Because Jamie concurs with his wife about liberty, the couple reject inheritance of cropland that he manages temporarily. The mistreatment of slaves impacts Claire with the unconscionable lynching of Rufus, a young worker impaled at the midriff by a foot-long hook. To treat the patient, she sweeps aside the embellishments on a dining table and replaces them with emergency supplies. Her gentle post-surgical offer of water indicates regard for the victim of Overseer Byrnes, whom she lambastes as a "real son of a bitch" (4:2). With concern for Rufus's recuperation, she has him bedded in her room, a violation of white protocol among African slaves.

The Cost of Elegance

By setting a vicious night-time struggle on the River Run front lawn, the *Outlander* TV series fuses gracious living with colonial greed. The choice of saving Rufus or allowing a mob to wreak havoc on a surgical patient forces Claire to choose euthanasia over an atrocity. Her offer of sedative tea conceals the deadly effects of yellow (also Confederate or Carolina) jasmine (*Gelsemium sempervirens*), a common decorative vine that contains poisonous strychnine. The theatrical chiming of midnight signals the handover of Rufus's corpse to roiling whites. The mob's menace begs the question: Which are the savages?

In the peaceful aftermath of potentially disastrous rock throwing, flaming torches, and mass violence, River Run returns to scrutiny at the prenuptial reception for Duncan Innes and Jocasta Cameron. The episode, entitled "Better to Marry than to Burn," restores to prominence the MacKenzie motto, *Luceo non uro* (I shine not burn), an allusion to the mob's threat to set fire to the estate and to Jocasta's grief at the burning death of daughters Seonag and Clementine during the Highland Clearances of 1746. Set across the Cape Fear from a welcoming pier, an opulent pavilion, a parallel of the garden pergolas at Versailles, provides space for guests to converse and dance the minuet and sarabande in a set piece reminiscent of Dresden china figurines. Columns covered in flowers and a central narthex topped with a woven metal dome complement the outdoor dance floor. Indoors, a table at the end of the foyer displays wedding gifts, evidence that Jocasta has retained favor among fellow planters.

Season five, episode eleven reveals a silent adoration of Ulysses for his mistress. Although he gained manumission on August 23, 1767, when Hector died, Ulysses stays close to Jocasta and interprets the world that she cannot see. His grasp on attorney Gerald Forbes in the parlor to stop him from suffocating her with a pillow forces Ulysses to flee a harsh law condemning slaves from laying violent hands on whites. In fall 1772, John Grey intercedes for Ulysses at Fraser's Ridge and offers a position as manservant for Grey's trip home to England. He declares Ulysses free as soon as he boards a British ship, but the dialogue hints that Ulysses's loyalties remain with his beloved Jocasta.

See also Racism; Slavery.

Source

Ashe, Samuel A., Stephen B. Weeks, and Charles L. Van Noppen, eds. *Biographical History of North Carolina*, eight vols. Greensboro, NC: Van Noppen, 1905 1917.

A New Voyage to Georgia. London: J. Wilford, 1737.

Prescott, Amanda-Rae. "*Outlander* Season 5 Episode 6 Review: Better to Marry Than to Burn," *Den of Geek* (22 March 2020).

Waddell, Alfred Moore. *A History of New Hanover County and the Lower Cape Fear Region 1723–1800*. Volume I. N.P.: n.p., 1909.

Rose Hall

A genteel Caribbean setting for the *Outlander* TV series and its most bizarre installment, Rose Hall at an estate on Montego Bay anchors Jamaican plantation history to West

Indian bondage and Creole witchery. A pseudo-genealogy of the MacKenzie clan incorporated Kenneth MacKenzie, an historical war chief elevated to the peerage in 1609 by Scots king James VI. After the Jacobite downfall at the Battle of Culloden on April 16, 1746, and subsequent Highland Clearances, a clairvoyant at Brahan Castle, Coinneach Odhar, known as "Warlock of the Glen," reputedly instilled hope in Highlanders that a Stuart monarch would return to the throne (Burke, 1883, 172). The prophecy kindles the obsessive crusade of fictional time traveler Geillis Duncan Abernethy.

The chronicle extracts from a muddled legend Geillis's belief that her lover, Dougal MacKenzie, war chief of Kenneth's clan, left a treasure chest on Selkie Island containing old coins, pearls, rubies, diamonds, and three magic sapphires. Following fairy tale numerology, the sapphires have power only in a triad. Geillis values the trio as key to the prediction that a Catholic Stuart will recover the British monarchy. In luxurious surroundings, she cossets two of the gemstones, lolls in a bath of goat's blood, and conducts a séance at the governor's reception to steal the third jewel from a fob, a memento worn by John Grey. In the background of a Machiavellian plot, she pretends to host Claire amid shadowy walkways and a lavish parlor at one of Jamaica's storied Georgian landmarks.

Outlander's authenticity stumbles from an embarrassingly amateurish denouement. In a roguish, feminine boudoir, she threatens the life of Young Ian Murray, whom she drugs with truth tea, massages with her toes, and sexually assaults. In the scramble to consult the sapphire, Geillis turns murderous by immuring Claire in a bedroom until Jamie rescues her. The final battle occurs under Rose Hall at Abandawe, a cardboardy cavern containing a glowing blue-green pool portal to a time slip. Above the magic waters stands a replica of the stones at Craigh na Dun, which concentrates earthly powers in the central monolith. While Jamie bashes Hercules, the slave security guard, and releases Ian, Claire surprises herself by slicing off Geillis's head, a crime previewed in Joe Abernethy's office from bones recovered from a slave burial ground.

The real Rose Hall Plantation in St. James parish nurtures a celebrated ghost, 17-year-old Annie Mary Patterson, a Haitian-born Anglo-Scots orphan trained by a nanny in poisons and voodoo, a West African religious tradition. The two-story stone-brick-and-hardwood mansion, built after 1770 by John and Rosa Kelly Palmer, headquartered a 650-acre plantation. The manse, wrapped in a balustraded porch above dual staircases, flourished during the rum and sugar boom that elevated Jamaica to England's richest Caribbean colony. Formerly staffed by 2,000 slaves, the estate collapsed in bankruptcy in 1792. Willed to a nephew, the property became entangled in conflicting legends of the murder of Annie's four husbands by stabbing and strangulation and the poisoning of enslaved African lovers, crimes of the fictional "White Witch of Rose Hall."

Source

Burke, Bernard. *Vicissitudes of Families*. London: Longmans, Green & Co., 1883.
Dash, Mike. "The Trial That Gave Vodou a Bad Name," *Smithsonian* (29 May 2013).
Donahue, Jennifer. "The Ghost of Annie Palmer: Give a Voice to Jamaica's 'White Witch of Rose Hall," *Journal of Commonwealth Literature* 49:2 (2014): 243–256.
MacKenzie, Alexander. *The Prophecies of the Brahan Seer*. Inverness, UK: A. & W. MacKenzie, 1888.

Scots Culture

Amid romantic stories of bravehearts, Samhain ghosts, blood offerings, fairies and changelings, and a magical white lady, Highlanders in the *Outlander* TV chronicle espouse homeland conventions that identify a region and nation. In David Hesse's

Warrior Dreams: Playing Scotsmen in Mainland Europe, he remarked that insurgents have required internal protection by a "warrior culture … since at least the Middle Ages," which included the reign of Macbeth of Alba from 1040 to 1057 (Hesse, 2014, 7). Hesse reiterates the popular figures of "a tartan-swathed figure of heroic strength, red-haired, red-bearded and spoiling for a fight" (*ibid.,* 70). Hesse notes the one-gendered backstory, promoted by Queen Victoria's journals. In European stereotypes of Highlander soldiery, "The Scottish dreamscape is gendered, the Scottish dreamscape is male" with a "primal masculinity" (*ibid.*).

In the vein of "a certain hairy belligerence," TV episodes detail Jamie's skill with claymore and dirk, his adoption of a tam and the nickname "Dunbonnet," reverence to patrons St. Michael and St. Andrew, and purchase of Claire's nuptial dress embroidered with a cascade of silver oak leaves, a global icon of longevity and strength (*ibid.*). In the opening of season five, the thistle stitched on Brianna Randall's wedding hem and scarf and topped with Ellen MacKenzie's heirloom pearls visualizes a vigorous Scots matri-lineage. In an interview with *Vogue* journalist Alexandra Macon, actor Sophie Skelton remarked, "We make a point of showing that this is one of Jocasta's dresses that has been reconfigured for the wedding. It's a hand-me-down," a version of woman-to-woman heir-looms (Macon, 2020). The prickly teasel epitomizes the motto of the Order of the This-tle: "Nemo me immune lacessit (No one attacks me with impunity, 3:4)," the Stuart motto that extends to the execution of rapists Stephen Bonnet, Arvin Hodgepile, and Lionel Brown.

Highlanders cherish the outré—the alleged mystic properties of herbs and teas, spirits inhabiting lochs and stones, fairies swapping sickly infants for sturdy offspring, and a puppet show of the Druidic powers of Craigh na Dun. In the opening episode, Frank relates the death of St. Odhran, an Irish monastic and follower of St. Columba to Iona, a famed Benedictine retreat a mile off western Scotland in the Inner Hebrides. At the historic abbey, which dominates the 2009 film *The Secret of Kells,* Odhran took the legendary role of voluntary foundation sacrifice on October 27, 548 CE, by choos-ing live burial beneath the church walls. Because the walls had repeatedly collapsed each day, masons needed a volunteer to stabilize the chapel, a superstition that figures in the Arthurian legend of Merlin and a prophetic Pendragon victory at Dinas Emrys, a fort in northwestern Wales.

ELEMENTS OF SCOTS HERITAGE

As with the BBC-TV series *Ballykissangel* and *Hamish Macbeth,* artistic details fit neatly into daily life, for example, the placement of a heather bouquet on the Fraser grave at Culloden moor, a bagpipe call to arms for Jacobite volunteers, honoring Murtagh's cairn with a rendition of "The Flowers of the Forrest," Rupert's storytelling of the water horse's human wife, and blood oaths at war rituals, weddings, and infant namings. At the MacKenzie gathering, a cyclical clan event at Castle Leoch, the sharing of the laird's loving cup exemplifies consistent drinking of wine, port, brandy, champagne, ale, and whisky for noteworthy occasions. Typically, the ritual ends with clan accord and a reel to fiddle music. During rent collection, broad camera sweeps reveal the quality of agrar-ian life amid stone fencing and barns with thatched roofs, where women perform the chore of "waulking wool," setting dyes with the ammonia in hot urine (1:5). On the search for Jamie in northwest Scotland, Murtagh Fitzgibbons Fraser and Claire appeal to the country folk's preference for fortunetelling, fire breathers, highland sword dances, and a bawdy tune sung by a cross-dressing Sassenach.

In question during the Fraser marriage, Scots androcentrism jogs along a tricky continuum based on eighteenth-century values and Claire's emergence from mid–1940s opportunities for women. Of the controversial belt whipping to punish her for disobedience to husband Jamie, actor Sam Heughan explained: "It's the way he's been brought up, and he's now got responsibility, and he's trying to do everything that's right," including adherence to a man-in-charge stereotype (Prudom, 2015). To ease modern viewers over a conflict between wife-beating and modern feminist values, author Diana Gabaldon concurred with Heughan: "In 1743 this was a very justified form of punishment that a husband would mete out" (Kennedy, 2016, 125). A return of misogyny in Jamie startled viewers of season five at River Run, where he belittles Claire's gender and drunkenly forces her into bruising intercourse in a barn stall, a revival of his earlier bestialism.

War Against English Imperialism

In an article for *Critical Military Studies,* Nataliya Danilova and Kandida Purnell assert that the native soldier remains "one of the key and abiding icons of Scottishness" (Danilova and Purnell, 2019, 4). In the fictional Claire's proposal to avert the fourth and final Jacobite Rebellion lies a prophecy—a beheaded laird and obliteration of the Scots clan system, land ownership, and Highland heritage, an upheaval that she knows from European history. Integral to Jamie's assumption of duty to a Jacobite regiment, comeuppance to war chief Dougal MacKenzie and lashings of Ross and Kincaid for dereliction of duty in 1744 continue the harsh military justice that had striped Jamie's back in October 1739 and antagonized him toward the English. Even in his hesitation to plot a complex hoax against the bonnie prince, Jamie trusts Claire's defense of fellow Scots and their perspective. The two tackle Prince Charlie's perverse Catholicism and sustain his fantasies of the divine right of kings and Stuart restoration.

Because of the Disarming Act and 1746 Act of Proscription, fictional Highlanders abandon their rebel plots. Illustrating a despairing older generation, Jamie disappoints Fergus, his teenage foster son, who expects a fifth revolt. Without dirk or sword, Jamie retreats to bow and arrow to kill a stag for the Lallybroch table. His silent hacking at the carcass emphasizes crude forest meals and symbolizes Scotland's disempowerment. Arrival in North American restores opportunities for pride and success, beginning with reverence to Gavin Hayes, whose hanging calls for a tavern singing of the Gaelic farewell "Eisd Ris" (Hear Him, 4:1).

Season five dramatizes the spunk and moral uprightness of Scots emigrants to North America. On settling Fraser's Ridge in North Carolina, Jamie dresses in standard kilt, brooch, sporran, and plaid and lights the fiery cross, a call to battle to survivors of Culloden and post-war imprisoning for treason. The chief ignites new fervor in Scots-American clan tradition and, on May 16, 1771, buoys spirits for the Battle of Alamance Creek. Unfortunately for émigrés, the brief combat sets Scot against Scot and costs the life of Jamie's godfather, Murtagh Fitzgibbons Fraser, the iconic leader of the poor and oppressed. The revival of the Rowan County Militia at the second cross lighting assembles men to rescue Claire and kill lawless pillagers, who begin their raid with destruction of the Fraser still, a token of Scots *joie de vivre.*

See also Birthing; Christianity; Gaelic; Heirlooms; Superstition; Weapons; Whisky.

Source

Danilova, Nataliya, and Kandida Purnell. "The 'Museumification' of the Scottish Soldier and the Meaning-Making of Britain's Wars," *Critical Military Studies* (2019): 1–19.

Hesse, David. *Warrior Dreams: Playing Scotsmen in Mainland Europe*. Manchester, UK: Manchester University Press, 2014.

Kennedy, Victoria. "The Way We Were: Nostalgia, Romance and Anti-Feminism," *Outlander's Sassenachs: Essays on Gender, Race, Orientation and the Other in the Novels and Television Series*. Jefferson, NC: McFarland, 2016, 117–129.

Macon, Alexandra. "An Exclusive First Look at Brianna and Roger's Huge *Outlander* Wedding," *Vogue* (7 February 2020).

Prudom, Laura. "'Outlander' Stars Break Down Claire and Jamie's First Fight, That Spanking Scene," *Variety* (5 April 2015).

Secondary Characters

Casting, the bulwark of the *Outlander* TV narrative, chooses expert character actors to play secondary roles—Mrs. Fitz, Stephen Bonnet, Geillis Duncan, Ned Gowan, Jocasta Cameron, Louis XV, Colum MacKenzie, Jenny Murray, and Young Ian. Supporting cast enacts smaller but no less integral parts—Maisri, Horrocks, Annalise de Marillac, Mr. Ward, Jared Fraser, the ever-faithful aide Elias Pound, Eppie the prostitute, John Quincy Myers, and Brighid the barmaid, Young Ian's first conquest. Some stand out for their uniqueness, particularly the elder Ian Murray (Steven Cree), the gentle, one-legged brother-in-law who counsels without scorn or wrangle; the rancorous malcontent Lionel Brown; and Willoughby (Yi Tien Cho, played by Gary Young), the love-starved Chinaman who writes poetry and autobiography that compensates for his celibacy. One paradox, War Chief Dougal MacKenzie (expertly portrayed by Graham McTavish), appears to combine the skill of the guerrilla warrior with coveting his brother's clan and maneuvering for favoritism on the bonnie prince's council. At a tense moment concluding season one at Rowan Cross, a satanical camera view of Dougal illuminates his wicked womanizing and plotting to bed Claire. The keen look into the inner Dougal accounts for deep sins in an ambitious man whom Claire labels a narcissist (2:9).

Some of the outstanding supporting roles establish memorable attitudes and relationships in a few scenes, especially perky Marsali Fraser (Lauren Lyle), contemplative Highlander Bryan Cranna (Martin Donaghy), snidely self-centered Geneva Dunsany (Hannah James), and Ulysses (Colin McFarlane), the see-all, know-all factotum of Jocasta Cameron Innes's River Run. During the worst of the Frasers' tenure in Paris in 1744, the amicable apothecary, Master Raymond (Dominique Pinon), sets an atmosphere of trust and friendship that heartens Claire much more than card-playing, gossip, and tea with bourgeois ladies. Similarly supportive of an altruistic healer, Mother Hildegarde (Frances de la Tour) gives Claire the praise she craves for treating the sick at l'Hôpital des Anges, an uplifting support that Claire passes on to daughter-in-law Marsali Fraser, her surgical assistant.

Suiting the Character

On a broader scale, Fergus 1 (Romann Barrux) and Fergus 2 (César Domboy) supply the Fraser household with a foster son and accomplice. He abets schemes to fool the bonnie prince, defraud Le Comte St. Germain (Stanley Weber), and serve as Jamie's proxy at La Maison de Madame Elise. A twentieth-century advocate returns her to an office shared with Joe Abernethy (Wil Johnson), who teasingly names her Lady Jane after the protagonist of *Lady Chatterley's Lover*, D.H. Lawrence's erotic novel challenged in a British court in 1960 and filmed in 1981. Partnered with Claire, Joe integrates Harvard's white-male-only medical school and encourages her return to Jamie. Seamlessly, the older Fergus greets and embraces Claire on her appearance at the Edinburgh market like a foster mother he hasn't seen in twenty years.

Infants supply the series with future glimpses in the birth and welcome to Germain and his sisters Joan and Felicité Fraser, Baby Clara Mueller, and Jeremiah "Jemmy" MacKenzie. One of the most convincing arrangements, selection of Willie 1, Willie 2 (Clark Butler), a rascal by age six, and Willie 3 preserves Jamie's likeness in heart and body to his only male offspring. A winsome babe in his pram, Willie 1 develops into a sturdy scrapper in Willie 2 before adopting his stepfather's aristocratic air and speech in Willie 3. Episodes picture Jamie looking for his own features in the three child actors and finding them in Willies 2 and 3.

On reunion with the twelve-year-old version, Claire and Jamie applaud the handsome appearance, reserved manners, and values that refuse to claim Jamie as father, even while he repels a Cherokee for wielding a tomahawk at Willie for theft. In a model of mirror images, camerawork depicts a swift slice to his left hand, a modified re-enactment of Corporal MacGregor's slicing of Fergus's left hand in 1752. The parallelism dramatizes the relationship of two scions with Jamie and his intuitive protection. A gift portrait in 1773 offers Jamie an opportunity to inform Brianna of her brother's existence and visual proof that the two children share blood and resemble their father.

Disappointments

At the beginning of season four, critic Kayla Kumari Upadhyaya penned a compliment to the series and its characters: "*Outlander* is truly a masterclass in chemistry.... It mixes ingredients in precise combinations and quantities to brilliant, complex results. The alchemy of this show, one that blends genres, tones, and emotions so deftly, is truly dazzling" (Upadhyaya, 2018). One example, Ned Dennehy, the actor who plays Lionel Brown, masters the free-floating hostility of the backwoods North Carolinian. He nails the characterization with rancorous spitting on the ground, a giveaway of the Faulkneresque, mad-at-the-world redneck.

A few actor choices fail to satisfy dramatic needs, especially the cartoonish Jerry and Millie Nelson, wooden Young Simon Lovat, and impassive Lieutenant Hamilton Knox, who hero worships Jamie. The worst, the whiny Mary Hawkins Randall (Rosie Day), appears to have an unalterable expression and voice tone. Even announcing her plans to marry Alex and bear a child, she registers restrained emotion. Fortunately, in a massive cast, the few failures make no inroads into viewer appeal.

A limited character actor in gesture and voice modulation, Nell Hudson manages a transformation in Laoghaire, the dogged villain of Claire's love life. From betrayer at the Cranesmuir witchcraft trial, Laoghaire sinks into ignominy by marrying Hugh MacKenzie, the cruel Simon MacKimmie, and the allegedly widowed Jamie Fraser. She appears to carry into middle age the delusions of a teenage crush. According to her description, her third family develops a peaceful home life through nightly storytelling to Jamie's stepdaughters, Marsali and Joanie. On meeting Brianna and voicing an aspersion of males, Laoghaire deduces Brianna's parentage and launches anew charges of witchery in the woman who allegedly conjured Jamie away. Apparently, the evil lies within, causing the character to seem as deranged as Black Jack Randall, Geillis Duncan, and Stephen Bonnet.

See also Stephen Bonnet; Murtagh Fitzgibbons Fraser.

Source

Carr, Flora. "Meet the Cast of *Outlander* Series Five Including the Witcher Star," *Radio Times* (13 March 2020).
Steinberg, Dawn. "How the Actors of 'Outlander' Got Cast," https://www.youtube.com/watch?v=hI5Ny69FWEg (2 June 2016).
Upadhyaya, Kayla Kumari. "*Outlander's* Alchemy Remains Spectacular in Its Hotly Anticipated Return," *AVClub* (4 November 2018).
_____. "*Outlander* Peddles a White Savior Narrative in Jamaica," *AVClub* (3 December 2017).

Slavery

Similar in motif to veteran Dave Robicheaux's contrast of the Vietnam War to the Civil War in the movie *In the Electric Mist with the Confederate Dead, Outlander* could not move the fictional TV chronicle west from Scotland and France without incurring the sins of the Americas. In the Caribbean, the Frasers meet slaves in holding pens, on the auction block, and in menial jobs at the governor's palace in Kingston, Jamaica. From Father Fogden in Haiti, Claire learns of Maroons or escaped slaves whom she later encounters in person at a Jamaican voodoo ritual. At the Kingston slave market, she cringes at a woman's branding and potential buyers gawking at the penis of Temeraire (Thapelo J. Sebogodi), a teenaged Ghanian named "bold." The charged atmosphere belies the actual eagerness of planters to add healthy breeders to their African stock. Historically, because of the high mortality rate in newborns and small children, in-house slave breeding in the West Indies had little influence on the total profits.

During the enslavement of blacks in British Jamaica from 1655 to 1787, investors acquired 600,000 or 40–50 percent of all abducted Africans. Most were as vulnerable as Temeraire. As liquid assets rose, bondsmen joined field gangs in their late teens and earned for whites the highest wealth in the Western world. History experts Trevor Burnard of Brunel University, London, and Kenneth Morgan of the Australian National University noted that "Prosperity or poverty depended on whether sufficient Africans could be purchased at reasonable prices and on whether they were long-lived and productive laborers" (Burnard & Morgan, 2001, 205). Market dealers, known as guinea merchants, sold lots in 1730 for £13–14 each or $3,127.45 in current value. Demand in 1765 raised prices to £51–56 per lot or $10,059.59.

PLANTATION LABOR

In the American South, enslavement varied in numbers from 15 percent of the population of Orange County, North Carolina, to 85 percent African captives in Brunswick County, the coastal plains northwest of the fictional Hector and Jocasta Cameron's River Run plantation. When the pound dropped in worth in 1768 at the time of Claire and Jamie's pioneering of Fraser's Ridge, the animalizing of African chattel resulted in the evaluation of each agrarian worker at £69–80 ($13,236.96). Inhumane laws limited manumission by altruistic men like Jamie and required the dismemberment of any slave who attacked whites. Nonetheless, the possibility of a gruesome execution in 1772 does not halt the fictional Ulysses from rescuing his mistress by breaking the neck of attacker Gerald Forbes.

Investment in slaves carried significant risk from epidemics and violence, possibilities that sci-fi novelist Octavia Butler surveys in the time slip story of Dana in *Kindred*. Two years after a slave revolt in Antigua on September 9, 1739, the Stono or Cato's Rebellion twenty miles southwest of Charleston, South Carolina, on the Edisto River began with a raid of arms and powder from Hutchinson's warehouse and the murder of two guards by seventy-six enslaved Angolan and Congolese rice laborers. On the march south toward Savannah to the beat of two drums, more slaves, like those who followed the Thracian gladiator Spartacus across Italy in 70 CE, joined the rebels and their leader Jemmy, a fact reported by a white post rider, Lieutenant Governor William Bull.

Violence backed by Spanish colonists in St. Augustine, Florida, caused arson of seven properties around Rantowles on the Wallace River and the murder of seventy people, twenty-three of them white men, women, and children. Some of the opposition force derived from local Cherokee and Chickasaw. Capture by militia resulted in a mass beheading, shooting, and gibbeting of forty black survivors and the mounting of heads on pikes as a warning of white retribution. One black escapee skulked at large for three years before execution. A flourishing slave population in the Carolinas ingrained in whites the fear of another uprising.

Bondage Laws

In the wake of the failed insurrection, comprehensive laws known as the Security Act of 1739 obscured the potential of bondsmen, who could unify into an army of rebels as vengeful and effective as Scots Jacobites. In mid–August, new regulations from the South Carolina Colonial Assembly demanded that plantation populations include ten percent white residents. In a Christian population, the laws required white males to arm themselves for Sunday church services when they were most vulnerable. The Negro Act of 1740 suppressed manumission and importation of African slaves from Angola and Congo and encouraged the breeding of black Americans. Legislation halted slave education, assemblies, gardening and herding, and personal earnings and travels.

By 1767, a year before the fictional Frasers reach North America, some 41,000 black North Carolinians functioned like farm beasts, even Eutroclus, the freedman bargee who navigates the Cape Fear with backbreaking toil. In the next quarter century, the number of slaves more than doubled to 100,783 or 25.6 percent of the total population of 393,751. Despite social disapproval, Claire and Jamie don't hesitate to rescue Wee Bonnie, Fanny Beardsley's biracial infant, and find a wetnurse in Brownsville to feed her. Without investigating the legal ramifications, they learn that the child will inherit Aaron Beardsley's land and trading post.

Season five, episode eleven introduces the dilemma of Ulysses, a black freedman whom the Frasers shelter. John Grey happily hires him as a manservant for the voyage to England, where Ulysses will be free. TV critic Amanda-Raw Prescott explained: "Within England in this era, slavery was legally unenforceable, and there was a growing movement to repeal the colonial slave codes as well" (Prescott, 2020). The statement shamed Americans for being reluctant to pursue abolitionism.

See also Details; Maroons; Piracy.

Source

Burnard, Trevor, and Kenneth Morgan. "The Dynamics of the Slave Market and Slave Purchasing Patterns in Jamaica, 1655–1788," *William and Mary Quarterly* 58:1 (January 2001): 205–228.
McCrady, Edward. *The History of South Carolina under the Royal Government, 1719–1775*. New York: Macmillan, 1899.

Prescott, Amanda-Rae. "*Outlander* Season 5 Episode 11 Review: Journeycake," *Den of Geek* (3 May 2020).
Smith, Mark M. *Stono: Documenting and Interpreting a Southern Slave Revolt*. Columbia: University of South Carolina Press, 2005.
Valentine, Genevieve. "'Outlander' Season 4 Premiere Recap: No Good Deed Unpunished," *New York Times* (4 November 2018).

Smuggling

In the golden era of smuggling, the *Outlander* TV series pictures a lucrative eighteenth-century money maker for anyone bold enough to engage in a capital felony against the English gouger. Before England drafted a coast guard to monitor trans-coastal trade, the venture began with an easy one-night sail from France or the Isle of Mann past British cruisers to seaside inlets. In the early 1740s, fictional War Chief Dougal MacKenzie stores goods at a Rowan Cross cave to fund the Jacobite rebellion. About the time of a three-year government ban on Scots distilling from 1757 to 1760, his nephew Jamie Fraser sets up a printshop in Edinburgh and imports whisky, brandy, cognac, rum, crème de menthe, and French wine as a free trader, a euphemism for booze runner.

According to literary expert Sam Baker, novelist Walter Scott, author of *Masters of Ballantrae* and *The Heart of Midlothian*, "brought smuggling into focus as a main criminal occupation of Scots" like the fictional Dougal and Jamie (Baker, 2011, 2). The novelist explained the Highlander's rationalization for robbing the treasury of its 1 percent malt and gin taxes. To prevent an insurrection of libertarians, dragoon regiments forcibly seized the excise. Scots peasants romanticized heroic Robin Hoods, who murdered six tax agents and assaulted 250 others to protect a lucrative stock. Under the rule of George I and George II, a constant consumer of Scotch whisky: "Smuggling was almost universal in Scotland, for people unaccustomed to imposts and regarding them as an unjust aggression upon their ancient liberties, made no scruple to elude them whenever it was possible" (Napton, 2018, 110).

By avoiding the Crown's heavy duties and taxation to pay for foreign imperialistic wars, Jamie risks confiscation of his premises and hanging by royal courts, but he maintains a sense of patriotic honor supported by clans and anti–English Jacobites. His sister Jenny Murray, who receives the profits, disagrees, pointing out that exposing Young Ian to unsavory scofflaws is no way to prepare him for a respectable career. Compounding the danger, Jamie's bribery of bureaucrat Sir Percival Turner, a customs superintendent, worsens the crime and places Jamie at risk of underworld retribution. John Barton's break-in at Jamie's quarters results in discord between Claire's self-defense and obedience to the Hippocratic Oath, under which she tries unsuccessfully to save the malefactor from brain death.

At John Barton's demise from unsuccessful trepanning, assistant Yi Tien Cho humorously seals the corpse in a cask of crème de menthe, a minty sweet anachronistic drink formulated in the 1880s as an after-dinner carminative. Because Jamie is certain true Scots will avoid a fussy, effeminate drink, he feels rid of evidence. In a glimpse of crime's longevity, Turner's accomplice, Harry Tompkins, follows Jamie to Jamaica on board the British man-o'-war *Porpoise*. Captain Thomas Leonard, a puffed-up military climber, threatens arrest in Kingston, where the punishment is hanging.

In North America, the animosity between fictional distillers, smugglers, and revenue agents prefigures the famed North Carolina moonshine trade in dry counties, where evangelicals forbid the sale of alcohol. The product that Jamie manufactures at Fraser's Ridge in the form of high quality Scots whisky gains screen credence as peasant crime in the films *Thunder Road, The Dukes of Hazzard, Coal Miner's Daughter,* and *Paper Moon.* The *Outlander* chronicle expands smuggling with Claire's one-time deal with Phillip Wylie. The bootlegged whisky passes through port cities, where Wilmington pirate Stephen Bonnet promotes himself to prominent insider trader to the wealthy of silks, lace, and other luxuries. In the sale of Brianna to Captain Howard, he escalates his crimes from smuggling to white slavery.

See also Stephen Bonnet; Whisky.

Source

Baker, Sam. "Walter Scott: Smuggler and Excise Man," Ninth International Conference on Walter Scott, Laramie, Wyoming, 2011.
Buxton, Ian, and Paul S. Hughes. *The Science and Commerce of Whisky.* Cambridge, UK: Royal Society of Chemistry, 2014.
Napton, Dani. *Scott's Novels and the Counter-Revolutionary Politics of Place.* Leiden, Holland: Brill, 2018.

Soldiery

The subject of training people for service in militias and armies recurs throughout the *Outlander* TV narrative. In the opening scenes, Claire and Frank Randall represent the intellectual side of the military, for which they study nursing and history. On Claire's arrival at Craigh na Dun on November 1, 1945, she encounters a castle regiment of Scots guerrillas in running conflict with the British Army, a different confrontation from what she observed between the Allies and Germans during World War II. With the Gaels in War Chief Dougal MacKenzie's band, Jamie Fraser learns asymmetric tactics: The Highland Charge, a close-packed wedge of Scots hurtling toward the British firing line, a contrast to the European method of marching and enfilade musketry in tight order under command of an officer that he learned as a mercenary. The styles illustrate the difference in English and Scots warrior tactics.

Outlander shares with the miniseries *Masada* and the *Rome* television series the grueling details of military life. After Jamie and Claire muster farm laborers from Lallybroch and Beaufort Castle, he intends to teach them strict discipline, regimental strategy, marching, and hand-to-hand combat from repeated drill with straw mannequins. In the midst of lining up and pivoting on Murtagh Fitzgibbons Fraser's command, Dougal interrupts the session with a mock assault certain to take heavy casualties in exchange for spooking the enemy. Stripped to the waist and daubed in mud, Dougal and his squad shriek their way down a hill at high speed to petrify Jamie's recruits. The sudden onset proves the psychological effect of the Highland Charge, which evolved during the days of battle-axes and two-handed swords. The close combat, perfected by Alasdair MacColla MacDonald and directed at lowland Scots in Argyll on September 1, 1644, resembled the uninhibited assault of the Germani at the Battle of Vosges in 58 BCE on Julius Caesar's legions.

Although Jamie persists in his methods and succeeds in burning cannon wheels during a commando raid, at Prestonpans and Culloden in 1745 and 1746, Jacobite soldiers flourish at Dougal's Celtic shock-and-awe gambit. At Prestonpans, in the words of Oxford-trained philosopher Alistair K. Macintyre, "General Cope's Government forces, wrong-footed by the Jacobites' new deployment, broke in panic as the Highland regiments on the front line surged out of the mist in full cry" (Macintyre). Culloden, however, reduced advantages for the Scots. After an initial discharge of muskets, the Scots threw them aside. The fictional aggressors come in low over boggy moorland amid gun smoke, parry bayonet muzzles with their targes, and thrust dirk and sword into enemy abdomens. In under an hour, grape shot "ripped off heads, smashed arms and legs ... a hailstorm of lead tearing flesh and breaking bones" (Newark, 2009).

Close-ups of the fictional Jamie in action picture him in full-throated roar, an anticipation of the Confederate rebel yell to startle Union forces during the American Civil War, an element of the time travel film *In the Electric Mist with the Confederate Dead*. Over flat ground, canister and cannon shot rapidly overwhelm the Jacobites. In a last-ditch tussle with a Redcoat, Jamie resorts to stifling him with a wad of turf, a symbolic weapon yanked from the roots of Scotland itself. A re-enactment of the Highlanders' defeat on May 16, 1771, at Alamance Creek, North Carolina, depicts the Findley brothers eager to test their mettle. The militia's loss proves primitive Celtic methods no match for English cavalry, cannon, and swivel guns.

See also British Army; Mercenaries; Militias; Weapons.

Source

Macintyre, Alistair K. "The Macintyres and the 'Forty-Five," https://www.electricscotland.com/Webclans/m/macintyre45.pdf.

Newark, Tim. *Highlander: The History of the Legendary Highland Soldier.* New York: Skyhorse, 2009.

Riding, Jacqueline. *Jacobites: A New History of the '45.* London: Bloomsbury, 2016.

Tomasson, Katherine, and Francis Buist. *Battles of the '45.* Rakuten, Japan: Pickle Partners Publishing, 2017.

Star Chamber

An English legal concept dating to the thirteenth century, the Star Chamber housed private court trials that the monarchy wished to conceal from the public, especially judgments of high-born aristocrats. In one of the most stunning scenarios in the *Outlander* TV series, depiction of a two-man trial in 1744 places Claire Fraser in the role of La Dame Blanche, a seer and sorceress. For maximum stage presence, she displays an emerald brocade dress with shoulder-to-hem panel sweeping grandly behind her. The screen setting combines a star-pocked blue dome above a dimly lighted hearing room centered with a zodiacal astrolabe ringed by the twelve months of the year, inscribed in gold Roman numerals. Behind a hidden passage, double doors set the tone of proto-science and mysticism with dragon shapes as well as celestial symbols and a triangle, a pagan representation of the soul.

Designer Jon Gary Steele assembled the set to enhance the high drama of suspects facing a fictional charge of sorcery, a capital offense. The mysterious chamber, guarded by black-hooded sentries, flickers with Roman torcheres, which illuminate marble wall panels and the arrival of King Louis XV and royal executioner Foret, a gaunt king's man dressed in black. The cryptic chamber attests to Louis's fascination with the occult and his obscuring from his subjects a hobby condemned by the Catholic church along with astrology, alchemy, divination, animism, and demonology. Based on scriptural commands in Exodus 22:18, Leviticus 20:27 and Deuteronomy 18:11–12, edicts from the Synod of Elvira, Spain, in 306 CE damned forms of pagan incantations and necromancy and excommunicated practitioners as heretics. The ousting of criminal cults remained zealous to the end of the Spanish Inquisition in 1826.

Under royal surveillance, the fictional apothecary Master Raymond, a seller of herbs, nostrums, and exotica, recalls a previous anti-witchcraft crusade under Louis XIV, who condemned "inheritance powder" (poison), enchantment, conjury, black masses, and restorative amulets. During a purge of the arcane from 1679 to 1682, the old king ordered interrogation of thirty-six underworld poisoners and enchanters and issued judgments in *lettres de cachet* (signed orders stamped with a royal seal). Punishments ranged from exile to fines, workhouse or galley slavery, life imprisonment, hanging, decapitation, or lethal torture. The most dramatic, burning alive, ended the career of Paris fortuneteller and witch Marie Bosse on May 8, 1679, and, on February 22, 1680, of her competitor, sibyl Catherine Deshayes "La Voisin" (the neighbor), a maven of chiromancy, abortion, child sacrifice, and alleged regicide.

Under the amiable Louis XV in 1744, a fictional Star Chamber hearing examines Raymond and his quasi-historic rival, the snide alchemist and avenger Le Comte St. Germain. Under Claire Fraser, the self-confessed Dame Blanche (white magician), the defendants answer charges of necromancy. To heighten Gothicism, the TV characterization pictures a glowering royal headsman, Monsieur Foret, a caged serpent, and two collections of illicit substances, alleged poisons confiscated from the defendants. After Raymond passes Claire's test by ordeal—drinking an unlabeled liquid—her loadstone amulet turns black, indicating the presence of a toxic substance. An eye-to-eye confrontation with St. Germain precedes his collapse from poison, ostensibly placed in the shared cup by Raymond.

Much of the series mysticism reflects fact. The historical Comte de St. Germain lived a shadowy collusion with Louis XV, communicated by coded letters with mystic Rosicrucian and Freemason brotherhoods, and died in Germany on February 27, 1784. The headsman's drawing and quartering of victims ended on March 28, 1757, with the torture, trial, and execution before City Hall in Paris of failed regicide Robert-François "Robert le Diable (the devil)" Damiens, the final victim. The royal liquidator, Charles Henri Sanson, tore the prisoner to pieces by attaching horses to his limbs and burned his torso at the stake. A witness, Venetian folk hero Giacomo Casanova, recoiled from the shrieking Damiens, but noticed that fashionable voyeurs did not blanch.

See also La Dame Blanche; Superstition.

Source

Mollenauer, Lynn Wood. *Strange Revelations: Magic, Poison, and Sacrilege in Louis XIV's France.* University Park: Pennsylvania State University Press, 2007.
Vineyard, Jennifer. "How *Outlander*'s Star Chamber Came Together," *New York* (23 May 2016).

Storytelling

Narrative imbeds oral lore and song with momentum and a longevity grounded in belief and repetition. In the *Outlander* TV narrative, episodes cover a gamut of tone, atmosphere, and genre as humorous as Jamie's recovery from war wounds in a brothel, as mystic as Margaret Campbell and Duncan Kerr's dazed foretellings, as historic as the building of Tryon's Palace, and as literary as Brianna MacKenzie's summary of novelist Herman Melville's *Moby Dick*. The series intrigues from the beginning with Claire's disappearance into the past at Craigh na Dun and alleged reappearance as the "white lady" on Selkie Island. Of the TV story line, *Outlander* producer Ronald Moore prefers deviations from the usual: "I'm always looking for surprise in a story, surprise in an ongoing series, taking the audience off-stride.... It can go in directions you're not expecting" (Ryan, 2016).

Episodic tellings personify nature and fate in Adawehi's dream of the white raven, Fanny Beardsley's visions of Mary Ann and Aaron's other murdered wives, Stephen Bonnet's orphaning, and Yi Tien Cho's autobiography, a proof of immortality. On an everyday level, Geillis Duncan anticipates Claire's engaging report of a nonstandard upbringing by Uncle Lambert, an archeologist. Whether episodic saga, cautionary tale, or personal anecdote, informative stories impact daily entertainment as well as private conversation, as with Frank Randall's display of erudition to Mrs. Baird in a recap of the macabre live burial of St. Odhran and the origins of Samhain and Yule. At Castle Leoch, the limpid solo recitation of "Bean Tighearna Bhail' 'n' Athain" ("The Woman of Balnain") by Welsh harper Gwyllyn the Bard illustrates the power of melody in a foreign language, which relates time travel similar to Claire's displacement.

Stories fill in difficult situations with narrative ease, especially Jamie's pensive parable of the grieving widowed greylag, an allegory of "wedded for life" (3:8). By recounting the elopement of Ellen MacKenzie and Brian Fraser during a clan gathering, Jamie lessens wedding night tensions with Claire while lauding his parents for cunning and audacity. For Frank, Mrs. Graham's details of concentrated power in Craigh na Dun gains his attention, but not his belief in an age-old time slip tale. Without belief, he takes no comfort from the prediction that Claire will return. Brianna maintains a similar opposition to time travel stories until she views Geillis Duncan's disappearance.

LOVE AND DEATH

For campsite entertainment, Rupert introduces the marriage of the kelpie or waterhorse to a human bride. The melodic fable features a mismatched union based on the need for warmth and safety, not unlike Claire's dependence on her husband for intimacy and security. The voice of Grant O'Rourke is a wise choice for fireside narrative, a suitable recounting of love and accommodation to entertain newlyweds. In the chill depths of the kelpie home, the loch acquires a chimney, an earthling's comfort that enables the waterhorse's wife to ward off cold while she fries fish for dinner. Rupert rounds out his version in mythic form, explaining the failure of a body of water to freeze in winter.

Other less sophisticated tellings fill the series with ancient beliefs in the Earth Mother, witches, demons, white ladies, saints, ghosts, and fairies. A Highlander by birth, despite classic education by a tutor, Jamie respects his people's oral traditions too much to refute a fear of the Black Kirk demons and belief in changelings, the substitution of a feeble baby for a robust child. At this point, according to scholar Marlène Charlier, "Claire realizes how much legends and folktales are relevant and can be dangerous" (Charlier, 2019, 16). Finding her saddened by a newborn's death in the chill forest, Jamie explains the lore of agrarian folk and repositions the small bundle in the tree crotch with a somber crucifix gesture. On return to an alien culture in Castle Leoch, Claire's reliance on her Scots husband's guidance ends with acquiescence to the past.

PROPHECY AND LIES

While the Frasers plot a way to manipulate Lord Simon Lovat at Beaufort Castle, Claire befriends his seer, Maisri, and uses narrative to advantage. To justify a belief that the clairvoyant can alter history, Maisri tells of a boy saved from drowning after his father-in-law damages his boat before a storm hits. The boy remains safe because he stays on shore. Similar to Claire's saving of Tammas Baxter from poison, the anecdote proves that seers have influence on dangers they perceive in the future. By restating Maisri's vision of a royal beheading awaiting Simon, Claire's spectral enactment alters a clan conference on Simon and Colum's support for the 1745 Jacobite rising.

In another glimpse of verbal performance, scriptural manipulation facilitates Laoghaire's twisted love plots. Her recounting of the biblical Ruth and Naomi (Ruth 1–4) precedes the other side of anecdote, a convoluted falsehood about Jamie. By implying that he has no love for his and Claire's unborn daughter, Laoghaire attempts to undermine Brianna's anticipation of meeting her birth father. The web of lies pictures Laoghaire as a rhetorical sorcerer capable of actuating jealousy. Intercalary views of Frank Randall accounting for wanting to marry mistress Sandy Travers deviates from Laoghaire's story of Ruth, one of the bible's beloved romantic heroines.

A Native American view of time travel, Wahkatiiosta's biography of Otter Tooth (played by Trevor Carroll) characterizes an Indian from the future who wishes to save the Iroquois from white oppression. The story follows the outlines of standard First Nations history—the naive acceptance of white settlers on traditional tribal lands. In Gothic style, Wahkatiiosta's version depicts Indian rejection of Otter Tooth's prophecy, which he dramatizes with face paint and an armed war dance. Miraculously, words spill out of his mouth after his death from a tomahawk blow to the skull and scalping.

Because Claire claims Otter Tooth's split cranium and opal, she possesses a true account of Native American history, a story of deracination. On parting with Young Ian, Jamie promises to respect the boy's choice of joining the Mohawk. The two, nephew and uncle, pledge *cuimhnich* (remembrance), the basis of folk narrative (4:13). Claire's subsequent meeting with Tebbe introduces her to a mulatto fearful of her powers to haunt her tormentors. By staring at Lionel Brown, she wordlessly exacerbates the rapist's terror of a reputed witch.

See also Superstition.

Source

Beard, Ellen L. "Satire and Social Change: The Bard, the Schoolmaster and the Drover," *Northern Scotland* 8:1 (2017): 1–21.

Charlier, Marlène. "La représentation des mythes et légendes dans la série Outlander," master's thesis, Université de Franche-Comté, 2019.

Mittel, Johannes. *Complex TV: The Poetics of Contemporary Television Storytelling*. New York: New York University Press, 2015.

Ryan, Maureen. "'Outlander' Boss Ron Moore on Eliciting Emotional Response, Season 2 and Surprising Storytelling," *Variety* (3 May 2016).

Watson, Roderick. *The Literature of Scotland*. London: Macmillan International Higher Education, 2016.

Stuart Dynasty

The contention undergirding the TV series *Outlander,* the fall of the Stuarts ended a royal line dating to 1371 with the crowning of Robert II, a Gaelic noble from Renfrewshire. A citation of the Roman poet Horace's "Pale Death visits with impartial foot the cottages of the poor and the castles of the rich," a grim overview of human mortality in the thirteenth episode, typifies the outlook of Mary Stuart, Queen of Scots, the mother of James I who abdicated in terror on July 24, 1567, (1:13). Elizabeth I had Mary decapitated twenty years later. Radical Jacobitism began in 1603 with the crowning of James VI of Scotland as James I of England to replace the childless Elizabeth. The unification of Scotland and England on May 1, 1707, under Queen Anne resulted in the sovereignty of Great Britain.

Enthronement of a Hanoverian, George I, in 1714 plunged the Jacobean era into more plotting, spying, and vicious political and pro–Catholic mutterings. Jacobites from the highlands raided England for four decades, in part because of national taxation, exclusion of Catholics from government, and a mounting backlash against sorcery, an obsession among uneducated Scots. The epoch saw the colonization of North America by the Scots diaspora, which included historic figure Hector Cameron, a survivor of the Battle of Culloden on April 16, 1746, and husband of the fictional Jocasta MacKenzie.

Because the British monarchy required a Protestant on the throne, Jacobites rioted in 1715 against the Whig contingent and its Hanoverian politics. Statelessness forced the Stuart household to harborage in Rome under the patronage of popes Clement XI, Innocent XIII, and Benedict XIII. Supporters rallied around Charles Edward Stuart, the bonnie prince and son and heir of the exiled James Francis Stuart and Maria Sobieska, a Silesian princess of Polish ethnicity. Significantly, until the last uprising, the prince, a Roman citizen, never visited Scotland, an anomaly stressed in *Outlander's* historical fiction by patriot Murtagh Fitzgibbons Fraser.

The introduction of the bonnie prince, played by Andrew Gower, depicts the Catholic pretender at age 24 as a ludicrous, effete dreamer who shores up dynastic idylls with

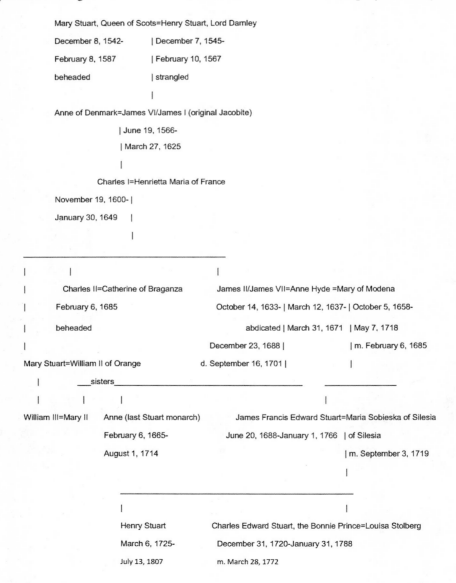

religious gabble, none of it scriptural or realistic. Historians Eveline Cruickshanks and Edward Corp justified the prince's management of the fourth Jacobite Rebellion from his Paris headquarters: "There were close links between the exiles in Saint-Germain and those in Paris, where the Catholic religious houses provided advice and assistance" (Cruickshanks & Corp, 1995, x). A self-absorbed would-be king, Prince Charles demands deference toward royalty from the fictional Jamie, who must kiss his hand and kowtow to nonsensical proposals for funding a Jacobite army. Appropriately located in Madam Elise's Paris brothel, the meetings remain low-level and abstract and involve heavy drinking and a backdrop of whorish blandishment.

To establish essential schemes, the fictional prince begins major comments with "Mark me," a suggestion of his insecurity as leader of men or a dynasty (2:3). On his arrival in Scotland in spring 1744 to lead the Highlander army, Claire and Jamie enter the final phase of a doomed war and attempt a last minute murder plot involving tea poisoned with yellow jasmine. Still loyal to the Jacobite ideal, in 1968, the Rev. Reginald Wakefield displays the banner and ironic Stuart motto "Nemo me impune lacessit" (No one strikes me without punishment, 3:4).

See also Bonnie Prince Charlie; Culloden; Hanoverian Dynasty.

Source

Cruickshanks, Eveline, and Edward Corp. *The Stuart Court in Exile and the Jacobites.* London: Hambledon Press, 1995.

Massie, Allan. *The Royal Stuarts: A History of the Family That Shaped Britain.* London: Thomas Dunne, 2011.

Superstition

Folk beliefs, particularly those of peasants, priests, and seafarers, inundate the *Outlander* TV chronicle from the beginning with vivid lore about omens, talismans, hexes, amulets, marks of the devil, love potions, magic rituals, premonitions, and coincidences. The series coordinates action with frequent references to illogical response to the unknown: Gavin Hayes's fear of *tannasgs* (ghosts), family suspicion of ravens as harbingers of death, letting blood from wounds to remove ill humors, Marsali's terror that Lionel Brown's ghost will haunt her, and a shapeshifter's transformation into a bear-man, a transcendence of anguish through fantasy. To stave off calamity and impose order from chaos in the bear-man's life, folksay permeates serious action. Utz Jeggle, a psychoanalyst at the University of Tübingen, called the method making "the unforeseeable to appear ... predictable," a blend of comedy and tragedy in mystic thinking (Jeggle, 2003, 81).

Jeggle clarified the unconscious justification of superstition as "private faith ... a way of managing irrationality" (*ibid.*). At Inverness in late October 1945, fictional Frank Randall, an expert in history and genealogy, incorporates arcane tales and events in the Druidic past that permeate hard-edged Scots history. Simultaneously, Claire acquiesces to Mrs. Graham's fortunetelling from oolong tea leaves and palmistry. A forked line introduces Claire's unpredictable future, but her Mount of Venus discloses love for both husbands, a prophecy that infuses the chronicle with spiritual transformation. At Frank's insistence, the Randalls observe the Druid circle dance until dawn, causing Claire to feel like a voyeur. The narrative implies that the Samhain ring ritual should remain private, not open to tourists.

The time traveler realizes from assimilation in eighteenth-century Scotland that she should guard her tongue and actions, especially against Father Bain, a grim Catholic priest who declares she smells of hell's vapors. An attempt to tell Glenna "Mrs. Fitz" Fitz-gibbons, the MacKenzie housekeeper at Castle Leoch, about falling through time confuses and terrifies an ignorant woman who knows only strange narrative ballads about Craigh na Dun. The cook determines that such events establish the malefaction of a demon or witch. The motif deepens into a major theme after Lindsey MacNeil dies of lily of the valley poisoning: He misidentifies the noxious plant as wood garlic and ingests its bulb at the ruined Black Kirk, a demon-ridden landmark.

Scholar Marlène Charlier comments on peasant trepidation: "Everybody but Claire believes in devil possession and that makes us think that the most important thing to do to make something real is to believe in it: magic can exist if everybody believes it exists" (Charlier, 2019, 7). After Claire restores Tammas Baxter from the same toxin with belladonna, she acquires a reputation at Castle Leoch for working miracles. Additional evidence of irrationality derives from War Chief Dougal MacKenzie's test with a drink from the liar's spring, a water source in a deep abyss reached by stone steps. Claire sips unscathed from a setting rich in cryptic nuance and the stench of hydrogen sulfide, a revered sign of Satan's presence.

WOMEN'S JUDGMENTS

The female coterie of season one conspires against Claire and her twentieth-century education. A crude ill-wish, a fetish that Laoghaire MacKenzie places under the Frasers' bed, appears as paltry as the black cockerel's blood smeared over Inverness lintels before Samhain, as ineffective as a love potion made of horse dung, and as pointless as Geillis Duncan's summons to the Earth Mother under the full moon. Purchased from Geillis, the bundle of sticks and bones illustrates the basis of a Celtic curse and the animus of Laoghaire, a frustrated lover whom Claire attempts to help with an incantation adapted from the 1939 film *The Wizard of Oz*. Beyond situational humor, faulty knowledge like the wariness Laoghaire acquires from Geillis unleashes near tragic judgments at Cranesmuir.

Incrimination at the witch trial by Laoghaire, the disgruntled housemaid Jeanie Hume, and Robena Donaldson, a changeling's mother, confronts Claire with charges of conjury and infanticide, gendered crimes that target females. A witness, Alistair Duffie, bases a complaint against Geillis on myths—glowing red eyes, hexes in the dark, hands summoning lightning, and wings to fly. Defense attorney Ned Gowan rebuts unfounded, imaginative testimony with a comparison to cats' intuition about sorcerers. Ned directs superstition against the locals, but batters a judicial panel and rowdy court audience inflamed with the opportunity to burn witches at the stake. Overriding the court's trust is a scriptural admonition from Exodus 22:18 about letting witches live.

NATURE'S MYSTIQUE

In the third season, episode nine, seagoing crews exhibit similar apprehensions, which outrank officers' orders. Captain Raines of the French brig *Artemis* instructs Claire on the value of ocean lore in securing a crew's loyalty. She, Marsali, and Jamie pose ill luck among sailors who reject females and redheads from passengers. Raines explains that the figurehead's bare breasts protect the ship from "an angry sea," a personification of evil in nature (3:9). At a stickier pass, the Frasers combat a possible atrocity on board because the crew intends to drown a "Jonah" (Jonah 1:8–12). Jamie's intervention saves Gavin Hayes from being bullied into self-sacrifice. Claire's return of a lucky rabbit foot to the corpse of Elias Pound, her fourteen-year-old medical aide on the English man-o'-war *Porpoise,* illustrates thanks for the boy's gratitude and respect for a young sea-goer dead from epidemic typhoid fever.

The TV narrative dramatizes storytelling enriched with the supernatural. At Fraser's Ridge, Claire observes the catastrophe that emerges from Old World misinformation, an unfortunate import by European emigrants. After watching Cherokee riders water their horses at a stream and sprinkle tobacco as a blessing, German settler Gerhard Mueller nurses recriminations that turn into mania. Certain his family lives under a Native American curse that kills his daughter-in-law Petronella and granddaughter Clara, he murders and scalps Adawehi, the Cherokee healer, and presents the evidence to Claire. Returning the story to reality, the Indians shoot fiery arrows at the Mueller house, killing Gerhard and his wife and burning the cabin.

See also Burial at Sea; Celtic Beliefs; La Dame Blanche; Storytelling; Witchcraft.

Source

Charlier, Marlène. "La représentation des mythes et légendes dans la série Outlander," master's thesis, Université de Franche-Comté, 2019.

Gallagher, Caitlin. "Jamie & Claire Sail to Jamaica on 'Outlander,' Exposing Sexist Superstitions That Keep Women Down," *Bustle* (12 November 2017).

Jeggle, Utz. "A Lost Track: On the Unconscious in Folklore," *Journal of Folklore Research* 40:1 (2003): 73–93.

Webster, Richard. *The Encyclopedia of Superstitions.* Woodbury, MN: 2008.

Taxation

The unconscionable levying of duties and taxes by eighteenth-century European monarchs underlay struggles at home and abroad. For the French, the erection and adornment of the royal palace at Versailles in season two initiated a class war that erupted on July 14, 1789, into the French Revolution and resulted in the guillotining of Louis XVI. In season four, episode five, the TV epic *Outlander* surveys the issue of colonial taxation for a similar malfeasance, the building of Tryon's Palace in New Bern, North Carolina. The resulting taxation forces the have-nots into revolt against a governor who cares nothing for the poor.

Hugh Allison, the current manager of Culloden battlefield, identified the clash of Jacobites with the British Army on April 16, 1746, as the beginning of New World independence. From a long-range view, he declared: "Its repercussions emptied English and French treasuries, which meant England's King George III called for more taxes in the American colonies, the impetus for the American Revolution" (Mailman, 2020). In 1765, the erection of the governor's mansion at New Bern and the monitoring of the Cherokee boundary line along the Little Tennessee and Watauga rivers precipitated a rebellion among the frontier taxpayers in Anson, Cumberland, Dobbs, Johnston, Orange, and Rowan counties.

In 1767, in addition to county and parish dues, levies against adult white male North Carolinians and all adult blacks reached 7 shillings (84 pence or three days' wages in current value) (Bassett, 1895, 150). The imbalance of disposable income overburdened backcountry settlers, who survived on barter rather than cash to retire poll and liquor levies. Shortage of cash thrust settlers into a dilemma. At Jamie's fictional meeting with potential tenants for Fraser's Ridge, Scotsmen complain of seizure of livestock, tools, and homes and abandonment of farmsteads to the Crown. Sheriffs charged a fee of 2 shillings and 8 pence (32 pence or £1 and 12 pence, nearly $32) for evicting the penniless and posting their property at Hillsborough auction houses, a profitable business for both sheriff and conveyancer. To attend court hearings, some pioneers had to travel up to 60 miles and pay their arrears in certificates pledging pelts, tobacco, grain, and other goods from commodities warehouses.

Compounding citizen complaints, dishonest sheriffs pocketed £49,000 in collected taxes (currently worth $107,179,660) rather than submit the funds to the public treasury. In episode eight, the fictional Governor William Tryon boasts that collection of the levy makes possible theater performances in Wilmington, an amusement for the elite. Simultaneously, the drive to amass state wealth presses the Regulator Movement toward desperation, climaxing in courtroom violence in Hillsborough. Murtagh's men retaliate against tax agents with tar and feathering, a barbaric punishment that Jamie observes firsthand.

In episode six of season five, Tryon admits the need for fiscal proceeds to establish his political credentials. Historian C.L. Hunter's *Sketches of Western North Carolina* (1877) exposed the underlying purpose, revealed three years after Tryon's departure on July 3, 1771, to the governorship of New York: "The entire subjugation of the country was the object of the British crown" (Hunter, 1877, 171). Too late, citizens discovered that the Battle of Alamance "[terminated] with cold-blooded murder" and killed the true patriots and martyrs to fair taxation (*ibid.,* 205).

See also Regulators; Smuggling; Governor Tryon; Regulators; Tryon's Palace; Whisky.

Source

Bassett, John Spencer. *The Regulators of North Carolina (1765–1771)*. Washington, DC: Government Printing Office, 1895, 141–212.
Hunter, C.L. *Sketches of Western North Carolina*. Raleigh, NC: Raleigh News, 1877.
Mailman, Erika. "The Popular Book and TV Series 'Outlander' Is Increasing Travel to These Scottish Sites," *Washington Post* (15 February 2020).

Time Travel

A sci-myth hybrid, Claire Randall's whisk from the twentieth to the eighteenth century in the *Outlander* TV epic launches the protagonist into period comparisons. According to Mary Russo, a literature professor at Hampshire College, passage among centuries initiates motifs and themes from disparate cultures. The stark contrasts parallel Offred's displacement in Margaret Atwood's *The Handmaid's Tale* and Elise McKenna's troubled musical career in *Somewhere in Time*. Time reversal dramatizes F. Scott Fitzgerald's story "The Curious Case of Benjamin Button," which Geillis Duncan mentions in season 3, episode twelve. By altering location in both time and place, Claire and her followers, Brianna Randall and Roger MacKenzie, investigate the foreign and strange and achieve new perceptions of ancient wisdom about danger and survival as well as a world devoid of pollution and species extinction.

The time slip narrative contrasts characters in terms of sensitivity to concentrated powers at Craigh na Dun. In analysis of the psychodrama, folklore specialist Erica Obey characterized the inborn gifts of Geillis, Claire, Brianna, and Roger, as "an inherited genetic characteristic, not requiring any arcana such as blood sacrifice," a claim that Geillis tests by burning husband Greg Edgars at the stone circle (Obey, 2002, 160). From an alternate perspective, experts Kirk Hampton and Carol MacKay view shards of emotions in symbolic travelers as ambiguous borders that transit may leave unchallenged, a residue that Claire recognizes in her loyalty to Frank and the Hippocratic Oath. Scholar Marlène Charlier separates the time slip in *Outlander* from fictional action: "It's finally the only big magical event that occurs in the series, the rest is rather realistic or at least non-magical … fantasy is just a backdrop in the whole story," an observation that also applies to novelist Octavia Butler's slave era time travel in *Kindred* (Charlier, 2019, 19, 20).

THE TABULA RASA

The time slip leaves travelers in a state of what Aristotle called the Περί Ψυχῆς or *tabula rasa*—a clean slate mentality dissociated from reality and open to a unique internal logic, a moral and ethical judgment compounded from competing world views. For Claire, in what Mary-Anne Potter at the University of South Africa at Pretoria termed "a simultaneous everything—and nothing-ness, existing in a state of synchronicity," female-oriented power enables her to interact with a more liberated ethos than the paternalistic 1700s applies to women (Potter, 2019, 282). Like Alice in Wonderland, Dorothy in Oz, and Wonder Woman, Claire disburdens herself of respectable behaviors and explores what novelist Les Daniels called "the wild dreams and desires which seem to have no place in our predominantly rationalistic and materialistic society" (Armitt, 2020, 172).

Similar to Dave Robicheaux's views on the Civil War in the backward-glancing film *In the Electric Mist with the Confederate Dead,* the 202-year gap in Claire's lives takes on deeper ramifications as she navigates more events. When she arrives at a reception in 1744 at Versailles, she learns that Captain Black Jack Randall, her husband's ancestor, did not die in the cattle stampede at Wentworth Prison. The orchestration of genealogy befuddles her with a dilemma—how to allow Jamie vengeance against his tormentor without killing off Jack before he can sire the line that produces Frank Randall. The argument riles Jamie, eroding his self-esteem and honor like the subsequent obsessions with killing pirate Stephen Bonnet, the despoiler of the hero's wife and daughter, and murdering Claire's abductors.

A dialogue between Jamie and Laird Colum MacKenzie enrages the older man with his nephew's certainty about the future of a Scots war with England. Jamie treads the difficult two-end path between justifying his prediction and confessing that his English wife knows the results of the Battle of Culloden. *New York Times* interviewer Jennifer Vineyard remarked on the heroine's two trips into the past. They begin with a buzzing at Craigh na Dun's central stone, which is not audible to Jamie, Young Ian, Mrs. Graham, or the ten Druidesses at Samhain. More information surfaces in 1968: "During (Claire's) most recent trip … she was more aware of the art and science of time travel, having read the journal of Geillis Duncan … (who learns that) only certain people have the genetic ability to do so" (Vineyard, 2018).

ADJUSTMENTS TO HISTORY

Casual communication forces time travelers of the Western Hemisphere to curb socializing with North Carolina planters. Claire's enlightenment about race, abolitionism, democracy, and equality causes River Run guests to back off, isolating her with Young Ian, who hates slavery and defends Indians against claims of atrocities. The enigma of adjusting history recurs in season four, when Brianna hurries to warn her parents that they may die in a cabin fire. Actor Sophie Skelton enlightened fans on the difficulties of avoiding anachronism: "Claire, Brianna, and Roger all have to monitor themselves 100 percent of the time when it's not just the three of them together—they have to change their language, their stance, their demeanor, any references they might make," even the American slang "okay," which dates to the early 1800s (Dibdin, 2020).

Beyond war and politics, Claire views time slip as a means of controlling disease. On the English man-'o-war *Porpoise* and at the Fraser's Ridge surgical practice, she chafes at contagion already contained in her own time. In 1770, she foresees control of infection by formulating penicillin, which she tests first on Jamie at Lallybroch to reduce fever. Advancing medical treatments more than two centuries, she protects Josiah and Keziah Beardsley during tonsillectomies by injecting them with her homemade antibiotic. She intends to shield casualties from the Battle of Alamance Creek on May 16, 1771, with the same therapy until Lionel Brown crushes her hypodermic syringe, a payback for her twentieth-century notions of marriage and female equality.

See also Allegory; Anachronism.

Source

Armitt, Lucie. *Fantasy*. New York: Routledge, 2020.

Charlier, Marlène. "La représentation des mythes et légendes dans la série Outlander," master's thesis, Université de Franche-Comté, 2019.

Dibdin, Emma. "*Outlander* Season 5 Will Have a Lot More 'Intimacy and Passion' Between Jamie & Claire," *Elle* (24 January 2020).

Obey, Erica. "Tall, Dark, and a Long Time Dead: Epistemology, Time Travel, and the Bodice-Ripper," *Worlds Enough and Time: Explorations of Time in Science Fiction and Fantasy*. Westport, CT: Greenwood, 2002, 157–166.

Potter, Mary-Anne. "'Everything and Nothing': Liminality in Diana Gabaldon's *Outlander*," *Interdisciplinary Literary Studies* 21:3 (2019): 282–296.

Vineyard, Jennifer. "'Outlander' Season 4 Is Nigh. Here's What to Remember," *New York Times* (2 November 2018).

Torture

Idle threats of fists, boots, swords, or knives raise the intensity of ordinary conversations in the *Outlander* TV series and usually end without force or bloodshed, as with War Chief Dougal's blind rage at his wife Maura's unexpected death from fever, Geillis Duncan Abernethy's dousing of Young Ian Murray with a flammable liquid in Abandawe, and Lord Simon Lovat's threat to chop out Claire's tongue for prophesying his execution. On a political level, the North Carolina Regulators disrupt court in Hillsborough on September 25, 1771, and raise the level of violence by coating corrupt tax agents with tar and feathers. After Jamie examines Judge Richard Henderson, who survives serious burns to the chest, he begins to see change in his godfather, Murtagh Fitzgibbons Fraser, who has breached the bounds of savagery.

For psychological reasons, torturers tend to stop short of murder or execution, for example, beating embezzler Edmund Fanning and dragging attorney William Hooper through Hillsborough streets. Deliberate crippling, the cause of Hugh Munro's mute communication, derives from Muslim fanatics slicing his tongue. They also pour boiling oil on his legs to force him to convert to Islam. The result of silencing Hugh returns to additional scenes, where he hand-signals important news and dangers to Jamie. The continued stress on Hugh parallels the loss of Fergus's left hand and the elder Ian Murray's lower right leg, combat amputations that constrain their agency and later terrify Jamie of losing his right leg to snakebite.

In a model of slow spiritual and physical death, unrelieved ennui, cold, disease, and hunger in Ardsmuir Prison punish traitors for the April 16, 1746, anti–English battle at

Culloden Moor. Jamie, their leader, clanks from place to place in leg irons and manacles that chafe his ankles and wrists. His former uniform jacket and shoulder wrap bear homely repairs and a pathetic mural of rips and ravels. Under the sobriquet MacDubh (son of the dark), he barters with warden John Grey for relief from anguish—drugs, blankets, watercress, and snaring privileges to replace with rabbits inconstant meals on prison rats. Jamie intends to ward off scurvy with watercress, a replacement of vitamin C unknown to Grey.

Lasting Damage

The prisoner transport to Virginia and the Caribbean severs Jamie's commitment to his godfather, Murtagh Fitzgibbons Fraser, whom he nurses with herbal oddments through fever, "la grippe," and rat bite (3:3). On departure from Murtagh in 1756, Jamie peers uneasily over a ragged blanket at his kin. Disheartened at parole to Helwater's stable groom, he summarizes his job as "shoveling shit" (3:3). The melancholy title of the next episode, "Of Lost Things," amplifies his sorrow at losing his Lallybroch family, Murtagh, wife Claire, and his unacknowledged son Willie, for whom he prays to St. Anthony. Unlike physical persecution, losses eat at his soul.

Mentally burdened and degraded at Wentworth Prison, Jamie suffers post-traumatic shock from rape by Captain Black Jack Randall and the maiming of his left hand with a hammer to the digits and spike through the palm. The loss of grasp disables his fighting hand, but mental agony affects him sexually, causing him to doubt his worth as husband and lover. Claire accepts from Brother Paul, a Benedictine monk at Father Anselm's abbey infirmary, the suggestion to make Jamie relive his anguish, a recommendation of physical rebuke that Ian Murray first proposed at Lallybroch. By coating Jamie in lavender oil and slapping him, she elicits the real man, a warrior not easily subdued by adversity or by a crazed maniac who applied saliva and lavender oil to accommodate sodomy.

The Tables Turned

Season five escalates torment in the lives of Fanny Beardsley, an abused wife, and Josiah and Keziah Beardsley, the twin indentured slaves of Indian trader Aaron Beardsley (played by versatile actor Chris Fairbank). At a Rowan County cabin, the script builds suspense with a slow revelation of Aaron's private hell. His punishment, described by writers Caroline Blyth and Jane Davidson-Ladd of the University of Auckland, epitomizes "the symbolic violence of misogynistic language, which marginalizes and objectifies women while eclipsing their social, sexual and religious oppressions" (Blyth and Davidson-Ladd, 2018, 145). In battlefield terms, "Sexual violence makes the foreign female captive a trophy and symbol of the conquest of her ethnic group," in this case, barren women (*ibid.*, 156).

According to Fanny, Aaron beat and killed his first four wives before striking her. She survives physical punishment because she conceives a child that he thinks is his. To repay a mad torturer, who lies paralyzed from stroke, she cuts his legs and burns his foot, which turns gangrenous, a symbolic rot. In her hands, he suffers for crimes against the twins, whom he acquired when they were two years old. To end his misery from bed sores and charred skin, Jamie gains Aaron's permission to shoot him in the head rather than amputate his foot. The stand-off concludes with reward—Claire's rescue of Fanny's infant, Wee Bonnie, whom Jamie proposes raising as their own.

In the season five finale, Marsali, a female avenger, comforts her stepmother for bruising, cuts, and rape by Arvin Hodgepile, Lionel and Cuddy Brown, and their marauders. Because Lionel immobilizes her with a rope noose, Claire retreats into a fugue state of an illusory Thanksgiving. After Jamie and his militia execute all but Lionel, the vicious abductor survives strapped to Claire's examining table. Although she refuses to execute him, Marsali zealously rids the family of a twisted stalker who joys in abusing wife Rose and Claire. Marsali plunges poisonous water hemlock into his neck below his venomous mouth, which spouts to the end his mockery of females. Of the Fraser's sufferings, critic Ariba Bhuvad takes hope: "This one horrible thing they all have in common now has somehow brought them closer, and there's a beauty in that" (Bhuvad, 2020).

See also Prisons; Violent Deaths.

Source

Bhuvad, Ariba. "*Outlander* Season 5, Episode 12 Recap: Never My Love," *Fansided* (11 May 2020).
Nagouse, Emma. "The Lamentation of Jamie Fraser: *Outlander*, Male Rape and an Intertextual Reading of Lamentations 3," *The Shiloh Project* (11 September 2017).
_____. "'To Ransom a Man's Soul': Male Rape and Gender Identity in *Outlander* and 'The Suffering Man' of Lamentations 3," *Rape Culture, Gender Violence, and Religion*. London: Palgrave Macmillan, 2018, 143–158.

Treasure

A predictable element in romantic adventures of sea dogs and pirates, a treasure box sets off multiple struggles in the *Outlander* TV narrative. The script extends a murky tale from Margaret Campbell, a crazed clairvoyant beaten into submission by her brother Archibald. The story, retold by tacksman Duncan Kerr, a fevered wanderer of the moors, discloses Geillis Duncan's insistence that War Chief Dougal MacKenzie deposited a family treasure box on Selkie Island north of the Scots mainland. The chest contains ancient gold and silver specie, pearls, red gemstones, diamonds, and three prophetic sapphires. Geillis values the three because they can reveal the date of the Stuart return to the English throne.

The epic uses the box as a contrast to treasured family. To clarify the identity of a *ban-druidh* (white witch) in Kerr's story, Jamie escapes Ardsmuir Prison and swims to the island. Although the MacKenzie crest—a horned stag head—identifies the box, he has no interest in oddments of treasure, only in recovering his wife. To prove his whereabouts, he keeps one sapphire for prison warden John Grey as proof of the venture. Simultaneous with his yearning, in 1768, Jamaica's governor Grey wears the single sapphire on a fob, a proof of longing for Jamie. Margaret foresees another aspect of love in a "200-year-old baby," a reference to Brianna Randall, Jamie and Claire's daughter, whom they conceived in February 1746 (3:12).

On the other side of the Atlantic at Rose Hall, Jamaica, the notorious Bakra (white woman)—Geillis Duncan Abernethy—seeks only the blue stones, which, according to folklore, can interpret oracles. She believes the three will ensure a Catholic Stuart takeover of the Anglican British crown. In a lavish boudoir, she soaks in goat's blood and, to impress Young Ian Murray, flaunts nudity, evidence of sybaritic extremes. A close-up of guest refreshments pictures her drugging, then seducing him with truth tea to learn the whereabouts of Dougal's treasure. At a reception of the new governor in Kingston, she organizes a séance and filches the third sapphire. Back home at Rose Hall, she locks Claire in a guest room while furthering the plot to recover a Stuart monarch, a perpetual fantasy.

See also Prophecy.

Source

Gordon, Diane. "'Outlander' Recap: Claire Encounters a Face from the Past in 'The Bakra,'" *Variety* (3 December 2017).

Levene, Dan. *A Port for Thieves—The Historical Fiction of Golden Age Piracy,* master's thesis, London South Bank University, 2019.

Martinelli, Dario. *What You See Is What You Hear.* Cham, Switzerland: Springer, 2020.

Tryon, Governor

The historical William Tryon, governor of North Carolina colony from 1765 to 1771, serves the *Outlander* TV series as a hardline loyalist, imperialist, and wily recruiter of settlers. Born in Norbury Park outside Surrey, England, on June 8, 1729, to Mary Shirley and Charles Tryon, he claimed court connections through grandfather Robert Shirley, 1st Earl Ferrers and councilor to Queen Anne. Arising from a military lieutenancy to colonel, Tryon earned field experience in Cherbourg, France, during the Seven Year's War. He displayed greed by jilting Mary Stanton, mother of his daughter Elizabeth, and by marrying a rich heiress, Margaret Wake, with whom he settled in Wilmington.

Tryon's reputation never rose above ambitious manipulator and brigand. During the Cherokee Wars, Indians called him the North Carolina Wolf. Promotion to a provincial governor on April 26, 1764, gave him a voice in opposing the Stamp Act of 1765, in creating a postal system, and in founding a favored partnership with Anglican clergy and fifty planters and merchants. The consortium foretells the groundwork of capitalism and the basis of American avarice that fed Tryon's ambitions. In *Sketches of Western North Carolina* (1877), historian C.L. Hunter described the governor as "an oppressive ruler and a blood-thirsty tyrant" (Hunter, 1877, 170).

Lead-up to Revolution

Tryon figured in a series of colonial decisions, including the move of the capital in 1766 from Edenton to New Bern. North Carolinians at New Bern and Wilmington formed a chapter of the Sons of Liberty that held mock funerals for the Stamp Act. In February 1766, a thousand men protested the closure of the ports of Brunswick and Wilmington and the Cape Fear River to trade and passenger service and organized a boycott of English merchandise in six counties. After Tryon confiscated three river vessels, Irish innkeeper and ferryman Cornelius Harnett and 500 rebels freed the boats and opened the coast. On March 31, 1766, the parliament of George III rescinded the Stamp Act.

During the completion of the gubernatorial mansion, Tryon stated that one thousand families of settlers drove their wagons west from Salisbury, a vast rise in the number of German and Scots-Irish emigrants. He named New Bern, set western boundaries with the Cherokee and their traders, and directed a militia to stem anti-tax protests in Hillsborough. In the new gubernatorial mansion, according to John Dalton Whitford, a columnist for the *New Berne Weekly Journal,* Tryon displayed his vanity in "court dress dazzling with gold lace, stars and ribbons" (Whitford, 1882). From spring 1768 to 1771, opposition to extravagance and illegal fees arose among settlers, who rioted under the direction of the Regulators. Tryon riposted by demanding a list of radicals by name. Whitford commented on the governor's greatest fault: "It was easier for him to rule by force than by the slow process of the law, or by compromise and persuasion" (*ibid.*).

At the fictional Wilmington theater gathering, Tryon reveals his mercenary nature by promising corrupt registrar and land agent Edmund Fanning a brick home if he survives emergency abdominal surgery. The registrar suffered injury on September 24, 1770, when Regulators attacked the colonial bureaucrat, dragged him through Hillsborough streets, and broke up the court and dispersed attorneys. The mob assault precedes Claire's fictional inguinal hernia operation on Fanning at the theater lobby, where she repairs the damage to his left torso wall. Head Regulator Murtagh Fitzgibbons Fraser states that petitions for tax redress will reach Tryon on September 30 and early October.

The Riot Act, passed on January 15, 1771, received discussion in season five, episode six, when the fictional Tryon attempts to suppress Regulators in Anson, Rowan, and Orange counties. At Burlington, 1,100 Redcoats, armed with cannon and swivel guns, defeated 2,000 dissidents on May 16, 1771, at the two-hour Battle of Alamance Creek, an unequal match of forces similar to the Scots attack on the British at the Battle of Culloden. At Tryon's request, the general assembly hanged six out of thirteen Regulators for provoking insurrection. To fund the militia, he raised poll taxes to eight pence and alcohol tax to two pence a gallon.

Gubernatorial Career

Sailing aboard the sloop *Sukey* to accept the New York governorship, on July 8, 1771, Tryon and Fanning left North Carolina. Tryon continued jockeying for high status and salary and purchased 40,000 acres from the Mohawks. He managed to fund a militia to guard city ramparts. The American Revolution involved him in unsuccessful strategies and blame for assaults on colonial women. To avoid violence, in October 1775, he sheltered on the war sloop *Halifax* in New York harbor. In September 1780, he revisited England for treatment of gout. He died in London on January 27, 1788, at age 58.

In the *Outlander* version, Jamie's decision to negotiate for a 10,000-acre land grant places him in a precarious spot between prosperity and gubernatorial coercion and taxation. *Vogue* interviewer Alexandra Macon characterized the deed signing as "a deal with the devil" (Macon, 2020). Tryon fawns over Jamie, flatters his ego, and inserts himself into Brianna and Roger's wedding. Quick to seize the moment, the governor takes Jamie aside to blackmail him—either capture Murtagh Fitzgibbons Fraser or lose Fraser's Ridge to confiscation. During a second nuptial, the union of Jocasta Cameron and Duncan Innes, Tryon again flexes his military muscle at Regulators for refusing a general amnesty. At Alamance Creek, according to star Sam Heughan, "He really pushed for this battle. He wanted to be seen as a great general and he wasn't" (Kosin, 2020).

See also Fraser's Ridge; Land Grants; Regulators; Tryon's Palace.

Source

Ervin, Samuel James, Jr. *A Colonial History of Rowan County, North Carolina.* Chapel Hill: University of North Carolina Press, 1917.
Haywood, Marshall Delancey. *Governor William Tryon and His Administration.* Raleigh, NC: E.M. Uzzell, 1903.
Hunter, C.L. *Sketches of Western North Carolina.* Raleigh, NC: Raleigh News, 1877.
Kosin, Julie. "Sam Heughan on *Outlander*'s Devastating Double Loss," *Elle* (30 March 2020).
Macon, Alexandra. "An Exclusive First Look at Brianna and Roger's Huge *Outlander* Wedding," *Vogue* (7 February 2020).
Whitford, James Dalton. "Rambles about Town: Tryon's Palace," *New Berne Weekly Journal* (3 December 1882).

Tryon's Palace

In December 1766, North Carolina assemblymen allotted £5,000 (currently $10,868,350) for the building of a Palladian three-story, seven-bedroom governor's mansion. Plans placed the structure in the neutral territory of New Bern, the new state capital overlooking the confluence of the Trent and Neuse rivers. Eastern aristocrats had to raise poll taxes to pay the upgraded cost of £10,000 ($21,736,700) for the colony's first permanent capitol. The symmetrical Georgian style with hip roof sketched by English architect John Hawks of Lincolnshire required three years' work. On February 23, 1767, he posted drawings and elevations to George III for approval.

The project took shape in red brick trimmed in marble, which outlined a Venetian entrance with central window and double arches of a coach house. Hand-carved doors and fretwork, wide stairs, and enclosed colonnades contributed to the outlay, as did masons and carpentry crews from Philadelphia, who hand-formed scrolled ironwork and nails. Landscaping encompassed a circular mall, main gate, lawn, cypress trees, fountains, and sixteen acres of formal gardens by French designer Claude Sauthier. For grand carriage entrances of uniformed men and hoop-skirted ladies, a continental allée led to George Street. Of the finished impression, T.B. Kingsbury, editor of the *Wilmington Messenger,* called it "substantial and massive" (Kingsbury, 1892).

THE REVOLT

In the TV epic *Outlander,* the palace amenities at New Bern appeal to the fictional Lord John Grey, who delights in English architectural style and the elegant tastes of wealthy aristocrats. In 1882, journalist John D. Whitford wrote in the *New Berne Weekly Journal,* "The noble court in Newbern had risen to refinement, luxury and splendor almost rivaling the Royal Court in England in its grandeur" (Whitford, 1882). For parties, balls, and receptions, delicacies simmered at the kitchen hearth and in deep-well cookers and a bake oven. Amid Tryon's social circle, Jamie and Claire use an amicable dinner party to meet historical politician John Alexander Lillington and sell Baron Penzler a ruby necklace. The historical Lillington, like palace visitor Colonel George Washington, earned military success during the American Revolution.

The heavy growth of Scots-Irish immigrants began filling the backcountry with vocal anti–English sentiment and protests of debtors' courts and missing county records of tax collections. Under the fictional Murtagh Fitzgibbons Fraser, Scots Regulators oppose the expenditure on a lavish showplace because outback pioneers and piedmont farmers had no vote in the project. Further frustrating them, tax agents and corrupt sheriffs overcharged, causing skirmishes in Rowan, Cumberland, Orange, Granville, and Anson counties among some 84 percent of Regulator supporters.

A GOVERNOR'S MANSION

Leaving temporary residence in Brunswick, the Tryons—Margaret Wake and William Tryon and ten-year-old daughter Margaret—took occupancy of the governor's palace in Craven County in early summer 1770. They funded furnishings themselves. After electing a speaker and administering oaths to officials, on December 5, he held the first government meeting in the west wing stable office, a mirror image of the east wing kitchen. To enlarge English authority, he began expounding on Anglicanism as the official colonial church and promoting rural parishes.

Regulators threatened in late February 1771 to burn the colonial capital as a demonstration to world dignitaries and travelers of the true cost of taxation. As enacted in season five, episode six, the Tryons occupied the palace for a year until their departure by ship for New York in late June 1771. Glowing receptions presented Margaret Tryon and her sister, Esther Wake, as social lions alongside the tyrannic governor. Under Governor Josiah Martin from August 12, 1771, to April 24, 1775, Tryon's Palace gained admiration from visitors and fewer complaints from Regulators. A sketch of the mansion adorned the 1775 North Carolina five dollar bill.

Source

Kingsbury, T.B., ed. "The Women and the Chicago Fair," *Wilmington Messenger* (17 March 1892).

Stewart, Bruce E. *Redemption from Tyranny: Herman Husband's American Revolution.* Charlottesville: University of Virginia Press, 2020.

Tryon Palace Commission. *Tryon Palace.* Charleston, SC: Arcadia, 2015.

Whitford, James Dalton. "Rambles about Town: Tryon's Palace," *New Berne Weekly Journal* (3 December 1882).

Unrequited Love

Romance and yearning spar with war for dramatic regard in TV episodes of *Outlander*. Models of separated lovers resonate with the daring of Isaiah Morton for sweetheart Alicia Brown, Fanny Beardsley's hidden romance with a slave, Alex Randall's death before he can wed Mary Hawkins, Frank Randall's fatal accident that ends his plan to marry Sandy Travers, Laoghaire's ache for Jamie, and the bonnie prince's regret that he can never have Louise de Rohan. One of the most poignant scenes in season one, Murtagh Fitzgibbons Fraser's mourning of his lost beloved, Ellen MacKenzie Fraser, enlightens Claire to a source of his dark despair and curt demeanor.

A potent revelation of private regrets, dialogue makes the most of actor Duncan Lacroix's command of a taciturn, often insulting character. A suggestion of parallel unrequited love derives from Marcus MacRannoch, the begrudging facilitator of Jamie Fraser's rescue from Wentworth Prison. Like Murtagh, Marcus gave Ellen an heirloom wedding gift—Scots freshwater pearls—as a token of his devotion. After marriage, he continues to admire her from afar, an example of wisdom through experience symbolized by the pearl's soft glow.

Gay Fervor

Similar in intensity to Texas Ranger Gus McCrae's pining for rancher Clara Allen in Larry McMurtry's *Lonesome Dove,* the motif of longing in season four, episode six of *Outlander* haunts Lord John Grey as painfully as it does Murtagh and Gus. In the gloom of Ardsmuir Prison, John seeks Jamie as a replacement for lover Gordon Dunsany and a source of passion, a heterosexual whom John can never have. During a loss of control, John grasps his beloved's hand, causing Jamie to threaten him with murder. To keep his love object close, John isolates Jamie from prisoners bound for indenturing in Virginia in 1756 and remands him as groom to the Dunsanys at Helwater, an obdurately marbled English estate. In a narrative triangle, Jamie learns from Isobel Dunsany her quiet pining for John, whom she admires for his devotion to King George II and the British Army, a career that limits him as husband material. None of the three guesses that Geneva, Isobel's engaged sister, will lock them all into an unconventional extended family.

New York Times journalist Jennifer Vineyard remarked on John's willingness to marry Isobel and raise her nephew William, grudgingly sired by Jamie with Geneva, the future wife of Lord Ellesmere. Vineyard added a jab at the ubiquitous Lord John: "Grey also used his position as the governor of Jamaica to help Jamie evade arrest. Now we wonder: Is there anything he wouldn't do to help a Fraser in need?" (Vineyard, 2018). On reunion with the Frasers in North Carolina, John's abiding passion for Jamie gives him reason for a long journey from Isobel's home at Mt. Kiziah in Lynchburg, Virginia, to Fraser's Ridge. In limbo after Isobel's death, while he recuperates from measles, he evokes a lengthy conversation with Claire, an overlong dialogue on jealousy that goes nowhere.

Permanent Loss

The television epic also investigates the Native American parallel of broken hearts by presenting Father Alexandre Perigault as sire of a biracial child reared by lover Johiehon. Blogger Tracy commented on the couple's influence on Roger MacKenzie and handfasted wife Brianna: "They guide others through tribulation, reaffirming their faith in love and each other in the process" (Tracy, 2019). The Mohawk equivalent of lovers' sacrifice takes on grotesque dimensions at the simultaneous burning of the two, who orphan their babe. The horror of self-immolation to the sounds of Samuel Barber's "Adagio for Strings" elucidates Roger's internal struggles with separation from Brianna, Jamie's vicious beating, and sale into slavery by Young Ian. Roger learns about depth of commitment from the gruesome execution at the stake, a jarring double death that expunges his grudge over trade to the Mohawk. Wiser from experience, he returns to embrace Brianna and their son Jeremiah.

Death and unrequited love enhance the drama of season five. By concluding Jocasta Cameron's wedding to Duncan Innes with Murtagh's marriage proposal, the chronicle chides the Scots leader for putting the demands of the Regulators before his affection for Ellen's younger sister. To epitomize his ardor for Jocasta, he beds her at River Run, arranges secret trysts at a hut on Fraser's Ridge, and presents a family crest as a nuptial gift. In his seventies, he earns Jamie's regret that he loses Jocasta to a lesser man. Jamie's empathy for his godfather crumbles at Murtagh's death on May 16, 1771, during the Battle of Alamance Creek. In a musical tribute, Jocasta sings "The Flowers of the Forrest," a moving Scots requiem. In extreme danger, Claire's mental fugue state unites the lovers by basing her wish fulfillment on a modern Thanksgiving dinner.

See also Couples; Friendship; Homosexuality.

Source

Gavin, Ann. "The Ultimate Ranking of Outland Season 4 Episodes, www.outlandercast.com/2019/03/ranking-outlander-season-4-episodes.html, 13 March 2019.
Tracy. "Episode 412: Providence," *Outcandour* (20 January 2019).
Vineyard, Jennifer. "How *Outlander*'s Revenge Scene Came Together," *Vulture* (19 June 2016).
_____. "'Outlander' Season 4 Is Nigh. Here's What to Remember," *New York Times* (2 November 2018).

Versailles

A mannered setting in France for the filming of *Dangerous Liaisons, Jefferson in Paris, Madame du Barry,* and *Casanova,* the historic château Versailles grounded season two of the *Outlander* TV epic. The royal residence began housing monarchs on May 6, 1682. Built from a two-story hunting lodge by Louis XIV, great-grandfather of Louis XV, the French classical château occupied 2,014 acres southwest of Paris. Under baroque architects Louis Le Vau, François d'Orbay, and Jules Hardouin Mansart, the world's largest and most splendid royal homestead acquired Doric columns, marble tiled courtyard, slated mansard roof, 1,250 chimneys, and meeting spaces for the chancellery.

In service to the entire court until the French Revolution on July 14, 1789, the expanding property influenced royal architecture, horticulture, and furnishings worldwide, including River Run in North Carolina. Versailles featured neoclassic elements—a color-coordinated garden facade, a 700-seat opera house, painted ceilings and parquet floors, and a mirrored hall lighted by chandeliers and 20,000 candles. Gilt flourishes adorned classical Corinthian pilasters and French doors. At age twelve, Louis XV settled at the estate on June 15, 1722, with his Hapsburg queen, Marie Leszczynska, after marrying her at Fontainebleau.

King and Queen

Although the TV series substitutes Drummond Castle in Perthshire and Wilton House in Salisbury for the French original, cinematographer Neville Kidd showcases versions of Versailles's Baroque garden paths, stairways, parterres, golden gate, four hundred sculptures, waterworks, Palladian bridge, and lighted fountains. For receptions and entertainments such as those that the fictional Frasers, Murtagh Fitzgibbons Fraser, Annalise de Marillac, and Louise de Rohan (played by Claire Sermonne) attend in 1744, the king (acted by Lionel Lingelser) decorated his ballrooms and salons with murals, crested hearths, and textured settees. He re-outfitted the residence to the delight of his historic mistress, Madame de Pompadour, whom he met in 1744 at a masked ball.

In public, Queen Marie, the former Silesian princess, bore eight daughters and two sons, notably the future king, Louis XVI. On advice from her gynecologist, in 1738, she ceased sharing the king's seven-room state apartment, but she continued living in shabby Versailles quarters and their two courtyards. While he preferred to enter his apartment through the Venus Room and to dine in private, she held audiences under a canopy. Protected by twelve security guards, she presided at court occasions and choral concerts with regal grace until her death at the palace on June 24, 1768.

Elements of Hubris

The fictional Louis XV sleeps in the Mercury Room under a brocade bed covering shot through with silver and gold threads. He impresses Claire with rare citrus fruits from Europe's largest orangerie, begun by his great-grandfather and augmented with palm, olive, lemon, and pomegranate plants among 1,000 bitter and sweet orange trees from Italy and Iberia. His outdoor tables offer colorful sweetmeats and grapes, which Claire samples. Special occasions exhibit the most frivolous fashions, makeup, and hairstyles of the age along with fireworks. Royal hangers-on number prominent bureaucrats and nobility, including Clarence Marylebone, the Duke of Sandringham, and Finance Minister Joseph Duverney.

While Jamie assesses horses for Sandringham on display at the palace stables, set at Gosford House in East Lothian, Claire strolls with Annalise and shows off a sumptuous brown coat dress with embroidered yellow gold underskirt. Airy outdoor walkways and trellises suit the encounter between the Frasers and Captain Black Jack Randall, whose British Army uniform sets him apart from lavish French couture. During Jamie's cultivation of new friend Duverney, their chess games occupy a palace library, for which Prague's Strahov Monastery substitutes. The same location served filming of *The Musketeers*.

See also Bourbon Dynasty; Star Chamber.

Source

Mair, George. "Scottish Castle Doubles for Magnificent Palace of Versailles Gardens," *Express* (28 October 2016).
Picon, Guillaume. *Versailles: A Private Invitation*. Paris: Flammarion, 2018.
"Versailles," http://en.chateauversailles.fr/discover/estate/palace.

Violent Deaths

Savage killings saturate literature on criminality, war, and resistance to British imperialism in Scotland, France, the West Indies, and the North American wilderness from the Carolinas to Shadow Lake, New York. For the *Outlander* TV series, the list of fictional deaths parallels dire situations involving jealousy, rape, conspiracy, tyranny, theft, extortion, sedition, vengeance, piracy, and the slaying of young kidnap victims:

method	*episode*	*place*	*name*	*killer*
ambush	(1:13)	countryside	Lennox	Redcoats
ambush	(5:12)	countryside	Cuddy Brown	Rowan County Militia
arrows	(4:5)	Mueller cabin	Gerhard Mueller	Cherokee
arrows	(4:5)	Mueller cabin	Rosewitha Mueller	Cherokee
asphyxiation	(5:5)	Hillsborough	Lt. Hamilton Knox	Jamie Fraser
beheading	(1:6)	Brockton	McGreavy	Highlanders
beheading	(2:11)	Belmont	Duke of Sandringham	Murtagh
beheading	(4:5)	Abandawe, Jamaica	Geillis Duncan	Claire Fraser
blade through the throat	(1:13)	Scots countryside	Redcoat messenger	Murtagh
blade through the torso	(1:13)	Lallybroch	Horrocks	Ian Murray
blade through the torso	(2:10)	Prestonpans	Jeremy Foster	Dougal
blade through the torso	(2:13)	Culloden House	Dougal	Jamie and Claire Fraser
bloodletting	(5:2)	Fraser's Ridge	Leith Farrish	Mrs. Farrish
brain injury	(3:7)	Edinburgh brothel	John Barton	Claire Fraser
broken neck	(5:10)	River Run	Gerald Forbes	Ulysses
burning	(2:13)	Craigh Na Dun	Greg Edgars	Geillis Duncan
burning	(4:12)	Mohawk village	Alexandre Ferigault	Mohawks
burning	(4:12)	Mohawk village	Johiehon	Mohawks
burning	(5:6)	Highlands	Clementina	Redcoats
burning	(5:6)	Highlands	Seonag	Redcoats
burning	(5:11)	Fraser's Ridge	Dutch family	Hodgepile's gang
car accident	(3:3)	Boston	Frank Randall	trauma
choked on turf	(2:13)	Culloden	Redcoat	Jamie Fraser

method	episode	place	name	killer
combat	(2:10)	Prestonpans	Kincaid	Redcoats
combat	(3:4)	Prestonpans	Gordon Dunsany	Jacobites
combat	(5:7)	Alamance Creek	Bryan Cranna	Redcoats
combat	(5:7)	Alamance Creek	Murtagh	Hugh Findlay
crucifixion	(1:5)	Highlands	two Scots	Redcoats
cyanide	(1:10)	Castle Leoch	Arthur Duncan	Geillis Duncan
drowned	(3:11)	Atlantic Ocean	Captain Raines, Murphy, Warren	gale
drowned	(4:7)	Atlantic Ocean	Marion	Stephen Bonnet
firing squad	(3:3)	Culloden	Frederick MacBean	Redcoats
firing squad	(3:3)	Culloden	Giles MacMartin	Redcoats
firing squad	(3:3)	Culloden	Gordon Killick	Redcoats
firing squad	(3:3)	Culloden	Rupert MacKenzie	Redcoats
goring to gut and thigh	(1:4)	forest	Geordie	wild boar
hanging	(1:15)	Wentworth Prison	Taran MacQuarrie	hangman
hanging	(4:1)	Wilmington	Gavin Hayes	hangman
hemorrhage	(3:4)	Ellesmere	Geneva Ransom	childbirth
internal hemorrhage	(2:10)	Prestonpans	Angus Mohr	Redcoat cannon fire
knifing in the gut	(3:1)	Culloden	Jack Randall	Jamie Fraser
knifing in the kidney	(1:2)	glade	Harry	Claire Fraser
knifing in the torso	(2:11)	Belmont	Albert Danton	Mary Hawkins
knifing in the torso	(5:12)	big house	Geordie	Arvin Hodgepile
mauled	(3:12)	Jamaica	Archibald Campbell	Maroons
pistol shot to the head	(3:4)	Ellesmere	Earl of Ellesmere	Jamie Fraser
pistol shot to the head	(5:3)	Rowan County	Aaron Beardsley	Jamie Fraser
poison	(1:3)	Cranesmuir	Lindsey MacNeil	accident
poison	(1:10)	Castle Leoch	Arthur Duncan	Geillis Duncan
poison	(2:7)	Star Chamber	Comte St. Germain	Master Raymond
poison	(5:12)	big house	Lionel Brown	Marsali
scalped	(4:3)	forest	Otter Tooth	Mohawk
scalped	(4:5)	Cherokee camp	Adawehi	Gerhard Mueller
shot	(5:6)	Highlands	Morna Cameron	Hector Cameron
shot in the head	(5:10)	Wilmington	Stephen Bonnet	Brianna MacKenzie
slit throat	(1:2)	glade	Redcoat deserter	Jamie Fraser

method	episode	place	name	killer
slit throat	(3:12)	Rose Hall, Jamaica	virgin boys, house staff	
slit throat	(4:1)	barge on the Cape Fear	Lesley	Stephen Bonnet
stake through the gut	(4:4)	Cherokee camp	Tskili Yona	Jamie Fraser
stake through the throat	(1:15)	Wentworth Prison	Marley	Jamie Fraser
sword through the gut	(5:2)	Hillsborough	Ethan MacKinnon	Lt. Hamilton Knox
tarring and feathering	(5:2)	Hillsborough	tax agent	Regulators
tomahawk to the chest	(5:12)	countryside	Arvin Hodgepile	Young Ian
witchcraft	(1:10)	Dougal's home	Maura MacKenzie	Geillis Duncan

For Claire's knifing Harry in the glade, slo-mo camerawork indicates her steely application of Angus Mohr's lesson in piercing the enemy in the kidney. At a significant moment in her relationship with War Chief Dougal MacKenzie, he realizes that she has seen men die violently in her past experience. More impromptu piercing ends Horrocks's extortion at Lallybroch, where Ian Murray revives his wartime acumen with a sword.

The approach of the Battle of Culloden on April 16, 1746, heightens preparations for violence and the staffing of a military field hospital. Laura Prudom, a *Variety* reviewer, remarked on the Prestonpans tragedy, a significant Jacobite victory: "The beloved double-act of Rupert and Angus is broken, with Angus dead and Rupert left in mourning for his best friend, casting a pall over the post-battle celebrations" (Prudom, 2016). Before Culloden, the husband-and-wife stabbing of Dougal's torso allies Claire with Jamie in the murder of a rabid Jacobite. Actor Sam Heughan observed, "Jamie and Murtagh ... were massacring people, and that's when it hits them what they've achieved, but also what they've lost" (*Ibid.*). At his parting from Claire at the stones, Jamie admits to committing murder and breaking trust.

A pirate's ferocity correlates buccaneering with disdain for human life. Roger MacKenzie recoils from the jettisoning of sick infant and adult passengers from the *Gloriana*, a sacrifice easily made by psychopath Stephen Bonnet to prevent an outbreak of smallpox. To save Morag and Jeremiah MacKenzie from the same fate, Roger hides mother and son in the hold. Although dressed in gentleman's outfit in season five, Bonnet extends his rapacity by slicing a victim's face through both eyes and stalking infant Jemmy MacKenzie, the new heir to River Run. Brianna ends the cyclical loss of life by Bonnet with a single rifle shot to his forehead. Predations continue in Hillsborough, North Carolina, where Regulators tar and feather a tax agent and Jamie asphyxiates Lieutenant Hamilton Knox, who learns that Jamie is shielding his godfather, Murtagh Fitzgibbons Fraser. The intentional slaughter joins other crimes that emerge from British imperialism.

At the season five finale, Jamie lights the fiery cross to summon the Rowan County Militia. To rescue Claire from serial rape, the company hunts down Arvin Hodgepile's outlaw gang, who pose as the Committee of Safety. At Jamie's command, all bandits suffer execution except Lionel Brown, who survives for questioning. Violent death awaits him in Claire's surgery, where he sneers at Marsali and demands food. Skillfully, she injects a water hemlock solution into his neck, a gentler demise than he deserves. Richard Brown admits his brother's wickedness, but assures Jamie that more bloodshed will follow in retribution.

See also Crime; Execution.

Source

Blyth, Caroline, and Jane Davidson-Ladd. "To Ransom a Man's Soul: Male Rape and Gender Identity in *Outlander* and 'The Suffering Man' of Lamentations 3," *Rape Culture, Gender Violence, and Religion* (2018): 143–158.

Crumlish, Callum. "*Outlander* Season 5: Star Reveals Which Death Shocked the Entire Crew—'Oh S**t,'" *Express* (26 October 2019).

Phillips, Jennifer A. "Jamie's 'Others': Complicating Masculinity and Heroism through His Foils," *Outlander's Sassenachs: Essays on Gender, Race, Orientation and the Other in the Novels and Television Series*. Jefferson, NC: McFarland, 2016, 54–67.

Prudom, Laura. "'Outlander' Recap: Sam Heughan Breaks Down the Victories and Losses of 'Prestonpans,'" *Variety* (11 June 2016).

Weapons

The *Outlander* anti-war TV production infuses human actions with the rancor and aftermath of combat in the field and the wild, where stalkers bring down wild boars with spears, rifles, and arrows. During a season one introduction to World War II, camera close-ups picture damage done by modern weaponry against Allied forces. Sounds of explosions and bursts of an artillery barrage threaten Claire during a night conflict. Musket fire jerks her back 202 years from Craigh na Dun on November 1, 1945, to a running skirmish in 1743 between Redcoats and Highlanders. Before she discovers that exploding shells are real, she surmises that the combatants are cinema actors armed with dirks and longswords, the armaments for which eighteenth-century Scots soldiers are famous.

The rapid change in fictional assault style puts Claire in danger of blade warfare. Hammered at a forge from iron or steel by an armorer, the finished broadsword required hardening and tempering at low temperatures to toughen the edge. Slow cooling enhanced flexibility. A one-on-one confrontation with Captain Black Jack Randall at a stream introduces her to the English saber, flaunted by Sergeant Frank Troy in the film *Far from the Madding Crowd*. A light, one-handed broadsword designed for thrusting, it evolved from the Renaissance rapier. Throughout the narrative, the androcentric blade represents misogyny, whether actualized with a weapon or the penis of a rapist.

Choosing Weapons

For protection from *en face* attack, fictional Highlanders adopt the lightweight targe, a 20-inch round shield or buckler. In 1739, the bonnie prince accepted a grand shield made of pigskin and jaguar hide on wood boards and graced with silver nails and, at center, the head of Medusa, the mythic gorgon whose stare turned mortals to stone. The standard targe features a detachable spiked boss at center, brass rivets, and leather arm loops in back to secure it to a wood circle. Jacobites wield pitchforks, pikes, and two-edged, 55-inch broadswords topped by a pommel, grip, and basket-shaped hilt to protect the hand. Unlike the slender English rapier or dueler's saber, the Scots broadsword found favor with shock cavalry into the Napoleonic era. After Highland disarming by Lord Cumberland in 1746, a few Scots buried their heirloom weapons on the heath.

Highlanders fighting in close combat parry with the targe against the British bayonet protruding from the plug of the Brown Bess flintlock musket, allegedly named for Elizabeth I. The tactic enables defenders to lunge with swords in wedge formation, called a Highland charge. Historically during a century of expansive colonialism, the muzzle-loading, 75-caliber English smoothbore armed the British with a 10.4 pound single shot carbine known as the Long Land Pattern Musket. Standardized in Birmingham from walnut, brass, and iron and warehoused in the Tower of London, it ranged up to 62.5 inches with a 46-inch barrel. The fictional dragoons under Captain Randall carry the 58.5-inch Short Land Pattern model weighing 10.5 pounds.

Marines like those under Captain Thomas Leonard on the English man-o'-war *Porpoise* relied on the 37-inch sea service flintlock, which weighed 9 pounds. By law, residents of the North American colonies maintained the flintlock or firelock along with paper cartridges and musket balls for instant ramming of each load with a scouring stick and discharge from the militia firing line. Thus, the English long gun served colonist and British adversaries during the Revolutionary War with a rifle effective up to 100 meters.

LEARNING SELF-PROTECTION

Fictional noncombatants press into use weapons more suited to their expertise, including Jamie's silent bow and arrow in the woods around Lallybroch, Laoghaire's discharge of a pistol at Jamie, and the hypodermic by which Marsali injects Lionel Brown's neck with poisonous water hemlock serum. Because of a raid by the Grants on War Chief Dougal MacKenzie's rent collection party, Angus Mohr trains Claire in the downward sweep of the *sgian dubh* (hidden dagger), a single-edged knife that she conceals in her hose or garter and later clips to her belt. The lightweight dagger with 3-inch blade and wood or horn hilt evolved from a covert Renaissance sleeve knife. By practicing a back stab into the kidney, she readies herself before the rape attempt by Harry, a Redcoat deserter, and kills him with a double thrust.

Boys prepare themselves for self-protection by observing weaponry, a focus of young Jamie's admiration for his father Brian's five-lobed Viking sword and Hamish's sword play with Dougal. Because of viewing Jacobite training sessions, Fergus displays skill in knifing a "filthy Redcoat" at the Battle of Prestonpans on September 21, 1745, and in learning to load and discharge a pistol (3:3). His single shot at a crow in 1752 rids Jenny's newborn son Ian of a death omen. At an unexpected hand-to-hand battle under Rose Hall, Jamaica, Claire's machete sweep in the Abandawe cave ends enmity against Geillis Duncan Abernethy, who threatens to kill Brianna. In the three skirmishes, adversaries have little time to prepare for attack.

NEW WORLD ARMAMENT

In North America, Scots immigrants arrive without their broadswords, which the British outlawed and confiscated under the Disarming Act of August 1, 1746. In the wilderness, they need weapons for hunting and warding off harm by wild animals and Native Americans bearing tomahawks, war clubs, and bow and arrow, which could be lighted for a fiery barrage. Jamie continues to rely on his dirk and urges Claire and Young Ian to stand ready with rifles against Cherokee attack. When the family presses north 700 miles from piedmont North Carolina to Shadow Lake, New York, an ambush causes Jamie to seize a tomahawk and press it to a Mohawk's throat. The quick action illustrates the Highlander's emergency adaptation to whatever weapon lies at hand. His trust in Scots weaponry motivates him to will his blades to grandson Jemmy MacKenzie.

In season five, Jamie admires Josiah Beardsley's skill as a hunter, a source of meat for the community and income from the sale of hides and pelts. Redcoat intervention in a peaceful settlement at Fraser's Ridge forces Jamie to re-arm with broadsword and dirk and to prepare for the Regulator Movement, a romanticized reclamation of Scots culture and manhood. For firepower, leader Murtagh Fitzgibbons Fraser urges his men to supply themselves with rifles. On the arrest of three Regulators after a raid in Hillsborough, North Carolina, Lieutenant Hamilton Knox loses sight of military ethics and skewers Ethan MacKinnon in the gut with a saber for spitting in an officer's face. The impromptu murder of an unarmed prisoner illustrates the effects of uncontrolled anger in an armed soldier, especially a respected career man.

The Battle of Alamance Creek on May 16, 1771, introduces fictional backwoodsmen and their antique muskets to an onslaught by efficient British armaments and three-pounder cannon. Loading with paper wadding and packing in grapeshot with a rammer ready the two field guns, one of which the Regulators capture. Tryon requisitioned from Fort Johnston near Southport six short muzzle-loading swivel guns or howitzers, which rest on a pivotal fork or stand for arcing grapeshot and small round pellets. The effective targeting of massed infantry remained a crucial tactic during the American Revolution.

The series contrasts the marksmanship of the MacKenzies. Brianna, whose stepfather taught her to shoot a rifle in girlhood, bests husband Roger, who despairs of his stunted binocular vision. The difference in skills proves advantageous to Brianna, who suffers for nearly two years with flashbacks to rape in a Wilmington inn. At Wilmington's east coast, her pistol misfire empowers pirate Stephen Bonnet to capture her. After armed family members subdue Bonnet and seek a court judgment, Brianna shoots him in the head while he awaits the penalty—drowning at the stake for his crimes. The one-bullet execution provides a feminist conclusion by enabling the victim to neutralize a manic stalker of the Fraser-MacKenzie household.

See also Culloden; Disarming Acts; Dueling; Heirlooms; Soldiery; Violent Deaths.

Source

Barks, Brenna A. "From *Waverley* to *Outlander*: How Scottish Dress Became Everyone's Dress," *Fashion, Style & Popular Culture* 5:3 (2018): 373–388.
Hoffman, Courtney A. "How to Be a Woman in the Highlands: A Feminist Portrayal of Scotland in *Outlander*," *The Cinematic Eighteenth Century*. New York: Routledge, 2017, 103–117.
"Sam Heughan Reveals Jamie's Season 3 Weapons," www.youtube.com/watch?v=Q01k-2SweAs, 5 September 2017.
Tise, Larry E., and Jeffrey J. Crow. *The Southern Experience in the American Revolution*. Chapel Hill: University of North Carolina Press, 1978.

Whisky

From the opening scenes of the *Outlander* TV series, strong drink invests action in eighteenth-century Scotland with variable solutions to fear, pain, fatigue, hunger, sepsis, joy, and amusement. According to essayist Charles Snodgrass, whisky "formed a fluid trajectory in a Scot's life" from infancy and daily fun to old age and funereal wakes (Snodgrass, 2016, 1). Fictional women take part in drinking strong spirits, for example, Donalda Gilchrest, the *ban dhuan* (song woman), who distributes "tipple" to the wool waulkers, Claire's defiance of misogynists at an Edinburgh bar in 1968, and Jocasta

Cameron sharing Scots whisky with guest Murtagh Fitzgibbons Fraser. Brianna Randall tastes drink from Jamie's still and on her wedding day, when the liquid symbolizes "something new" (1:5, 5:1). Geillis Duncan's stout pull on Ned Gowan's flask in Thieves Hole, Cranesmuir's underground cell, illustrates the use of whisky to ward off cold and fear. At Fraser's Ridge, Brianna and Marsali Fraser take an evening glassful in relief that toddler Jemmy has not disappeared. The mutual drink encourages female fellowship and loosens Marsali's inhibitions about divulging the cruelties of her father, Simon MacKimmie.

Armed patrols in fall 1743 quaff personal stashes of whisky. While War Chief Dougal MacKenzie's outriders belt down swallows to suppress hunger, Claire pours from a flask to disinfect the gunshot through Jamie's right shoulder. Conviviality at the MacKenzie gathering increases when men drain Laird Colum MacKenzie's loving cup to pledge allegiance to their kin. At a tense post-wedding scene, Claire proposes whisky to tranquilize nerves and admits to a hangover from spending the day before her nuptials deep in drink. Near Wentworth Prison in a taproom scene of gambling and ale tossing, the cost in coins to Angus Mohr and Rupert MacKenzie buys information from guards that aids Claire in setting Jamie free from Black Jack Randall's dungeon.

For the West Indian elite, Governor John Grey's reception in Jamaica displays hospitality with trays of brandy and champagne, the upscale beverages that Jamie imports to Kingston on the French brig *Artemis* for his cousin, Jared Fraser. In his townhouse, camera shots of a large staff, indoor murals, fine furnishings, and lavish draperies indicate that Jared's Paris business is profitable. Jamie's knowledge of vintages proves useful at Ardsmuir Prison, where he identifies the *vin de bourgogne* that flavors a pheasant entree. His refined palate elevates him above the ragged jacket and chains that confine him.

HARD TIMES

For Claire's tedious setting of Jamie's crushed left hand at Father Anselm's abbey, the patient prefers whisky to laudanum as an anesthetic and analgesic. Meanwhile, his companions sip from their flasks to stifle worry about his hunger strike. Strong drink recurs in his toast to Claire at the Paris celebration in 1744 of decoding the bonnie prince's letter, a shred of progress toward suppressing the Jacobite rising. For Ross and Rupert after the Battle of Prestonpans on September 21, 1745, sorrow for comrades Kincaid and Angus calls for a shared belt from a leather-covered canteen. The survivors' duet of "Down among the Dead Men" makes a pun on war casualties and empty bottles, which carousers toss under the table.

Although whisky predominates in Scots libation choice, situations limit the servings of strong drink to whatever lies at hand. At a fractious farewell between siblings Colum and Dougal MacKenzie, wine replaces whisky for Dougal, who offers a last sip to his beloved big brother. Unfortunately for Dougal, gulps from the bottle fail to anesthetize grief at Colum's suicide, accomplished by a vial of poisonous yellow jasmine. In season three, episode two, Fergus prefers French wine to whisky for treating a hand amputation, an ethnic choice that differentiates him from Scots like Jamie, Ross, Rupert, and Dougal.

SHORT SUPPLY

The opening of season four on a hanging in Wilmington in 1767 dramatizes Jamie's report that whisky is more difficult to locate than rum on the North Carolina coast, a shortage that Aunt Jocasta Cameron and Murtagh Fitzgibbons Fraser regret. To the request of Gavin Hayes for a parting "wee dram," Jamie can offer only a flask of rum, a carryover from adventures in Jamaica, where sugar plantations supply distilleries of the native Caribbean beverage (4:1). In a poignant salute to the hanged man, Lesley and his comrades raise their tankards to Gavin and sing a Gaelic farewell, "Eisd Ris" (Hear him), marked by pounding of ale cups and hands on the table (*ibid.*).

The return to a macho tradition of liquid valor dating to the 1400s foretells Jamie's intent to brew Scotch whisky at his home on Fraser's Ridge. The hit-or-miss project asserts Highlands resistance to British taxation of two pence per gallon (around 50¢ in current value). In comparison with the barrels of strong drink at Castle Leoch, Jamie's subsistence efforts from distilling barley require more experimentation and longer aging. On an evening at River Run with Jocasta, Murtagh declares that he prefers the original Scots brew.

Jamie's contribution of a wilderness sour mash beverage to mountain culture foretells a frontier enterprise for Scots immigrants to Appalachia, where whisky serves as tranquilizer, sterilizer, and currency. Bypassing excise levies, single malt liquor enlarges profits from local barley or rye and evolves into "corn squeezins," the original American whisky. High-proof bootleg spirits gain the name "white lightnin'" and "moonshine" from illicit distilling of powerful homebrew by night at hidden stills to elude confiscation by tax agents.

WHISKY IN USE

At the 1968 gathering on Grandfather Mountain, Brianna Randall avoids risk by asking insiders where to buy non-tax-paid whisky. On her excursion with Roger MacKenzie to the clan rally, she buys moonshine in one of three dry counties—Avery, Caldwell, or Watauga, a district in which adherents of fundamentalist religion outlaw sale and consumption of spirits. Guests at her wedding at the big house in 1770 play a tippling game that reveals their degree of inebriation, a fun time for the Fraser community. In competition with woozy males, Marsali impresses a ring of participants with "The Pheasant Plucker Song," a test of sobriety of unknown origin. Improvement in the taste of the brew encourages Jamie, who dispatches supplies with the Rowan County Militia to boost enlistment.

To ease a murderous feud at Brownsville in season five, episode four, Captain Roger MacKenzie, an inexperienced militia officer, opens a keg at Lionel and Richard Brown's trading post. Shared drink quietens nerves for working out a deal over Isaiah Morton's seduction of Alicia Brown, a convoluted romance similar to the Celtic tale of Tristan and Isolde. The afternoon quaff takes on an affable air with Roger's singing of "Bonnie Laddie, Highland Laddie." The halyard shanty, children's game, and folk seduction dialogue, rewritten in 1786 by Robert Burns and first published in 1855, gained authentication in 1881 as a regimental quick march. Drink returns to multiple uses to calm Alicia from attempted suicide, at a Hillsborough pub where Jamie rewards his men with free whisky, and, in episode nine, during Roger's easing snakebite pain in his father-in-law.

In an unusual ploy, Claire serves as go-between to improve still profitability. She negotiates a deal with rake Phillip Wylie to arrange the smuggling of Jamie's whisky. In hopes of locating pirate Stephen Bonnet to kill him for mauling his wife and raping his daughter, Jamie accepts the arrangement for Alexander Malcolm, the alias under which he smuggled liquor in Edinburgh. At the handover of whisky at Wylie's Landing, the ruse turns into a brawl rather than a sale, a demonstration of the tie between illicit booze and violence.

See also Smuggling.

Source

Gopaldas, Reshma. "*Outlander* 'Perpetual Adoration' Recap: Jamie and Claire, Penicillin, Murder & a Cat," *Entertainment Weekly* (15 March 2020).

Pierce, Daniel S. *Tar Heel Lightnin'*. Chapel Hill: University of North Carolina Press, 2019.

Snodgrass, Charles. "Whisky: The Spirit of Scottish National Identity," https://www.thebottleimp.org.uk/wp-content/uploads/2017/08/TBI2016-Supplement-3-Whisky-The-Spirit-of-Scottish-National-Identity-Charles-Snodgrass.pdf, April 2016, 1–5.

Witchcraft

The theme of sorcery resonates throughout the *Outlander* TV narrative in peasant beliefs and fears of collusion with Satan. The subject appears at Craigh na Dun in late October 1945 with Frank Randall's interest in Druid beliefs, which Jamie later identifies at Beaufort Castle as "the power of the old ones" (2:8). Females like herbalists Claire Fraser and Geillis Duncan, typical victims of accusations, expose themselves to accusers by displaying agency, a violation of androcentric societies and a source of toxic gossip. Artistic renderings of witches on broomsticks implied the use of brooms as supernatural phalluses. In season one, episode 11, the thump of drums and onlookers' chants accompany prejudice among the fictional Cranesmuir church court judges and attendees. Defended by English attorney Edward "Ned" Gowan, the negation of the Witchcraft Act of 1653 by a House of Lords repeal in 1735 ensures that Claire receives legal counsel.

Educated in American colonial history, Claire knows the dire outcomes of the Salem witch trials administered by fanatic Puritans in 1692–1693. Defendants at Massachusetts court hearings tended to be widows or lone women lacking fathers, uncles, sons, or brothers to protect them from charges of necromancy. With a touch of sarcasm, authority Valerie Estelle Frankel, an English professor at San Jose City College, explained an underlying reason: "In medieval times any outspoken woman might be accused and murdered—the witchfinders inherited the women's property after all" (Frankel, 2015, 161). Her version of seventeenth-century court justice rests on imperialist greed, a factor that grounded the Jacobite and Regulator revolts and the American Revolution.

WITCHES AND LAW

The fictional Claire may not be aware that Henry VIII defined the occult as a felony in 1542 and that Elizabeth I passed the Act Against Conjurations, Enchantments, and Witchcrafts in 1563. The Renaissance legislation wrested power over trials from the church to the Crown and, under royal court sentence, consigned the practitioner to the Queen's executioner. A parallel Scots law of 1563 remained valid until emendation in 1735 under a Protestant monarchy that equated Catholic ritual with spells and conjury. A reversal in criminality charged claimants with accusing anyone of practicing magic or charming victims. Both enchanter and client risked the death penalty or, at the least, a year in prison. Subsequent legislation fought superstition and ignorance among religious fanatics and attendees at séances and healing rituals.

Outlander bases characterization on the historical Geilis (or Gillis) Duncane. She served as maidservant to David Seaton, deputy bailiff of Tranent east of Edinburgh, until her arrest in 1589 and court appearance at the North Berwick Witch Trails in November 1590. Torture with thumbscrews and a head rope for practicing herbalism preceded imprisonment and interrogation. Before a judge, she claimed she could fly and identified her management of the North Berwick Kirk witches' sabbath on the previous Michaelmas, September 29, 1590. In an era when 87 percent of witch trial defendants lost their cases, an executioner strangled Geilis on Edinburgh's Castle Hill, on January 27, 1591, for conspiracy to murder James VI of Scotland. Authorities burned her remains to extinguish evil powers.

Adaptation to TV

The herbalist's tragic biography inspired the fictional Geillis Duncan and her claim of diablerie and murdering her husband Arthur. In 1743, Jamie's questions about the smallpox scars on Claire's and Geillis's left upper arms indicate his inability to shake peasant superstitions. At Wentworth Prison, his evil nemesis, Captain Black Jack Randall, reveals a gullible side in response to Claire's curse and pinpointing the time and date of his death. The manipulation of believers continues at Beaufort Castle in season two, episode eight, when Claire playacts Maisri's vision and unsettles Lord Simon Lovat from his maneuver to seize Lallybroch. Claire and Maisri predict Lovat's actual beheading for treason in London on April 9, 1747.

In season three, the three-masted Portuguese frigate *Bruja* and French brig *Artemis* carry direct references to the occult female. The Portuguese term *bruja/bruxa* names an empowered, fierce enchantress, crone, or hag. The practitioner of Wicca (*brujeria* or black magic) tends to rely on a familiar—an owl, a symbol of wisdom, or a cat, a representative of sly deceit. Athenians honored Artemis and her Anatolian alter ego Hecate, a protector of the home from hexes and evil spirits. Cultists raised shrines at crossroads and entranceways and formulated curatives, aphrodisiacs, abortifacients, and poisons from monkshood (aconite), nightshade (belladonna), dittany (marjoram), and mandragora (mandrake), a hallucinogenic treatment for depression, convulsion, and madness. On the island of Aegina, worshippers held mystic rituals and chanted spells to Artemis. Renaissance obsessions with wizardry colors William Shakespeare's tragedies *Hamlet, Othello,* and *Macbeth,* the fantasy *The Tempest,* comedies *The Merry Wives of Windsor* and *The Comedy of Errors*, and the history plays *Richard III, Henry V,* and *Henry VI.*

Lunar Witchery

The twin of the god Apollo, Artemis protected virgin girls from seduction and guarded women during parturition, two functions of Claire's nurse care and counseling Mary Hawkins, Louise de Rohan, Petronella Mueller, Brianna, Marsali, Fanny Beardsley, and Alicia and Rose Brown. The connection of Artemis with the moon and the female 28-day cycle anticipates Claire's gaze heavenward on December 24, 1968, at the Apollo 8 moon orbit. Her 1767 reunion with Jamie reprises stargazing on deck of the *Artemis,* a romantic moment that incorporates memories of Bree and a favorite children's book, *Goodnight, Moon.* In subsequent episodes, the moon appears ominous, as though damning the pre-war negotiations at Beaufort Castle. The night sky illumines the evil the

Frasers combat in Kingston, Jamaica, at Rose Hall and Abandawe against a real sorcerer, Geillis Duncan Abernethy, who admits murdering husband Arthur Duncan and summoning the Earth Mother to destroy Maura MacKenzie.

In season three, episode twelve, TV viewers learn the real deception that spares Geillis death at the stake, a standard punishment in 141 Scots cases involving the black arts. Her lover, War Chief Dougal MacKenzie, substitutes the remains of an elderly woman, Granny Joan MacClellan, for immolation while Geillis relishes the horror as it unfolds. A barely suppressed accusation of witchcraft reemerges at the big house on Fraser's Ridge when Marsali views an autopsy, an alarming surgery on the remains of Leith Farrish that revives Laoghaire's assertions of Claire's sorcery. Without defending herself, Claire reminds her daughter-in-law that reasoning skills have advanced beyond the Cranesmuir debacle. The statement refers to the growth of rational thought and curbs on anti-female rhetoric. Superstition emerges once more in the conclusion of season five when Tebbe and Wendigo Donner confide that Claire's abductors fear her powers. Her prediction that they will die within hours proves prophetic after Jamie tracks the outlaw gang and orders their execution.

Source

Barry, Jonathan, Owen Davies, and Cornelie Usborne, eds. *Cultures of Witchcraft in Europe from the Middle Ages to the Present*. London: Palgrave Macmillan, 2017.

Carlton, Genevieve. "What 'Outlander' Didn't Tell You about Scottish Witchcraft," *Ranker* (16 May 2018).

Frankel, Valerie Estelle. *The Symbolism and Sources of Outlander*. Jefferson, NC: McFarland, 2015.

Paterson, Laura. "Executing Scottish Witches," *Scottish Witches and Witch-Hunters*. London: Palgrave Macmillan, 2013, 196–214.

Wright, Thomas. "King James and the Witches of Lothian," *Ainsworth's Magazine* 10 (1846): 247–254.

World War II

The *Outlander* TV epic consolidates combat for its pernicious and lasting effects on humankind, a mental burden represented at Inverness by swipes of cockerel's blood over the inn door. In a flashback to shipping out from England by train to the Allied front in 1939, Claire Randall parts willingly from husband Frank, an intelligence officer who bears a surname reflecting the Norse "wolf shield." He offers to intercede with a transfer, but she prefers patriotic duty to king and country to preferential treatment. Over a six-year separation relieved by ten days of reunion, he dislikes the upside down arrangement of husband in London and wife nearer danger from German aggressors. His implication that she had a fling with a Scots lover at the front implies adultery, a common temptation over long deployments. Ironically, the sexual alliance occurs, but two centuries in the past from holy wedlock that precedes Claire's union with Frank.

Glimpses of Claire's wartime experience picture her in uniform apron soaked in ruddy spurts, watching a pick-up baseball game, and tutoring recruits about keeping their feet dry, which she repeats to eighteenth-century Scots. She befriends American soldiers after D-Day by introducing them to English black pudding and compares English war rations to American Delmonico steaks, buttered baked potatoes, tomatoes, and chocolate ice cream, a model of international stereotypes. In her tent, she sleeps on an army cot set in mud. Dazed by gruesome nurse care of the wounded, she sips from a wine bottle while reflecting on the Allied celebration in Paris on May 8, 1945, V-E Day. Jamie's shoulder brooch—"Je suis prest"—brings to mind the insignia of the American

Airborne and the dramatic ironies of men facing a cataclysm for which they can never be ready (1:9).

MENTAL BURDENS

Claire's post-traumatic stress disorder summons a living model of the dragonfly in amber. Analyst Jorie Lagerwey at University College Dublin remarked that "Time travel conceit allows for an anachronistic heroine to take her post–World War II values, deeply coloured by the knowledge and experience she gained doing the meaningful public work of nursing during the war, to a time when patriarchy was absolute, unlabeled, and unquestionable" (Lagerwey, 2017, 209). In aggressive therapy to save a soldier at a dilapidated hospital filmed at Dunmore Park, Falkirk, Claire clamps a femoral artery to stop bleed-out from his right leg, a proof of life's fragility. In an opposing view, helplessness in night combat against Germans paralyzes her into a fetal position, which she reprises at a Jacobite training camp during a flash forward to the 1940s. Allied rescuers remark on a lone female crouched by the roadside, an unusual sight before the deployment of women to war zones.

Along with other obstacles, in eighteenth-century Scotland, Claire misses iodine, merthiolate, and penicillin, fallbacks against infection that saved Allied men from gangrene. Her recall of period terminology—commando raid, food rationing—period film—*The Wizard of* Oz, *Casablanca*—and swing music—"I'm Gonna Get Lit Up" and "Shuffle Rhythm"—draws compassion and affection from a loving Scots husband, the foundation of a classic screen romance. His solace targets memories of the dead men she has encountered, including a rotting Highlander corpse in the woods in the tenth episode of season two and an Allied casualty begging for his mother. Managing a Jacobite medical facility before the Battle of Prestonpans on September 21, 1743, she acknowledges to Scots volunteers her experience in undisclosed wars and the free-floating doubts that rattle nurses before casualties arrive. Her honesty and Alice McMurdo's prayer of the rejuvenating Psalm 91 strengthen them for bloody work.

THE NEW WOMAN

At moments in the series, Claire retrieves the chutzpah that got her through a six-year conflict. The English-Scots confrontation revives her bent for blasphemy and swearing "Jesus H. Roosevelt Christ" and impinges on thoughts and doubts. In a clutch of Harvard professors, she steels herself to ignore contempt for women's wartime service. The animus of Gerhard Mueller toward Cherokees hints at German atrocities during the 1930s and 1940s. His gift of Adawehi's scalp astonishes Claire, who gently wraps the remains and burns it in the fireplace, one of the recurrent motifs of fire and heat that renew her strength.

Characters recall Roger MacKenzie's orphaning in World War II at the death of spitfire pilot Jerry and Marjorie MacKenzie and the boy's fostering by the Rev. Reginald Wakefield. In season two, episode thirteen, the adult Roger reclaims a toy one-seater British Spitfire in the Wakefield attic, a relic of boyhood that stirs memories of orphaning at age seven and rearing by a foster father. During saber rattling by Russia, a Cold War fighter jet over the Wakefield yard causes Claire to damn "another fucking war," a proof of her wounded psyche and repugnance for World War II and the Battle of Culloden, which separates her from Jamie (2:1). Season three compounds her gloomy thoughts with details of Jamie's sufferings at Culloden, Ardsmuir Prison, and Helwater Estate. At Fraser's Ridge, in seasons four and five, she prophesies war with the British over American independence. Her grim foretelling bears a veteran's tone.

See also Combat Nursing; Claire Fraser.

Source

Hoffman, Courtney A. "How to Be a Woman in the Highlands: A Feminist Portrayal of Scotland in *Outlander,*" *The Cinematic Eighteenth Century*. New York: Routledge, 2017, 103–117.

Lagerwey, Jorie. "The Feminist *Game of Thrones*: *Outlander* and Gendered Discourses of TV Genre," *Women Do Genre in Film and Television*. London: Routledge, 2017, 198–212.

West, Kelly. "*Outlander*'s Diana Gabaldon on Setting World War II as Claire's Backstory," *Cinemablend* (29 July 2014).

Glossary

Word/Phrase	Meaning	Speaker	Episode
A&P	American grocery chain	Millie Nelson	(3:2)
a chiusle	my blood kin	Jamie	(5:8)
Adawehi	religious leader	Tawodi	(4:5)
ad hoc	temporary	examiner	(1:11)
aff	off	bar entertainer	(3:4)
affaire de coeur	illicit romance	Louise de Rohan	(2:4)
affidavit	sworn statement	John Grey	(3:13)
a-ghraidh	dear	Jenny	(1:12)
alors	therefore	Fergus	(5:9)
anaphylaxis	severe allergic reaction	Claire	(5:5)
anisomelia	limbs of unequal length	Claire	(5:10)
Aniyunwiya	the Cherokee	Tawodi	(4:4)
astrolabe	a circular device that tells time	John Grey	(5:8)
autochthonous	aboriginal or native	Dean Tramble	(3:5)
bairn	baby or child	Jamie	(1:3, 1:12)
Bakra	a white woman (also spelled Buckra)	Portuguese crew	(3:12)
		Young Ian	(4:1)
bambin	toddler	Joseph Duverney	(2:4)
ban-druidh	healer or witch	Jamie	(3:3)
bannock	flat barley or oat quick bread	Letitia	(1:2, *passim*)
bawbag	scrotum	Angus	(2:10)
bawbee	halfpenny	Ned Gowan	(1:5)
beal	growl	Angus	(1:5)
bedevil	taint	Jenny	(1:14)
bee gum	a hollow blackgum tree	Jamie	(4:9)
belay	halt	Captain Raines	(3:10)
besom	ill-natured woman	Jamie	(2:8)
bhalaich	boy	Murtagh	(5:7)
bicker	brawl	Dougal	(1:6)
birkie	cocky fellow	Jamie	(1:3)

Word/Phrase	Meaning	Speaker	Episode
black coral	a sea plant known to have mystic healing properties	Geillis	(3:12)
black pudding	sausage	Claire	(3:1)
Bob's your uncle	and so it is	Geillis	(3:12)
bollocks	testicles	Ned Gowan	(3:8)
bonny	pretty	Jamie	(1:3, *passim*)
bon soir	good evening	Jamie, Madame Jeanne	(3:6)
boyo	sonny	jailer	(1:15)
Brahan seer	Coinneach Odhar, a clairvoyant at Brahan Castle, called "Warlock of the Glen" for predicting a Stuart return	Geillis	(3:12)
braw	healthy	Laoghaire, Murtagh	(1:4, 2:9)
		Ian, Jenny	(3:2)
breeks	pants	Reginald Wakefield	(2:1)
		Dougal	(2:10)
		Jamie	(3:13)
broadsheet	wanted poster	Redcoat, Jamie	(4:11, 4:13)
bugger	pest	Jamie	(1:7)
bugger off	fuck off	Angus	(1:5)
bum	ass	Claire	(5:9)
burn	creek	Jamie	(1:7)
ca' canny noo	go easy now	Angus	(1:5)
cacciatore	hunter style	Claire	(3:4)
caisteal dhuni	black castle	Bryan Cranna	(5:2)
caithris	lament	Lesley	(4:1)
canny	smart, perceptive	Horrocks, Murtagh	(1:12, 4:5)
canty	lively	Jamie, Roger	(3:6, 4:3)
ceilidh	folk reel	Roger	(4:3)
Charon	a water man who rows the deceased over the River Styx to the Greek underworld	Roger	(5:9)
cheetie	kitty	Jamie	(5:5)
ciochan	breasts	Dougal	(1:7)
Cirein-cròin	huge sea monster in Gaelic lore	Stephen Bonnet	(4:7)
clarty	dirty	Jamie	(1:5, 2:5)
cleekit	crochet	Young Ian	(4:4)
clink	coins	brothel madam	(1:7)
clype	tattler	Young Ian	(3:8)
Co-Burn	Cockburn, capital of Grand Turk	Annekje	(3:10)

Word/Phrase	Meaning	Speaker	Episode
cockade	a ribbon rosette indicating militia membership	Jamie	(5:7)
cock-a-doodle-dooed	drunk	Angus	(1:5)
cockstand	erection	Young Ian	(3:7)
coggie	wood drinking cup	Claire	(1:14)
commencez	begin	Fergus	(5:3)
composing stick	tray to hold type	Fergus	(4:8)
conjure woman	sorcerer	Eppie, Tebbe	(5:10, 5:12)
coof	clown	Rupert	(1:7)
coorie	snuggle	Dougal, Buck	(1:7, 5:7)
cosh	niche	Lesley	(3:6)
cotter	tenant farmer	Murtagh	(2:2)
		Jamie	(2:9)
cribbage	a card game with unusual scoring	Geneva	(3:4)
crivvens	gosh	Jenny	(1:13)
crural index	the ratio of tibia length to femur	Claire	(3:5)
cuimhnich	remember	Jamie	(4:13)
cullion	contemptible person	Lord Lovat	(2:8)
cunny/cunt	vagina	young MacDonald	(1:10)
		Jack Randall	(1:12, 1:15)
		Laoghaire	(3:8)
		sailors	(3:9)
		Geillis	(3:12)
cutthroat razor	straight or open razor	Jamie	(5:1)
dall	dung cake used for fuel	Jamie	(3:8)
danke	thank you	Gerhard Mueller	(4:5)
Danu	Celtic goddess	Stephen Bonnet	(4:1, 4:7, 4:9)
de meme, enchanté	likewise pleased	Claire	(3:6)
deo gratias	thanks be to God	Jamie	(5:3)
dinna	don't	Jamie	(1:4, *passim*)
doldrums	motionlessness	title	(3:9)
doocot	dove house	Fergus	(3:2)
dun	brownish gray	Samuel Lewis	(3:2)
	fort	Young Ian	(3:6)
dragoon	mounted soldiers	Frank, Jack	(1:8, 2:5)
dreich	dreary	Laoghaire	(2:8)
dry county	a district that bans alcohol sales	Roger	(4:3)
eaglais dhubh	black church	Geillis	(1:3)
earwigs	insects (*dermaptera*)	Geillis	(1:11)

Word/Phrase	Meaning	Speaker	Episode
eau de femme	womanly smell	Jamie	(5:11)
e'e	eye	Claire, Roger	(1:14, 4:3)
Ehhaokonsah	dogface	Mohawk	(4:12)
eisd ris	Hear him	Jamie, Lesley	(4:1)
fae	from	Dougal	(1:6)
fallow	uncultivated	Lieutenant Wolff	(4:2)
fartleberry	excrement on the anus	Gavin Hayes	(3:11)
fash	fret	Mrs. Fitzgibbons	(1:3, *passim*)
fathom	a nautical measure of six feet	crew	(3:10)
feart	scared	Laoghaire	(2:8)
fenghuang	mythical bird of virtue feathered in five colors: black, green, red, white, yellow	Yi Tien Cho	(3:9)
flux	menstruation	Geillis, Murtagh	(1:2, 2:6)
	diarrhea	Jamie	(4:1)
footling	breech birth	Jenny	(1:13)
forbye	besides	Dougal	(1:5)
fou	drunk	wool waulker	(1:5)
frae	from	bar entertainer	(3:4)
Francis Stephen	the Holy Roman Emperor who precedes Louis XV of France as Duke of Lorraine	Taran MacQuarrie	(1:13)
Frau Klara	Mrs. Claire	Rosewitha Mueller	(4:5)
frog/frog-eater	Frenchman	Cpl. MacGregor	(3:2)
		Stephen Bonnet	(4:1)
		Joanie	(4:7)
gab/gob	mouth	Angus, Colum	(1:7, 1:10)
		Rabbie	(3:2)
Gaberlunzie tokens	licenses to beg	Jamie	(1:8)
galley	ship's kitchen	Captain Leonard	(3:10)
ganakti	healer	Claire	(4:5)
gang thegither	belong together	bar entertainer	(3:4)
gant	gasp	Angus	(1:5)
Geordie	King George	Stephen Bonnet	(4:7)
gey very		Murtagh, Jamie	(2:9, 3:3)
ghoistidh	godfather	Jamie	(5:1, 5:7)
gill	one-cup drink	bar entertainer	(3:4)
glaikit	simple-minded	Rupert	(1:15)
gomeril	fool	Mrs. Fitzgibbons	(1:3)
gralloch	gut the deer	Jamie	(4:6)

Word/Phrase	Meaning	Speaker	Episode
grog	watered rum	Lt. Leonard	(3:10)
Hacienda de la Fuente	fountain house	Father Fogden	(3:11)
half six	6:30	Jamie	(5:7)
hanger	brandisher of a long penis	Claire	(1:14)
ha'penny	a half-cent	Jamie	(4:5)
haverin'	babbling	Dougal	(1:5)
hedge whore	beggar prostitute	Lionel Brown	(5:12)
heehaw	nothing	Murtagh	(2:14)
helm a-lee	turn the ship downwind	Captain Raines	(3:10)
Herr	Mister	Mother Hildegarde	(2:3)
		Gerhard Mueller	(4:5)
Hogmany	New Year's Eve	Jeanie Hume	(1:11)
		Jamie	(3:8)
hornie-gollachs	earwigs (*dermaptera*)	Geillis	(1:11)
hud	hold	Murtagh	(1:7)
Iain Og	Young John	Iain Og Findlay	(5:3)
ilka	each	Jocasta	(5:8)
ill-faured	coarse, ugly	Taran MacQuarrie	(1:15)
in drag	in harness	Laoghaire	(4:7)
in flux	during the menstrual cycle	Murtagh	(2:6)
inguinal hernia	bulging intestine in the groin	Claire	(4:8)
jeunes filles	girls	Madame Jeanne	(3:6)
jessies	British soldiers	Angus	(1:9)
Jonah	a curse on a ship	crew	(3:9)
jouk	twitch	Jamie	(1:3)
journeycake	cornbread	Claire	(5:11)
keek	peek	Angus, Laoghaire	(1:7, 2:8)
ken/kent	know/knew	Mrs. Fitzgibbons	(1:2, *passim*)
kine	cattle	Geordie	(1:4)
kirk	church	Rupert	(1:3)
kitling	brat	Peggy	(3:6)
kittle-hoosie	brothel	Brighid	(3:7)
K-rations	packaged meals during World War II	Allied soldier	(2:9)
la grippe	influenza	Jamie	(3:3)
leannan	my darling	Jamie	(4:9, 5:1)
lilt	sing	Jocasta	(5:8)
limmer	rascal	Dougal	(1:5)
lugs	ears	Angus, Jenny	(1:5, 1:14)

Word/Phrase	Meaning	Speaker	Episode
lyam-hounds	bloodhounds	Geillis	(1:11)
MacDubh	son of the dark	prisoners	(3:3, 3:6)
ma chèrie	my dear	Hildegarde, Louise	(2:7)
		Fergus	(3:12)
m' annsachd	my bessing	Jamie	(4:9)
ma petite fleur	my little flower	Jamie	(5:11)
maroon	escaped slave	Father Fogden	(3:11)
menage a trois	three-person sexual experience	Fergus	(3:7)
merde	shit	Fergus	(4:11)
		Madame Jeanne	(3:6)
mess	dine	Claire	(3:10)
m'fhuil	bleeding	Jamie	(5:8)
midden	dungheap	Jamie	(2:5)
mo charaid	my friend	Murtagh	(4:5)
mo cridhe	my heart	Jenny, Jamie	(1:12, 5:7, 5:11)
moi	me	Fergus	(3:7)
mollies	homosexuals; sissies	young MacDonald	(1:10)
		Murtagh	(3:3)
mon ami	my friend	Fergus	(3:7)
mon amour	my love	Fergus	(4:12)
mon canard	my duckling	Fergus	(3:12)
mon coeur	my heart	Fergus	(3:10)
mon fils	my son	Jamie	(3:7, 3:10)
mo nighean donn	my brown-haired lass	Jamie	(1:9, *passim*)
morbid sore throat	diphtheria	Jamie	(4:1)
muckle	big	Murtagh, Claire	(1:7, 1:14)
muddle	pressing juice from herbs [misspelled in Closed Caption]	Jeanie Hume	(1:11)
mull	kiss	singers	(1:5)
multure	the miller's percentage	singers	(1:5)
mun	must	Roger	(2:13)
Murphy's sign	an intake of breath during a gallbladder examination	Joe Abernethy	(3:4)
necrosis	dead tissue	Claire	(3:5)
neep-heids	turnip heads, slang for Redcoats	Murtagh	(3:3)
nether mouth	vagina	Peggy	(3:6)
nicht	night	Robena Donaldson	(1:11)
nighean na galladh	bitch	Jamie	(5:3)

Word/Phrase	Meaning	Speaker	Episode
nvwadohiyadv	harmony	John Quincy Myers	(4:3)
old nick	Satan	Jamie	(1:3)
oolong	Chinese tea	Claire	(1:1)
ordinary	pub	citizen	(5:5)
orlop	bottom deck	Thomas Leonard	(3:10)
Ozzie and Harriet	a television series from 1952 to 1966 based on a real couple	Joe Abernethy	(3:5)
palfrey	gentle horse for a lady to ride	Geneva	(3:4)
paps	breasts	Dougal	(1:5)
parfum d'amour	fragrance of love	Jamie	(5:11)
Pavlova	meringue dessert filled with berries and whipped cream	Claire	(3:2)
piebald	patchy	wool waulker	(1:5)
piece de resistance	main element	Fergus	(3:7)
pintle	penis	Claire	(1:14)
plight troth	pledge truth	Roger	(4:8, 5:2)
pogue	shirker	Taran MacQuarrie	(1:13)
poltroon	coward	William Dunsany	(3:4)
ponce	prance	Angus, Jamie	(1:7, 2:9)
pooter	loiter	Murtagh	(2:9)
Procrustes	mythic Greek robber who cut victims to fit his bed	Jamie	(9:5)
procurator fiscal	treasury officer	Dougal	(1:3)
p'tit garçon	little boy	Fergus	(5:11)
puckled	bedeviled	Ned Gowan	(1:5)
puddock	frog [misspelled in Closed Caption]	Geillis	(1:11)
puggie	monkey	wool waulker	(1:5)
quelle performance	what a deal	Fergus	(3:7)
quick-march	the British military march at 140 beats per minute	Gordon Killick	(3:1)
quitrent	a land tax on leased property	Jamie, Governor Tryon	(4:1)
radge	loose woman	Buck MacKenzie	(5:7)
Ràibeirt	Rupert	Jamie	(3:1)
rake	lecher	Mrs. Tryon	(5:6)
ratling	mouse	Geillis	(3:12)
reddish	bloody	Jack Randall	(1:6)
reiving	stealing	Jamie	(1:9)
robe rouge	red dress	Louise de Rohan	(2:2)
rowe	argue	Claire	(1:14)

Word/Phrase	Meaning	Speaker	Episode
Samhain	Celtic Halloween	Mrs. Baird	(1:1)
sasine	seizure	Lord Lovat	(2:8, 2:13)
schlaf kindlein	sleep baby	Petronella and Rosewitha	(4:5)
scunner	loathsome person	Ned Gowan	(1:11)
		Taran MacQuarrie	(1:13)
		Angus Mohr	(1:14)
selkie	mythic seal folk	Duncan Kerr	(3:3)
a seventy-four	a 74-gun man-o'-war	Captain Raines	(3:10)
sha	'tis so, an interjection prefacing a remark	Jamie	(1:1, 1:8, 2:1, 2:2)
shagger	sexual exploiter	Rupert	(1:2)
		young MacDonald	(1:10)
sgian dubh	hidden dagger	Dougal	(1:8)
ship's fever	typhus	Captain Leonard	(3:9)
signet	authority	Ned Gowan	(1:11)
siyo genali	greetings, friend	John Quincy Myers, Jamie	(4:4)
skelp	slap or smack	Jamie, Rupert, court examiner	(1:3, 1:9, 1:11)
		Jenny	(1:14)
skint	broke by gambling	Rupert	(1:15)
slàinte mhaith	to your good health	Highlanders	(1:1, *passim*)
Slàn leat	Farewell	Jamie	(3:1)
slater	woodlice	Claire	(1:3)
sleekit	sly	Rupert, Jocasta	(1:5, 4:13)
smiths	metal workers	Jamie	(2:9)
smout	twit, underling	Dougal, Murtagh	(1:6, 2:4)
		Lord Lovat	(2:8)
soiree	evening party	Geillis	(3:12)
soixante-neuf	simultaneous male-female oral sex	Jamie	(2:4)
sonsie	robust, good-natured	Murtagh	(1:14)
splints	swollen legs on horses	Jamie	(2:5)
sporran	money pouch	Jamie	(1:7, 2:3)
squeaker	baby	Peggy	(3:6)
stand down	yield	Taran MacQuarrie	(1:13)
		Harry Tompkins	(3:7)
steek	shut	Rabbie MacNab	(3:2)
sterling	minted coin	Jamie	(3:8)
stock	necktie	Claire	(3:7)

Word/Phrase	Meaning	Speaker	Episode
stottin'	bouncing	Angus	(1:5)
stramash	fracas	Taran MacQuarrie	(1:13)
		Maisri	(2:8)
		Jamie	(4:1)
strath	wide valley	Claire	(1:14)
sun king	Louis XIV	Mother Hildegarde	(2:7)
swive	fornicate	Dougal	(1:5)
swivet	quandary	Jamie	(1:3)
tacksman	tenant, landholder	Dougal, Jamie	(1:4, 2:9)
tanist	power based on the worthiest kin, chosen laird during a chief's lifetime	Murtagh	(1:4)
tannasg	ghost	Lesley	(4:1)
tatterdemalion	bum	Gavin Hayes	(3:11)
Tawodi	hawk	Tawodi	(4:4, 4:5)
teuchter	rural Gaelic-speaking Highlander	Cpl. MacGregor	(3:2)
thon	those	Dougal	(1:5)
thousand-yard stare	shell shock	Brianna	(5:8)
thrapple	throat	Dougal	(1:6)
todger	penis	Murtagh	(1:5)
tolbooth	a municipal jail in Edinburgh	Taran MacQuarrie	(1:13)
		Brianna Randall	(3:4)
Tom-faced	drunken	Horrocks	(1:13)
Tommies	Redcoats	Claire	(1:6)
tossel	penis	Taran MacQuarrie	(1:15)
tripe	guts	Jamie	(5:9)
trobhad	come	Murtagh	(1:1)
trow	vow	Roger	(2:13)
tskili	evil	John Quincy Myers	(4:3)
		Adawehi	(4:4)
tulach ard	battle cry of "the high hill"	Dougal, Jamie	(1:1, 2:9, 2:10)
		Roger	(4:3)
tumshie	fool	Angus	(2:10)
turner	coin worth two cents	Ned Gowan	(1:5)
Tynchal	boar hunt	Rupert	(1:4)
unyirdly	supernatural	examiner	(1:11)
vinho de porto	fortified port wine	Kenneth McIver	(3:12)
wanking	fornicating	Angus	(1:4)
watch	home guard	Murtagh	(1:5)
waulking	cleansing new wool of impurities	Donalda Gilchrest	(1:5)

Word/Phrase	Meaning	Speaker	Episode
wede	take by death	Jocasta	(5:8)
wee man	penis	Angus, Rupert	(1:5, 2:11)
wellies	rubber boots	Roger	(2:13)
wheesht	silence	Jamie	(1:7)
whist	a card game won by taking tricks	Jamie	(5:6)
with bairn	pregnant	Geillis	(1:4)
yona	bear	John Quincy Myers	(4:3)
		Adawehi	(4:4)
yona dihi	bear killer	Nawohali	(4:4)
yupa	(*Anadenanthera peregrina*) a West Indian and South American hallucinogen smoked in a pipe	Father Fogden	(3:11)
zam gau	traditional Chinese acupuncture	Yi Tien Cho	(3:9)

A Guide to Herbalism

From the early middle ages, the Celtic medical tradition dominated Gaelic speakers of the Highlands with a mix of myth, verse, and scripture and studies of local plants, such as Hawthorn berries, a general tonic, and fennel, for relief of bloating. Like Native American healers, white witches, charmers, leeches, and midwives passed folklore through families, forming medical dynasties respected for powers over illness bordering on magic.

plant	use	patient	provider
althea officinalis (blue mass pills)	constipation (5:2)	Parrish	wife
althea officinalis (marshmallow)	chronic cough (2:2)	Alex Randall	Claire
	antidote to poison (2:4)	Claire	Claire
balm of Gilead (*Commiphora gileadensis*)	broken wrist (5:11)	Rose Brown	Claire
barberry (*Berberis vulgaris*)	abortion (2:4)	Louise de Rohan	Claire
belladonna (*Atropa belladonna*)	antidote to poison (1:3)	Tammas Baxter	Claire
	combat wounds (5:7)	casualties	Claire
bitter cascara (*Rhamnus purshiana*)	poisoning (2:3)	enemies	Master Raymond
	poisoning (2:4)	Claire	Comte St. Germain
	mimic smallpox (2:6)	Jamie, workers	Claire
chamomile (*Chamaemelum nobile*)	chronic cough (2:12)	Alex Randall	Mary Hawkins
cherry bark (*Prunus avium*)	wound pain (1:2)	Jamie	Mrs. Fitzgibbons
coltsfoot (*Tussilago farfara*)	chronic cough (2:12)	Alex Randall	Claire
comfrey (*Symphytum officinale*)	wound pain (1:2)	Jamie	Mrs. Fitzgibbons
	wound pain (5:12)	Lionel Brown	Claire
fennel (*Foeniculum vulgare*)	belly pain, gas (1:!0)	Arthur Duncan	Claire
garlic (*Allium sativum*)	sterilizing bandages (1:2)	Jamie	Mrs. Fitzgibbons

plant	use	patient	provider
ginger (*Zingiber officinale*)	chronic cough (2:12)	Alex Randall	Mary Hawkins
	seasickness (3:9)	Jamie	Claire
guelder rose (*Viburnum opulus*)	aching amputation (1:12)	Ian Murray	Claire
hellebore (*Helleborus occidentalis*)	abortion (2:4)	Louise de Rohan	Claire
Humulus lupulus (hops)	sleeplessness (2:2)	Jamie	Master Raymond
Jesuit bark (*Cinchona*)	malaria (4:9)	Lizzy Wemyss	Claire
juniper (*Juniperus communis*)	gut infection (5:7)	casualties	Claire
kelp (*Nereocystis lueteana*)	source of dietary iodine (5:10)	patients	Claire
lady's mantle (*Alchemilla mollis*)	promote conception (1:13)	Claire	Jenny, Granny MacNab
lavender (*Lavandula spica*)	burn (1:16)	Jamie	Jack Randall
	despair (1:16)	Jamie	Claire
	pain (1:16)	Jamie	Jack Randall
laudanum (*Papaver somniferum*)	finger surgery (1:16)	Jamie	Claire, Brother Paul
	chronic cough (2:12)	Alex Randall	Mary Hawkins
	trepanning (3:7)	John Barton	Claire
	surgery (4:2)	Rufus	Claire
	combat wounds (5:7)	casualties	Claire
mandrake (*Mandragora officinarum*)	mental illness (3:7)	Margaret	Archibald Campbell
milk thistle (*Cirsium vulgare*)	chronic cough (2:12)	Alex Randall	Mary Hawkins
	rat bite (3:3)	Murtagh	Jamie
mistletoe (*Viscum album*)	mental agitation (3:7)	Margaret	Claire
monkshood (*Aconitum napellus*)	murder (2:3)	enemies	Master Raymond
mugwort (*Artemisia vulgaris*)	contraception (2:3)	Suzette	Master Raymond
nepeta cataria (catnip)	sleeplessness (2:2)	Jamie	Claire
nettles (*Urtica dioica*)	mimic smallpox (2:6)	Jamie, workers	Claire
onion poultice (*Allium cepa*)	treat infected snakebite (5:9)	Jamie	Claire
opium (*Papaver somniferum*)	anesthetic (1:6)	Redcoat	Redcoat surgeon
orris root (*Iris germanica*)	pain, swelling (1:2)	Jamie	Mrs. Fitzgibbons

plant	use	patient	provider
penicillium (*Asomycota fungus*)	infection (5:5)	Graham Menzies	Claire
		Josiah	Claire
		Kezzie	Claire
	infected snakebite (5:9)	Jamie	Claire
pennyroyal (*Mentha pulegium*)	antiseptic (5:7)	casualties	Claire
peppermint (*Mentha piperita*)	morning sickness (4:1)	Marsali	Claire
peppermint oil (*Mentha piperita*)	headache (3:9)	Manzetti	Claire
poppy syrup (*Papaver somniferum*)	rape, shock (2:4)	Mary Hawkins	Claire
raspberry leaf (*Rubus idaeus*)	promote conception (1:13)	Claire	Jenny, Granny MacNab
rosehip (*Rosa moyesii*)	promote conception (1:13)	Claire	Jenny, Granny MacNab
rose madder (*Rubia tinctorum*)	mimic smallpox (2:6)	Jamie, workers	Claire
rosemary (*Salvia rosmarinus*)	mimic smallpox (2:6)	Jamie, workers	Claire
tansy (*Tanacetum vulgare*)	mental agitation (3:7)	Margaret	Claire
thornapple (*Datura stramonium*)	cough of asthma (1:5)	Ned Gowan	Claire
	chronic cough (2:12)	Alex Randall	Claire
tormentil (*Potentilla erecta*)	trepanning (3:7)	John Barton	Claire
Valeriana officinalis (valerian root)	insomnia (1:3)	Arthur Duncan	Geillis Duncan
	sleeplessness (2:2)	Jamie	Master Raymond
	mental agitation (3:7)	Margaret	Claire
watercress (*Nasturtium officinale*)	scurvy (3:3)	prisoners	Jamie
water hemlock (*Cicuta douglasii*)	migraine, suicide (5:8)	Young Ian Murray	himself
	murder (5:12)	Lionel Brown	Marsali
water pepper (*Persicaria hydropiper*)	aching amputation (1:12)	Ian Murray	Claire
willow bark tea (*Salix alba*)	pain, inflammation, fever (1:2)	Jamie	Mrs. Fitzgibbons
			Geillis Duncan
	measles (4:6)	John Grey	Claire

plant	use	patient	provider
witch hazel (*Hamamelis virginiana*)	sterilizing bandages (1:2)	Jamie	Mrs. Fitzgibbons
wood betony (*Stachys officinalis*)	emmenagogue (1:3)	pregnant girls	Geillis Duncan
yarrow (*Achillea millefolium*)	trepanning (3:7)	John Barton	Claire
yellow jasmine (*Gelsemium sempervirens*)	assisted suicide (2:12, 2:13)	Colum	Claire
	euthanasia (4:2)	Rufus	Claire
yupa (*Anadenanthera peregrina*)	euphoria (3:11)	Claire, Yi Tien Cho	Father Fogden

Source

Carr-Gomm, Philip, and Stephanie Carr-Gomm. *The Druid Plant Oracle.* New York: St. Martin's Press, 2008.
Gehring, Abigail. *The Illustrated Encyclopedia of Natural Remedies.* New York: Skyhorse, 2020.
Comrie, John D. *History of Scottish Medicine to 1860.* London: Ballière, Tindall & Cox, 1927.

A Guide to Place Names

Achnasheen (1:14)	town west of Inverness where Redcoats arrest Jamie
Adjumako (4:2)	Rufus's coastal home in Gold Coast (Ghana)
Arbroath (3:6)	port at center of Scotland's east coast
Ardsmuir (3:3, 4:5)	fictional prison in northwestern Scotland
Ayr (4:7)	harbor southwest of Edinburgh
Balnain (1:3)	Scots village southwest of Inverness
Balriggan (3:8, 4:7)	Laoghaire's fictional cottage on the western edge of Fraser holdings
Banffshire (4:5)	Brian Fraser's home east of Inverness
Beauly (2:9)	a town west of Inverness and location of Beaufort Castle
Belmont (2:11)	fictional estate of the Duke of Sandringham filmed at Drumlanrig Castle in Dumfries
Bois de Boulogne (2:6)	site in eastern Paris of Jamie's duel with Jack
Brockton (1:2)	fictional Scots village occupied by Lord Thomas and his dragoons
Brownsville (5:4, 5:12)	fictional community in Granville, County, north of Raleigh, North Carolina
Brunswick (4:8)	North Carolina village west of Wilmington where Governor Tryon lived until completion of Tryon's Palace
Carfax Close (3:7)	alley off High Street in Edinburgh
Castle Leoch (1:1)	fictional stronghold northwest of Dundee on the coast of the North Sea set at Doune Castle
Cocknammon Rock (1:1)	fictional setting of an ambush on Dougal's band
Compiegne (1:2)	Claire's alleged family home in north central France
Corrieyairack (3:1, 3:12)	military camp in the central highlands where John Grey tries to assassinate Jamie
Cranesmuir (1:11)	fictional village set at Culross on the River Forth northwest of Edinburgh
Crieff (2:8)	Prince Charles's first Jacobite camp west of Perth, Scotland
Cross Creek (4:2)	beginnings of Fayetteville, North Carolina
Culloden Moor (1:1, *passim*)	bog east of Inverness
Falkirk (2:12)	site of a Jacobite victory west of Edinburgh
Findhorn River (1:8)	river east of Inverness and Culloden, Scotland
Florrach (1:4)	fictional hiding place for Scots rustlers

Fort William (1:2, 1:6, 1:12)	fortress on the east coast of Loch Linnhe, the fictional flogging site, filmed at Blackness Castle on the Firth of Forth
Fraser's Ridge (4:9, *passim*)	10,000 acres spread over Caldwell, Wilkes, and Watauga counties in western North Carolina
Glen Rowan Cross (2:14)	fictional sandstone cave where Dougal hides supplies
Gold Coast (3:12)	West African source of black slaves now called Ghana
Grand Turk (3:10)	Caribbean isle north of Haiti supplying water to passing ships
Granite Falls (5:4)	town in southeastern Caldwell County, North Carolina, and home of Isaiah Morton
Haiti (3:10)	island where Claire rejoins Jamie and arranges a wedding for Fergus and Marsali
Harvard (2:1, 3:2)	American university northwest of Boston on the Charles River
Haslemere (2:11)	fictional British outpost on the way to Inverness
Hillsborough (5:2)	town east of Greensboro, North Carolina, in Orange County
Innse-Gall (1:12)	island of the central Outer Hebrides that Jamie claims is his home
Inverness (1:1, *passim*)	North sea town on Moray Firth, the site of Claire and Frank's second honeymoon, filmed at Falkland, Fife
Kingussie (2:8)	gathering place for Lallybroch men in the center of Scotland
Le Havre (2:1, 2:6)	French port northwest of Paris where the Frasers witness sailors dead from smallpox
Les Perles (3:13)	fictional coast in colonial Georgia
l'Hôpital des Anges (2:3)	fictional charity hospital near Notre Dame Cathedral on the Seine River in Paris
Lochaber Bridge (1:13)	site of the Watch's ambush on the Chisholm rent party north of Fort William
Loch Fannich (1:4)	lake at Ross-shire in northwestern Scotland
Lynchburg (4:6)	site of Mt. Josiah, Isobel Dunsany Grey's home in central Virginia
Monach Isles (2:8)	outer Hebrides cluster where Lord Lovat tries to secure Ellen MacKenzie from marriage
Nairn (2:12)	northern Scotland port and camp site of Cumberland's army
Ocracoke (5:10)	island northeast of Wilmington off North Carolina's Pamlico Sound
Old Leanach Cottage (2:1)	thatched-roof house at Culloden that survived the battle in 1746
New Bern (4:6)	North Carolina state capital and site of Tryon's Palace on the Trent River
Perth (2:9, 2:10)	location of a Jacobite victory north of Edinburgh
Prestonpans (2:10)	site of a significant Jacobite triumph on the Firth of Forth
River Run (4:2)	fictional plantation on the Cape Fear River northwest of Fayetteville, North Carolina
Rose Hall (3:12)	Jamaican great house on the northwestern coast at Montego Bay
Rowan County (5:3)	vast area of west central North Carolina containing Salisbury and Alamance Creek
St.-Louis-du-Nord (3:11)	port in northwestern Haiti south of the island of Tortuga
St. Ninian's Spring (1:6)	fictional site at Finnich Glen west of Edinburgh near Loch Lomond

Seaford (2:3)	birthplace of Mary Hawkins at Sussex, in southeastern England
Skye (1:1)	Inner Hebrides island off Scotland's northwestern coast
Thunderton House (2:12)	Prince Charles's headquarters at Batchen Lane, Elgin, on Scotland's north central coast
Tilbury Fort (4:5)	English prison east of London on the Thames inlet
Versailles (2:2)	French royal enclave and palace southwest of Paris
Wilmington (4:1)	North Carolina's major Atlantic port on the Cape Fear River
Woollam's Creek (4:5)	fictional North Carolina setting of Murtagh's forge
World's End (3:6)	real pub on High Street northeast of Edinburgh's Old Town

A Guide to Outlander
Aphorisms

Bees that have honey in their mouth have a sting in their tail.	Jamie (4:1)
The bravest are surely those who have the clearest vision of what is before them, glory and danger alike, and yet notwithstanding go out to meet it. (Thucydides)	Jamie (5:12)
A dream for some can be a nightmare for others.	Jamie (4:1)
Even the devil has standards.	The Reverend Wakefield (2:1)
Excessive taxation brings out the savage in all of us.	Claire (4:1)
Fair's fair.	Jamie (1:7)
Honor and courage are matters of the bones.	Jamie (5:12)
How careful we'd be if we kent which goodbyes were our last.	Jocasta (5:8)
If you bed a vixen, you have to expect to get bit.	Jamie (1:9)
Jamais pris vivant. (Never be taken alive)	Ian (1:12)
Je suis prest. (I am ready)	Fraser motto (1:3, 1:9, 2:9)
Je suis prest. (I am ready)	Brianna (5:1)
Luceo non uro. (I shine not burn)	MacKenzie motto (1:3, 5:6)
A man most often makes his own luck.	Stephen Bonnet (4:1)
A man's life springs from his woman's bones and in her blood is his honor christened.	Jamie (5:12)
Memories, they remain raw even longer than wounds.	Colum (2:12)
Nemo me impune lacessit. (No one strikes me without punishment)	Stuart motto (3:4)
Nothing is lost.	Jamie (4:1)
One man fighting for his home is worth one hundred fighting for pay.	Edmund Fanning (5:2)
Pale Death visits with impartial foot the cottages of the poor and the castles of the rich. (Horace)	Jamie (1:13)
Poor men must bleed for rich man's gold and always will.	Mrs. Findlay (5:3)
Some ghosts can only be banished by speaking their names and foul deeds aloud.	Jamie (4:1)
Some things don't change.	Claire (1:7)
Still waters run deep. (Curtius)	Jamie (1:7)
A story told is a life lived.	Yi Tien Cho (3:9)

There is the law, and there is what is done.	Governor Tryon (4:1)
There's always a war comin'.	Murtagh (5:1)
Time, space, history be damned.	Claire (5:2)
War tastes bitter no matter the outcome.	Jamie (2:10)
What's one more sin to a sinner?	Colum (2:12)
When has it ever been easy?	Jamie (3:8)
When it comes to politics, there's not much difference between makin' the right friends and the right enemies.	Jamie (5:1)

Historical Chronology

October 28, 1636	Harvard opened under the name New College.
1653	The Witchcraft Act declared sorcery, charms, enchantment, and witchery felonies under English law.
1663	Charles II initiated a system of colonial land grants.
September 6, 1686	Jean-Baptiste Lully's *Acis et Galathée* opened at the Paris Opera.
November 11, 1688	A bloodless coup ousted James II of England/James VII of Scotland and the Stuart dynasty and replaced it with the House of Orange.
October 9, 1701	Yale opened under the name Collegiate School.
March 23, 1713	After defeat in North Carolina, the Tuscarora fled north to New York.
August 1, 1714	George I established the Hanover dynasty in England.
September–November 1715	Jacobite rebels led the first of three revolts.
mid–May 1718	Pirate Stede Bonnet blockaded Charleston Harbor.
September 28, 1718	Colonel William Rhett fought pirate Stede Bonnet at the Battle of Cape Fear River in Wilmington, North Carolina.
June 1719	The second Jacobite revolt failed.
1735	The House of Lords repealed the 1653 Witchcraft Act.
1740	Samuel Richardson wrote *Pamela,* the first English novel.
late 1741	Johann Sebastian Bach published the Goldberg Variations, a series of 30 musical inventions.
August 4–5, 1741	Because of tropical fevers, the English failed at invading Santiago, Cuba.
July 23, 1745	The warship *Elisabeth* carried Bonnie Prince Charlie to the Isle of Eriskay to muster an army to fight the British.
August 1745	George II offered a £30,000 reward for the Bonnie Prince.
September 21, 1745	The prince and his Jacobites overwhelmed the English General John Cope at Prestonpans.
November 1745	The Jacobites triumphed at Carlisle.
December 4, 1745	A subsequent victory at Carlisle buoyed the Jacobite spirit.
January 17, 1746	Jacobites overran British forces at Falkirk.
March 1746	Prince Charles made his headquarters at Thunderton House, Batchen Lane, Elgin.
April 15, 1746	The 25th birthday of William, Duke of Cumberland, preceded the fallback of Jacobites to Inverness.

April 16, 1746	Some 2,000 Jacobites died on Culloden Moor during the pro–Stuart Rebellion.
June 28, 1746	Prince Charles, posing as Betty Burke, fled to the Isle of Skye.
July 23, 1746	George II established a lottery granting a trial to only one-fifth of Jacobite prisoners.
August 1, 1746	The Act of Proscription demolished the feudal clan system and forbade Scots ownership of weapons.
September 20, 1746	The bonnie prince fled by the frigate *L'Heureux* to France.
April 9, 1747	Lord Simon Lovat died of beheading for treachery.
1765	English law suspended Scots whisky distilling.
early spring 1768	The mustering of militias began suppressing the colonial Regulators, who attacked Hillsborough.
October 5, 1770	Violence in New Bern resulted in the maiming of Inferior Court Judge Richard Henderson and District Attorney William Hooper.
October 6, 1770	Regulators at Hillsborough sacked Edmund Fanning's home.
January 15, 1771	The Riot Act stopped the Regulators from gathering and attacking legislative buildings.
May 16, 1771	Governor William Tryon attacked 2,000 Regulators at Alamance Creek south of Burlington, North Carolina.
June 20, 1771	The North Carolina Supreme Court ordered the hanging of six Regulators at Hillsborough.
July 3, 1771	Governor Tryon left North Carolina by the sloop *Sukey* to assume the governorship of New York.
November 23, 1774	Wilmington formed a Committee of Safety for New Hanover, County.
April 18, 1775	Paul Revere rode to Lexington to warn of a British invasion at Lexington and Concord.
April 19, 1775	The British arrested Paul Revere.
September 23, 1775	At Salisbury, Rowan County formed a Committee of Safety.
1786	Robert Burns wrote "Freedom and Whisky."
July 14, 1789	The storming of the Bastille initiated the French Revolution.
December 19, 1843	Charles Dickens issued *A Christmas Carol*.
January 1861	*The Atlantic Monthly* published Henry Wadsworth Longfellow's "Paul Revere's Ride."
March 31, 1889	The Eiffel Tower reached completion in Paris.
September 28, 1928	Scots bacteriologist Alexander Fleming discovered penicillin.
September 1, 1939–September 2, 1945	Allied forces fought World War II.
June 18, 1940	The Eiffel Tower closed during the Nazi occupation of Paris.
June 6, 1944	Allied forces landed at Normandy and invaded France.
August 19, 1944	The Allies liberated Paris.
May 8, 1945	The Allies celebrated victory in Europe
December 21, 1945	George S. Patton died in Heidelberg, Germany, from complications of a car accident.

April 18, 1949	The Republic of Ireland attained freedom.
June 21, 1949	President Harry Truman named Georgia Neese Clark the nation's first female Treasurer of the United States.
November 1, 1955–April 30, 1975	The United States fought the Vietnam War.
1956	American movie-goers popularized *The Searchers* and *Carousel*.
1956	Miss Clairol color bath came on the market.
August 1962	Drummer Ringo Starr joined the Beatles.
December 9, 1965	Charles M. Schultz wrote *A Charlie Brown Christmas*.
1966	*Batman* debuted on television.
June 27, 1966	*Dark Shadows* began a weekday TV soap opera.
December 24, 1968	Apollo 8 orbited the moon.

Source

Bassett, John Spencer. *The Regulators of North Carolina (1765–1771)*. Washington, DC: Government Printing Office, 1895, 141–212.

Ervin, Samuel James, Jr. *A Colonial History of Rowan County, North Carolina*. Chapel Hill: University of North Carolina Press, 1917.

Hunter, C.L. *Sketches of Western North Carolina*. Raleigh, NC: Raleigh News, 1877.

"Newbern, October 5," *Virginia Gazette* (25 October 1770).

Rumple, Jethro. *A History of Rowan County, North Carolina*. Salisbury, NC: J.J. Bruner, 1881.

Snodgrass, Mary Ellen. *Civil Disobedience: An Encyclopedic History of Dissidence in the United States*. New York: Routledge, 2009.

Whitford, James Dalton. "Rambles about Town: Tryon's Palace," *New Berne Weekly Journal* (3 December 1882).

Bibliography

Primary Sources

Arthur, John Preston. *Western North Carolina: A History*. Raleigh, NC: Edwards & Broughton, 1914.

Ashe, Samuel A., Stephen B. Weeks, and Charles L. Van Noppen, eds. *Biographical History of North Carolina*, eight vols. Greensboro, NC: Van Noppen, 1905–1917.

Bassett, John Spencer. *The Regulators of North Carolina (1765–1771)*. Washington, D.C.: Government Printing Office, 1895, 141–212.

Burke, Bernard. *Vicissitudes of Families*. London: Longmans, Green & Co., 1883.

Comrie, John D. *History of Scottish Medicine to 1860*. London: Ballière, Tindall & Cox, 1927.

Ellis, H.D. "Some Steps in the Evolution of the Apostle Spoon." *Burlington Magazine for Connoisseurs* 23:125 (August 1913): 283–285, 287.

Ervin, Samuel James, Jr. *A Colonial History of Rowan County, North Carolina*. Chapel Hill: University of North Carolina Press, 1917.

Godfrey, Thomas. *The Prince of Parthia*. Boston: Little, Brown, 1917.

Haywood, Marshall Delancey. *Governor William Tryon and His Administration*. Raleigh, NC: E.M. Uzzell, 1903.

Hunter, C.L. *Sketches of Western North Carolina*. Raleigh, NC: Raleigh News, 1877.

Johnson, Charles. *A General History of the Pyrates*. London: Thomas Warner, 1724. Kingsbury, T.B., ed. "The Women and the Chicago Fair." *Wilmington Messenger* (17 March 1892).

MacGibbon, David, and Thomas Ross. *The Ecclesiastical Architecture of Scotland*. Edinburgh: D. Douglas, 1897, 330–337.

Mackenzie, Alexander. *History of the Frasers of Lovat*. Inverness, Scot.: A. & W. Mackenzie, 1896.

_____. *The History of the Highland Clearances*. Edinburgh: Mercat Press Books, 1883.

_____. *The Prophecies of the Brahan Seer*. Inverness, UK: A. & W. MacKenzie, 1888.

McCrady, Edward. *The History of South Carolina under the Royal Government, 1719–1775*. New York: Macmillan, 1899.

A New Voyage to Georgia. London: J. Wilford, 1737.

"Newbern, October 5." *Virginia Gazette* (25 October 1770).

"The Physicians of the Western Islands." *British Medical Journal* (19 May 1906): 1178.

Rumple, Jethro. *A History of Rowan County, North Carolina*. Salisbury, NC: J.J. Bruner, 1881.

Stewart. Alexander. *'Twixt Ben Nevis and Glencoe: The Natural History, Legends, and Folk-Lore of the West Highlands*. Edinburgh: William Paterson, 1885.

The Tryals of Major Stede Bonnet and Other Pirates. London: Benjamin Cowse, 1719.

Waddell, Alfred Moore. *A History of New Hanover County and the Lower Cape Fear Region 1723–1800*. Volume I. N.p.: n.p., 1909.

Whitford, James Dalton. "Rambles about Town: Tryon's Palace." *New Berne Weekly Journal* (3 December 1882).

Wright, Thomas. "King James and the Witches of Lothian." *Ainsworth's Magazine* 10 (1846): 247–254.

Secondary Sources

Armitt, Lucie. *Fantasy*. New York: Routledge, 2020.

Bangley, Bernard. *Butler's Lives of the Saints*. Brewster, MA: Paraclete, 2005.

Barry, Jonathan, Owen Davies, and Cornelie Usborne, eds. *Cultures of Witchcraft in Europe from the Middle Ages to the Present*. London: Palgrave Macmillan, 2017.

Bennett, Tara. *The Making of Outlander: The Series*. New York: Random House, 2019.

Bernier, Olivier. *Louis XV*. Tokyo: New Word City, 2018.

Bilby, Kenneth. *True-Born Maroons*. Gainesville, FL: University Press of Florida, 2008.

Black, George F. *Surnames of Scotland*. Brighton, UK: Churchill & Dunn, 2015.

Borman, Tracy. *Witches: James I and the English Witch Hunts*. New York: Vintage, 2014.

Brown, Ian. *Performing Scottishness: Enactment and National Identities*. London: Palgrave Macmillan, 2020.

Butler, Lindley S. "Stede Bonnet." *South Carolina Encyclopedia*. Charleston: University of South Carolina, 2016.

Buxton, Ian, and Paul S. Hughes. *The Science and Commerce of Whisky*. Cambridge, UK: Royal Society of Chemistry, 2014.

Byrne, Katherine, Julie Ann Taddeo, and James Leggott, eds. *Conflicting Masculinities: Men in Television Period Drama*. New York: Bloomsbury, 2018.

Carr-Gomm, Philip, and Stephanie Carr-Gomm. *The Druid Plant Oracle.* New York: St. Martin's Press, 2008.

Cavanaugh, Thomas Anthony. *Hippocrates' Oath and Asclepius' Snake: The Birth of the Medical Profession.* Oxford, UK: Oxford University Press, 2017.

Chopra, Ruma. *Almost Home: Maroons between Slavery and Freedom in Jamaica, Nova Scotia, and Sierra Leone.* New Haven, CT: Yale University Press, 2018.

Colvin, Howard. *Architecture and the After-life.* New Haven: Yale University Press, 1991.

Crosby, Janice C. *Cauldron of Changes: Feminist Spirituality in Fantastic Fiction.* Jefferson, NC: McFarland, 2000.

Cruickshank, Janet and Robert McColl Millar, eds. *Before the Storm.* Aberdeen, Scotland: Forum for Research on the Languages of Scotland and Ulster Triennial Meeting, Ayr, 2017.

Cruickshanks, Eveline, and Edward Corp. *The Stuart Court in Exile and the Jacobites.* London: Hambledon Press, 1995.

Duffy, Christopher. *The '45: Bonnie Prince Charlie and the Untold Story of the Jacobite Rising.* Columbus, OH: Phoenix, 2007.

Evans, Richard, ed. *Prophets and Profits: Ancient Divination and Its Reception.* New York: Routledge, 2017.

Fletcher, LuAnn McCracken, ed. *Literary Tourism and the British Isles: History, Imagination, and the Politics of Place.* Lanham, MD: Lexington Books, 2019.

Frankel, Valerie Estelle, ed. *Adoring Outlander: Essays on Fandom, Genre and the Female Audience.* Jefferson, NC: McFarland, 2016.

_____. *Outlander's Sassenachs: Essays on Gender, Race, Orientation and the Other in the Novels and Television Series.* Jefferson, NC: McFarland, 2016.

_____. *The Symbolism and Sources of Outlander.* Jefferson, NC: McFarland, 2015.

Fusick, Katherine. *Ladies in Rebellion: Women of the 1715 and 1745 Jacobite Risings.* Baltimore: University of Maryland, 2017.

Gehring, Abigail. *The Illustrated Encyclopedia of Natural Remedies.* New York: Skyhorse, 2020.

Gibson, Marion. *Rediscovering Renaissance Witchcraft.* New York: Routledge, 2017.

Gregor, Walter. *Notes on the Folk-Lore of the North-East of Scotland.* Sydney, Wales: Wentworth, 2019.

Gregory, E. David. *The Late Victorian Folksong Revival.* Lanham, MD: Rowman & Littlefield, 2010.

Harrod, Mary, and Katarzyna Paszkiewicz. *Women Do Genre in Film and Television.* New York: Routledge, 2017.

Heath, Mary. "Villains and Heroes: An Analysis of *Outlander's* Portrayal of Sexual Violence." Master's thesis, Arizona State University, 2019.

Hesse, David. *Warrior Dreams: Playing Scotsmen in Mainland Europe.* Manchester, UK: Manchester University Press, 2014.

Hilmes, Michele. *Network Nations: A Transnational History of British and American Broadcasting.* New York: Routledge, 2012.

Hobby, Blake, ed. *The Grotesque.* New York: Infobase, 2009.

Holder, Geoff. *The Jacobites and the Supernatural.* Stroud, UK: Amberley, 2010.

Hurry, Jamieson B. *Imhotep: The Egyptian Father of Medicine.* Clifton, NJ: African Tree Press, 2012.

Kline, Wendy. *Coming Home: How Midwives Changed Birth.* Oxford, UK: Oxford University Press, 2019.

Kobatchnik, Amnon. *Blood on the Stage, 1600 to 1800.* Lanham, MD: Rowman & Littlefield, 2017.

Lansky, Bruce. *100,000+ Baby Names.* New York: Da Capo, 2019.

Martinelli, Dario. *What You See Is What You Hear.* Cham, Switzerland: Springer, 2020.

Massie, Allan. *The Royal Stuarts: A History of the Family That Shaped Britain.* London: Thomas Dunne, 2011.

McAllister, Margaret, and Donna Lee Brien. *Paradoxes in Nurses' Identity, Culture and Image: The Shadow Side of Nursing.* Abingdon, UK: Routledge, 2020.

Merrens, Harry Roy. *Colonial North Carolina in the Eighteenth Century: A Study in Historical Geography.* Chapel Hill: University of North Carolina Press, 1964.

Mittel, Johannes. *Complex TV: The Poetics of Contemporary Television Storytelling.* New York: New York University Press, 2015.

Modleski, Tania. *Loving with a Vengeance: Mass Produced Fantasies.* New York: Routledge, 1982.

Mollenauer, Lynn Wood. *Strange Revelations: Magic, Poison, and Sacrilege in Louis XIV's France.* University Park: Pennsylvania State University Press, 2007.

Moseley, Rachel, Helen Wheatley, and Helen Wood. *Television for Women: New Directions.* London: Routledge, 2017.

Napton, Dani. *Scott's Novels and the Counter-Revolutionary Politics of Place.* Leiden, Holland: Brill, 2018.

Newark, Tim. *Highlander: The History of the Legendary Highland Soldier.* New York: Skyhorse, 2009.

Nicholas, Christy Jackson. *Stunning, Strange and Secret: A Guide to Hidden Scotland.* Meath, Ireland: Tirgearr, 2014.

Oates, Jonathan. *Battles of the Jacobite Rebellions: Killiecrankie to Culloden.* Havertown, PA: Pen and Sword Military, 2019.

Olson, Christopher J, and CarrieLynn D. Reinhard. *The Greatest Cult Television Shows of All Time.* Lanham, MD: Rowman & Littlefield, 2020.

Percy, Sarah. *Mercenaries: The History of a Norm in International Relations.* New York: Oxford University Press, 2007.

Picon, Guillaume. *Versailles: A Private Invitation.* Paris: Flammarion, 2018.

Pierce, Daniel S. *Tar Heel Lightnin'.* Chapel Hill: University of North Carolina Press, 2019.

Plank, Geoffrey. *Rebellion and Savagery: The Jacobite Rising of 1745 and the British Empire.* Philadelphia: University of Pennsylvania Press, 2015.

Radford, Mona A., and Edwin Radford. *Encyclopaedia of Superstitions*. New York: Home Farm Books, 2013.

Reynolds, William R. *The Cherokee Struggle to Maintain Identity in the 17th and 18th Centuries*. Jefferson, NC: McFarland, 2015.

Riding, Jacqueline. *Jacobites: A New History of the '45*. London: Bloomsbury, 2016.

Ross, Anne. *Folklore of the Scottish Highlands*. Stroud, UK: History Press, 2000.

Royle, Trevor. *Culloden*. New York: Pegasus, 2017.

Smith, Mark M. *Stono: Documenting and Interpreting a Southern Slave Revolt*. Columbia: University of South Carolina Press, 2005.

Snodgrass, Mary Ellen. *Civil Disobedience: An Encyclopedic History of Dissidence in the United States*. New York: Routledge, 2009.

_____. *World Clothing and Fashion*. New York: Routledge, 2015.

Stewart, Bruce E. *Redemption from Tyranny: Herman Husband's American Revolution*. Charlottesville: University of Virginia Press, 2020.

Stratton, Curtis H. *War Coin: A Brief History of Mercenaries and Their Impact on World History*. Privately published, 2019.

Streets, Heather. *Martial Races: The Military, Race and Masculinity in British Imperial Culture, 1857–1914*. Manchester, UK: Manchester University Press, 2011.

Swaminathan, Srividhya, and Steven W. Thomas. *The Cinematic Eighteenth Century*. New York: Routledge, 2017.

Tabrasham, C.J. *Scotland's Castles*. London: B.T. Batsford, 1997.

Tise, Larry E., and Jeffrey J. Crow. *New Voyages to Carolina: Reinterpreting North Carolina History*. Chapel Hill: University of North Carolina Press, 2017.

_____. *The Southern Experience in the American Revolution*. Chapel Hill: University of North Carolina Press, 1978.

Tomasson, Katherine, and Francis Buist. *Battles of the '45*. Rakuten, Japan: Pickle Partners Publishing, 2017.

Watson, Roderick. *The Literature of Scotland*. London: Macmillan International Higher Education, 2016.

Webster, Richard. *The Encyclopedia of Superstitions*. Woodbury, MN: 2008.

Whyte, Donald. *A Dictionary of Scottish Emigrants to the U.S.A.* Baltimore, MD: Genealogical Publishing, 1998.

Woodard, Colin. *The Republic of Pirates*. Orlando, FL: Houghton Mifflin, 2007.

Electronic Sources

"Cairns of Scotland." www.scotland.com/blog/cairns-of-scotland.

Carey, Meredith. "*Outlander* Filming Locations Around the World." www.cntraveler.com/gallery/outlander-filming-locations-around-the-world, January 27, 2019.

"Gosford House." www.thecastlesofscotland.co.uk/the-best-castles/stately-homes-and-mansions/gosford-house/.

"Greek Medicine." https://www.nlm.nih.gov/hmd/greek/greek_oath.html.

Macintyre, Alistair K. "The Macintyres and the 'Forty-Five." https://www.electricscotland.com/Webclans/m/macintyre45.pdf

McCreary, Bear. "*Outlander*: Return to Scotland." https://www.bearmccreary.com/#blog/blog/outlander-return-to-scotland/, July 19, 2016.

Norton, Rictor. "Popular Rage (Homophobia): The Gay Subculture in Georgian England" (16 August 2009), http://rictornorton.co.uk/eighteen/homophob.htm.

Peck, Ashlee. "*Outlander*'s Scottish History." *FamilyTree*, www.familytreemagazine.com/entertainment/26578/#.

"Sam Heughan Reveals Jamie's Season 3 Weapons." www.youtube.com/watch?v=Q01k-2SweAs, 5 September 2017.

Snodgrass, Charles. "Whisky: The Spirit of Scottish National Identity." https://www.thebottleimp.org.uk/wp-content/uploads/2017/08/TBI2016-Supplement-3-Whisky-The-Spirit-of-Scottish-National-Identity-Charles-Snodgrass.pdf, April 2016, 1–5.

Steinberg, Dawn. "How the Actors of 'Outlander' Got Cast." https://www.youtube.com/watch?v=hI5Ny69FWEg (2 June 2016).

"Versailles." http://en.chateauversailles.fr/discover/estate/palace.

Walbert, David. "Disease and Catastrophe." *Anchor*, https://www.ncpedia.org/anchor/disease-and-catastrophe.

Periodicals, Dissertations, and Chapters

Albiniak, Paige. "House of Tutor: Dialect Coach Brings Gaelic Authenticity to *Outlander*." *New York Post* (22 August 2014).

Alter, Alexandra. "A Best-Seller Again, after a Boost from TV." *New York Times* (3 October 2014).

Apperley, Tom. "Counterfactual Communities: Strategy Games, Paratexts and the Player's Experience of History." *Open Library of Humanities* 4 (2018): 1–22.

Avina, Alyssa. "*Outlander*: 10 Behind-the-Scenes Secrets You Never Knew about the Makeup." *ScreenRant* (7 October 2017).

_____. "*Outlander*: 10 Things That Are Historically Accurate (And 10 Things That Aren't)." *ScreenRant* (24 April 2019).

Baker, Sam. "Walter Scott: Smuggler and Excise Man." Ninth International Conference on Walter Scott, Laramie, Wyoming, 2011.

Bales, Brittany, "Viewing History Through a Lens: The Influence of Film on Historical Consciousness." Master's thesis, East Tennessee University, May 2020.

Barks, Brenna A. "From *Waverley* to *Outlander*: How Scottish Dress Became Everyone's Dress." *Fashion, Style & Popular Culture* 5:3 (2018): 373–388.

Beard, Ellen L. "Satire and Social Change: The Bard,

the Schoolmaster and the Drover." *Northern Scotland* 8:1 (2017): 1–21.

Bell, Bethan. "Burial at Sea." *BBC News* (19 December 2016).

Bell, Carrie. "*Outlander* Author Diana Gabaldon on the Season-One Finale, and What Changes to the Book Were Hard to Swallow." *Vulture* (1 June 2015).

_____. "'Outlander' Postmortem: All Hail King Louis XV!" *Yahoo Entertainment* (14 May 2016).

Bellas, Athena. "*Outlander*'s Tactile Caress: A Multisensory Romance." *Continuum* 33:5 (2019): 507–524.

Bénédic-Meyer, Diane. "La construction d'un tissage émotionnel au féminin dans la série *Outlander*." *TV/Series* 15 (2019).

Benson-Allott, Caetlin. "No Such Thing Not Yet: Questioning Television's Female Gaze." *Film Quarterly* 71:2 (2017): 65–71.

Bhuvad, Ariba. "*Outlander* Season 5, Episode 12 Recap: Never My Love." *Fansided* (11 May 2020).

Bianchi, Diana, and Adele D'Arcangelo. "Translating History or Romance? Historical Romantic Fiction and Its Translation in a Globalised Market." *Linguistics and Literature Studies* 3:5 (2015): 248–253.

Brigley Thompson, Zoë. "From Safe Spaces to Precarious Moments: Teaching Sexuality and Violence in the American Higher Education Classroom." *Gender and Education* 32:3 (2018): 1–17.

Brinson, Susan L. "TV Rape: Television's Communication of Cultural Attitudes toward Rape." *Women's Studies in Communication* 12:2 (February 2015): 23–36.

Bucksbaum, Sydney. "'Outlander' Producer Defends Graphic Rape Scene: 'We Wanted to Do It Justice,'" *Hollywood Reporter* (21 May 2016).

_____. "'Outlander' Team Breaks Down That Violent Act of Revenge and 'Powerful' Scene Viewers Didn't See." *Hollywood Reporter* (18 June 2016).

_____. "'Outlander' Team Talks Black Jack's 'Chilling' Moment of Rage, Mary's Loss and Claire's Redemption." *Hollywood Reporter* (25 June 2016).

Burnard, Trevor, and Kenneth Morgan. "The Dynamics of the Slave Market and Slave Purchasing Patterns in Jamaica, 1655–1788." *William and Mary Quarterly* 58:1a (January 2001): 205–228.

Burt, Kayti. "*Outlander*: Does Jamie Die in the Books?" *Den of Geek* (20 April 2020).

_____. "*Outlander* Season 4 Episode 1 Review: America the Beautiful." *Den of Geek* (5 November 2018).

_____. "*Outlander* Season 5 Ending Explained." *Den of Geek* (10 May 2020).

_____. "*Outlander*: La Dame Blanche Review." *Den of Geek* (1 May 2016).

Byrne, Katherine, and Julie Anne Taddeo. "Calling #TimesUp on the TV Period Drama Rape Narrative." *Critical Studies in Television* 14:3 (September 2019): 379–398.

Byrne-Cristiano, Laura. "'Outlander' Season 1, Part 2: Superfans Talk Must Haves." *Hypable* (31 March 2015).

Carey, Meredith. "*Outlander* Filming Locations around the World." *Conde Nast Traveler* (27 January 2019).

Carlton, Genevieve. "What 'Outlander' Didn't Tell You about Scottish Witchcraft." *Ranker* (16 May 2018).

Carpenter, Perry. "Why 'Outlander' Season 5 Needs To Include More Steamy Scenes Between Jamie And Claire." *Showbiz Cheatsheet* (7 August 2019).

Carr, Flora. "Meet the Cast of *Outlander* Series Five Including the Witcher Star." *RadioTimes* (13 March 2020).

Cateridge, James. "What If Your Future Was the Past?" *International Journal of Scottish Theatre and Screen* 11:1 (2018): 67–83.

Charlier, Marlène. "La représentation des mythes et légendes dans la série *Outlander*." Master's thesis, Université de Franche-Comté, 2019.

"Claire Fraser Becomes a Doctor: Medical Education and Developments from 18th Century Scotland to 20th Century America." *LordsLadiesandLore* (2018).

Cliffe, Nicole. "*Outlander* Recap: Indecent Proposal." *Vulture* (1 October 2017).

Cohn, Paulette. "Author Diana Gabaldon Reveals Why the Death on Tonight's *Outlander* Is a 'Turning Point' for Jamie." *Parade* (29 March 2020).

_____. "Jamie Faces Death in This Week's *Outlander*—Diana Gabaldon Discusses the Episode's Symbolic Role Reversals." *Parade* (19 April 2020).

_____. "*Outlander*'s Jamie and Claire Just Rejected Their Last Chance to Raise a Child Together—Diana Gabaldon Explains Why." *Parade* (8 March 2020).

Coleman, Tyrese. "How Outlander Has Avoided the Stereotypes of Its Source Material." *BuzzFeed News* (22 October 2017).

Cornelius, Jim. "The Doom of the Clans." *Frontier Partisans* (16 April 2016).

Coventry, Laura. "*Outlander* Costumes—Jamie's Jacobite Style." *Scots Magazine* (1 March 2019).

Crawford, Amy. "The Gentleman Pirate." *Smithsonian* (31 July 2007).

Crouch, David. "Places around Us: Embodied Lay Geographies in Leisure and Tourism." *Leisure Studies* 19:2 (2002): 63–76.

Crumlish, Callum. "*Outlander* Season 5: Jamie Fraser Star Sam Heughan Speaks Out on Show Ending 'We'll See,'" *Express* (11 November 2019).

_____. "*Outlander* Season 5: Star Reveals Which Death Shocked the Entire Crew—'Oh S**t,'" *Express* (26 October 2019).

Danilova, Nataliya, and Kandida Purnell. "The 'Museumification' of the Scottish Soldier and the Meaning-Making of Britain's Wars." *Critical Military Studies* 5:2 (2019): 1–19.

Dash, Mike. "The Trial That Gave Vodou a Bad Name." *Smithsonian* (29 May 2013).

Davis, Sherri Sutton. "The Heroic Journey in *Outlander*: Tracing the Mythic Path." Ph.D. dissertation, Fayetteville State University, 2005.

Deanie, Marc. "Referendum Riddle Over Hit Series UK No-Show." *The* (London) *Sun* (14 August 2014).

Debnath, Neela. "*Outlander*: Did Frank Randall

Believe Claire's Time Travel Story?" *Express* (30 October 2019).

_____. "*Outlander*: How Are Frank Randall and Black Jack Related?" *Express* (19 November 2019).

_____. "*Outlander*: How Did Ian Murray Lose His Leg? The Heartbreaking Story." *Express* (5 November 2019).

_____. "*Outlander*: What Happened to Brian Fraser? Tragic Backstory Explained." *Express* (12 November 2019).

_____. "*Outlander*: What Happened to Ellen Fraser? The Tragic Backstory of Jamie's Mother." *Express* (7 November 2019).

Del Mar Rubio-Hernández, María, and Irene Raya Bravo. "The Erotization of the Male Body in Television Fiction: *Outlander* as a Case Study." *Océanide* 10 (2018): 1–9.

Delgado, A.J. "*Outlander* Slams Christianity." *National Review* (8 September 2014).

Derakhshani, Tirdad. "'Outlander' Highland Fling." *Philadelphia Inquirer* (17 August 2014): C5.

Desowitz, Bill. "'Outlander' Season 2: How Designers Nailed the Glam 18th Century Paris Look (Emmy Watch)." *IndieWire* (22 April 2016).

Devine, Thomas M. "La nation écossaise s'est construite dans la lutte contre l'angleterre." *L'Histoire* 2:468 (2020): 13–23.

Dibdin, Emma. "*Outlander* Season 5 Will Have a Lot More 'Intimacy and Passion' Between Jamie & Claire." *Elle* (24 January 2020).

_____. "*Outlander*'s Governor Tryon Was a Very Real Person Set on Stopping the Regulator Movement." *Town&Country* (17 February 2020).

Donahue, Jennifer. "The Ghost of Annie Palmer: Give a Voice to Jamaica's 'White Witch of Rose Hall,'" *Journal of Commonwealth Literature* 49:2 (2014): 243–256.

Donelan, Carol. "'Sing Me a Song of a Lass That Is Gone': Myth and Meaning in the Starz Original Series *Outlander*." *Quarterly Review of Film and Video* 35:1 (2018): 31–53.

Donnelly, Laura. "The Disappearing of Clan Murray." *Outlander Locations* (11 September 2019).

Donvito, Tina. "Obsessed with the *Outlander* Theme Song? Here's Why It's So Special, Especially Season 5's Version." *Parade* (23 March 2020).

Doran, Sarah. "How Outlander Fans Helped Diana Gabaldon Change the TV Portrayal of Jamie Fraser's Assault." *Radio Times* (1 June 2017).

Dossena, Marina. "The Prince and the Sassenach." *Reference and Identity in Public Discourses* 306 (2019): 43–66.

Dowling, Amber. "'Outlander' Review: A Female Character Stays Afloat in a Sea of Masculine Energy in Episode 10." *IndieWire* (26 April 2020).

_____. "'Outlander' Review: A Season 5 Wedding Sets Up All Kinds of Family Drama." *IndieWire* (14 February 2020).

_____. "'Outlander' Review: Claire and Jamie Rush Through Jamaica in a Semi-Repetitive Storyline." *IndieWire* (3 December 2017).

_____. "'Outlander' Review: Tumultuous Waters Rip Claire and Jamie Apart." *IndieWire* (19 November 2017).

Dresbach, Terry. "*Outlander* Secrets, Part 10: The Big, Big Problem with Jamie's Kilt." *Elle* (10 June 2016).

DuPlessis, Nicole M. "Men, Women and Birth Control in the Early *Outlander* Books." *Outlander's Sassenachs: Essays on Gender, Race, Orientation and the Other in the Novels and Television Series.* Jefferson, NC: McFarland, 2016, 82–96.

EllenandJim. "*Outlander*, Season 4, from *Drums of Autumn*: The Colonialist American Past, a Book of Fathers & Ghosts." *EllenandJim* (10 February 2019).

Eringaard, Charlene. "Dinna Fash Yourself, Sassenach: Dialect Translation in *Outlander*." Master's thesis, Leiden University, 2019.

Faircloth, Kelly. "*Outlander*: Damn This Show Took a Dark Turn." *The Muse* (18 May 2015).

Ferguson, Brian. "London gets Scots makeover for *Outlander* Premiere." *Scotsman* (10 March 2015).

_____. "*Outlander* Success Belies Lack of Investment." *Scotsman* (1 February 2015).

Fletcher, LuAnn McCracken. "'Scott-land' and *Outlander*: Inventing Scotland for Armchair Tourists." *Literary Tourism and the British Isles: History, Imagination, and the Politics of Place.* Lanham, MD: Lexington Books, 2019, 191–220.

Frankel, Valerie Estelle. "Being Lord John: Homosexual Life in Georgian London." *Outlander's Sassenachs: Essays on Gender, Race, Orientation and the Other in the Novels and Television Series.* Jefferson, NC: McFarland, 2016, 68–81.

Fremont, Maggie. "*Outlander* Recap: Operating Theater." *Vulture* (23 December 2018).

_____. "*Outlander* Season Premier Recap: Take a Vow." *Vulture* (14 February 2020).

Fretts, Bruce. "Behind 'Outlander,' on Starz, True Hearts in the Highlands." *New York Times* (16 April 2015): 18.

_____. "'Outlander' Costume Designer Terry Dresbach on 8 Memorable Outfits." *New York Times* (15 April 2015).

_____. "The 'Outlander' Show Runner, Ron Moore, on That Harrowing Season Finale." *New York Times* (30 May 2015).

Gallagher, Caitlin. "Jamie & Claire Sail to Jamaica on 'Outlander,' Exposing Sexist Superstitions That Keep Women Down." *Bustle* (12 November 2017).

Galle, Jillian E., Elizabeth Bollwerk, and Fraser D. Neiman. "The Digital Archaeological Archive of Comparative Slavery." *Monticello Department of Archaeology,* 2007.

Garfinkle, Robert A. "The Moon in Mankind's History and Lore." *Luna Cognita.* New York: Springer, 2020, 1–50.

Gavin, Anne. "Fairies, Folklore, Witchcraft & Waterhorses—The Symbolism & Superstitions of *Outlander*." *Outlander Cast* (25 October 2016).

_____. "Freedom & Whisky—The Real Story behind *Outlander*'s Episode 3.05 Title." *Outlander Cast* (10 October 2017).

_____. "Outlandish Locations: A Look at Midhope Castle—*Outlander*'s Lallybroch." *Outlander Cast* (17 April 2019).

_____. "The Ultimate Ranking of *Outlander* Season 4 Episodes." *Outlander Cast* (13 March 2019).

Gilje, Paul A. *To Swear Like a Sailor: Maritime Culture in America, 1750–1850.* Cambridge, UK: Cambridge University Press, 2016.

Gold, John R., and Margaret M. Gold. "The Graves of the Gallant Highlanders." *History & Memory* 19:1 (Spring/Summer 2007): 5–38.

Goodman, Gemma, and Rachel Moseley. "*Outlander*: Body as Contested Territory." *Conflicting Masculinities: Men in Television Period Drama.* New York: Bloomsbury, 2018.

Gopaldas, Reshma. "*Outlander* 'Perpetual Adoration' Recap: Jamie and Claire, Penicillin, Murder & a Cat." *Entertainment Weekly* (15 March 2020).

_____. "*Outlander* Season 5 Finale Recap: In 'Never My Love' Claire Struggles to Survive and *Outlander* Breaks Us." *sheknows* (10 May 2020).

Gordon, Diane. "'Outlander' Recap: 'Of Lost Things' Introduces the Dunsanys, Another Child for Jamie and a New Love Story." *Variety* (1 October 2017).

_____. "'Outlander' Recap: Claire Encounters a Face from the Past in 'The Bakra.'" *Variety* (3 December 2017).

Greenberg, Stephen J. "Claire Fraser, RN, MD, OMG: History of Medicine in the *Outlander* Novels and Series." *Journal of the Medical Library Association* 108:2 (April, 2020): 310–313.

Gurung, Regina. "'Outlander' Season 4 Episode 4: Alarming Prophecy Suggests a Vulnerable Character May Soon Die." *Entertainment Weekly* (27 November 2018).

Hågbäck, Moa. "[..] If Only You Behaved Like the Loyal British Subjects You're Supposed to Be: National Identities and the Function of the Past in Starz's *Outlander*." Master's thesis, Linnaeus University, 2019.

Hahn, Kate. "How *Outlander* Is Taking the Art of Love (and War) to Paris in Season 2." *TV Insider* (29 March 2016).

Hallemann, Caroline. "Everything We Know So Far about *Outlander* Season 5." *Town & Country* (2 January 2020).

_____. "How *Outlander* Created a Whole New Breed of Superfan." *Town & Country* (7 February 2020).

_____. "Is *Outlander*'s Fraser's Ridge a Real Place?" *Town & Country* (11 February 2010).

_____. "*Outlander* Author Diana Gabaldon Sees Claire's New Ring as the Show's Way of 'Apologizing,' to Readers." *Town & Country* (10 December 2018).

_____. "*Outlander*'s Caitriona Balfe Shares a Rare Behind-the-Scenes Video of Sam Heughan." *Town & Country* (23 April 2020).

_____. "*Outlander*'s Terry Dresbach on the 'Terrifying' Challenge of Designing This Season's Native American Costumes." *Town&Country* (25 November 2018).

_____. "See the First Photo of Sam Heughan Introducing *Outlander*'s Newest Furry Cast Member, ADSO." *Town & Country* (24 May 2019).

Herrera, Hannah. "Shifting Spaces and Constant Patriarchy: The Characterizations of Offred and Claire in *The Handmaid's Tale* and *Outlander*." *Zeitschrift für Anglistik und Amerikanistik* 67:2 (2019): 181–196.

Hess, Amanda "How Movies and TV Address Rape and Revenge." *New York Times* (14 January 2017): AR1.

Hill, Libby. "'Outlander' Recap: Claire and Jamie Play God, Poorly." *Los Angeles Times* (7 May 2016).

_____. "'Outlander' Season 1 Finale Recap: Jamie Is Broken." *New York Times* (30 May 2015).

Hix, Lisa. "True Kilts: Debunking the Myths about Highlanders and Clan Tartans." *Collectors Weekly* (15 November 2017).

Hoffman, Courtney A. "How to Be a Woman in the Highlands: A Feminist Portrayal of Scotland in *Outlander*." *The Cinematic Eighteenth Century.* New York: Routledge, 2017, 103–117.

Hughes, Roxanne. "*Outlander*: Diana Gabaldon Shocks Fans with ALARMING Jamie Fraser Reveal." *Express* (18 September 2019).

Hughes, Sarah. "Highland Flings and Time Travel: Have You Been Watching *Outlander*?" *Guardian* (20 May 2015).

Hurley, Laura. "Is *Outlander* Finally Going to Burn Fraser's Ridge in Season 5 Finale?" *CinemaBlend* (3 May 2020).

Ingham, Alexandria. "Explaining Murtagh's Change of Character in *Outlander* Season 5." *Claire&Jamie* (March 2020).

_____. "*Outlander* Season 5: Who Is Lionel Brown in 'The Fiery Cross?,'" *Claire&Jamie* (December 2019).

Javaid, Aliraza. "Feminism, Masculinity and Male Rape: Bringing Male Rape 'Out of the Closet,'" *Journal of Gender Studies* 25:3 (2016): 283–293.

Jean-Philippe, McKenzie. "*Outlander*'s Theme Song 'The Skye Boat Song' Was Changed Again for Season 5." *Oprah Magazine* (18 February 2020).

Jeggle, Utz. "A Lost Track: On the Unconscious in Folklore." *Journal of Folklore Research* 40:1 (2003): 73–93.

Jones, Michelle L. "Linked.. through the Body of One Man: Black Jack Randall as a Non-Traditional Romance Villain." *Adoring Outlander: Essays on Fandom, Genre and the Female Audience.* Jefferson, NC: McFarland, 2016, 71–81.

Jones, Trahern, and Lindsay Jones. "A Tour of Old Parisian Hospitals." *Student Hospitalist* (March 2012).

Karda, Ni, and Made Fany Renjana. "The Exposures of Scottish Culture in Diana Gabaldon's *Outlander*." *Jurnal Ilmiah Mahasiswa FIB* 1:4 (2015).

Keen, Suzanne. "Probable Impossibilities: Historical Romance Readers Talk Back." *Style* 52:1 (2018): 127–132.

Kennedy, Victoria. "The Way We Were: Nostalgia, Romance and Anti-Feminism." *Outlander's Sassenachs: Essays on Gender, Race, Orientation and the Other in the Novels and Television Series.* Jefferson, NC: McFarland, 2016, 117–129.

Kissell, Rick. "Ratings: Starz Drama 'Outlander' Returns Twice as Big as Series Premiere." *Variety* (12 April 2016).

Kosin, Julie. "*Outlander* Season 3 Episode 9: Jamie & Claire Are Separated Again." *Bazaar* (12 November 2017).

_____. "Sam Heughan on *Outlander*'s Devastating Double Loss." *Elle* (30 March 2020).

Lagerwey, Jorie. "The Feminist *Game of Thrones: Outlander* and Gendered Discourses of TV Genre." *Women Do Genre in Film and Television.* London: Routledge, 2017, 198–212.

Larson, Mary. "A Brief History of Nursing and Diana's Impressive Choices for Claire." *Outlander Cast* (1 September 2015).

Lash, Jolie. "'Outlander' Stars Dive into That Season 5 Wedding and Fiery Cross Scene." *Hollywood Reporter* (16 February 2020).

Lawson, Richard. "*Outlander* Is as Odd and Enveloping as Ever in Season 2." *Vanity Fair* (8 April 2016).

Leach, Yvonne D. "*Outlander* from Book to Screen: Power in Gender." *Outlander's Sassenachs: Essays on Gender, Race, Orientation and the Other in the Novels and Television Series.* Jefferson, NC: McFarland, 2016, 130–152.

Leeds, Sarene. "'Outlander' Season 3 Premiere: One Relationship Ends in a Sexually Charged Duel." *MarketWatch* (10 September 2017).

Leigh, Devin. "The Origins of a Source: Edward Long, Coromantee Slave Revolts and the History of Jamaica." *Slavery & Abolition* 40:2 (2019): 295–320.

Lenker, Maureen Lee. "*Outlander* Recap: Is It the American Dream or Nightmare?" *Entertainment Weekly* (4 November 2018).

LeSavage, Halie. "Sam Heughan Explains Jamie and Claire's 'Most Intimate' *Outlander* Moment Yet." *Glamour* (20 April 2020).

Levene, Dan. "A Port for Thieves—The Historical Fiction of Golden Age Piracy." Master's thesis, London South Bank University, 2019.

Lopez, Araceli R. "Gazing at Jamie Fraser." *Outlander's Sassenachs: Essays on Gender, Race, Orientation and the Other in the Novels and Television Series.* Jefferson, NC: McFarland, 2016, 44–53.

López-Cordero, Ivette M. "A Walk through the Standing Stones: The Historical Novel, Gender and the Supernatural in Diana Gabaldon's *Outlander*." Master's thesis, University of Puerto Rico at Mayaguez, 2019.

Lutkin, Aimee. "Here's a Study of Sexual Violence in TV and Movies." *Jezebel* (17 October 2017).

MacLean, Coinneach. "The 'Tourist Gaze' on Gaelic Scotland." PhD thesis, University of Glasgow, 2014.

MacLean, Diane. "Gaelic Television: Building Bricks Without Straw." *International Journal of ScottishTheatre and Screen* 11:1 (2018): 6–28.

Macon, Alexandra. "An Exclusive First Look at Brianna and Roger's Huge *Outlander* Wedding." *Vogue* (7 February 2020).

Mailman, Erika. "The Popular Book and TV Series 'Outlander' Is Increasing Travel to These Scottish Sites." *Washington Post* (15 February 2020).

Mair, George. "Scottish Castle Doubles for Magnificent Palace of Versailles Gardens." *Express* (28 October 2016).

Martinelli, Marissa. "How *Outlander* Keeps Getting Tangled Up in Real-Life U.K. Politics." *Browbeat* (14 July 2016).

Mitchell, Hilary. "14 Scottish Places All 'Outlander' Fans Must Visit." *BuzzFeed* (21 May 2015).

Moxey, Sarah. "Review: A Global Force." *Scottish Affairs* 27:2 (2018): 262–265.

Murillo, Stella. "Half-Ghosts and Their Legacy for Claire, Jamie and Roger." *Adoring Outlander: Essays on Fandom, Genre and the Female Audience.* Jefferson, NC: McFarland, 2016, 144–161.

Murphy, Shaunna. "'Outlander' Just Broke the Mold with Jamie's Sexual Assault: Here's Why,'" *MTV News* (30 May 2015).

Nagouse, Emma. "The Lamentation of Jamie Fraser: *Outlander,* Male Rape and an Intertextual Reading of Lamentations 3." *The Shiloh Project* (11 September 2017).

_____. "'To Ransom a Man's Soul': Male Rape and Gender Identity in *Outlander* and 'The Suffering Man' of Lamentations 3." *Rape Culture, Gender Violence, and Religion.* London: Palgrave Macmillan, 2018, 143–158.

Neill, Anna. "Buccaneer Ethnography: Nature, Culture, and Nation in the Journals of William Dampier." *Eighteenth-Century Studies* 33:2 (Winter 2000): 165–180.

Nicolaou, Elena. "The True Story of the North Carolina Regulators Seen in *Outlander* Season 5." *Oprah Magazine* (17 February 2020).

_____. "What Diana Gabaldon's *The Fiery Cross* Tells Us about *Outlander* Season 5." *Oprah Magazine* (16 February 2020).

Noorda, Rachel. "From *Waverley* to *Outlander*: Reinforcing Scottish Diasporic Identity through Book Consumption." *National Identities* 20:4 (2018): 361–377.

Nurczynski, Melissa Anne. "Fortune Favors the Brave." Master's thesis, University of Texas at El Paso, 2019.

Nussbaum, Emily "Out of Time: Remaking History on 'Outlander' and 'The Americans,'" *New Yorker* (11 April 2016).

Nwaubani, Adobe Tricia. "When the Slave Traders Were African." *Wall Street Journal* (20 September 2019).

Obey, Erica. "Tall, Dark, and a Long Time Dead: Epistemology, Time Travel, and the Bodice-Ripper." *Worlds Enough and Time: Explorations of Time in Science Fiction and Fantasy.* Westport, CT: Greenwood, 2002, 157–166.

Ormond, Melissa. "Gender, Fantasy, and Empowerment in Diana Gabaldon's *Outlander*." Master's thesis, DePaul University, 2009.

Osborne, Kristin O'Neill. "This Noble Ruin: Doune Castle's Relationship to Popular Culture and Heritage." Dissertation, Ohio University, 2018.

"*Outlander*'s Depiction of Bonnie Prince Charlie 'a Travesty,'" *Scotsman* (13 February 2019).

Paoletti, Ciro. "The Battle of Culloden: A Pivotal Moment in World History." *Journal of Military History* 81:1 (2017).

Parker, Emily. "*Outlander,* Season 3, Episode 10—'Heaven and Earth,'" *Sweatpants & Coffee* (21 November 2017).

Paterson, Laura. "Executing Scottish Witches." *Scottish Witches and Witch-Hunters.* London: Palgrave Macmillan, 2013, 196–214.

Pera, Mariam "An Interview with Diana Gabaldon." *American Libraries* (8 January 2015): 20–21.

Perkins, Claire, and Constantine Verevis. "Transnational Television Remakes." *Continuum* 29 (2015): 677–683.

Phillips, Jennifer A. "Jamie's 'Others': Complicating Masculinity and Heroism through His Foils." *Outlander's Sassenachs: Essays on Gender, Race, Orientation and the Other in the Novels and Television Series.* Jefferson, NC: McFarland, 2016, 54–67.

Pittock, Murray. "Arran Johnston, 'On Gladsmuir Shall the Battle Be! The Battle of Prestonpans 1745,'" *British Journal for Military History* 5:1 (2019): 73–75.

Pollard, Tony. "Shooting Arrows." *Writing Battles: New Perspectives on Warfare and Memory in Medieval Europe.* New York: Bloomsbury, 2020, 177.

Poniewozik, James "*Outlander* Is Many Kinds of Show, All in One Kilt." *Time* (2014): 1.

Potter, Mary-Anne. "'Everything and Nothing': Liminality in Diana Gabaldon's *Outlander.*" *Interdisciplinary Literary Studies* 21:3 (2019): 282–296.

Prescott, Amanda-Rae. "*Outlander* Season 5 Episode 11 Review: Journeycake." *Den of Geek* (3 May 2020).

_____. "*Outlander* Season 5 Episode 6 Review: Better to Marry Than to Burn." *Den of Geek* (22 March 2020).

Prudom, Laura. "'Outlander' Finale: Ron Moore on Tackling Rape Scenes Truthfully." *Variety* (30 May 2015).

_____. "'Outlander' Postmortem: The Past Catches Up to Jamie at Lallybroch." *Variety* (25 April 2015).

_____. "'Outlander' Recap: Sam Heughan Breaks Down the Victories and Losses of 'Prestonpans,'" *Variety* (11 June 2016).

_____. "'Outlander' Stars Break Down Claire and Jamie's First Fight, That Spanking Scene." *Variety* (5 April 2015).

_____. "'Outlander' Stars Break Down the Desperate Deals of 'The Hail Mary,'" *Variety* (25 June 2016).

_____. "'Outlander' Stars on 'Surprising' Season 2 Twists, Parisian Politics and Changing History." *Variety* (8 January 2016).

_____. "Starz's 'Outlander' Woos Women with Strong Female Protagonist." *Variety* (7 August 2014).

Radish, Christina. "*Outlander* PaleyFest Interview: Caitriona Balfe, Tobias Menzies, Ronald D. Moore, and More." *Collider* (14 March 2015).

_____. "Sam Heughan Talks 'Outlander' Season 5, What's Next for the Frasers, and His 'Bloodshot' Role." *Collider* (16 February 2020).

Raterink, Eline. "The '*Outlander*-effect' on Social Media: Screen Tourists' Perceptions of Scottish Cultural Heritage Sites." Master's thesis, Radboud University, 2019.

Reiher, Andrea. "'Outlander' EPs Break Down Claire's 'Survival Mechanism' in Season 5 Finale." *Variety* (10 May 2020).

_____. "'Outlander' Recap: 'Perpetual Adoration' Slows Season 5 Action Down." *Variety* (15 March 2020).

_____. "'Outlander' Recap: 'The Company We Keep' Finds Jamie and Claire Caught in Brown Family Drama." *Variety* (8 March 2020).

_____. "'Outlander' Recap: Why Jocasta Feels It Is 'Better to Marry Than Burn,'" *Variety* (22 March 2020).

_____. "'Outlander' Season 4 Premiere Recap: Jamie and Claire Meet 'America the Beautiful,'" *Variety* (4 November 2018).

Rice, Lynette. "Maria Doyle Kennedy on Jocasta rejecting Murtagh on *Outlander*: 'Devastating,'" *Entertainment Weekly* (22 March 2020).

Robertson, Calum. "Celebrating a Scottish Past: Construction, Contestation and the Role of Government." *World Archaeology* 50:1 (2018): 337–346.

Robinson, Joanna. "*Outlander* Continues to Struggle with Its Biggest Challenge in Season 4." *Vanity Fair* (14 January 2019).

_____. "*Outlander* Star Sam Heughan on Jamie's Devastating Loss." *Vanity Fair* (30 March 2020).

_____. "*Outlander*: The Surprising Inspiration Behind That Dazzling, Show-Invented Bath Scene." *Vanity Fair* (4 December 2017).

_____. "*Outlander*'s Thanksgiving Episode Gives the Book's Native Americans a Much-Needed Update." *Vanity Fair* (26 November 2018).

Roblou, Y. "Complex Masculinities: The Superhero in Modern American Movies." *Culture, Society & Masculinities* 4:1 (2012): 76–91.

Roots, Kimberly. "*Outlander*'s [Spoiler] Breaks Down the Scene That Nearly Made His Corpse Cry." *TVLine* (29 March 2020).

Rumburg, Delilah "How TV Can Help Improve Our Understanding of Sexual Violence." *Time* (22 September 2016).

Ryan, Maureen. "'Outlander' Boss Ron Moore on Eliciting Emotional Response, Season 2 and Surprising Storytelling." *Variety* (3 May 2016).

Salto, Cattia. "*Outlander*: Dance of the Druids." *Terre Celtiche* (1 April 2018).

_____. "*Outlander*: Wool Waulking Songs." *Terre Celtiche* (11 April 2018).

Shacklock, Zoë. "On (Not) Watching *Outlander* in the United Kingdom." *Visual Culture in Britain* 17:3 (2016): 311–328.

Sharpe, Victoria. "The Goddess Restored." *Journal of the Fantastic in the Arts* 9:1 (1998): 36–45.

"Sir Francis Drake's Body 'Close to Being Found off Panama,'" *BBC News* (25 October 2011).

Solis, Sandi. "Culloden and Wounded Knee: Genocide, Identity and Cultural Survival." *Outlander's Sassenachs: Essays on Gender, Race, Orientation and the Other in the Novels and Television Series.* Jefferson, NC: McFarland, 2016, 17–29.

_____. "The Good, the Bad and Lord John Grey:

Observations on Desire, Sex, Violence, Lust, and Love." *Adoring Outlander: Essays on Fandom, Genre and the Female Audience.* Jefferson, NC: McFarland, 2016, 82–93.

Stegall, Sarah. "The Beaton: Healing as Empowerment for Claire Beauchamp." *Outlander's Sassenachs: Essays on Gender, Race, Orientation and the Other in the Novels and Television Series.* Jefferson, NC: McFarland, 2016, 97–104.

Stewart, Malcolm. "The Decline of Scottish Clans." *The Corvette* 3:2 (2016): 7–22.

Still, Jennifer. "'Outlander' Season 5 Finale Recap: 'Never My Love,'" *Decider* (11 May 2020).

Strachan, Hew. "Scotland's Military Identity." *Scottish Historical Review* 85:2 (2007): 315–332.

Swaminathan, Srividhya, and Steven W. Thomas. "How to Be a Woman in the Highlands: A Feminist Portrayal of Scotland in *Outlander*." *The Cinematic Eighteenth Century.* New York: Routledge, 2017, 113–127.

Terrero, Nina. "'Outlander' Costume Designer Dishes on Those Dazzling Clothes." *Entertainment Weekly* (2 April 2015).

Tracy. "Episode 412: Providence." *Outcandour* (20 January 2019).

Trendacosta, Katharine. "Is the UK Missing Out on *Outlander* Because of the Scottish Referendum?" *Gizmodo* (18 September 2014).

Tryon Palace Commission. *Tryon Palace.* Charleston, SC: Arcadia, 2015.

Upadhyaya, Kayla Kumari. "*Outlander* Bungles the Conflict in 'Savages,'" *AVClub* (2 December 2018).

_____. "*Outlander* Peddles a White Savior Narrative in Jamaica." *AVClub* (3 December 2017).

_____. "*Outlander*'s Alchemy Remains Spectacular in Its Hotly Anticipated Return." *AVClub* (4 November 2018).

Valentine, Genevieve. "'Outlander' Season 3, Episode 11: The Most Unlikely Places." *New York Times* (26 November 2017).

_____. "'Outlander' Season 3, Episode 9: Sailing Takes Them Away." *New York Times* (12 November 2017).

_____. "'Outlander' Season 4, Episode 2 Recap: Southern Hospitality." *New York Times* (11 November 2018).

_____. "'Outlander' Season 4, Episode 9: Fraser Hospitality." *New York Times* (31 December 2018).

_____. "'Outlander' Season 4, Premiere Recap: No Good Deed Unpunished." *New York Times* (4 November 2018).

_____. "'Outlander,' Season 4, Episode 3 Recap: Mysterious Encounters." *New York Times* (18 November 2018).

Villarreal, Yvonne. "As Jamie Fraser in 'Outlander,' Sam Heughan Was Destined to Live in Grief." *Los Angeles Times* (20 March 2018).

Vincenty, Samantha. "Everything We Know about *Outlander* Season 5." *Oprah Magazine* (7 February 2020).

_____. "The *Outlander* Cast Tells Us What to Expect from Season 5." *Oprah Magazine* (10 February 2020).

_____. "The True Story Behind *Outlander*'s Villainous Governor Tryon." *Oprah Magazine* (17 February 2020).

Vineyard, Jennifer. "Actor Tobias Menzies on the 'Outlander' Death We All Knew Was Coming." *New York Times* (25 September 2017).

_____. "Have a Compelling Story, Will Travel." *New York Times* (3 November 2018: C6).

_____. "How *Outlander* Made Those Sea Journeys Feel So Incredibly Real." *Elle* (28 November 2017).

_____. "How *Outlander*'s Revenge Scene Came Together." *Vulture* (19 June 2016).

_____. "How *Outlander*'s Star Chamber Came Together." *New York* (23 May 2016).

_____. "'Outlander' Finally Unveiled Jamie's Big Secret. Here's How the Writers Did It." *New York Times* (5 November 2017).

_____. "'Outlander' Season 4 Is Nigh. Here's What to Remember." *New York Times* (2 November 2018).

_____. "'Outlander' Takes Manhattan." *New York Times* (2 November 2018).

_____. "What to Remember before the 'Outlander' Season 3 Premiere." *New York Times* (8 September 2017).

Virtue, Graeme. "*Outlander*: 'Game of Thrones Helped Open the Door for Us,'" *Guardian* (21 March 2015).

Vogels, Nina. "The Time Traveler as 'Outlander,'" bachelor's thesis, Utrecht University, 2018.

Waard, Jolien de. "Adapting Claire's Feminist Beliefs and Female Agency: A Comparison Between the First *Outlander* Novel and Its Television Adaptation." bachelor's thesis, Utrecht University, 2018.

Walker, Eilidh. "*Outlander* Wins Two People's Choice Awards." *Creative Scotland* (8 January 2016).

Walker-Arnott, Ellie. "*Outlander* Season Two: Who Is La Dame Blanche?" *RadioTimes* (1 May 2016).

Watson, Alan D. "A Consideration of European Indentured Servitude in Colonial North Carolina." *North Carolina Historical Review* 91:4 (October 2014): 381–406.

Weaver, Nicole. "Why 'Outlander' Doesn't Have Americans Playing Cherokee and Mohawk Characters." *Showbiz CheatSheet* (6 October 2018).

Webb, Claire. "Discover the Real Castle Leoch and Outlander's Stunning Scottish Locations." *RadioTimes* (29 June 2017).

Weekes, Princess. "The Problem of *Outlander*'s Historical Narrative." *The Mary Sue* (8 October 2018).

West, Kelly. "*Outlander*'s Diana Gabaldon on Setting World War II as Claire's Backstory." *Cinemablend* (29 July 2014).

Wilkinson, Amy. "*Outlander* Recap: Castle Leoch." *Entertainment Weekly* (17 August 2014).

_____. "'Outlander' Recap: 'Lallybroch,'" *Entertainment Weekly* (26 April 2015).

_____. "'Outlander' Recap: 'The Watch,'" *Entertainment Weekly* (3 May 2015).

_____. "*Outlander* Recap: La Dame Blanche." *Entertainment Weekly* (30 April 2016).

Williamson, Penelope. "By Honor Bound: The Heroine as Hero." *Dangerous Men & Adventurous Women.* Philadelphia: University of Pennsylvania Press, 1992, 125–132.

Wilson, Christina. "*Outlander* Is Set to Boost Tourism." *Glasgow Evening Times* (29 July 2014): 13.

York, Patricia S. "Why the Pineapple Became the Symbol of Hospitality." *Southern Living* (3 March 2017).

Zemler, Emily. "How *Outlander*'s Costume Designers Took Jamie and Claire into the New World." *Elle* (10 December 2018).

Zhukov, Georgy K. "In *Outlander* Season 1, the Duke of Sandringham Has a Duel in Which They Appear to Fire Blanks at Each Other." *Reddit* (2018).

Index

Numbers in **bold** indicate main entries